Songsters and Saints

Unidentified young singer, self-accompanied on banjo. Some of his contemporaries, the "songsters and saints" of this book, recorded their secular and sacred vocal traditions thirty years later. Unknown photographer, 1890s. *Valentine Museum, Richmond, Virginia.*

Songsters and Saints

Vocal traditions on Race records

PAUL OLIVER

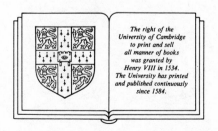

The right of the
University of Cambridge
to print and sell
all manner of books
was granted by
Henry VIII in 1534.
The University has printed
and published continuously
since 1584.

CAMBRIDGE UNIVERSITY PRESS
Cambridge
London   New York   New Rochelle
Melbourne   Sydney

Published by the Press Syndicate of the University of Cambridge
The Pitt Building, Trumpington Street, Cambridge CB2 1RP
32 East 57th Street, New York, NY 10022, USA
296 Beaconsfield Parade, Middle Park, Melbourne 3206, Australia

First published 1984

Printed in Great Britain at the University Press, Cambridge

Library of Congress catalogue card number: 84-1699

British Library Cataloguing in Publication Data
Oliver, Paul
Songsters and saints.
1. Music, Black 2. Music, Popular (Songs etc)
I. Title
780'.42   ML128.B45

ISBN 0 521 24827 2 hard covers
ISBN 0 521 26942 3 paperback

Contents

Illustrations

The assistance of the staff of the following libraries in providing illustrations, is greatly appreciated: Photographic Collection, the Library of Congress, Washington, D.C.; The Harding Collection, The Bodleian Library, Oxford; The Valentine Museum, Richmond, Virginia; and the Manuscript Department, William R. Perkins Library, Duke University, Durham, N.C.

Acknowledgments

This book is really the result of a combined effort, for so much of the work has been done by my wife, Val. She has listened (often willingly) to hundreds of recordings of songs and sermons; she has typed up the manuscript, checked the notes and sources. To have done this in California while the spring sunshine and the glistening water of San Francisco Bay beckoned meant a sacrifice which only she and I can recognize; my greatest debt is to her.

A number of people were immensely generous with their time and interest. The book was largely made possible with the invaluable help of David Horn, Assistant Librarian at the University of Exeter and Rosemary Mieckle of the audio-visual division. David ensured that I had access to the expanding American Studies and Popular Music sections while Rosemary made tape copies of innumerable items in the University's holdings, a large proportion coming from the collection of Roger Misiewicz. To all of them, my warmest thanks.

I am deeply indebted to Anthea Williams, who brought her methodical approach to the task of researching the great Harding collection of sheet music of American popular song; thanks too, to the staff of the Bodleian Music Library for making it possible for us to work on the collection. No one has been more interested in the progress of the work than John Cowley, who has brought numerous papers and references to my attention and copied out details in his immaculate hand. To him a special word of appreciation. Tony Russell, Karl Gert zur Heide, Bruce Bastin and Brian Davis have also freely given useful information and help on the way for which I am most grateful.

One of the most attractive aspects of working in this field is the generosity of enthusiasts and collectors in passing on data of likely interest, copying items in their collections, assisting with illustrations or transcriptions. The process has continued over a long period, during which time a great many friends have contributed in various ways. It would be invidious to attempt to name them; I hope that this book will be regarded as an expression of my thanks to all of them, as well as being a means of acknowledging the pleasure that these singers and preachers on Race records have given me over so many years.

Finally, a special word of thanks to Rosemary Dooley and Penny Souster for their interest, advice and editing.

A note on the transcriptions

All transcription of vocals on Race record must be a compromise between the song or speech as it is heard and the means of conveying the words in text. In this book the verses of songs are indented, and choruses are further indented. Spoken asides by the performer, or spoken and shouted comments by his companions or members of a congregation are indicated in parentheses (Yes, Lord!). Sung responses by members of a group or congregation are shown by italics in parentheses (*ain't never been told*). Gaps in delivery are shown by a dash –; omitted passages in a transcription by dots . . . Repeated lines, sometimes with minor variations in the words, are marked by a numeral in parentheses representing the number of times that the line is sung (2) or (3). When a couplet is followed by a brace and a numeral in parentheses, repetition of the couplet is intended. The word "etc." following a phrase or part line is used where a longer chorus is repeated.

Peculiarities of accent and dialect, diction and timbre present many difficulties in transcription. The problem is exacerbated by the poor quality of recording of some records, notably on the Paramount Race series, and the surface condition of some copies of 78 rpm records, which in all cases are over fifty years old. Some words or phrases that remain unclear are indicated with square brackets around the suggested transcription. Diacritical marks are not employed and no attempt has been made to find equivalents for dialect, but the elision of some vowels or consonants (ev'ry, ma'am, 'em) and certain other common characteristics have been marked by apostrophes or other conventional means. In certain instances, stresses on specific syllables, or the use of falsetto and antiphonal singing has been suggested by italics or broken underlining, these have been explained where they occur in the text. In a few cases square brackets have also been used to explain a word that has been omitted in the song.

A number of songs consist of many stanzas and some sermons are of considerable length when transcribed. Regrettably, but in the interests of manageable length, partial transcriptions only have been included. Finally, every attempt has been made to be accurate but the meaning of some words or phrases remains debatable in some instances. I shall be interested to learn of any alternative interpretations.

The Half Ain't Never Been Told
An introduction

Tell it over again – (*ain't never been told*)   (3)
The half ain't never been told.

> Dear brothers and sisters,
> We come before you at this hour,
> To tell you about the half ain't never been told.
> Our text is found in the Book of the First Kings,
> The tenth chapter and the seventh verse,
> And reads as follows:
> "Howbeit I bel*ieved* not the *words*,
> Until I *came* and mine eyes had *seen* it,
> And *behold* – the *half* was not told *me*;
> Thy wisdom and prosperity
> Exceedeth the *fame* which I heard . . ."

Before he began to preach, Reverend F. W. McGee led his congregation in a snatch of gospel song, their sung response lines overlapping antiphonally with his own, while the sweeping glissandi of a broad-toned trombone and the cross-rhythms of guitar, piano and percussion contributed to the exhilarating sound. As the stanza ended, the tension was sustained with his powerful delivery of the story of the visit of the Queen of Sheba to the Kingdom of Solomon. Members of the congregation shouted their approval and sang or moaned in accord, while, with a strong and trembling voice, he lingered on specific words to an implied beat. His sermon was an allegory, an appeal for understanding, discernment and judgment, and was addressed not only to the congregation present but to the thousands of black people who purchased phonograph discs of preaching in the 1920s.

The Half Ain't Never Been Told was recorded on a June day in 1928 and was issued soon after in the Victor record series produced exclusively for sale to blacks in the United States. [1] Though its purposes were undoubtedly different, the theme of the sermon, when heard again today, could well have been on the subject of these "Race records" (as Ralph Peer, an astute recording executive, first termed them). When Reverend McGee preached this sermon he had already recorded on four separate occasions, and the company had found that his discs were beginning to challenge the popularity of those by such preachers as Reverend J. M. Gates, Reverend A. W. Nix and Reverend J. C. Burnett. Their issues were appearing in the Race series of such rival companies as Okeh,

1

Columbia and Vocalion. Though there were scores of titles by preachers and their congregations available, they did not constitute the only forms of black religious vocal traditions on record. Groups that sang spirituals in the manner of the nineteenth-century Fisk Jubilee Singers, like the Pace Jubilee Singers or the Elkins Payne Jubilee Singers, were prolific, though they were challenged by the newer harmonizing quartets such as the Birmingham Jubilee Singers or the Excelsior Quartet. Contrasting with their carefully rehearsed techniques were the gospel songs of guitar-playing street evangelists like Reverend Edward Clayborn or Blind Willie Johnson.

Some of the quartets, the Norfolk Jazz Quartet for example, also sang harmonized secular songs which proved to be popular. But black purchasers of secular records were more drawn to those by the vaudeville and stage artists like Edna Hicks or Viola McCoy, and especially to those who used current black idioms: Ethel Waters or Lizzie Miles, for instance. Standby's of black entertainment were the duets who acted out domestic relationships in song, in the manner of Butterbeans and Susie or Coot Grant and Kid Sox Wilson. Among the professional entertainers were some who included a large number of blues in their repertoires, among them Sippie Wallace, Bertha "Chippie" Hill or Ida Cox, and the acknowledged outstanding exponents of the genre, Gertrude "Ma" Rainey and Bessie Smith.

Though most of the stage singers used jazz band support there were also many records of self-accompanied singers, veterans of the Southern road shows, who carried several decades of tradition in their records – Jim Jackson, Blind Blake or Papa Charlie Jackson. And there were the country blues singers, who were also generally self-accompanied; Blind Lemon Jefferson, Lonnie Johnson or Barbecue Bob among them, though one or two, like Texas Alexander, seem to have come straight from the cotton fields and were accompanied by other musicians. Small Southern bands, including the Memphis Jug Band or Cannon's Jug Stompers were likewise recorded extensively and, in mid-1928, there were pianists such as Will Ezell and Meade Lux Lewis whose records indicated the arrival of another idiom, which was to appeal particularly to the blacks who had migrated to the Northern cities.

When Reverend McGee made *The Half Ain't Never Been Told* the issue of Race records had reached a plateau of around a thousand titles a year, a rate that was to continue until the Depression hit the industry. In the diversity of records there was "wisdom" – and wit, humor, conflict, disappointment, misery. There was "prosperity" too, a richness and variety of forms, styles, idioms and interpretations. In the ensuing few years these were to increase as new singers were brought to the recording studios and other talent was found on location in the South. For a dozen years a remarkable documentation of black vocal traditions was purchasable on commercial releases.

How the recording of black artists commenced in 1920 and how records that were made specifically for a black audience were marketed through the Race series is a story that *has* been told, a number of times.[2] But it has been narrated in the context of writing which has been devoted to only a part of the music forms that were on disc: the blues. Writers on the blues have been impelled to "tell it over again" as the music over the years has assumed an international significance. From being a music of a racial sub-culture in the United States it became, from the late 1950s, the root and stem of modern popular music. This growth in importance of the blues has resulted in a distorted image, for, if the story of the blues has been told at length and in detail, as far as black music as a whole is concerned it is a half-story, though one that has become very persuasive. Before any consideration of the other half of black song, the half that "ain't never been told" is possible, it is necessary to review how this bias came about.

As early as 1926 a collection of blues music composed by W. C. Handy was published which included an historical and critical introduction by Abbe Niles. Fifteen years later Handy wrote his autobiography. An account of the stage career of the singer Ethel Waters, the reminiscences of the Chicago bluesman Big Bill Broonzy and my short study of Bessie Smith were the only books on the subject until the close of the 1950s.[3] This is not to say that the blues was wholly ignored in previous writings: in fact it figured in two specific genres – the literature of American folk music, and the literature of jazz. Both were to have a bearing on the positions taken in blues writing, and both were to have some influence on the way in which writers on the blues perceived the music.

Blues verses appeared in addresses made to folklore societies before the First World War. Soon after, a number of articles on folk song were published by Howard W. Odum, E. C. Perrow, Will H. Thomas, Walter Prescott Webb and John A. Lomax which contained verses marking the growing popularity of blues within Southern folk communities.[4] Thomas W. Talley's book of *Negro Folk Rhymes*, "wise and otherwise", appeared in 1922 but, among more than 350 songs and fragments, only a handful of blues verses were included. Only four years later, in their second book, Howard Odum and Guy B. Johnson gave prominence to the blues which they had collected orally from singers in the Carolinas and adjacent regions, and considered the influence of the new blues recordings on the folk tradition. Dorothy Scarborough relied mainly on an interview with W. C. Handy for her review of blues in her discussion of *Negro Folk-Songs* of 1925. Three years later, Newman I. White, in a copious work, included many blues fragments collected during the war years in Alabama and North Carolina, concluding that Scarborough, Niles and Odum and Johnson had "pretty well exhausted the subject".[5]

Folklorists placed great importance upon material collected "in the field", and almost none on material recorded commercially. Concerned much more with the songs than with the singers, they frequently showed little interest in the names and occupations of those from whom the songs were "recovered". Some folklorists took heart that, as Newman White wrote in 1928, "the vogue of the blues is already on the wane";[6] others regarded the evident growth in its popularity with no enthusiasm. It was, they believed, detrimental to the survival of the other, and probably older, black folk idioms. They were, however, paying more attention to secular song than had their predecessors.

Formerly, it had been the spirituals which had dominated most folk song collecting from black sources and, indeed, they continued to be highly regarded, with two volumes compiled by James Weldon Johnson, and collections of *Mellows* published by R. Emmett Kennedy being among those that appeared in print in the 1920s.[7] A boom in compilations of Negro songs and spirituals reflected, in part, the success of the writers of the "Negro Renaissance" and the negritude of Harlem and Paris which created a ready market. Blues was even being recognized as an element in the folk song of America and was making its appearance in anthologies with a few examples quoted with the spirituals and work songs.[8]

Enthusiasm was sustained in the 1930s by the work of John A. Lomax and his son Alan Lomax who published a succession of anthologies of American folk song which included representative coverage of traditional black spirituals, ballads, work songs and blues. These they frequently drew from their collections in the field for the Library of Congress and, particularly, from the singing of Leadbelly (Huddie Ledbetter).[9] Rather than go to the field recordings, let alone to commercial records, other folklorists used the Lomaxes' books as sources: B. A. Botkin, for example, edited a series of voluminous "Treasuries" of folk tales and songs which took examples from the Lomax works or from the Library of Congress albums. One, of *Mississippi River Folklore*, had a song section under the general title "Where the Blues Began" which contained no blues at all. Renewed field work in the 1950s enlarged the scope but Harold Courlander, while drawing valuably on his recordings in Alabama, was uneasy in his treatment of blues in *Negro Folk Music U.S.A.* which appeared in 1963.[10] Five years afterwards it was still possible for a much acclaimed first edition of a work on the study of folklore in America by Jan Harold Brunvand, to omit any reference to blues in its sections on folk song and ballads. Again, as late as 1972, Duncan Emrich, former head of the Folklore Section of the Library of Congress, included a 200-page section, "Folk-Songs and Ballads", in his own vast compilation of American folklore which did not so much as mention blues. Seeking signs of recognition of the music they liked and hoping for information and appraisal that would enlarge their knowledge and understanding of the music, blues enthusiasts felt poorly served by the folklorists.[11]

On the other hand, they had some reason to be grateful to the writers on jazz, at any rate after 1939. When Frederic Ramsey Jr. and Charles Edward Smith published a collection of essays, *Jazzmen*, which firmly established the importance of New Orleans in the history of jazz, prophetically they emphasized "that from any aesthetic point of view the background of the blues, and consequently of jazz, has as much validity in its own field as any other form of art". In Europe, serious writing on jazz began well before the Second World War, but it was Iain Lang's *Background of the Blues*, published by the Workers' Music Association in 1942, which pointed to a new direction. Concise and informed, it was first of all a history of jazz, but one which gave prominence to the importance of blues. Lang unequivocally stated his position that "the blues is not the whole of jazz, but the whole of the blues is jazz. It has no existence apart from this idiom." [12]

It was an opening developed by the anthropologist Ernest Borneman who maintained that "the blues is truly the heart of jazz and . . . jazz, without the blues, will expire". Support for Borneman's view, which gave firm recognition of blues, though still as a part of jazz, came in 1949 with the publication of *Shining Trumpets* by Rudi Blesh. Advancing a classification of archaic, classic, post-classic, contemporary, decadent and sophisticated blues he combined temporal and aesthetic terms within one system. [13] It was confused, but did begin to differentiate between blues types and styles and to introduce criteria. For Rudi Blesh, blues represented a precursor of jazz, but he also gave prominence, like the editors of *Jazzmen* before him, to boogie woogie as an element in "Hot Piano". So did Marshall Stearns when, some years later in 1956, he wrote what was to remain for a long time the definitive history of jazz; he included the swing and bebop eras which Blesh did not, but trimmed back his coverage of blues – placed *before* minstrels, spirituals or ragtime – to less than ten pages. Most jazz magazines also gave some space to blues, but seen from the position of the blues collector, jazz writing, though acknowledging its importance, placed the genre in a subordinate position. Blues was perceived as an influence on the development of jazz or as an ingredient in a more important whole.

With the publication of a history of the rural blues tradition through the lives and works of some principal exponents, *The Country Blues* by Samuel Charters, and my survey of the content of blues as it reflected aspects of black American life, *Blues Fell This Morning*, the position changed. Blues was shown to have origins, development and traditions of its own. [14] Between 1960 and the present over a hundred books on blues and related fields have been published. In these, references to jazz are seldom made, and then only in the context of instrumental accompaniment to blues singers. Similarly, folk songs and folk traditions, both sacred and secular, are only lightly acknowledged, playing a subordinate role to what is now seen as the dominant music, namely blues. In this process representatives of the blues in jazz histories or folk song are relegated to minor positions: Leadbelly is hardly mentioned; boogie woogie and hot piano is virtually ignored; the "classic blues" singers are classic no more and recognized only as jazz singers or performers on the vaudeville stage. Values as expressed by the folklorists and jazz writers have been reversed and blues criticism has developed its own measures of quality. Charley Patton and Tommy Johnson, unmentioned in any jazz book, have been considered among the "greatest" blues singers, while even in 1977 Bessie

Smith's singing was still being dismissed as "predictably dull".[15]

Distancing the blues from folk song or jazz, the authors of blues books and articles expanded its scope to accommodate a wide range of distinctions among singers and traditions. Like jazz authors, blues writers became obsessed with "style", seeking to identify singers according to the modes of singing or playing that they represented, and producing simple taxonomies which made differentiations by state, region and period of recording.[16] Among the scores of blues books are to be found many that are broader in intention: histories, analyses of content, considerations of blues lyrics as poetry, and a few biographies. The "cross-over" of white and black traditions, a sociological analysis of modern urban blues, the relationship of blues to soul and the influence of blues on pop music, even the phenomenon of world-wide blues appreciation itself, have been the subject of studies.[17]

If length restrictions have made a number of these books little more than outlines of their subject, the range is commendably wide. The enthusiasts' desire for ever more information was met by specialist magazines which afforded space for discographies, interviews with singers, and reviews of records and concerts. Commencing in 1963 with the English *Blues Unlimited*, regular publications followed in France, Germany, Belgium, Sweden, Australia and eventually, with *Living Blues*, even in the United States.[18] So great was the importance played upon data in articles and record sleeve notes that in 1979 a massive biographical dictionary of blues singers, based largely on these sources, took pride that "each entry has been condensed to the bare facts, without embellishment".[19]

Because blues writing ultimately snowballed there was, it seems, less time for reflection. Theoretical studies of the blues in the first fifteen years were few, written mainly by Europeans. American writers concentrated on portraits of the singers in action; or they notated blues vocals and accompaniments so that intending white "blues" performers might perform like their idols. Distance from the blues milieu may have afforded the European writer some measure of detachment and a perception of blues within a broader conceptual framework, while the proximity of American writers to live performers in clubs and concerts, could have shaped their preferences.

Recently however, one or two books have been published in the United States which have applied scholarly analysis to the blues and the blues-producing culture. *Early Downhome Blues* by Jeff Todd Titon offered a detailed examination of forty-four songs by thirty-five rural blues singers. Small though the sample was, Titon drew important conclusions as to musical structure and the use of formulaic patterns and word groups in blues lyrics. Another important work, *Big Road Blues* by David Evans, employed ethnomusicological techniques which included extensive interviewing and recording to recreate the field of influence of a prominent singer (Tommy Johnson), the essence of a local tradition, and the importance of a single theme in giving that tradition shape. These and other works since the late seventies have brought a narrower but sharper focus to the subject.

Perceiving blues as central to black secular song has had the effect of minimizing, even totally ignoring, other vocal traditions, or of placing them in a relationship dependent upon their bearing on blues. Blues writers have more than compensated for the earlier neglect of blues in studies of Afro-American music, to the extent that there are now major gaps in other areas of scholarship. This is particularly marked as far as sacred song is concerned, the number of works on the subject published in the last forty years being surprisingly small. Most concentrated on ante-bellum studies; even Lydia Parrish's collections made in the Georgia Sea Islands and published in 1940 were of "Slave songs". Arguing that spirituals were encoded messages concerning freedom or the desire to return to Africa, Miles Mark Fisher's study of slave songs was somewhat myopic.[20] When writing his sprawling but insightful account of "how the Afro-American spiritual was hammered out", John Lovell Jr. was perhaps too personally involved. But other works offered more considered and carefully documented studies of slave music traditions; none more so than Dena Epstein's *Sinful Tunes and Spirituals*, a painstaking reconstruction of black folk music to the Civil War.[21]

Epstein

The "peculiar institution" of slavery continues to exert its fascination. In the 1970s a number of reappraisals of conditions and social patterns in the South during the slavery period were published. Several of these, like Fogel and Engerman's contentious economic history of slavery using cliometric techniques, and Herbert Gutman et al.'s vigorous rebuttal of their conclusions, or Gutman's own major work on the black family during and after slavery, make no mention of song or music. They might have had a place in the latter, but would have had no relevance to statistical analysis. Other books reviewing the same period, like Eugene Genovese's study of the "world the slaves made", John W. Blassingame's survey of plantation life in the ante-bellum South, or Albert Raboteau's *Slave Religion*, all considered song while discussing slave society.[22] Such has been the emphasis on slave song within slave culture, and so searching has been the study of that culture, that we are now in the curious position of knowing more today about this inter-relationship than we do of the relationship between post-Reconstruction song, or even early gospel song, and their cultural contexts.

In spite of its popularity and continued growth, black church song of the past half-century has been given scant recognition by scholars, apart from one or two important theses. Dedicated to "all the gospel singers who didn't sell out" Tony Heilbut's racy account of personalities in the competitive world of post-Second World War gospel was a useful sketch. The autobiography of Mahalia Jackson and sundry record notes extend the meagre literature, while some current studies by Doug Seroff are concentrating on the evolution of black Jubilee quartets and gospel groups.[23]

Research in secular black song and musical forms apart from the blues has not been totally lacking, even if it has been relatively limited. Traditional songs, ring games, and "plays" from the Sea Islands were noted from Bessie Jones, fife and drum bands were recorded in Mississippi and Tennessee, work songs by black inmates of the Southern prison units were collected while "toasts" and other street ritual and speech were seriously examined. Such studies, based on field work and often augmented by recordings, showed that black song and music traditions of a very diverse nature continued, in some instances, well into the 1970s.[24]

A great deal of this research has been based on active recording in the field. Unfortunately, the significance not only of making such recordings, but also of issuing them has been recognized in almost inverse ratio to the availability of material. As ethnomusicological methods have become more refined, the older generation of informants and singers have declined in numbers.

Field recording probably commenced, as far as black song was concerned, with the cylinders believed to have been made by Howard Odum in Mississippi in 1904. But neither these nor the Edison cylinder recordings made in Virginia during World War I by Natalie Curtis Burlin have been recovered. Developed systematically in 1926 by the first curator of the Archives of Folk Music at the Library of Congress, Robert W. Gordon, many cylinder recordings were made in Darien, Georgia in 1926. Some six years later the Library of Congress sponsored field trips throughout the South undertaken by John A. Lomax and Alan Lomax, augmented later by other collectors, to create a vast, but very largely unissued, and now in many cases unissuable, archive. In 1950 Harold Courlander and Frederic Ramsey Jr. recorded on location in the South. After 1960 field work in the blues, made independently of jazz or folklore research and including the active seeking and "re-discovery" of blues singers in the South, became a firmly established practice. Veteran singers were recorded and their blues issued, and a lively program of reissues of early recordings commenced.[25]

Formerly, any blues reissues were almost exclusively linked with jazz and, even in the sixties, what was virtually a blues catalog was issued as the "Origin Jazz Library". Most such reissue programs were collector-inspired, financed and marketed by minor companies, with names that underscored the authenticity of their releases. That they covered a wider scope than did the published writings on the subject was partly due to the competitive nature of the reissue market itself. Blues series laid great importance on rarity, and many notes stressed the obscurity of the titles. In order to appeal to a restricted audience, producers with a genuine interest in, for example, black religious music had to resort to curious devices: an album of evangelists was released as *The Rural Blues – Sacred Tradition*; another of services, as *Traditional Jazz in Rural Churches*. Directed at potential purchasers who were of different ethnic origin, economic position, social status, and of a different generation from those working-class blacks for whom the original 78s were intended, the immense quantity of reissue albums has created an inbalanced picture of Race records, weighted heavily in favor of the blues.[26]

The term "Race records" for issues directed solely to the black purchaser, was in use by Okeh as early as January 1922. Several other major record

Representative labels of some of the principal companies who issued Race records including examples from the Okeh 8000, Paramount 12000 and Columbia 14000 series. *Paul Oliver collection.*

companies began to issue Race series: Columbia commenced in 1921 while Paramount (owned by the Wisconsin Chair Company) merged with the only label to have black ownership, Black Swan, and commenced its Race series in 1922; the following year Victor joined the lists. By the end of 1922 Race records were being distributed in many Northern cities and as far south as Alabama. They were distinguished by numerical series, so that even in the general catalogues they were, in effect, segregated lists. Many of these also had separate series for hillbilly or country music, and some differentiated between jazz and blues/religious issues. Most incorporated at least part of their jazz catalogue in the Race series, and blues records were almost wholly within them.

Entertainers who worked in the black shows were the first to be recorded, but as early as July 1921 a vocal quartet recorded a couple of spiritual titles and soon religious records were proving to be as popular as the secular releases. The record companies advertised in newspapers like *The Chicago Defender* which reached the black readership, and began to issue flyaway leaflets and full catalogs of their issues. Typically, they distinguished between Vocal Blues, Religious, Spirituals, Hot Dance, Sermons and Novelties, though within the categories the selection was often broad.

Jo Baker Received Acclaim in First Paris Engagement

By MAURICE ROCHAMBEAU

(Published by The Chicago Defender, through special arrangement with Jack Goldberg, managing director of Odd Talking Pictures, producers of Josephine Baker's great film production, The Siren of the Tropics.)

CHAPTER VII

(body text largely illegible)

HIT AND MISS

By SALEM TUTT WHITNEY

NOTHING could be more expensive or descriptive of an actor's theatrical life than hit and miss. The uncertainty of the game seems to be its most fascinating element. An actor hits when he thinks to miss and misses when he thinks to hit.

(body text largely illegible)

Read This Column and Send for Mail

THE THEATRICAL EDITOR.

Ethel Waters to Open at Parisian Nite Club Jan. 1

Paris, France, Dec. 27.—Ethel Waters, noted American blues singer, recently closed a highly successful engagement at the Palladium in London, will open at Lou Mitchell's premier of the Plantation night club.

(body text largely illegible)

Talkies Put in the Bijou in Nashville

By W. R. ARNOLD

Nashville, Tenn., Jan. 3.—Christmas night saw moving-talking pictures making their initial bow at the Bijou theater before a large and well filled house. Through the efforts of Manager Milton Starr talking pictures were brought to the popular Fourth Ave. playhouse.

(body text largely illegible)

W. James Writes of Ownership of Dallas Theater

Dear Sir — *(body text largely illegible)*

(Signed) WYATT D. JAMES.

Here and There With Bob H

(body text largely illegible)

Thank You!

The theatrical editor wishes to thank the many friends who sent New Year's cards. He appreciates your kindness and wishes all of you a very happy and a highly prosperous New Year.

THE THEATRICAL EDITOR.

New York Bands Tour Midwest

New York, Jan. 2.—Two local orchestras are scheduled to make a tour of the Midwest and the West as they have received good advance booking.

(body text largely illegible)

New Show Playing in Houston, Texas

Houston, Tex., Jan. 3.—A new production featuring "Miss Hannah From Savannah," the hottest gal in Dixie, with a red hot chorus of girls is playing the Washington theater and will be in the Lone Star state until about the first of March, then they are homed for the Golden West.

Virginia Four & Victor Recordings

New York, Jan. 2.—The Virginia Four recently completed the recording of four records for the Victor company, which are to be released Jan. 15.

(body text largely illegible)

Ida Cox Complains of Untrue Rumors

Dallas, Tex., Jan. 2.—Ida Cox and "Raisin' Cain" company are in their second week at the Central theater with Miss Cox slightly ill because she ate the stew with a low-necked dress on. She states that she would not be with the show this week but the management of the theater insisted that she go on with the production.

(body text largely illegible)

Record companies advertised regularly in *The Chicago Defender* and other black newspapers.

Expanding their markets and responding to the evident demand in the South the companies began, as early as 1924, to employ talent scouts to find rural singers and to send field units to record them. The locations were usually urban – Atlanta, New Orleans, Dallas or Memphis for example, and the factors which influenced the selection of performers and issue of recordings were variable. Nevertheless, the diversity of singers, entertainers, jazz bands, preachers and other black artists represented on these records was remarkable.

Recording of black artists falls into a number of phases, which were defined by factors that were both social and economic. This first phase continued for a decade but the effects of the Depression were deeply felt by the industry. There were only three issues a week in 1933 when the first phase ended, and a great many artists, and specific Race labels, appeared for the last time on disc. Recovery of the industry in 1934 was marked by some changes in emphasis in the kind of material recorded; though both sacred and secular issues continued to be released, there was an increase in urban-based blues and more sophisticated gospel singing. This second phase came to an enforced end with the combined effects of Government controls on shellac, and a ban on recording initiated by J. C. Petrillo, President of the American Federation of Musicians, who sought to inhibit the supposedly damaging effect of juke-boxes on the employment of musicians for live performance.[27]

With the end of World War II and the rescinding of the ban, another phase began. The former "majors" were unable to respond to changing tastes and were desultory in their recording of new artists, leaving a gap which scores of small concerns in California, Texas, Tennessee and the East Coast were quick to fill. "Rhythm and Blues" replaced the term "Race record" to cover a wide span of musical forms from rural guitar to urban piano, "jump" numbers, to harmonized vocals. Aided greatly by the very juke-boxes that Petrillo hoped to eliminate, and boosted by the disc-jockeys who played "R & B" records for hours at a stretch over the ever-expanding stations beamed to black audiences, the industry boomed. The terms might change, but the range of sacred and secular musical and song types within "Race" and "R & B" music remained as wide, and broadly similar categories continued into the 1960s. Recording venues differed, but again, the practice of using talent scouts in the field as well as urban recording centers persisted. From the mid-fifties the 45 r.p.m. "single" replaced the 78 disc, while the long-playing record made inroads into the black market. The "l.p." matched the sophistication of the new vogue for "Soul" singers whose songs were replacing the blues in popularity with black audiences, and was to be a useful vehicle during the most recent phase for tapping the growing white audience for blues in the 1960s. This last phase remains with us to the present.[28]

As might be expected, the phases of recording black music do not correspond in all details with the changing nature of the music itself. But as the fortunes of the Race record production relate to the position of blacks within

the national economy and as the nature of black folk song relates to their
social condition, there are discernible connections.

Few attempts have been made to make a comprehensive analysis of all the
forms of black song (let alone of instrumental music) which appeared on disc
through all these phases. Nor has there been adequate consideration of how
representative these were of the music in both the urban and the rural contexts
of the times, nor whether their appearance or absence from record was a
reflection of their popularity within the black community. How perplexing the
recorded evidence may be, can be ascertained from a comparison between
such material recorded for the Archives of Folk Music of the Library of
Congress as is accessible, and that on commercial record from the same
period. Only a small fraction of the Archive material appears to have been
blues, while the titles by many popular artists of the thirties were exclusively in
that idiom. Yet, when the commercial issues of Race records and field
recordings made for research or archival purposes are heard in parallel and
placed in sequence, a number of continuous threads can be erratically traced
over some fifty years. Documentary evidence does not suggest that these were
necessarily new traditions; some had a history which, though not without
change, was longer than that of the blues. Insofar as work songs, ragtime
dances, ballads, game songs, spirituals and folk sermons existed in the
nineteenth century, they can be said to pre-date all blues forms. But they also
existed in parallel with the growth of the blues, long enough to be recorded
even a quarter of a century after the end of World War II.

In 1977, Lawrence W. Levine published *Black Culture and Black Consciousness*, which expanded on a process already begun by Harold Courlander's
Negro Folk Music U.S.A. and to some extent by LeRoi Jones (Imamu Amiri
Baraka) in *Blues People* in 1963 – the relationship of black music to its cultural
setting.[29] Levine's book was larger in scope, extending to folk tales and jokes,
but it was also illustrated with literally hundreds of examples of songs from all
periods. Levine reunited what had been forcibly separated in the fight for
recognition of the blues as a music with its own identity – its place within a
larger picture of black song, both sacred and secular. These various forms
were seen as being direct expressions of the culture that produced them and
Levine's book was a remarkable work of synthesis and creative interpretation;
its weakness was that it relied almost entirely for its examples, whether
spirituals, gospel, folk song or blues, on the writings of other folklorists and
collectors.

This means that while the inter-relationship of folk culture and black
society was incisively demonstrated, the examples employed did not extend
our knowledge of the range of folk song that has been recorded. Field
recordings and commercial recordings must be seen as complementary, giving
as full a picture as can be recovered of the music of earlier phases. But how
extensive were they? Recent work by John Cowley has revealed a considerably

larger range of field recordings than hitherto noted, but most of these, unlike the commercial recordings, have not been issued in any form. How extensive the combined resources are, may be ascertained from the comprehensive discographies compiled for the first two phases.

Fortunately, the range of records available in all the Race series, or recorded in the field for archive purposes in that period, is very fully listed in Dixon and Godrich's *Blues and Gospel Records 1902–1943*, and Brian Rust's *Jazz Records 1897–1942*. They do not constitute a complete discography of all Race records for certain forms such as some of the Jubilee groups, comedians and some parodists, and most choirs have been excluded, in addition to those artists who did not perform in a "distinctively black-style American folk music" idiom. This begs a number of questions at the more sophisticated end of the song spectrum, where there are some deliberate omissions, but in all folk forms the Dixon/Godrich discography is as complete as present scholarship permits. Similarly, the more sophisticated types of dance music and vaudeville entertainment are not covered in Rust's *Jazz Records* (though many are listed in his other discographies) but all black jazz-blues singers are included, often duplicating in areas of uncertain definition the entries in *Blues and Gospel Records*. With these exceptions apart, the listing of relevant Race records for the first two phases is all but complete, augmented by full and annotated label listings of the Columbia and Paramount Race series, and the Victor Master listing.[30]

Examination of the many thousands of titles listed in these sources for the period 1920 to 1940 confirms that whole areas of black vocal tradition have been overlooked, or at best have received a few tangential references. Among sacred vocal traditions, the hundreds of recorded sermons have been virtually unnoted, while the scores of jubilee and gospel quartets who recorded, often over fifty titles each, have been grossly neglected. Apart from Bessie Smith and Ma Rainey there has been little attention given to the vaudeville blues singers, almost none to the entertainer-duetists.[31] Though the folk idioms of rural and Southern singers have occasionally been remarked, it has always been in the context of blues; their importance as representatives of other traditions has been minimized. The neglect is not confined to vocals on Race records; some attention has been paid to the jug and washboard bands, though not to the string bands that these folk instruments augmented. Their more sophisticated successors, the "hokum" bands have been disregarded. There are no studies of harmonica players of the period, no serious examination of the range of piano styles and performances, from the earlier vaudeville blues accompanists to the boogie woogie soloists.[32] Other themes, too numerous to mention here, await research. That similar studies are needed in the later phases of recording is no less evident.

From the folklorist's point of view, recordings in the field, unadulterated by contact with external influences will give a truer picture of song traditions in their authentic form than will commercial records. To some extent this must

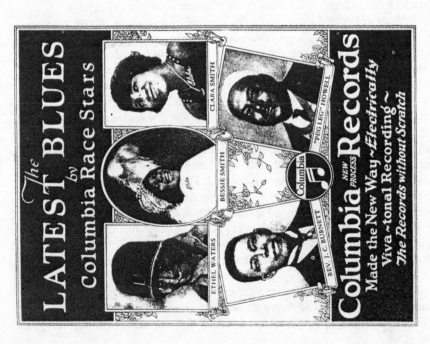

Columbia placed Reverend J. C. Burnett and songster "Peg Leg" Howell with their principal jazz-blues stars on the cover of their 1927 catalog. *Paul Oliver collection.*

Among the records listed in a 1928 Victor "fly-sheet", or record catalog supplement, was Reverend F. W. McGee's *The Half Ain't Never Been Told.* Others were by Richard "Rabbit" Brown and Elder Burch. *Paul Oliver collection.*

be true, though it is clear from field recordings made for Harold Courlander, Harry Oster and others that the influence of issued discs is to be found even in the remotest rural contexts. Unlike the books and articles that have been written on black music, and unlike the records that have been reissued or produced for specialized interests, Race records were purchased by the culture that produced the music. Subject to the influence of the record executives they may have been, but they were issued as a response to market forces and popular demand. Made by black performers for black audiences they constitute a significant guide to the traditions that were relevant to that society as well as delineating the contours of a new popular music.

In view of the sequence of phases in recorded music, it is possible to make a study of any one of them, but there are obvious strong arguments for commencing with the earliest phase. Not only might it provide a base on which to build, but it also makes the study of continuity and change more practicable. Moreover the first phase of recording has its own logic: it was the period when virtually the only records in any form which represented black vocal traditions were those on commercial labels, the small number of unissued cylinders apart. Race records are therefore not only an important index to the music of black Americans early in the century, they are the sole source from which we may deduce what many of their traditions sounded like in performance.

This book is concerned with the folk vocal traditions on Race records in the first phase. As such however, the first phase is immediately contracted, for no recordings of folk performers were made before 1924 and relatively few before 1926. As the decline in recording brought about by the Depression further reduced the number in the early 1930s, the effective span covered by this book is little more than five years. Nevertheless it was an extremely productive period, during which literally thousands of Race recordings were issued – far too many for a comprehensive study to be made in one volume of the total compass of song forms represented on them.

Rather than make a vertical division between the sacred and the secular traditions, I have drawn a horizontal distinction between the folk and the semi-sophisticated traditions in both. Such a division, necessary in view of the quantity of material is not without its problems of definition. Limitations in previous research have meant that some assumptions concerning "folk" character have had to be made based on delivery, repertory, style, place of origin and fragmentary information which may later require modification. In the study of vocal traditions other than blues or jazz song, difficulties have been met where the singers on record have made a substantial number of blues as well as other song types; similarly some predominately secular performers have also recorded religious titles. Between the folk idioms of the fundamentalist Baptist or Sanctified congregations and the more sophisticated forms of sacred song the distinction is at times blurred. But rehearsed, arranged and harmonized performances, whether by Sacred Harp singers, religious quartets or gospel and church choirs, have been omitted. Vaudeville singers, jazz-blues singers and others with jazz accompaniments, whether they have a minimal blues element in their repertoires or not, I have considered as being appropriate to a subsequent work.

Where jug bands and similar small groups are concerned the policy of inclusion/exclusion in Dixon and Godrich has not been precisely followed. If the nature of their recorded repertoire clearly indicates a link with other folk traditions including religious ones, I have included them, but a marked jazz orientation in their work has meant that they have been omitted. More problematic is the position of the "hokum" groups, but their somewhat knowing and sophisticated approach, and the presence among them of some known professional stage performers have led me to exclude them. Reference to stage performance and professional entertainment highlights another difficulty in that singers who worked with the traveling minstrel and medicine shows could also be regarded as "professionals". However, these were essentially folk entertainments and both the careers and the repertoires of their principal representatives on record indicate their appropriateness to the present study.

Inevitably, some links with other traditions are evident, such as the adaptation by vaudeville singers of folk songs, or the use of stage material by folk artists. This "crossover" problem particularly applies to parallel and overlapping forms of song common among both black and white folk performers. Some mention has been made of examples of this, but the full extent of linkages and the significance of the cultural exchanges that they indicate, constitute appropriate areas for future research. This will be possible when the corresponding hillbilly and Old Time music traditions have also been fully listed and examined.[33]

Apart from being an overview of vocal traditions that appeared in the Race series when black folk performers were first recorded, this book is also concerned with questions of the sources and currency of these idioms during the preceding thirty years. Part of my purpose has been to show how the recordings of the first phase related to the folk songs of that earlier period. For indications of the songs of the late nineteenth century that were influenced by, or entered the tradition, there is only the printed sheet music of the era on which to draw; for secular examples I have used the largely untapped resources of the Harding Collection at the Bodleian Library; for sacred items, early gospel songbooks and sheets.

As for the folk songs current during the first two decades of this century, the only resources available are the published collections of the folklorists. They are of varying kinds and quality. Thomas W. Talley's *Negro Folk Rhymes* may have been recollected from the late nineteenth century – they correspond rarely with other collections or with the recordings. As neither their sources nor the dates when they were noted were given, they leave many questions unanswered. More valuable in this respect was the extensive collection of black song made in the field by Howard Odum in the Carolinas and Mississippi in 1904–6. E. C. Perrow's collection also dates from this period but it was primarily drawn from white sources. Both Dorothy Scarborough and Newman Ivey White had numerous informants in the South who extended their collections, with many of those included in White's work dating from the First World War. Shorter collections by Will and Gates Thomas and John A. Lomax add further examples from black sources, but the early items included in the voluminous, and mainly white, Frank C. Brown collection from North Carolina were mostly from secondary sources.[34]

Fragmentary though some of these collections are, in total they comprise a not inconsiderable body of black folk song, of which a large number were to be found on Race records during the first phase. Yet, no matter how carefully the songs had been transcribed, or occasionally the music notated, the quality of timbre and pitch, the measure of individual folk artistry and invention, the skill – or otherwise – of the instrumental accompaniments were not, and could not have been, captured. Quite simply, the *sounds* of black song were missing. The closest approximation of those sounds we are ever likely to obtain is from records; it is their grooves cut over fifty years ago that can bring to life the shadowy figures from whom the songs were initially collected.

So, Race records have been the basic resource for the present study; they have always provided the starting point for any line of enquiry, and they have been the basis for the questions that have arisen. From them I have formed the broad classifications represented by the chapters, groupings which facilitate the presentation of an argument or help to show the connections between specific idioms, but which are not in themselves complete. Though they constitute only a part of the wealth of song and music which was available on Race records, it is my hope that the half that "ain't never been told" will eventually be told in full. When it is, perhaps their respective qualities will be recognized and new criteria applied which will not be determined by the perspectives of conventional scholarship in folk song, jazz or blues.

omits – rehearsed, arranged Sacredly .
– Vaudeville, jazz-blues ; jazzy jug bands !
– hokum

Do the Bombashay

Dance songs and routines

A tall man with proud features beneath his white skull cap, Joshua Barnes "Peg Leg" Howell was a familiar figure on Atlanta's Decatur Street. He played guitar and sang in a crackling, somewhat lugubrious voice, which was enlivened when he was joined by Eddie Anthony or another fiddler to play a stomping dance. Shot in the leg by an angry brother-in-law back in 1916, Howell was an amputee. The incident had ended his career on a farm and made it necessary for him to earn his living by his music. Born some eighty miles south-east of Atlanta in 1888, he had also worked in a fertilizer plant, made and sold moonshine liquor, and "just messed around town". Moving to Atlanta in 1923, he played on the street for coins outside Bailey's Theater. He was heard by the talent scout Dan Hornsby who arranged for him to record for Frank Walker of Columbia when the latter brought a field unit to Atlanta in November 1926 to record a number of preachers and religious artists. The small group of titles by Peg Leg Howell were the first they made of a rural black folk singer.[1]

His choice for his first song was probably unexpected: *Coal Man Blues* was hardly a conventional blues; it began as a ballad which described a railroad accident before slipping into the song of a street vendor hawking coal from his wagon:

> Let me tell you something that I seen,
> Coal man got run over by the 5.15;
> Cut off his arms and it crushed his ribs –
> Did the po' man die? No the po' man lives.
> > Hard coal, stovewood man,
> > Hard coal and the stovewood man.
> > I ain't got but a li'l bit left,
> > If ya don't come get it, gonna burn it myself.
> Sell it to the rich an' I sell it the po', (3)
> Sell it to the nice brown that's standin' at the do'.
> > Furnish your wood, furnish your coal, (3)
> > Make you love me, doggone your soul.[2]

Among the other titles that Howell recorded on that date was *New Prison Blues* which he had picked up from a fellow convict in 1925 when he was serving time for selling bootleg liquor. When the unit came back in April the

18

following year, Peg Leg was joined by his "Gang": Eddie Anthony sawing
away at the fiddle placed high on his shoulder, and Henry Williams strumming
guitar. Their pieces included a sixteen-bar song with suggestive "baker shop"
lyrics, *Jelly Roll Blues*, which had been around for some years. Ferdinand
"Jelly Roll" Morton had copyrighted a version in 1915, though he claimed to
have composed it in 1905. The opening strains of *Original Jelly-Roll Blues* by
Morton's Red Hot Peppers indicate that it was essentially the same theme as
the one that Howell had heard "a fellow named Elijah Lawrence" sing.

Returning to Atlanta in the fall, the Columbia unit continued to visit twice a
year until early in 1929. Over this period Howell recorded some thirty titles, of
which all but two were issued in the Columbia 14000 Race Series. Many of
these were of blues; some slow and lugubrious, like *Walking Blues*, or *Broke
and Hungry Blues*. Many of Howell's blues verses dated back to the earliest
stanzas noted by collectors: verses in *Rocks and Gravel Blues* and *Turtle Dove
Blues* were noted by John A. Lomax in 1908 when he collected them from the
Mississippi levee woman Dink as she was washing for the levee workers on the
Brazos River in Texas.[3] Others he may have learned from a record, or they
shared a common ancestry, like *Hobo Blues*, which was closely related to
Charles Davenport's celebrated song and "showcase" piano piece, *Cow Cow
Blues*. Sometimes he developed a blues-like theme from fragments of work
song, or, as in the case of *Please Ma'am*, from the pleading of a rejected man.
Perhaps the only blues to be recorded which was built from just one or two
lines repeated in various forms, it suggested a field holler (or "over and over"
as the repetitive field hand's songs were sometimes called) and bore out his
simple statement: "I heard many of my songs around the country. I picked
them up from anybody – no special person."[4] Its fragmentary lyrics echoed
the words and sentiments of songs that had been in currency long before: *Oh
My Babe, Take Me Back* and *Honey Won't You 'llow Me One More Chance*.
Some of his songs were blues in name only; *Skin Game Blues* for example,
which was a gambling song describing the fortunes of a player in the game of
Georgia Skin:

> Went out to the skin game last night,
> Thought I'd have some fun,
> Lost all the money that I had, baby,
> Pawn my special gun,
>> Had to pawn my special gun,
>> Says I pawn my special gun, lovin' baby,
>> Pawn my special gun.
>
>> Says you better let the deal go down,
>> Skin game comin' to a close
>> And you better let the deal go down.
>
> Says, gambled all over Missouri,
> Gambled all through Spain, babe,
> Police come to arrest me, babe,

> And they did not know my name.
>   And they did not know my name, (3)
>   Better let the deal go down,[5]   etc.

Skin Game was evidently a song which Howell had worked up from other sources; it related to old songs in both white and black traditions like *The Roving Gambler* and *The Coon-Can Game*, to which he had added a chorus based on the calls of the "pikers".

Certain of Howell's blues have been recognized as exceptional, and as an important figure in the Georgia tradition he has been included in every history of the blues: his *Low Down Rounder's Blues* has been quoted by Sackheim, Oakley and Titon in their various books. *Rolling Mill Blues* was one which I included in *Blues Fell This Morning*; there I related the closing of the mine to the closures of the Depression, but in fact the reference was much older. Howell's couplets began:

> The rollin' mill, babe it done broke down,
> Ain't shippin' no iron to town.
>
> The longest train I ever seen
> Run round Joe Brown's coal mine,
>
> The engine was at the coal mine hill
> And the captain never left town.
>
> The train run off the track last night,
> And it killed my lovin' Corinne.
>
> Her head was found in the drivin' wheel
> And her body have never been seen . . .[6]

The lyrics appear to have derived from a song cluster known to white singers, which included *In the Pines* and *The Longest Train*. After studying 160 versions of the song on record or in print, Judith McCulloh was of the opinion that the coal mine references were to those in Dade County, Georgia, owned by Governor Joseph Emerson Brown in the 1870s. The railroad accident with its gruesome image of the head found in the driver's wheel, but the body untraced, was fixed in the folk mind and, Judith McCulloh suggests, probably originated in the Reconstruction period.[7] Howell it seems, was synthesizing verses that had been in currency for over half a century. About half of his recordings were blues, excellent examples of the idiom that had developed in his maturity. But the other half of his recorded repertoire was a mixture of elements from many sources, which marked Peg Leg Howell as a typical songster of his generation.

As early as 1911 the collector Howard Odum noted in his epoch-making paper the terms used by black performers to describe themselves. "In general 'songster' is used to denote any Negro who regularly sings or makes songs; 'musicianer' applies often to the individual who claims to be expert with the banjo or fiddle" while the "music physicianer" was a traveler who was a

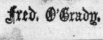

J. H. CAVE.

Pages of a nineteenth-century "Songster". *Paul Oliver collection.*

combination of both. At almost the same time Will H. Thomas noted the term "songster"; seventy years later both "songster" and "musicianer" were still in use, though "music physicianer" – probably a medicine show term – had been discarded.[8]

As early as 1821 the term "songster" was being used for small songbooks of ballads, broadsides and popular songs. As Malcolm Laws noted "during the 19th Century hundreds or perhaps thousands of different songbooks were printed and sold throughout America. Most of them contained the word 'songster' in the title, sold for about a dime, and were of pocket size." *The Forget Me Not Songster*, *The Arkansas Traveler Songster* and the *Uncle True Songster* were typical. It is likely that the term was soon applied to those who sang their songs, while "musicianer" was used by extension.[9]

The good songster was expected to be a good musicianer too, when the need arose – which it did most frequently at country barbecues and dances; the kind of social function described in the background chatter between Peg Leg Howell and Jim Hill on *Chittlin' Supper* with its skilful mandolin imitation of a piano and its stumbling humor: "Bring me some of those ole best pan chittlin's in here. What do I care for expenses – uh? I'd soon as spend a dime as not – uh . . ."[10]

Songsters were entertainers, providing music for every kind of social occasion in the decades before phonographs and radio. They were receptive to a wide variety of songs and music; priding themselves on their range, versatility, and capacity to pick up a tune, they played not only for the black communities, but for whites too, when the opportunities arose. Whatever else the songster had to provide in the way of entertainment, he was always expected to sing and play for dances. This over-riding function bound many forms of black secular song together. Social songs, comic songs, the blues and ballads, minstrel tunes and popular ditties all had this in common, and whether it set the time for spirited lindy-hopping or for low-down, slow-dragging across a puncheon floor, the music of black secular song could almost always be made to serve this purpose. It was the regular beat that provided the pulse for the dance and the cross-rhythms of vocal and instrumental that inspired the shuffles, shimmies, hip-shakes and shoulder rolls.

Before much serious attention was paid to the songs of black Americans, their dances were the subject of white interest and mimicry. Charles Dickens, who visited "Almack's" cellar dive in the notorious Five Points district of New York in April 1842, was one of several writers who gave graphic descriptions of "a regular break-down". He saw "the corpulent black fiddler, and his friend who plays the tambourine, stamp upon the boarding of the small raised orchestra in which they sit, and play a lively measure" to which the young mulatto girls and their beaux responded. "A lively young negro who is the wit of the assembly, and the greatest dancer known" dashed in: "Instantly the fiddler grins, and goes at it tooth and nail; there is new energy in

Published in 1840, *Jim Along Josey* was a popular minstrel song and dance, performed by Edmund Harper, John Diamond and John N. Smith in imitation of blacks.   *Paul Oliver collection.*

the tambourine" and the young black stepped: "single shuffle, double shuffle, cut and cross-cut; snapping his fingers, rolling his eyes, turning in his knees, presenting the backs of his legs in front, spinning about on his toes and heels like nothing but the man's fingers on the tambourine: dancing with two left legs, two right legs, two wooden legs, two wire legs – all sorts of legs and no legs . . ." and finishing by "leaping gloriously on the bar-counter and calling for something to drink".[11]

It is suggested by Hans Nathan in his detailed study of Dan Emmett and the origins of, as he decorously termed it, "Negro Minstrelsy", that the dancer Dickens saw was John Henry Lane, the celebrated "Juba"; he may have been, but there were many black dancers on whom the minstrels modelled their steps. They drew upon Scots and Irish sources too, and it is still arguable how much the "Ethiopian jigs" were derived from the Irish jigs, with their rapid footwork and almost motionless upper body and arms. As for the term "jig", it had a long history in Britain, where it had been used for the vigorous "capering" and satirical dances with songs and "rare discord of bells, pipes and tabors" since the late seventeenth century. Charles Read Baskervill concluded that "in spite of changing modes 'jig' remained an accepted term for dance song" through the seventeenth century.[12]

To what extent black capering and jigging were based on African steps remains questionable, though some West African dances have characteristics in common with early descriptions of American dancing. Violent dancing with shoulder and elbow snaps, and with the knees drawn up to the chin in swift, jerking movements is typical of the Ewe of the former Gold Coast (Ghana), for instance. White minstrel troupes drew inspiration from black rural dancing, and though many forms of dance must have had a short life there are some indications that others persisted. The dances of the slave quarters were a source of interest and amusement for whites.[13] Recalled one ex-slave, James Lucas, who was born in 1833: "us could dance about all night. De old-time fiddlers played fast music and us all clapped hands and tromped and swayed in time to de music, . . . Marster and Mistis laugh fit to kill at de capers us cut." Another ex-slave, James W. Smith, from Palestine, Texas recalled that "there am dancing and singing mostest every Saturday night. He had a little platform built for the jigging contests. Colored folks come from all around, to see who jig the best" and he described one man who "was the jiggingest fellow ever was . . . he could put the glass of water on his head and make his feet go like triphammers and sound like the snaredrum".[14]

For such dances the music was provided by fiddle, banjo and tambourine, or home-made instruments when better ones were not available. "Us take pieces of sheep's rib or cow's jaw or a piece of iron, with a old kettle, or a hollow gourd and some horsehairs to make a drum . . . they'd take the buffalo horn and scrape it out to make the flute. That sure be heard a long ways off. Then they'd take a mule's jawbone and rattle the stick across the teeth", Wash Wilson, another one-time slave, explained. As for the dances: "they wasn't no special name to them. There was cuttin' the pigeon wings – that was flippin' your arms and legs round and holdin' your neck stiff like a bird do. Then there was going to the east and going to the west – that was with partners and sometimes they got to kiss each other . . . And there was calling the figures and that meant that the fiddler would call the number and all the couples got to cut that number." [15]

These and numerous other testimonies of ex-slaves indicate that in the first half of the nineteenth century jigs and capers were a common feature of black dancing. If the slaves performed novelty dances imitating bird and animal movements, set dances, such as cotillions, were also danced by them, as they were by the families of their white owners. Black musicians played for both races, as Prince Johnson, from Clarksdale, Mississippi explained: "De same old fiddler played for us dat played for de white folks. And he sure could play. When he got dat old fiddle out you couldn't keep your foots still." The songs that accompanied the dances were often simple: "It goes sort of like dis: 'Turn your pardner round! Steal round de corner, 'cause dem Johnson gals is hard to beat! Just glance round and have a good time! Dem gals is hard to find!'" Robert Shepherd from Athens, Georgia, remembered. [16]

From the two thousand interviews in the *Slave Narrative Collection* of the Federal Writers' Project of the WPA, the vast, thirty-one volume collection of *The American Slave* compiled by George Rawick, [17] and the many other anthologies of slave narratives, a very full picture of music and dance in the ante-bellum years could, and should, be compiled. Unfortunately, no such comprehensive interviewing was conducted concerning black life in the Reconstruction, or indeed after, and detailed descriptions of their secular music during these periods are thin on the ground. In the interim a great many changes must have taken place in some elements of black dance and its related songs and music. Even so, several aspects appear to have persisted, among them the vigorous dancing with animal and bird-like movements, whirling arms and rapid footwork of the solo jigs. The instrumental music of fiddle and banjo continued, while the improvising of instruments from any suitable materials, from the jawbones and ribs of animals, to household utensils like the washtub, scrubbing board and stoneware jar remained common throughout the South. [18]

Black musicians still played for the white balls in the big plantation houses, and this too, remained a tradition throughout the century; others played in the barns or on the cornshucking grounds of the plantations and farms for the Saturday night frolics. They performed the tunes for the quadrilles and cotillions, set dances and barn dances of the white rural communities and from their simple platforms "called the sets". Their skill and timing was appreciated enough for them frequently to take precedence over white musicians, as many nineteenth-century illustrations indicate. Servants and hands who watched the white folks dancing were sometimes permitted to hold their own dances within the Big House, which meant that they had access both to the dances and to the music of the balls, and could copy them.[19]

Rural dance traditions of this kind die hard – they persisted to the 1940s all over the South and can still be witnessed in some areas. Fifty years ago they were customary. Among the recordings of "Old Time Fiddle Tunes" and other country music issued in the 1920s there were scores, even hundreds, of examples. White musicians like Fiddling John Carson, Riley Puckett, Gid Tanner and a great many others extensively recorded country dance music, but the records of a number of black musicians also captured something of the quality of the shared tradition. While these individual Race records do not illustrate all the instruments they employed, or the dance forms that they had performed, they do create a composite picture of the instrumental accompaniment to early dances, while the lyrics make connexions with early traditions. For example, Henry Thomas, who was a Texas guitarist born around 1880 and believed to be one of the oldest rural black singers on record, performed what was already, in his terms, an *Old Country Stomp*, singing couplets or single lines repeated:

> Get your partners, promenade,
> Promenade all around the town.
>
> Hop on, you started wrong,
> Take your partner, come on the train.
>
> I'm going away, I'm going away,   (2)
>
> Miss Ginnie eat, Miss Ginnie talk,
> Miss Ginnie eat with knife and fork.
>
> Goodbye boys, fare you well,   (2)
>
> I'm goin' back to Baltimore,   (2)[20]

His guitar accompaniment was essentially rhythmic, but between the vocals he played the melody on the quills; apart from Big Boy Cleveland who recorded a single title, he was the only singer to record on this folk instrument. "In my childhood I saw many sorts of 'quills'. The quills were short reed pipes, closed at one end made from cane found in our Southern cane-brakes", wrote Thomas W. Talley in 1922. He differentiated between the five-note "little set" of quills and a "big set" with more reeds. "The reed pipes were made closed at one end by being so cut that the bottom of each was a node of the cane. These pipes were 'whittled' square with a jack knife and were then wedged into a wooden frame, and the player blew them with his mouth." It was an old tradition: George W. Cable, wrote in 1886 of "the black lad, sauntering home at sunset behind a few cows that he has found near the edge of the canebrake whence he has also cut his three quills, blowing and hooting, over and over".[21] Henry Thomas played his quills between calling sets in a jaunty, shrill but clear melody. At one point he used a verse of ante-bellum date, once recalled as "jawbone eat, jawbone talk, jawbone eat with knife and fork" which was collected in Virginia and elsewhere, but which he now ascribed to "Aunt Ginnie".[22]

When Foggy Jones
     comes to Town,
   All de Coons
       for miles aroun'
   From Pickaninny's
        to Parson Brown,
   dey all join in de
              Cake Walk.

One-man band playing banjo, drums, cymbals and harmonica on harness. From the cover of *Foggy Jones*, a cakewalk by Jos. Gearen, 1900. *Paul Oliver collection.*

Another musician, Sam Jones, from Cincinnati, who styled himself "Stovepipe No. 1" was a "one-man band" who played guitar, harmonica (on a rack or neck-harness, as Thomas had probably played his quills) and a stovepipe into which he blew to produce a resonant and acceptable bass melodic line. He recorded in cities as far apart as St. Louis, Richmond (Indiana), New York and Atlanta but his themes, including those that were unissued, were rural and similar to white dance tunes. *Cripple Creek* and *Sourwood Mountain* were typical Appalachian songs, on which he called sets:

> Me and my wife and a bob-tailed hound
> Goin' away to Bagentown,
> Me and my wife and bob-tailed hound
> Take a lil ride and go to town,

he sang on *Cripple Creek*; and on *Sourwood Mountain*

> I've got a gal on the Sourwood Mountain,
> Swing your partners all the way round . . .
>
> Raise hands [up], circle to the right,
> Promenade all the way round . . .

His calls were similar on his recording of *Turkey In the Straw*:

> Change hands up, circle to the right,
> Promenade all the way round;
> Swing the girl you love the best,
> Please let mine alone . . .[23]

Turkey In the Straw was an old reel from Dan Emmett's Virginia Minstrels called *Old Zip Coon*. First published in the 1830s and probably performed as early as 1829 on the stage, it derived from Irish hornpipes. A century after its first performance it was recorded by Peg Leg Howell, with his companion Eddie Anthony on violin. Their *Turkey Buzzard Blues* was rough country music of the kind which may have inspired the imitations of the minstrel shows. Played in the black quarters it was, perhaps, too earthy for the white balls. Whereas Stovepipe No. 1 only called the sets, Howell and Anthony hollered the verses in rasping voices and played guitar and fiddle in a strongly syncopated fashion.

> Have you ever went fishin' on a bright summer's day,
> Standin' on the bank, see the little fishes play,
> Hands in your pockets, and your pockets in your pants,
> See the lil bittie fishes do the Hootchy-Kootchy dance.
>
> I had an ole hen, had a peg-leg,
> Fattest ole hen that ever laid an egg,
> Laid more eggs than the hen around the barn,
> Says "Another lil drink won't do me no harm".
>
> Sugar in the gourd, cain't get it out,   (3)
> Way to get sugar – roll it all about.[24]

The Hootchy-Kootchy, or belly dance, had been introduced by the dancer "Little Egypt" at the Chicago Columbia Exposition, or World's Fair, in 1893 where her erotic movements created a sensation. *Sugar In the Gourd* was another song fragment that was known from the East Coast to west Texas. In these, as in other dance songs, an underlying vein of ribaldry was there to be found by those who had a mind to.

Play-parties, where immense gatherings of country folk came together for dancing and feasting, were a common feature of Southern rural entertainment, especially when the nights were short in the height of summer and in the cool of long evenings. In some regions, as in Mississippi in the 1870s and 1880s, huge picnics and barbecues, sometimes attracting thousands of blacks and their families to a single event, were held in the summer. Numerous bands provided music for the dancing that took place on platforms built for the purpose. Railroad companies offered excursions from Jackson to Vicksburg, Mississippi, sometimes with a riverboat trip to complete a circular tour. Music for dancing entertained the excursionists who crowded into the towns on the way. In 1880 the *Hinds County Gazette* questioned the right of any railroad to "pour fifteen hundred howling excursionists upon any peaceful community". Picnics continue in Mississippi still, if on a reduced scale.[25]

Singing and dancing that was most typical of the period was to be heard in the converted barns of rural settlements, and the grimy dance halls of black belt towns and waterfront dives. In a sharply, but sympathetically, observed article written in 1876, Lafcadio Hearn described the dance halls of the Cincinnati levee, where in one, "a well-dressed neatly-built mulatto picked the banjo, and a somewhat lighter colored musician led the music with a fiddle, which he played remarkably well and with great spirit". The dancing ranged from jigs with the customary water-glass on the head of the dancer, to a quadrille and an old Virginia reel. "The dancing became wild; men patted juba and shouted, the Negro women danced with the most fantastic grace . . . the musicians began to sing; the dancers joined in; and the dance terminated with a roar of song, stamping of feet, 'patting juba', shouting, laughing, reeling."[26]

Patting juba, or producing rhythms by beating the palms on the knees, hips, thighs, chest and other resonant parts of the body had been known since the earliest days of minstrelsy and continued as "pats" well into the present century. Combined with foot tapping they provided opportunities for parti-cipants, whether seated or dancing, to create complex cross-rhythms against the music of fiddle and banjo, and to introduce syncopated time into the per-formance.[27] Such syncopation was already evident in *Civil Rights Juba*, which was published as early as 1874, while *Rag Baby Jig*, included in the "Banjo Companion" of a decade later, hinted at the direction which black dance music and song was taking. It seems likely that the origins of piano ragtime lay in the dance music of the string instrumentalists of the 1880s. By 1885 the pioneer ragtime pianist Scott Joplin was living in St. Louis where he would have been able to hear folk instrumentalists performing for dances. Later, at the Chicago World's Columbian Exposition, he met Plunk Henry, a banjo player who had been born in the 1850s and who was, according to Rudi Blesh, one of the very early group in the Mississippi Valley who developed the rudiments of piano ragtime from banjo syncopation.[28]

None of the recordings of dance tunes mentioned so far were to banjo accompaniment; though banjo players made Race recordings, their instru-ment was already considered old-fashioned; the guitar was as popular in the twentieth century as the banjo had been in the nineteenth. Though Gus Cannon – Banjo Joe – played his *Madison Street Rag* in a percussive fashion which may reflect the style of the folk banjo rags from which the piano forms partly derived, the guitar rags of a performer like Blind Blake showed the

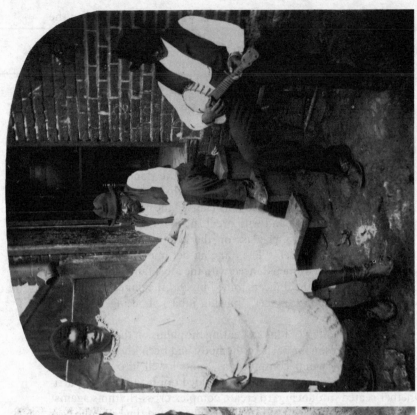

"Happy John", a veteran banjo-player, photographed by McCrary and Branson, 1897. *Library of Congress collection.*

"Sally In Our Alley" Stereo photograph by B. L. Singley, St. Louis, 1897. A girl in high boots dances to banjo accompaniment. Inside the door a beer keg stands on a table. *Library of Congress collection.*

superiority of the instrument for free-flowing dance rhythms. "Now we goin'
to do the old country rock" he stated on *West Coast Blues* – which was
certainly not a blues and more likely to have referred to the East Coast than to
the West:

> First thing we do –
> Swing your partners – promenade –
> See-saw to the right.

> Swing that gal over there with the blue dress on, – an'
> Bring her right on back to me.
> If she starts to funny foolin'
> Well its done got sweet to me . . .

listen.? [handwritten]

He talked over the fast rag with its swinging, deft fingering, lazily commenting
on his own prowess:

> It's done got good to me,
> It's good to the last drop,
> Just like Maxwell House coffee – yes
> Just boot that thing . . .[29]

Blind Blake, believed to have been born in Jacksonville, Florida in the mid-
1890s, traveled extensively, singing in the streets and playing at work camps.
He acquired a formidable technique and displayed it in many recordings of
guitar ragtime, including *Wabash Rag*, *Sea Board Stomp*, *Hot Potatoes*, *South
Bound Rag* and *Blind Arthur's Breakdown*. He also recorded *Dry Bone Shuffle*,
a rag with an unknown player of the bones providing a clattering, brisk
accompaniment.

> Let's go, bones – Whip it bones, – do it a long time
> Jus' like getting money from home,
> That's the way I like it –
> Play them bones boy – that way it's hot.
> Play 'em boy – get'n good to me.
> Let's have a bit of Charleston in it . . .[30]

commented Blind Blake. His rapid dance had breaks and suspensions of
rhythm in which the dancer could hold a step or the bones could play a brief
solo interlude. A folk rhythm instrument, the "bones" were popularized in
the minstrel show as early as 1843 by Frank Brower of the Virginia Minstrels.
Smoothly carved, slightly curved pieces of animal shin bone were held
between the first and second, and second and third fingers so that they could
be vibrated against each other. Wooden spoons and even fire-tongs were
employed for this same purpose, on occasion.[31]

Spoken comments on the dance steps, sometimes interspersed with local or
oblique asides appear frequently on guitar rags. William Moore, who claimed
on his *Barbershop Rag* to be the "only barber in the world can shave you and
give you music while he's doin' it", was a resident of Tappahannock, Essex

A boy demonstrates steps to the picking of a new guitar. Unknown photographer, c. 1900.   *Valentine Museum, Richmond, Virginia.*

County on the Rappahannock River in Virginia, where he moved from Georgia in 1904 at the age of eight. *Ragtime Crazy*, an old buck-and-wing dance theme was played to one of the melodies erroneously associated with the fandango and often called the "Spanish flang-dang" by country guitarists. Interrupting the flow with "stop-time" breaks, he invited the dancers to invent "crazy" steps:

> . . . Come on Bubber, bump it up and down a little bit, sonny,
> Yes Sir – Take those scroungers out of my face –
> Give you a bottle of milk when you get home –
> . . . now I'm goin to put it on while you take it off,
> Take it slow and easy, Big Boy.
> Look out Johnny, save a little bit of that corn.
> Now let's go crazy folks, for a minute.
> Step on it chillen – look foolish –
> Cross-eyed and ev'rything –[32]

It seems likely that the guitar rags developed in the rural areas at much the same time as the pianists of Sedalia and St. Louis were developing piano ragtime. Both could have shared sources, but the guitar players may have derived their rags from the banjo and fiddle reels and dance tunes of the earlier generation when the new instrument became readily and cheaply accessible. The American firm of C. F. Martin originated the American-made guitar as early as 1833, but it was not primarily a folk musician's instrument until Orville Gibson began to manufacture for the popular market in 1894. Mail order guitars were soon made in competition; by 1908, Sears Roebuck were marketing a standard size guitar for only $1.89 – inclusive of an extra set of strings, a capo, book of chords and a fingering chart. Several other models were available for less than five dollars. But it was Gibson and Martin's steel-strung guitars introduced in 1900 which were ideal for playing outdoors or at noisy dances. As the guitar notes could be sustained in a manner which was not possible on the banjo, with its short, staccato sounds, the guitar was particularly suited to the sliding and shuffle dance steps which were popularized in the 1890s.[33]

Ragtime, though viewed by the composers of piano rags as being a special and distinct music, was associated in the popular mind with a variety of song and music types of the day, from the "coon songs" which had their origins in the minstrel show, to the ragtime songs of vaudeville and concert hall and the instrumental music of the brass bands. Jim Reese Europe, C. Luckyeth Roberts and Will Marion Cook were among the prolific black composers whose instrumental and piano ragtime were closely related to the craze for cakewalks and two-steps. If they may not have been derived from the plantation jigging contests for the award of the cake, they certainly derived from the "walkarounds" and "cakewalks by the entire company" which were a concluding feature of many large minstrel shows. The strains of the ragtime compositions of trained musicians like Joplin, Tom Turpin and James Scott were probably based on the sets of the quadrilles, cotillions and other popular ball dances. Sousa's marches, the two-steps, cakewalks and quadrilles combined with the popular "coon" songs of the 1890s to stimulate a period of unprecedented excitement over new dances.[34] Some of these were still reflected in some degree in the songs of folk musicians thirty years later: Jim Jackson, for instance, whose markedly syncopated jig rhythm must have been close to the folk origins of the dances he mentioned on *Bye, Bye, Policeman*:

> Now first thing honey is the Bombashay,
> Oh turn right round, go the other way.
> To the Worldly Fair, the Turkey Trot,
> Oh, don't that girl think she's very hot?
> She puts her hand on her head
> And let's her mind rove on –
> Stands way back, lookin' to stop –
> Oh! She dance so nicely, and politely
> She do the Pas-a-Ma-La . . .[35]

A guitar player born in Hernando, Mississippi, Jim Jackson spent most of his life there, on the road, or in Memphis. In performance his song was rural Southern in character but the words were directly from the original *Pas Ma La* by Ernest Hogan, published in 1895.

> Fus yo' say, my niggah, Bombashay
> Then turn 'round and go the other way
> To the World's Fair and do the Turkey Trot,
> Do not dat coon tink he look very hot?
>   Hand upon yo' head, let your mind roll far,
>   Back, back, back and look at the stars,
>   Stand up rightly, dance it brightly
>   That's the Pas Ma La.[36]

Possibly French Creole in origin, and known as La Pas Ma Lé, the dance had been gently parodied by a black composer, Irving Jones, as the *Possumala Dance* a year earlier. In the mid-1890s it was widely popular.

The dreamy image of "put your hand on your head and let your mind roll on" persisted in the folk memory, to crop up in a number of songs, including Gus Cannon's *Walk Right In* – "sit right down, and honey, let your mind roll on". "Looking at the stars" and the three backward steps that accompanied the pose, gave an endearing and amusing effect to the dance, which continued to enjoy a fair measure of popularity for some fifteen years.

According to Max Hoffman's 1897 song, *Bom-ba-shay*, it was a "reg'la honalula dance" which incorporated the "possum a la", but which may have had some links with the impending annexation of Hawaii. In 1909 the Bombashay still appealed, if William Jerome's *That Spooney Dance* is an indication: "Oh that Spooney dance, oh that Cooney dance, Sweet lovin' Bombashay, just steals your heart away . . ." But only a year later Ed Rogers and Saul Aaronson were dismissing it in favor of the new dance *Alabama Bound*: "You may talk about your Salome dance and your Cubanola glide, your Pas'mala and your Bombashay have got to stand aside . . ." The Alabama Bound dance described in the song was one where the dancers were held close in the manner of the Bunny Hug and others of the new, and shocking, close-couple dances: "Come babe, look into my eyes, and roll them round and round; I'm feelin' oh so funny, won't you hug me honey, to dat

Alabama Bound."[37] The back-arching abandonment of the Turkey Trot and the breast contact of the Grizzly Bear were erotic in their day and banned from the politer dance halls. As Jim Jackson lamented in another song:

> 'Cause when I woke up this morning she's gone . . .
> She made ma mad, I felt so sad,
> I would not tell you even the reason why;
>   Oh, how she loved to dance that old Grizzly Bear
>   I guess she's gone to Frisco to dance it there –
> 'Cause when I woke up this morning, she's gone,
>   She's gone, gone, gone . . .[38]

In a period when the invention of new dances was an important part of popular culture, a professional song writer like Perry Bradford was quick to seize upon folk dances and to compose jazz songs with instructions on how to perform the dance. Songs such as *Ballin' the Jack*, by Chris Smith (1913) and *Walkin' the Dog* by Shelton Brooks, published four years later, were among the best known, but many others gave details of the new steps. Perry Bradford had seen a dance in Jacksonville, Florida which in 1907 he published as the *Jacksonville Rounder's Dance* "but people didn't like the title because 'rounder' meant pimp, so I wrote some new lyrics in 1919 and renamed it *The Original Black Bottom Dance*". Like his *Bullfrog Hop* of 1909 or *Messin' Around* of 1912 this gave instructions: "Hand on your hips and do the Mess Around, Break a leg until you're near the ground". Often in his songs he mentioned the titles of other dances that he had already published, doubtless with an eye to the sales of sheet music. The Black Bottom, the song stated, "started in Georgia and it went to France" which acknowledged both its origins and its rapid international appeal when cleaned up for the ballroom.[39] Though Smith's *Ballin' the Jack* was an exception, dance vocals seldom give instructions on *how* to dance in the songs, though they frequently exhorted the dancers to break into specific, named steps. In the folk tradition it seems, it was assumed that the steps themselves would be known. There are hints in *Georgia Rag* by Blind Willie McTell, that he was well aware visitors came to "Darktown" to pick up the dances. McTell was a highly accomplished performer on the twelve-string guitar; its resonance was ideal for the "dancing at house parties in Statesboro, in the smaller outlying towns like Register, Portal and Metter, and at farm houses out in the country" in rural Georgia where he played. He was attracted to Atlanta, as were many other rural musicians:

> Down in Atlanta on Harris Street
> That's where the boys and girls do meet,
>   Doin' that rag, that Georgia Rag
>
> Out in the Alley, in the street
> Every little kid, that you meet,
>   Doin' that rag, that Georgia Rag – (swing that Georgia Rag boy)
>   Buzz around like a bee,

> Shake it like a ship over sea,
> That wild rag, that crazy rag
> Better known as the Georgia Rag.

> Come all the way from Paris, France
> Come to Atlanta to get a chance,
> To do that Rag, that Georgia Rag

> Peoples come from miles around
> Get into Darktown t' break 'em down,
> Doin' that rag, that Georgia Rag.[40]

Country musicians in and around Atlanta recorded a large number of dance tunes, suggesting that there may well have been some justification for the frequent linking of the name of a dance step and the state of Georgia in the title or lyrics of a song. Sinuous, often lascivious, undulating movements and thrusting of the hips had been known for years as the "bumps and grinds". One song, the *Georgia Grind* was published with music by Albert Grimble in 1913: a later version appeared in 1926 by pianist Jimmy Blythe. Blythe's composition was recorded by several singers and bands that year, including Louis Armstrong's Hot Five, and even Duke Ellington's Washingtonians – among the very first titles made by each of them, when their music still reflected an earthier origin. Henry Williams, a rough country guitarist and associate of Peg Leg Howell, recorded *Georgia Crawl* with fiddle player Eddie Anthony.

> Run here papa – look at Sis
> Out in the backyard jus' shakin like this –
> Doin' the Georgia Crawl – ooh Georgia Crawl
> We don't need nobody tryin' to do the Georgia Crawl.

> Old Miss Sadie, old and grey
> Did the Georgia Crawl till she died away,
> Doin' the Georgia Crawl etc.[41]

An "Instrumental hit" called the *Georgia Crawl* had been published in 1912, and it could have been the dance on which Blythe based his tune. But Williams and Anthony might themselves have heard the Louis Armstrong record and based their "Crawl" on it; at least once one of the pair sings "Georgia Grind" rather than "Crawl". Another recording, *Too Tight Blues*, by Peg Leg Howell and his Gang – which included Anthony and Williams – is one of the most successful at capturing the spirit of the country dance, with its marked swing, strumming guitars, scraped fiddle and spoken exchanges or shouted comments throughout the performance:

> Grab your gal, fall in line,
> While I play this rag o' mine.
> Too Tight, this rag o' mine. (Listen boy – Yeah?)

> Too tight, ain't cha 'shamed?
> Too tight, shakin' that thing,
> Too tight, this rag o' mine (no way of gettin' to it, boy)

Peg Leg Howell, guitar (right) with fiddle player Eddie Anthony, and probably, Henry Williams, playing in an Atlanta street, c. 1928. *George Mitchell collection.*

and the singers urge the dancers and themselves on with

> like Maxwell House coffee – Good to the last drop! –
> Give 'em a little Charleston boy . . .[42]

But the dance had earlier been recorded by Blind Blake – well known in
Georgia – with similar words; he recorded it again a year after Howell. The
Maxwell House reference had also appeared on Blake's *West Coast Blues*.
Certainly Howell was aware of popular recordings of the day: his *Peg Leg
Stomp*, though played as a country dance, was based on *Bugle Call Rag*, which
had been recorded by Red Nichols and His Five Pennies some months earlier.
If there was plenty in the folk tradition to be milked by the composers it is also
evident that rural musicians sometimes derived, if at one or two stages
removed, from published and recorded dance tunes. It is by no means certain
that all the dances referred to in the recordings of folk musicians, any more
than those in sheet music, actually existed as separate steps. Another Atlanta
guitarist, Robert Hicks who played for customers at a barbecue stand and was
known as Barbecue Bob, sang of the "Scraunch". But it seems from his verses
that it was a combination of other popular steps of the period:

> Down in Dixie there's a dance that's new
> Ain't much to it an' it's easy to do,
>   Called doin' that Scraunch, – oh doin' that Scraunch
>   Just wiggle and wooble it, honey when you do the Scraunch.
>
> You wiggle and a-wooble it, an' you move it aroun'
> Ball the jack and you go to town,
>   And does that Scraunch,[43]   etc.

Subsequent verses follow a familiar form of describing a girl who's the "best in
town", and the inevitable "grandmom and grandpapa at the age of eighty-
three, they the best scraunchers you ever did see . . ."
   Some dances had a relatively long life, and certain steps and movements
were readily transposed to a variety of dance tunes which, in themselves, only
enjoyed a brief vogue. The shimmy-shake, in which the shoulders, breasts,
hips and knees of the dancer were shaken in a rippling movement may have
first appeared on stage with the Hootchy-Kootchy. But it was popularized for
white audiences and for dancers who were brave enough, by Gilda Gray, who
slipped the straps of her chemise from her shoulders while dancing in a
Western cabaret. "I'm shaking my shimmy, that's what I'm doing", she is
reported to have explained, and such was the success of her dance that she
wore a heavily sequinned chemise to show off her shakes.[44] Similarly, Ballin'
the Jack, with its flexed legs, knees together movement left and right, followed
by vigorous revolving or twisting, and the Eagle Rock movement with
extended arms and bird-like flapping, were also popular for a long time. Most
celebrated of all the dances, and the one which appears to have typified the
1920s to generations afterwards, was the Charleston. Though it is questionable that it derives from "An Ashanti ancestor dance" as LeRoi Jones has

hinted, it was undoubtedly current before 1905 when Noble Sissle learned it
in Savannah, Georgia. Its back kicks, leg-shakes, crossed arms and knocked-
kneed movements were spectacular and the dance gave the greatest opportunities for performers to "do the breakaway" and invent new steps to its jaunty
rhythm.[45]

As a dance the Charleston encouraged competition. In country districts as
well as in city dance-halls, dancers competed to win prizes and, perhaps more
important to them, the admiration and envy of other dancers, as their parents
had with the cakewalk and their sons and daughters were to do with the Lindy
Hop. It also invited competition from the musicians, and *Charleston Contest*
by Too Tight Henry seems to have been more of a demonstration of his own
ability and a brag that might provoke a challenge, than a competition between
dancers. "Too Tight" Henry Castle was born in Georgia in 1899 and traveled
with both Blind Blake and the Texan Blind Lemon Jefferson. In Memphis he
played with Jed Davenport and other musicians who must have respected his
accomplishment. He spoke about his early life briefly in his two-part
Charleston Contest recording, on which he played a twelve-string guitar and
imitated the voice of an imaginary companion, "Chappie", who asked:

C. Say listen here Too Tight, they tell me you-all gonna have a Charleston Contest out
your way tonight?
TT. Yeah boy, I heard 'em talkin' 'bout it.
C. Well, thing I want to know is, who is gonna play for 'em?
TT. Well, I heard them say they wanted to get ole Henry L. Castle to play, I guess
that's me myself . . .

He invited "Chappie" to sit beside him and listen to his imitation on guitar of
"that old hawg man bring that ole hawg he got down from his job".

C. Hey, boy, if you do that again I'm gonna have you run out of town.
TT. Yeah that's what they told me at the Mill when I keep on playing the Charleston –
But you know one thing, Chappie, when I was a poor boy first started out playin'
music, an' tried to travel from town to town and I didn't have any money . . .
C. What did you do, Too Tight?
TT. Oh well I'd go out to the freight yard and the first thing I saw lined out
smokin' . . . and when she got out yonder on that long old lonesome freight I just
could imagine if I had one of them ole browns of mine there to shake that thing
with me – how we could keep time with that ole locomotive engine like so with this
twelve-string guitar . . .

He continued by recalling "when I was a lil old boy comin' along I used to see
ole mens playing the git-tar – and you know they said they could play a guitar,
and keep time with the strings and beat the drum and never lose a note but . . .
well, they didn't do anything but tap the strings occasionally and wear the piss
out on the wood – but ole Too Tight never did on the steel . . ." He was
apparently referring to the folk custom in which a second musician played an
accompanying rhythm on the fingerboard with straws. Promising to Chappie
that "you'll get a chance to see ole Sister Hooper shake that can of hers" he

displayed his skill by referring to "that fool rag that mandoline he got" and imitating it on the guitar. Then he imitated the banjo player, "that ole feller doin' his Charleston now". Chappie asked,

C. I want to know how many you got in that string band you got over there?
TT. Oh well, ain't nobody but me, myself Henry L. Castle, ole Too Tight . . .
C. I don't care if you got you and your whole family, you sure is killin' me . . .

To each exchange Henry Castle swung into an exciting, if individualistic chorus or played a fast break, the equivalent of the dancer's "breakaway".[46]

In the breakaway dancers often devised new steps that briefly caught on with their contemporaries, establishing a "rage" or "craze" for a few weeks, or even months, before being superseded by another, more audacious or more fetching, step. Many of the dances noted by Marshall Stearns must have had their origins this way, and many that exist as name only and are otherwise undescribed in his work must have enjoyed a vogue that was briefer than that of the tunes to which they were danced.

"Say Pal," asked Papa Charlie Jackson on *Skoodle Um Skoo*, "do you know anything about that new dance they got over in town?" ("No I don't") "It's a dance they call Skoodle um skoo – let's go –

> Now I know a lady, name of Sue, she like to know just what to do
> Now sit right over there, sweet mama, I'm gonna tell you just what to do,
> I'm gonna tell you just before you go . . .
>
> You got to skoodle um skoo, oh' baby got to skoodle um skoo
> Come on mama, got to skoodle um skoo, skoodle um, skoodle um skoo

and so on. "It's a wonderful dance . . ." he commented in an instrumental passage, but though there were several verses there was scarcely a hint of the steps. Jackson, who came from New Orleans, played banjo, which was already something of an anachronism. But he played so energetically at a brisk tempo and with a bright sound that he remained one of the most popular of the artists recording for Paramount. His banjo playing was probably the closest to that of the previous century that could be heard on disc. When the theme was recorded again in 1928, a year later, it was by the raucous Seth Richard, from Georgia, who played a twelve-string guitar and kazoo:

> Aw skoodledum doo, oh baby, let's skoodledum doo
> Come on mama, let's skoodledum doo, skoo-doo-doo,
>   Mama, Mama, have you forgot
>   The night I had you in the vacant lot?
> Skoodledum doo – skoo doo-doo.[47]

Though the tune was the same, and the playing ideal for dancing, there was no mention of any dance in it. Like Blind Blake's more complex *Skeedle Loo Doo*, to which it was somewhat related, any specific steps associated with the tune appear to have been forgotten, though it was the kind of rag-based number which would have encouraged dancers to invent steps of their own.

On a number of recordings with strong dance music the vocal contributions were often minimal. The Kansas City team of Winston Holmes and Charlie Turner, who both played guitars on *Kansas City Dog Walk*, put their efforts into an exhilarating dance music, the rhythms of one offset by the sliding notes of the other. "I'm goin' down to the Yeller Front and walk the dog all night long . . .", commented Holmes, pointing out a woman on the floor: "she can strut" and concluding in the final ragtime choruses "all right, now . . . let's shut the windows, pull down the blinds . . . let's get messin' . . ." The strutting "walking the dog" had been a hit when danced by John Sublett, known professionally as Bubbles, of the Buck and Bubbles tap dance team; he claimed to have invented it in 1910 when he was eight years old. But it almost certainly started life as part of the plantation and minstrel show "walk-arounds" in which the strutting steps to ragtime music were an invitation to display.[48]

Dancing was a release, an opportunity to vent emotions and to forget worries and pressures. Another guitar duet, Pink Anderson and Blind Simmie Dooley, who performed for picnics and country dances around Spartanburg, South Carolina implied this in a fast ragtime dance song, *Gonna Tip Out Tonight*. Sang Simmie Dooley in his hard nasal voice, to comments and encouragement by Anderson and against strong bass runs on the guitars:

> Gee, I'm feelin' mighty lonesome,
> Gee, I'm feelin' mighty homesome,
> My gal quit me an' I don't know what ter do (what you do?)
> She even tol' me from the start
> If I go I would break her heart,
> Every time I think about her, makes me feel so blue.
> This mornin' I received a note (got a letter from her: I read it.)
> And this is what the answer I wrote (what you say?)
> "Go on gal, sing them blues to me
> I'm sweet as any man can be,"
> She even tol' me to ma face (what?)
> That any ole rounder sure can take my place.
> Says "I'm gettin' tired of your lowdown ways,
> I'm goin' back to my baby's days.
> Go on girl, honey you can't [change your] luck,
> I'm gonna tip out tonight, I'm gonna strut my stuff,
> I mean I'm gonna straw my stuff." [49]

Rural dances could be held in the open or in converted barns and warehouses; as the demand increased "jukes", or drinking and dancing parlors, were constructed in the rural regions. Often closed during the week they were open for dances on Friday and Saturday nights. Crude frame buildings clad in clapboard and roofed with corrugated iron, they were crowded to capacity. A bare table or a plank across barrels formed a bar; if they were lucky the guitarists were provided with stools. Often the function would be in a private house, with the meagre furniture pushed back to the walls and a big fire outside. "You can tell where the dances are to be held by the fires", wrote the black anthropologist Zora Neale Hurston, "Huge bonfires of faulty logs and slabs are lit outside the house in which the dances are held. The refreshments are parched peanuts, fried rabbit, fish, chicken and chitter-lings. The only music is guitar music and the only dance is the ole square dance." As she recalled from her work in Florida, "one guitar was enough for a dance, to have two was considered excellent. Where two were playing one man played the lead and the other seconded him. The first player was 'picking' and the second 'framming', that is, playing chords while the lead carried the melody by dextrous finger-work. Sometimes a third player was added, and he played a tom-tom effect on the low strings."[50] Hezekiah Jenkins, with a guitar accompaniment that was rather less accomplished than those described by Zora Neale Hurston, conveyed the atmosphere of a similar function:

> Went to a dance last Saturday night
> And what I mean this dance was tight,
> Given by a man named Lovey Joe
> In a small room 'bout two by fo'.
> And in this room they was thick as peas,
> You could hardly tell the he's from the she's
> And when the band began to play, I could hear them say,
>   "Oh, shout you cats, do it, stomp it, step you rats,
>   Shake your shimmy, break a leg,
>   Grab your gal and knock 'em dead,
>   Oh, do that thing!
>   Hey, hey, everybody sing."
> They got so good they threw away they hats,
>   I could hear 'em hollerin' "Shout you cats!"
> In came the cop 'bout half past fo'
> I felt sure we was booked to go,
> He said "everybody, fall in line!"
> They kep' on dancin', paid him no mind.
> A great big feller 'bout six foot tall,
> Grabbed the cop and slammed him up 'gainst the wall,
> The cop said "Buddy, everything Okay?" Listen to what I say –
>   "Oh, shout you cats, do it, stomp it,[51]   etc.

Though the song was in a sense a stereotype, it was authentic enough to fit with the experience of his audience. Jukes were rough places, hot, noisy and dusty. In the excitement of the dance and the close proximity of the dancers jealousies were inflamed and tempers flared. Many musicians who played the jukes have spoken of nights that ended in violence, with the dances broken up by "the law". During the Prohibition era "bootleg" liquor was sold in the jukes, which often had additional rooms for gambling, or where local girls could "turn a trick" or two. As Sam Chatmon, one of the band who called themselves the Mississippi Shieks explained, his group would play in one room for a dance, while gambling was taking place in another. "Sometimes the law would come, and all of them was in there in the gambling room, they had to pay a fine. You'd spy more pistols laying on the floor when the law come in. You could just look anywhere and find a pistol or a big, long knife laying down on the floor, some of them stuck up under the heaters. You seen the houseman tell the law to come by to keep him from having a lot of trouble. Guys what got pistols on 'em, if the law come and take their pistols, they wouldn't have nothing to act with." [52]

Not all the dances and hops were wild ones, and not all the dancers armed. Nor, for that matter, were all the dances vigorous with kicking steps and flapping arms. Some were "glides" and "slides" with slower movements in which the dancers kept their feet close to the floor. At what stage such dances as these became popular is difficult to determine; perhaps because they were less spectacular than high-stepping versions of barn dances and the like, they seem not to have been noted by early observers. Or they were the dances that were labeled often as "lascivious", their body and leg contact offending nineteenth-century proprieties. The "slow drag", which has long been associated with the cluster of dances performed to the blues, appears to have been first identified in one of Scott Joplin's earlier compositions, *Sunflower Slow Drag*, published in 1901. On the Slow Drag, Marshall Stearns, historian of *Jazz Dance*, who described many dances of the period, was vague: referring to the "Congo" hip movements of the Slow Drag, which are otherwise unspecified, he grouped it with the "Snake Hips and other social dances of the Negro folk". These, the "Afro-American vernacular, that is the basic dances of the Negro as the Strut, Shuffle, Sand and Grind" receive scant description. [53]

In 1911, Scott Joplin wrote his three-act ragtime opera, *Treemonisha*, with its action set in 1884. It concluded with "A Real Slow Drag" by the entire company: "hop and skip, now do that slow, – do that slow drag". With the sheet music came directions on dancing the Slow Drag which "must begin on the first beat of each measure. When moving forward, drag the left foot; when moving backward, drag the right foot". Sideways movements to left or right were accompanied by dragging the opposite foot; "when prancing your steps must come on each beat of the measure. When marching and when sliding, your steps must come on the first and third beat of each measure." One was to hop and skip on the second beat and "double the schottische step to fit the slow music". It was an elaborate set of movements appropriate for a dance finale, but in the country dances it was less complicated. The cornet player Charlie Love was more succinct: "They did the Slow Drag all over Louisiana, couples would hang onto each other and just grind back and forth all night." He was talking about 1903, but it could have been 1953, or perhaps 1873. [54]

When the barber William Moore played his *Old Country Rock* it was as a slow drag rather than as the Eagle Rock. The rocking movement from side to side as the dancers shifted weight from the ball of one foot to that of the other set the pace of the music, with long notes squeezed on the strings encouraging the slides of the slow drag.

> Come on Bill, let's take 'em for an Old Country Rock,
> Let's go back down on the Rappahannock, down Tappahannock
>   way . . .

He talked lazily over the guitar in a low voice with marked cadences:

> Rock me sister, rock me, Rock me till I sweat –
> Jump back folks and let your pappy rock –
> Pappy knows how – Chillen rock –
> Sister Ernestine, show your pappa how you rock,
> Mighty fine boys; rock it, rock it till the cows come home . . .

It was, he said, "too sad, I mean too sad for the public"; meaning that it was "happy" music in the use of slang inversions, such as "too bad" for "so good", which were current at the time.[55]

With the popularization of the blues, as both song form and dance, slow dragging became increasingly evident at black dances. The beat of the blues, and its frequent use of medium and slow tempos were ideally matched by the shuffle, rock and drag dances. They were also suited to cramped spaces, where "dancing on a dime" was a physical necessity. In the cities, in particular, where dances were often held in private premises and living rooms, slow drag blues were less noisy, and less of a threat to weak structures in timber framed tenements. Not that these were issues that were likely to have been given much consideration at "parlor socials" and "rent parties". Arranged in back rooms with local instrumentalists, especially pianists, to provide the entertainment, these events have been frequently described. The black poet Langston Hughes went to many "in small apartments where God knows who lived – because the guests seldom did – but where the piano would often be augmented by a guitar, or an old clarinet, or somebody with a pair of drums walking in off the street. And where awful bootleg whisky and good fried fish or steaming chitterlings were sold at very low prices. And the dancing and singing and impromptu entertaining went on until dawn came in at the windows." They were working-class functions, for attending which a small charge was made that would help pay the rent of the hostess; functions where he met "ladies' maids and truck drivers, laundryworkers and shoe shine boys, seamstresses and porters".[56]

William Moore recorded *Old Country Rock* and his other guitar rags for dancing with spoken commentaries like *Ragtime Crazy*, *Barbershop Rag* and *Raggin' the Blues*, in January 1928; later that year a number of recordings of similar type, but with spoken comments addressed to the dancers over a boogie woogie piano accompaniment, enjoyed a vogue. They were often modeled on Clarence Pine Top Smith's *Pine Top's Boogie Woogie*, and were recorded by pianists who sought to create the atmosphere of the rent party. Romeo (Iromeio) Nelson, Charles Avery and Speckled Red (Willie Perryman) were among them, but the number of pianists was legion. Sometimes one would emerge from the obscurity of Harlem or the Chicago South Side, to make a title or two – like Jim Clarke, whose only recorded item was *Fat Fanny Stomp*:

> . . . When I say 'Hold it!' this time, I want everybody to gully . . .
> Gut that thing, I mean gully,
> Hold it! Oh, gully . . . gully, gully low . . . gully like you live!
> Sister Fullbosom, you sure guttin' that thing . . .
> When I say hold it this time I want everybody to Sally Long
> Hold it! – Sally Long, Sally Long your fanny gal, Sally that thing,
> Shake your fat fanny – that's what I'm talkin' about . . .[57]

Though the Sally Long seems to have enjoyed a brief vogue in the late 1920s and is mentioned in several recordings, its name may have derived from the 1830s when William Whitlock and T. G. Booth sang of Sally King and Lucy Long in a dance song which included the lines "Take your time Miss Lucy Long, rock de cradle Lucy, take your time my dear". Other dances recur over many decades, those that were based on the actions of animals and birds being frequently revived by name, and in all probability in movements also. "Turkey Trot" was definitely used as a name to describe a dance in the 1850s while even *Scratchin' the Gravel*, which Perry Bradford mentioned in *The Bullfrog Hop* of 1909 and made into a dance-song (introduced, inevitably by "Slewfoot Jim") in 1917, had published as "Trike de toe and heel – cut de pigeon wing, scratch gravel, slap de foot – dat's just de ting" in *Sich a Gitting Up Stairs* in the 1830s.[58]

With house rent parties and boogie woogie, dances on Race records slip easily into the blues, bridged by the knowing, good-time music popularized as "Hokum". Of the many recordings, like Mozelle Alderson's *Tight Whoopee*, or Lil Johnson's *House Rent Scuffle*, *Come on Mama* by Georgia Tom and Hannah May (Jane Lucas) must serve to illustrate the persistence of traditional dance steps and striking imagery, and the teasing, challenging strutting of the dancer as she responded to the cheerful piano and guitar routine played by Tom Dorsey and Big Bill Broonzy:

> Come on mama, do that dance for me –
> Do the Mississippi Rub and the Mobile Bay,
> Turn right around and go the other way –
> Come on mama do that dance for me.
> > Oh, do that dance, oh do that dance,   } (2)
> > Come on mama, do that dance for me.   }

(See how you like this step – watch this shimmy I'm gonna shake – how do you like this mess around?)

> Put your hand on your hips, let your mind roll on
> Rather like you did the day you was born.
> > Come on mama, do that dance for me,
> Do the Blacksnake Wiggle and the Possum Trot,
> Scratch the gravel in a vacant lot.
> > Come on mama, do that dance for me,
> > O, do that dance.   etc.

(the snake hips . . . what do you think about them?)
>Now there's an old sister about seventy years old,
>Don't know how to do it, she done got cold . . .
>>Come on mama, do that dance for me.
>Now her hair turned grey, nose turned blue
>Some day this thing's gonna happen to you
>>Come on mama, do that dance for me.
>>Do that dance   etc.[59]

Played and sung by a good 'musicianer', or 'songster', almost all black secular songs could be adapted to dancing, and they generally were. Those whose lyrics referred to the dance steps, or the functions where music was played, were clearly intended for dancing, but they are often no more suitable than many other pieces on which an experienced performer could draw. They do, however, contain phrases and references to specific dances that give clues as to their date or origin, and this helps in establishing the lineage of the tradition. Because the requirements for a good dance piece – a swinging rhythm and a beat that lightens the steps of the dancers – have not substantially changed since the early nineteenth century, there has been an identifiable continuity in the dance songs and routines that has not always been matched in other song types. The interplay between folk custom and published sheet music, and between the traditional and the new, which relates folk idiom to popular song has to be borne in mind when the sources of other items in the songsters' repertoires are pursued.

2

Under the Chicken Tree
Songs from the ragtime era

A year after he published his important collection of *American Negro Folk Songs* in 1928, Newman I. White examined the sources of the material in an obscure article in the journal *American Speech*. Many of the 680 items that he and his collaborators had gathered from numerous informants a dozen and more years before were of minstrel origin. He deduced that "the Negro learned them from the white man and on request sang them back to the white man because the Negro knew it was what the white man wanted. After a while, as in the case of all other similar borrowings, he forgot that they were not originally his own." [1] Some in fact might have been originally black songs for many of the early minstrel entertainers based their performances on direct observation of black folkways. Not only dances but scraps of song and dialogue were drawn from life, and a number of minstrels who lived in, or came from, the South were in a position to learn directly from slaves and house servants. It is possible that song fragments or stanzas were cycled and re-cycled, later black singers being attracted to verses that were once the property of their forefathers. Be that as it may, Newman White considered that of the 680 songs, 104 showed "traces of the ante-bellum minstrel song".

Also significant in his reckoning were some fifty-eight items "showing traces of coon songs, vaudeville songs and ballets" which, numbered with twenty-two examples of white traditional folk song, and the minstrel songs already mentioned, represented in total over twenty-seven per cent of his collection. "Coon Song means to the Negro any popular song, not religious, composed by a white man about the Negro", he wrote. "Nor can the echoes of these songs in the Negro secular song be always distinguished from the influence of the 'ballet'. A 'ballet' by a semi-literate Negro or white man is sold at a fair or picnic and passes at once into oral tradition which sooner or later, by the immemorial process of repetition, amalgamation, addition and garbling, absorbs it into the current of genuine folk-song." [2]

Newman White's perceptive comments have gone unremarked, but they are borne out by the evidence of the repertoires of the songsters. He assumed though, that the authors of the coon songs were white whereas many of the most popular pieces among black songsters on record were, in fact, black in origin. Though the snatches of dance songs have given support to his belief that many were of ante-bellum minstrel origin, few songs that pre-date the

47

ragtime era of the 1890s were recorded by black songsters. An exception was
Champagne Charlie, which dates from as early as 1868 but which, in Sigmund
Spaeth's words, "up to 1895 or thereabouts . . . was just the last word in
devilishness".[3] The composition of an English music hall writer, George
Leybourne, *Champagne Charlie* was not the only Leybourne song to be
popular with black musicians; his *If I Ever Cease to Love* became an anthem
for the New Orleans marching bands. Originally a mechanic in the British
industrial Midlands he performed his song at the 'Canterbury Arms', a public
house in London's Lambeth Marshes – subsidized by a firm of champagne
merchants who appear to have shipped the song, as well as the bubbly, to New
York:

> The way I gain'd my title's By a fashion which I've got
> Of never letting others pay, However long's the shot,
> For whoe'er drinks at my expense, Is treated all the same,
> "Fifth Avenue" or "Bow'ry Style", I make them take Champagne.
>   Champagne Charlie is my name, Champagne Charlie is my name.
>   Good for any game at night, my boys,   (2)
>   Champagne Charlie is my name,   (2)
>   Good for any game at night, my boys,
>   Who'll come and join me in a spree?[4]

At his last recording session, Blind Blake made a version to an even simpler
tune, adapted in a form which would have appealed to black audiences as
much for the idioms as for the incongruity of their drinking champagne in the
Depression year of 1932.

> I went to see my true love, never been there before,
> Her shoes and stockings in her hand,
> And her feet all over the floor.
>   Champagne Charlie is my name,   (2)
>   Champagne Charlie is my name, by golly,
>   And robbin' and stealin' is my game.
>
> I went down to Louisville,
> And I h'ain't been there before;
> And a great big bully knocked me down,
> And I didn't go back no more.
>   Champagne Charlie   etc.
>
> I went to see a young lady,
> I ain't been there before,
> She feed me out of her [pork] pig-trough
> And I ain't goin' back no more . . .[5]

It's "devilishness" in the nineties related the song in popular taste to the
"bully", "coon" and ragtime songs of the day. Most famous, but not
necessarily the first, of the bully songs was sung by May Irwin in 1895 in *The
Widow Jones*. She had encouraged the sports writer Charles E. Trevathan to
put words to a tune which he had heard black singers perform in Tennessee.

But it also seems likely that the song was being performed at much the same time by Mama Lou, the stout and aggressive singer in the celebrated brothel in St. Louis run by Babe Connor, where *Ta Ra Ra Boom Der Re* was also born. Whatever the original source – and both may have derived from a folk song current among blacks – it was an instant success for May Irwin.[6] The cover for the sheet music of *The Bully Song* was a grotesque caricature of a razor-toting, thick-lipped, prognathous black man in exaggerated clothes. Many other variants were published: *The New Bully*, in four different versions and with different "authors", *De Bully's Wedding Night* and *Dere's a Bully Gone To Rest*, all in the space of a year 1895–6.[7] Though it was recorded many times by popular and hillbilly singers it appeared on Race records only as a fragment in Henry Thomas's *Bob McKinney*, and then to the tune of *Pallet on the Floor*, and as *I'm Looking for the Bully of the Town* by the Memphis Jug Band. They selected it for their second session, but they sang only a couple of stanzas and excluded the refrain:

> I'm lookin' for the bully, the bully can't be found,
> I'm looking for the bully, for the bully of this town.
> Oh he's a bad man, he was the baddest man in town
> I'm looking for the bully of the town.[8]

Paul Allen's popular *New Coon in Town*, published in 1883, may have given the name to the genre of "coon songs" which appeared in large numbers a dozen years later. Portraying blacks in stereotypical imagery, the coon songs made them the butt of a crude humor which laughed at physical characteristics of color and hair and, in W. K. McNeil's words, "an unusual, often incorrect use of language and a love of song, ostentatious names, laziness and shiftlessness"[9] let alone an appetite for watermelons, chicken and sharp razors.

Coon songs and ragtime were closely related in the nineties, with many such songs containing syncopation in the music and scoring that was of a ragtime character. Other coon songs were closer to the Victorian tradition of "heart" songs and sentimental ballads, often depicting the "coon" or the "darkey" as a subject of pity and sugary sympathy, or as naive and simple. Over 600 songs in the coon and bully vein were published in the last five years of the nineteenth century, and the flood only slightly abated in the next decade. As W. F. Gates complained in an article, "Ethiopian Syncopation; the Decline of Ragtime" in 1902, "jerky note groups by the million, 'coon poetry' by the ream, colored inks by the ton", were being produced in a "flood of 'rag-time' abominations, that sweeps over the country".[10] Whilst many of the songs were nauseating in the sentimentality and in the crudity of their stereotyping, there were some which showed a measure of sensitivity in their lyrics or melodies, and a few which had genuine musical merit.

Some of the earliest composers of coon and ragtime songs were black, including Ernest Hogan, whose *All Coons Look Alike To Me*, caused much bitter reproach; Hogan in fact, had intended to soften the impact of a song which was originally composed as "All pimps look alike to me". A "Medley-Schottische" in one version it was almost as popular as the same composer's *Pas Ma La*. Another black composer who was "passing for white" was Ben Harney, whose *You've Been a Good Old Wagon But You've Done Broke Down* and *Mister Johnson, Turn Me Loose* were widely acclaimed for their authenticity of idiom. But though the former Harney title was recorded by Bessie Smith, neither Harney nor Hogan left any impact on black song such that their compositions appeared much on Race records, and neither seems to have influenced black folk vocal traditions.[11]

A number of other black composers seem to have appealed much more to folk musicians; Chris Smith was one of them. He was born in Charleston, South Carolina in 1879 and as a boy worked in a bakery. A natural entertainer, he performed as singer and dancer both locally and with visiting shows. With his friend Elmer Bowman he left the South to tour. "Elmer and me left Charleston with a white man", Edward Marks reported him as saying. "We was still in short pants. This man, he was an old actor man that turned to doctoring, and he was to pay us 6 dollars a week. He used to take axle grease and put it up in tin boxes and sell it for a nickel a box for a rheumatism cure for

"True Lovers of the Muse": young musicians playing mandolin and guitar. Detroit, Michigan, 1902. *Library of Congress collection.*

colored people. If you want to know how many miles it is from Georgetown, South Carolina to Columbia, it is seventy-nine. Elmer and I had to walk it when this old man wouldn't give us our wages." [12] As young men they formed a vaudeville act which lasted until World War I. Smith's early songs included *The Sounds of Chicken Fryin' In the Pan, Dat's Music To Me* and, as early as 1900, at the age of twenty-one he wrote *Never Let the Same Bee Sting You Twice*. It was recorded over a quarter of a century later by Richard "Rabbit" Brown, a New Orleans-born guitarist and boatman. Though Smith's song was written as a light and wry comic number, Rabbit Brown took it seriously, and in his rough, lugubrious vocal projected it as a piece of folk wisdom.

> I been worried all the time,
> I never have a satisfyin' mind.
> Life to me is a sad mistake,
> Me and my wife we done separate.
> If one have lovers that are kind and true,
> I'm gonna tell you something that you all must do.
> I've been studyin' nearly all my life,
> Keep the same bee that stung me from stinging me twice.
>> Never let the same bee that sting you,
>> Never let it sting you twice.
>> That's if you want to be happy,
>> Keep up with this kind of life.
>> Oh when you out upon your honeymoon,
>> And your trouble and your sorrows rose in a balloon,
>> Go out with a girl,
>> But you must remember your wife,
>> Never let the same bee that stung you, sting you twice. [13]

Elmer Bowman, Smith's partner in the writing of a number of songs, died in New York in 1916 when he was less than forty years old. One of his compositions in collaboration with Smith, *I Ain't Poor No More*, had been a hit in the same year as *Never Let the Same Bee*, but a more widely known song was their joint *I Got de Blues* composed in 1912. That year, too, he wrote *Beans! Beans! Beans!* for which Smith composed the music, a comedy number whose irony and surreal exaggerations impressed two songsters who recorded in Charlotte, North Carolina: James Albert, who was called "Beans" Hambone, and his partner El Morrow, folk musicians with rough voices and with guitars that "sound like they were home-made, making the whole performance seem like a field recording rather than one for commercial sale", as Richard Spottswood observed. He surmised that the song was almost certainly from the nineteenth century pre-blues tradition. Albert introduced himself on the record: "This is 'Beans' now, fixin' to play you all a beautiful little number entitled 'Beans'. You sing this from Gener-resurrection to the Revolution. . . ." When you came to his house, he asserted, "you won't find no stew beef, no pork and spice, . . . no ham, no eggs . . ."

> They give you beans for your breakfast,
> Give you beans for your dinner

DEDICATED TO

LITTLE SADIE JONES.

POSSUMALA DANCE

OR

MY H·O·N·E·Y

WORDS AND MUSIC

BY

Irving

Jones.

4

NEW YORK:

WILLIS WOODWARD & CO.,

842 & 844 BROADWAY.

COPYRIGHT MDCCCXCIV BY WILLIS WOODWARD & CO.
LONDON : ENTERED AT STATIONERS HALL.

CHARLES SHEARD & CO., 192 High Holborn. W. C. London.

In spite of its subject, the music for Irving Jones's *Possumala Dance* had a sedate
cover, with a portrait photograph of its composer. *Harding Collection,*
The Bodleian Library.

Beans for suppertime.
They give you fried beans, boiled beans,
Stew beans, baked beans,
Beans brand [an' I]
Got sick from eatin' beans.
Oh the doctor brought beans,
Had pills looked like beans,
Wrote out a 'scription for 'beans, beans, beans'.
And they taste like beans,
Then they act-a like beans, beans, beans.
They will work you like beans too,
Some a'liman beans, beans, beans,
A mess of pork and beans,
Spoon stickin' in your beans,
David had a mess of beans, beans, beans.
Old David had beans, beans,
Some a'lima beans,
You seen the pinto beans,
Adam had a mess of beans,
Swear Eve had beans,
She had a garden full of beans.
Old Norah had beans, beans,
He had a ark full of beans.
Parson Paul had beans, beans,
Some a'liman beans,
I died from eatin' beans, beans, beans,
Undertaker brought beans,
Had a coffin full of beans,
His hearse was full of beans, beans,
To the graveyard eatin' beans,
Dug my grave in beans, beans, beans.
Let me down with bean strings,
Covered me up with bean hulls,
Preached my funeral in beans, beans, beans . . .[14]

The song was ideal for the folk songster, permitting extemporized lines to be added at will as they suited the audience and the circumstances of the performance.

Neither Chris Smith, nor Elmer Bowman nor Cecil Mack was the most popular composer with the folk songsters. That honor goes to one of their most prolific, but woefully neglected, contemporaries, Irving Jones. As early as 1894 Irving Jones had published *Possumala Dance*, a version of the *Pas Ma La* which pre-dated the Hogan composition by a year. Its content linked with folk songs in the black tradition, describing a "colored hop" where the house was crowded to the doors. "In came a big coon . . . with diamonds loaded from head to feet; I think they called him 'Sloo-foot Pete', He was the coon who ran the ball; the dance was held at Bad Land Hall . . ."

When in came a big coon looking for a fight
Said he, "My name is George Good Health,

I'm so bad, I'm afraid of myself."
He pulled his gun, began to shoot,
All the darkies they began to skoot,
Such cutting and shooting I never saw –
One coon fell clear through the floor . . .

After the police came in, "slipped the nippers on his hands" and called for
the patrol wagon, "he began to sing:

"Nobody knows how bad I am, honey, honey,
Nobody knows how bad I am baby, baby . . ."

The song is significant in many ways; it clearly used the "coon song"
terminology which ensured its publication at the time, and it described the
fracas at a dance which fitted the "bully" image. But it also drew from folk
sources. In 1892, just a couple of years before, "a fragment" had been
collected by Gates Thomas in south Texas:

In came a man was tall and fat,
He had on a Stetson hat,
Said his name was Billy Gelef,
He had got so bad he was skeered of hisself.

"the remaining stanzas of the song, forgotten, recount a 'coon can' game in
which Billy is at first spectator and later a participating hero",[15] Thomas
wrote, many years later. The song that George Good Health commenced to
sing may have also been drawn from the tradition, or it may have been the
inspiration for a new song. At any rate, it clearly linked with Jim Jackson's *I'm
a Bad, Bad Man*:

I'm a bad, bad man, from bad, bad lands,
Nobody knows how bad I am,
I don't care for police, judge and jury,
I'm a man from the bad, bad lands.[16]

Both the name of the man who put on the dance and the location of the
function were themselves probably already in the folk tradition. If not, Irving
Jones was instrumental in introducing them to subsequent composers,
including Perry Bradford, who's *Rules and Regulations* "Signed Sloo-foot
Jim" of 1911 became "Razor Jim" when recorded by Edith Wilson eleven
years later.

   The theme of the police raid was a perennial one in black song, and was the
subject of Blind Sammie's *Razor Ball* – played and sung by Blind Willie
McTell under a pseudonym.

Down at the Razor Ball, given at the Razor Hall,
Sloofoot Mose and old Cross-eyed Joe
Didn't go in at all,
They hung around outside, this is what they spied: (what was it?)
   Big crap game, in the hall, started in to fight,
   Joe got drunk, mad with em all,
   When Eddie turned out the light

> Mike took Charlie, Charlie shot his automatic, when
> Charlie grabbed a gal and he crossed [all] skin,
> Police came and pulled a haul
> Down at the Razor Ball, I mean Ball,
> Down at the Razor Ball.
> Doin' that shimmy-sha-wabblin', shakin'
> Shimmeshawabblin', quit shakin' your hips
> Down at the Razor, I mean Ball, down at the Razor Hall.[17]

His song continued with other crap games and fights at the ball, sung and played with Willie McTell's customary speed and deft precision. In the manner of playing it was a dance theme, but the subject of the affray at the ball was one which occurred in ragtime songs of the turn of the century. Irving Jones's *Possumala Dance* was scored with ragtime syncopation. It had indirect connexions with *Razor Ball*, though McTell's song, substantially altered in transmission, may have been derived from the recording made in 1925 by Sara Martin as *Down at the Razor Ball.*

During the next three or four years Irving Jones composed and published a number of songs, some of which, like *The Black Four Hundred* (1897) were intended either to attract, or mildly to parody, the wealthier blacks. His earlier songs have a certain middle-class appeal like *The Blackville Derby Ball* (1898) or *Get Your Money's Worth* (*Instructions From the Boss*) of the year before. In the same year he wrote a song in which a woman dismisses her wastrel husband – a theme which was to be popular on the black vaudeville stage – *Take Your Clothes and Go.* Its success encouraged a rejoinder, *Let Me Bring My Clothes Back Home*, which soon slipped into the popular tradition. Howard Odum collected it only a few years after publication and considered it "characteristic in its adaptation of the 'coon' song into a negro song".

> The burly coon, you know
> He packed his clothes to go,
> Well, he come back las' night,
> His wife said, "Honey, I'm tired o' coon,
> I goin' to pass for white".

When her partner became mad "because his color was black" he promised to get a job if she wouldn't quit him;

> I'll wuk both night an' day,
> An' let you draw my pay.
> Baby, let me bring my clothes back home.
> When you kill chicken, save me the bone;
> When you buy beer, give me the foam.
> I'll wuk both night an' day
> An' let you draw the pay.
> Baby, let me bring my clothes back home.[18]

Another version, collected a few years later by Gladys Torregano of New Orleans and published in 1923 by Walter Prescott Webb was essentially the same song. Henry Thomas recorded it in a medley entitled *Arkansas* in 1927 but felt compelled, or was persuaded by the record executive, to bowdlerize it: "coon" became "beans" and "white" became "green", a subterfuge which would have been transparent to those of his listeners who knew the song.

> Albert turn round, pack his trunk and go –
> Yes, he came back home las' night –
> He' wife said "Honey I'm done with beans
> I'm gonna pass for green."
> "Oh my little honey don't you make me go,
> I'll get a job, if you 'llow me, sho'
> All crapshooters I will shun,
> Good little baby, jes' let me work.
> > When you buy chicken, all I want is the bone,
> > When you buy beer, be satisfied with foam:
> > I'll work both night and day,
> > I'll be careful what I say –
> > Honey (What?) Please, let me bring my clothes back home . . ." [19]

Rejection, which was to be a dominant theme in black theatrical duets, was often the subject of Jones's songs at this time, including *You Don't Handle Nuff Money For Me*, *You Ain't Landlord No More*, and *There Ain't No More Use to Keep On Hanging Around*, all published in 1898–9. Money, or the lack of it, also figured prominently in his songs, with *I'm Livin' Easy*, *I'm Lending Money to the Government Now*, *Mr Dingy Don't be Stingy* and *My Money Never Gives Out* being published in 1900. The latter song was in the form of a fantasy in which the singer dreamed that he was wealthy:

> My money never gives out,
> Rich food is making me stout,
> 'Cause every meal, for quail on toast, I shout –
> I live good all the time
> I don't drink no cheap wine . . . [20]

A veteran banjo player from Red Banks, Mississippi, Gus Cannon, who was seventeen at the time the song was published, was living near Clarksdale when he recorded the song nearly thirty years later. With its jaunty rhythm it was a favourite theme and, in his version with his own Jug Stompers, it had markedly syncopated choruses.

> There's a certain yeller joker lives around this town
> Just as lazy as lazy can be,
> While as long as they shake it there, he hangs around.
> "I love my hop" says he.
> Early one morning this joker ran away
> To roam the world, was said,
> "Then I go back to bed, man, I keep up my head
> I don't care if I never wake up." . . .
> "Now if my money was stacked high,
> I believe to my soul it would touch the sky.

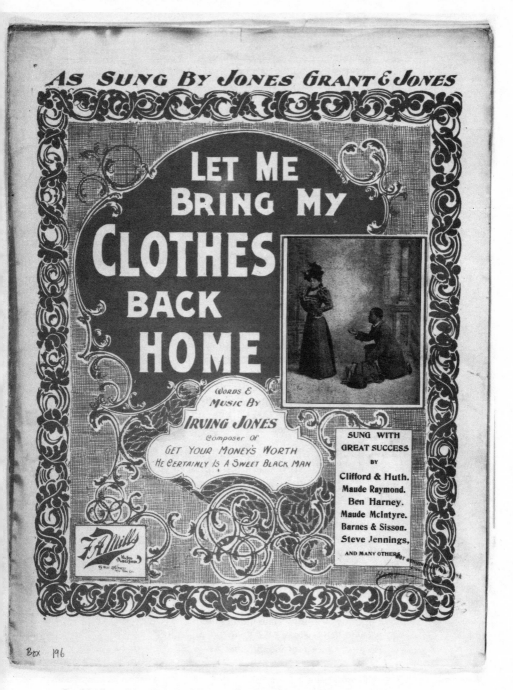

Let Me Bring My Clothes Back Home was performed by many entertainers. A lemon yellow rococo design was chosen for the cover, with an illustration of the theme. *Harding Collection, The Bodleian Library.*

> I'd polish my teeth with diamond dust
> I don't care if the bank is bust,
> For my money, don't never run out,
> Rich food is making me stout
> Well ev'ry good evenin', for quail on toast, I shout.
> Now I'm living good all the time
> I don't drink", he says, "no cheap wine
> Well it's almost certain, my money well, it never run out . . ."[21]

Gus Cannon was illiterate and he could not have learned the song direct from the sheet music without the help of an intermediary – Alec Lee perhaps, an older musician who taught him other songs. *My Money Never Gives Out* was advertised, with a short extract, on the back cover of another fantasy piece by Irving Jones, written in the same year, 1900, *The Ragtime Millionaire*. Apart from its interest as a song it may be the first by a black writer to make reference to the blues – not as a song form but as a condition. It assumes, since it makes a joke about it, understanding of the usage by the listener: "from wearing blue-white diamonds I have got the blues/ thousand dollar bills to me look like the daily news/I have solid gold knobs on all of my doors and carpets made of money tacked on all of my floors . . ."

> I am the ragtime millionaire,
> I haven't got a thing but money to spare,
> I live through this expensive world with ease,
> I know I'm goin' to die with money disease,
> I am the ragtime millionaire,
> More popular than the man in the President's Chair –
> Ev'ry rich man in town takes his hat off to me,
> I'm the ragtime millionaire.[22]

The Tappahannock barber, William Moore, no doubt entertained his clients with his version of the song, suitably updated, expressing his dreams of owning a new car. He seems to have had some knowledge of *My Money Never Gives Out* for certain key lines have been incorporated in the song.

> Mr Henry gonna send me a Ford T. [mark]
> Everybody else gonna take my [junk]
> Gonna put a little sign on it "In God we Trust"
> I don't mean to have no fuss,
>   All you little people take your hat off to me,
>   Because I'm a ragtime millionaire.
>   I'm a rag, I'm a rag,
>   I'm a rag, I'm a ragtime millionaire,
>   All you little people take your hat off to me,
>   Because I'm a ragtime millionaire.
>
> Some of these boys say that I'm gonna be late,
> No, if you please – I got a '28.
> Some boys say they goin' t' catch me at last
> But all I have to do is just to step on the gas,
>   All you little people take your hat off to me,   etc.

A sympathetic caricature of Irving Jones on stage appeared on the bright red cover of his *The Ragtime Millionaire*. Two of Irene Mackey's Trio performed in blackface. *Harding Collection, the Bodleian Library.*

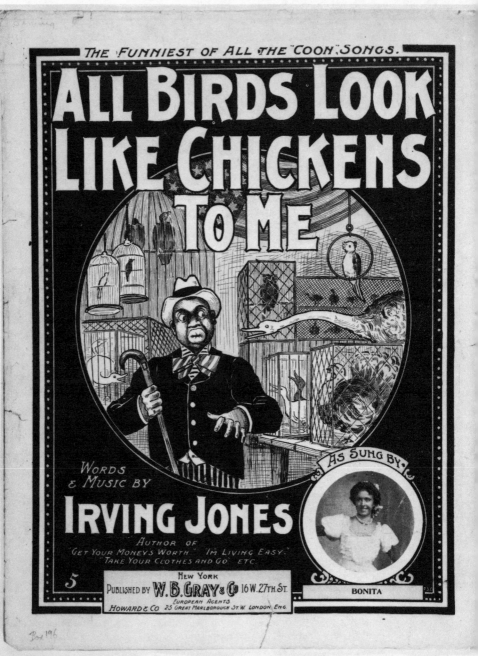

For the cover of *All Birds Look Like Chickens To Me* by Irving Jones, publisher
W. B. Gray resorted to coon stereotype. *Harding Collection, The Bodleian Library.*

> Every tooth in my head is solid gold,
> Make those boys look icy cold.
> I brush my teeth with diamond dust
> And I don't care if the bank would bust.
>   All you little people take your hats off to me
>   'Cause I'm a ragtime millionaire.[23]

At the turn of the century Irving Jones complied with the current trend in coon songs with *I Don't 'llow No Coon To Hurt My Feelings*, and *If They'd Only Fought With Razors In the War*. "A splendid little War" as John Hay called it, the war with Spain was followed by the "insurrection" in the Philippines. When Governor William Taft's "little brown brothers" received assurances of eventual independence and a positive future for them was being planned, Irving Jones wrote *I Want a Filipino Man* with more than a touch of irony. Some of his songs had a hint of social comment in the comic disguise: *Every Coon In Town Is Broke, Home Ain't Nothing' Like This, I Feel Like Sending Home For Money* and *I Never Seen Such Hard Luck Before* being among his contemporary songs. The occasional song which made the stereotyped jokes about black tastes still proved to be popular: *All Birds Look Like Chickens To Me* was clearly intended to mock Ernest Hogan's *All Coons Look Alike To Me*. In 1926 it was recorded by one Sweet Papa Stovepipe – probably McKinley Peebles, a New York street singer who was two years old when Irving Jones's song was published as:

> All birds look like chicken to me,
> Crows look like black hens to me,
> Some birds are raised for a prize
> But a knife and fork make 'em all one size.
> You people say quails are chickens you see
> But they look like Lilliputian hens to me.

Quails seem to have been a personal symbol for high living to Irving Jones. Not surprisingly, Peebles had changed two lines to make more sense in his frame of reference which presumably did not include *Gulliver's Travels*:

> . . . Quails are like chickens to me
> They look like little fat hens to me . . .[24]

While he still composed in the established coon song genre, Irving Jones seems to have found devices for making popular songs while giving a twist to the themes. *Under the Chicken Tree* certainly accorded with the stereotype of the minstrel coon drooling over chicken in gravy. But it is an image which in this song only takes shape as a dream. It was recorded by Earl McDonald's Original Louisville Jug Band in 1927. One member of the band, Lucien Brown claimed the song as his own: "There was one thing though, *Under the Chicken Tree* and *Rocking Chair Blues*, these were my numbers that I had worked out everything for. Earl just took them over because it was his band." Jug player and leader Earl McDonald took the vocal on Irving Jones's 1908 song, for which the music was written down by Kerry Mills.

I had a dream last night it almost turned me white,
I dreamed that hens and roosters grew on trees.
I dreamed on a great big ranch, on ev'ry hen tree branch,
The eggs were just as thick as bumble bees.

I stepped down in the yard,
And shook one tree right hard,
And 'bout one hundred fowls come tumblin' down.
Just as soon as they had died, I had them quickly fried
With the gravy oozing out all nice and brown –
   It was under the chicken tree,
   Under the big fricassee,
   Eggs was droppin' from every blossom,
   I lost all my taste for the meat they call 'possum'.
   Hounds, hogs, everything,
   Looks like feathers, shaking that wing;
   Eggs was dropping, wings was floppin',
   Under the chicken tree.[25]

Though his verse kept close to Irving Jones's lyrics the chorus was slightly different: Jones had written for example, "All kinds of money and ev'ry other thing looked like chicken feathers to me" which made slightly more sense, though sense was not too important in a depiction of a dream. The differences suggest that the song did not derive directly from sheet music but through oral transmission. It was probably a fairly popular theme with jug bands; as early as 1924, guitarist and nose-whistle player Buford Threlkeld, known as "Whistler", had recorded *Chicken Tree* with his Jug Band in St. Louis, but the item remained unissued.

At least one more song by Irving Jones appeared on Race record when Lil McClintock made his *You Must Think I'm Santa Claus*, which I have previously discussed in *Screening the Blues*. It, too, was slightly altered; where Irving Jones had written

If you think I'm a Christmas Tree,
You have certainly made a frost,
Because I give you presents, honey,
Once in a while, don't think I'm Santa Claus.

Lil McClintock sang:

You need not think that I'm a human being,
It's nothing but a fraud.
'Cause I bring you a present ever' once in a while,
Don't think I'm Santa Claus.

Apparently he did not know the other verses of the song, and instead built up a medley which, as Richard Raichelson has shown, was of verses and chorus from four songs. The others were *By the Watermelon Vine – Lindy Lou* by Thomas S. Allen, published in 1904, *Keep a Little Cozy Corner in Your Heart for Me* (sung as "a closer corner" by Lil McClintock) which was published a

'Cuff Boys'

year later with words by Jack Drislane and music by Theodore F. Morse, and a snatch of *Everybody Works But Father* of the same year.[26] This latter song was written by Jean Havez, but it had been adapted from an earlier music hall song in England which in the previous year, 1904, had been published there as by S. Lehman and, by a coincidence, with words by C. W. McClintock. The medley, which did not have the internal logic in the piecing together of the themes that was sometimes the case in the medleys by Henry Thomas or Jim Jackson, was recorded under the modified title of the Irving Jones' song, *Don't Think I'm Santa Claus*. It was among the last of his compositions. He had, in fact, published *I've Lost My Appetite for Chicken* that same year, in 1904, though *Under the Chicken Tree* came out four years later; perhaps his appetite for coon and ragtime songs had also waned, even if the memory of some of those that he had published survived in the folk tradition for thirty years.

Though other black song writers of the ragtime period composed items which appealed to songsters, none seems to have been as popular as Irving Jones. Few other composers of such importance within a genre have been so neglected by historians of popular music. What was the reason for the attraction of his compositions among songsters? Undoubtedly the catchy tunes and swinging rhythms had much to do with their appeal, making them both memorable and relatively easy to pick up from a few hearings. Though the songs at first sight seem to fit the current clichés, the author of *When a Coon Sits in the President's Chair* and *St. Patrick's Day is a Bad Day for Coons* had a certain pointed wit which indicates that he was using a popular song idiom to get in a barb or two. As the lyrics of *I'm Living Easy, You Needn't Think I'm a Regular Fool* or *He Certainly Is a Sweet Black Man* confirm, he also had an ear for authentic idioms of black speech of the times.[27]

Nevertheless, his songs were unlikely to have been learned directly from sheet music by songsters, many, perhaps the majority, being illiterate and few, if any, being able to read music. Songsters were generally working class; Gus Cannon was a field hand, ditch digger and eventually, in his words "a gumball-raker" for the streets of Memphis. Henry Thomas was a street singer, Frank Stokes was a blacksmith, Willie McTell and Arthur Blake were both blind. Only William Moore, as a barber, was a little more socially advantaged.

In 1910, when most songsters were active as musicians, illiteracy among blacks was extensive. Georgia, from where many songsters came, reported over 300,000 black illiterates over the age of ten, while those in Alabama, Mississippi and Louisiana were in excess of a quarter of a million in each state, all of them representing up to forty per cent of their respective black populations. This meant, nonetheless, that six out of ten blacks in many Southern states could read to some extent, and they may in turn have passed on the words of popular songs.[28]

In Edward Marks' recollection, Irving Jones "was a musical illiterate, and probably lost more tunes than he actually sold. (A clique of white 'composers' known as the 'the cuff boys' used to haunt the colored clubrooms for the blk. minstralay

special purpose of picking up songs.)" When *Take Your Clothes and Go* was published by Marks "we really had something",[29] but Jones also published many of his songs with F. A. (Kerry) Mills and several with Leo Feist in New York and Charles K. Harris of Chicago and Milwaukee. Harris had made a hit with his song *After the Ball* – hummed to a pianist who transcribed it for him as he could not write a note of music himself – and later wrote *Hello Central Give Me Heaven* which had its effect upon black blues and popular song. He had, wrote Charles Hamm, "an uncanny ability to judge which songs of his (and other composers) were most likely to sell well quickly" and this "made him one of the most successful and powerful publishers of popular song in America". Feist, composer of a "darkey lamentation" *Let Me In, Dat's All* and other coon songs, was also a successful publisher.[30]

John Stark, the publisher of *Maple Leaf Rag*, among many rags by Scott Joplin, James Scott, Artie Matthews and other pianists, staked his reputation and the money that he had acquired from peddling ice-cream and pianos on their music. He had a low opinion of the methods employed by his competitors in the publishing field in securing markets, though he was not above denigrating them in circulars which he sent to the dealers in sheet music, and naming names in the process. "Leo Feist – nettled at seeing a competitor's 'hits' going faster than his own filled up the Woolworth's 5 and 10ct. stores with music on sale. S. H. Knox of Buffalo was induced to put music in his sixty-eight 5 and 10ct. stores scattered throughout the country. The New York Music Co. (Albert Von Tilzer) actually sends a man to these 10ct. stores to sing and push their pieces. It is said that Chas. K. Harris sold Knox 50,000 pieces at one order", he accused.[31] It is by no means unlikely that some of Irving Jones's songs were included in Charles Harris's order for the Kress stores, or that *The Ragtime Millionaire* and *My Money Never Gives Out* were among those that Leo Feist placed in Woolworth's. His songs were certainly popular: *Take Your Clothes And Go* sold 100,000 copies in less than two years.

However, it is far less likely that the shelves were ransacked for suitable material, and live performance must have played a major part in the popularization of most songs. Though the minstrel show may be seen as a grotesque parody of black song, speech and dance, it had wide appeal among black audiences. Before the Civil War, shows with "Pure Plantation Melodies" were being presented by "Slave troupes" who were "earning their freedom by giving concerts under the guidance of their Northern friends" and in the season of 1865–6 Booker and Clayton's Georgia Minstrels, "the Only Simon Pure Negro Troupe in the World" drew large audiences to their evocations of plantation life; the members of the troupe had been slaves in Macon, Georgia.

Charles Callender, a white tavern owner and promoter, brought together the talents of black entertainers like Charles Hicks, Billy Kersands and Bob Height to form a famous company of Georgia minstrels; later Hicks and Kersands broke away to form their own troupes, and by the mid-1870s there were some thirty black minstrel shows working the states. When Callender sold out to J. H. Haverly in 1878 the new promoter "presented the black minstrels not as entertainers but as representatives of the plantation Negro put on exhibit"[32] with scenes of levee and canebrake on stage. Lew Johnson's many companies, the competing Hicks and Sawyer companies, Billy Kersand's Minstrels, W. C. Cleveland's Colored Minstrel Carnival and many others traveled throughout the country, performing in Wyoming, Nevada, California as well as in the Eastern and Southern states. In his detailed account, Robert C. Toll lists over a hundred black companies who were working between the end of the Civil War and 1890, some short-lived, but others famous and successful.[33]

Black troupes frequently toured in their own sleeping and baggage cars, performed under canvas, in barns or, as their number increased, in theaters. They were popular in the South in the years of Callender, Hicks and Sawyer and the Booker and Clayton Georgia Minstrels, and this popularity was shared by the later companies that were active in the present century until after World War II. Many black song writers got their training and their experience in the minstrel shows, as did James Bland, the composer of *Carry Me Back to Old Virginny* and *Oh Dem Golden Slippers* who was a greatly reputed performer with Sprague's Georgia Minstrels and, later, with Haverly. Ernest Hogan combined with Henry Eden to form Eden and Hogan's Minstrels in 1890, "a great company and noted for its fine parades" as "Old Slack", Ike Simond, a "banjo player comique" recalled in his *Reminiscence and Pocket History of the Colored Profession from 1865 to 1891*. He remembered the popular song writer Sam Lucas, composer of *De Day I Was Sot Free, Shivering and Shaking Out In the Cold*, and a number of religious items including *Put On My Long White Robe*, all of which he wrote from 1878 to 1879. Lucas performed with Callender's Minstrels, with Sprague and with Haverly's Black Hundred of 1879. "He told me he would never black his face again, and as I have met him in nearly every city of the United States since that time I don't think he ever has", Simond commented.

One such meeting was significant in the present context. The Sam Jack Creole Company was formed in Boston in 1890 to go on tour; included among the cast were Sam Lucas and Irving Jones. Simond "happened to drop into Sam T. Jack's Creole Car while en route to Chicago" where he found several members of the company "engaged in a game of dice. Irving Jones was holding stakes and by the way he turned flip flaps and growled from the bottom of his bread basket I could see that he would not get left." Ike Simond's typically fragmentary account did not give details of the show, though it did reveal Irving Jones as an astute gambler. "The Creole Show" had a large cast, with sixteen beautiful girls "in attractive groupings of shapely femininity" as the Indianapolis *Freeman* reported in 1890. It played Boston, New York and a season at Sam Jack's Opera House during the Chicago World's Fair of 1893. Though it did not include a plantation setting it did have the first part of a minstrel show, breaking with convention by having a woman as "Interlocutor". A burlesque, "The Beauty of the Nile, or Doomed by Fire" included Irving Jones in the part of Zeno.[34]

From these and other indications, including contemporary photographs, it is evident that Irving Jones knew Sam Lucas, who had earlier worked with James Bland, and hence had an introduction to music publishing, and that he was a performer before composing the *Possumala* in 1894. Later, in the 1890s, Jones was a member of John Isham's Octoroons, and in 1899 he played with Will Marion Cook's "Jes Lak White Folks". A season with Black Patti's troubadours followed, before he teamed with Charley Johnson, as "The Two Cut-Ups". At the turn of the century, he was regularly touring with a song and dance team under the name of Jones, Grant and Jones, while the publication of *One More Drink and I'll Tell It All* in San Francisco in 1901, and *You Needn't Think I'm a Regular Fool* in Denver, Colorado in 1905 may give a clue to the extent of his travels. A member of the Clef Club, New York in 1912, he continued to entertain with his "droll comedy" playing Chicago's Grand Theater in 1919. When he was sixty in the 1920s he was still touring the Radio Keith-Orpheum theaters. He died in 1932 in New York.[35]

Though other song writers composed works which were picked up by the songsters and recorded many years later, the instance of Irving Jones not only helps to clarify how the songs and dance themes related to the minstrel, carnival and traveling shows of the late nineteenth century, but also how the sheet music became popularly and cheaply available. If it is scarcely possible now to trace how a specific song like *My Money Never Runs Out* became a part of the repertoire of Gus Cannon's Jug Stompers, it is not difficult to see how such pieces could have been heard, enjoyed, learned and absorbed by the songsters, especially those who themselves performed in the traveling shows in the intervening years.

As the twentieth century advanced, black composers rose on the tide of popularity for the "all-colored" Broadway shows and the appeal of jazz. New markets among whites were opened up, and some more sophisticated writers were aware of a social responsibility to their race. James Weldon Johnson and his brother J. Rosamund Johnson came from an educated family and wrote songs which eschewed all the clichés of the coon and minstrel genres. "We wanted to clean up the caricature" Rosamund Johnson specifically stated.[36] The new audience was fascinated by depictions of what they assumed to be authentic black folkways. For a pushing composer who had an eye for the music sheet and publishing market, like W. C. Handy, Perry Bradford, George Thomas or Spencer Williams, the absorption, borrowing and reabsorption of traditional songs, especially those that provided the basis of a blues or near-blues composition, was extremely tempting. Abbe Niles noted that the writers of the different versions of *Hesitating Blues*, published in 1915, W. C. Handy, and Smythe and Middleton, used "slightly different arrangements". Early blues composers were quick to arrange, or "improve" the songs they adapted as Handy described his deliberate introduction of "flat thirds and sevenths (now called 'blue notes') into my song", when writing *St. Louis Blues*. At that time "the tango was the vogue. I tricked the dancers by arranging a tango introduction, breaking abruptly then into a low-down blues."[37] *St. Louis Blues* was recorded by Bessie Smith and other stage blues singers, but was rarely found in the folk tradition: Jim Jackson made one version (backed, as it happens, by *Hesitating Blues*) and the Mississippi Shieks recorded *Shooting High Dice* to the tune of *St. Louis Blues*. The tune of another early published example, *Dallas Blues* by Hart Wand, was adapted by Kid Cole for his *Niagra Falls Blues* (sic) but, in general, composed blues of this type were far less appealing to the songsters than were songs drawn from the folk tradition. Thus the song variously known as *It Ain't* / *Ain't* / or *Taint Nobody's Business (Biz-ness) If I Do* was recorded by Sara Martin and Anna Meyers in 1922 and by Bessie Smith, Lena Wilson and Alberta Hunter the following year. But the version published by Porter Grainger which they performed was an arrangement of a song which was current in the tradition at least since the first decade of the century. It was collected as *Tain't Nobody's Bizness But My Own* by Howard Odum, which, in his opinion, represented "the more reckless temperament of the wanderer".

> I went to see my Hanner
> Turn tricks in my manner
> Tain't nobody's bizness but my own.
>
> Don't care if I don't make a dollar,
> Jes'so I wear my shirt an' collar
> Tain't nobody's bizness but my own.[38]

Though the words did not directly correspond, the stanzas scan in a way which suggests that the recording made by the songster Frank Stokes, or in the following instance by Mississippi John Hurt, to a rolling guitar accompaniment derives from the original song:

> Ain't nobody's dirty bizness
> How my baby treat me,
> Nobody's bizness but my own.
>
> Some of these mornings, gonna wake up crazy,
> Gonna grab my gun, kill my baby,
> Nobody's bizness but mine.
> Ain't nobody's dog-gone bizness,   etc.
>
> Some of these mornings gonna wake up boozy,
> Gonna grab my gun, gonna kill ole Susie,
> Nobody's bizness but mine.
> Goin' back to Pensacola,
> Goin' by my babe and run 'im over,
> Nobody's bizness but my own.
>
> Say baby did you get that letter,
> If you take me back I'll treat you better,
> Nobody's bizness but mine.
> Ain't nobody's dog-gone bizness,[39]   etc.

When the folk tradition survived, to be adapted or modified as the songster chose to suit his personal style and the instrumental technique or accompaniment which he had devised, it was also subject to the scoring of the professional composer. When in turn the arrangement was recorded by a popular vaudeville or theater blues performer and marketed as a Race record it was prone to being absorbed, if in modified form, back into the tradition. The passage of decades and the processes of oral transmission, aided or, indeed, complicated by those of record distribution, led to the incorporation of whole songs or even single verses from the tradition into new contexts. The subject clearly demands much more research, but a single example may serve to illustrate the complexity of the interrelationship of tradition, published song and recording, as well as the songster's involvement in his material as he adapted it to suit his chosen context.

In 1920 W. C. Handy published *Long Gone* with words by the black song writer Chris Smith, based on a Kentucky folk song, known variously as *Lost John*, *Long John* or *Long John Dean*. The sheet music claimed that it was "Another 'Casey Jones' or 'Steamboat Bill'". Everyone was singing its seven verses but "eventually you will sing Long Gone with a hundred verses" – an acknowledgment of the reworking of songs in oral tradition. Abbe Niles stated that the story was based "on an actual event" in which a black trusty at the jail in Bowling Green, Kentucky was to be the victim of a test on the efficiency of a pack of new bloodhounds. John Dean fixed "a steep trap in a barrel on its side, over which he jumped as he started; the lead hound followed the scent into the barrel and the trap; the rest stopped to investigate", by which time Long John was well away. The story probably came from Handy who had embroidered a version he had given to Dorothy Scarborough which she retold in a paper to the Texas Folk-Lore Society. In this, Long John was escaping from "a Joe Turner" (presumably the legendary "long-chain man" who escorted convicts to prison) and made use of a barrel to decoy the dogs.[40] The incident did not appear in either the song as rewritten by Handy, or in the versions collected or recorded. Jim Jackson's version of *Long Gone* begins with verses that are close to Handy's but departs with a couple of stanzas apparently incorporated from another song:

> Now you all have heard the story 'bout Long John Green,
> Bold bank robber from Bowling Green,
> They put him in jail and he stayed thirty days,
> Late last night he made his getaway.
>> He's long gone, from old Kentucky,
>> He's long gone, wasn't he lucky?
>> He's long gone – what I mean
>> He's long gone from Bowling Green. (repeats chorus)
>
> They sent for the high sheriff to bring him back
> Went and put the police hounds on his track,
> The dog-gone police hounds lost his scent
> And nobody knows where Long John went.

He's long gone, from old Kentucky,   etc.

"I ain't gonna tell ya how I got here,
But I got here just the same."
If you see him running the first five miles
You'd swore he wasn't lame.
He'd stop in the woods, catch his wind,
Heard a stick crackin' and he lit out again,
"I ain't gonna tell you how I got here,
But I got here just the same." [41]

Papa Charlie Jackson's version was typically direct, and he kept to both tune and theme throughout. The opening verses described how Lost John waited for the Dixie Flyer – "he missed the cow-catcher when he caught the blind". Reaching a "country woman's house" he was invited in with the words "I'll send for the porter and I'll buy some beer", but Lost John replied:

"Never mind woman, don't you buy no beer
The hounds is on my trail and I can't stay here."
John jumped up on the top of the hill,
Says "The hounds ain't caught me and they never will,
    Now I'm long, long gone."

Now the funniest thing, I ever have seen,
Lost John coming through the Bowling Green.
Stone bare-footed, no shoes on his feet,
Beggin' everybody for the bread and meat,
    Now he's long, long gone.

Lost John made a pair of shoes of his own,
Just as good a shoes as was ever were worn,
Had heels in front, and heels behind,
You couldn't tell whichaway Lost John's gwine.
    Now he's long, long gone.

He was standin' on the corner, talkin' to his brown,
He doubled up his fist and knocked the police down.
The police jumped up, said "Whichaway did he go?"
The last time I see him he was in the Gulf of Mexico.
    Now he's long, long gone.

They took ol' Lost John and they put him in the pen,
Now the son-of-a-gun is out and he's gone again.
    Now he's long, long gone.

Now if anybody should ask you who composed this song,
Tell 'em Papa Charlie Jackson and idle on –
    Now he's long, long gone . . . that's all. [42]

In a compact form, with short lines of a few beats each, *Long Gone* was used as a work song; no fewer than five recordings were made of it by Lightnin' Washington and his gang for the Library of Congress at Darrington State Farm, Texas in 1933–6. While they were linked with them textually, the versions on Race records were in other respects structurally different.

Connexions can be made with the published song copyrighted by Chris Smith and W. C. Handy but it is not clear whether such similarities as there are, arose from awareness of the published form at first or second hand, or whether their song incorporated verses that had already been current in the tradition. Dennis "Little Hat" Jones, a Texas singer and guitarist who worked in and around San Antonio, was far removed from the probable source of the song, and though he lived in the same state as the convicts of Darrington his *Kentucky Blues* was quite distinct from their work song. In his refrain he was clearly drawn to the image of the submarine slipping away unseen from its enemies; a more telling use than Smith and Handy's text which merely had "a gang of men" try to capture Dean "so they chased him with a submarine".

> Well whiles we here tryin' to have our fun
> 'Spose the law jumped up and said "Nobody run!"
> Well you know I'm long gone, from Kentucky,
> Long gone, an' got away lucky,
>   Cause I'm gonna leave so keen,
>   I'll be just like a submarine.
>
> Well, my woman poked her head out the window of the bed'
> Said "Please don't let 'em kill Mister Little Hat dead."
> I said, "No use to worryin' sweet mama, I ain't gonna be here long",
> Tell her not to sing this worryin' song,
>   'Cause I'm gonna leave so keen,
>   I'm gonna be just like a submarine.
>
> Well an officer you know the man they call him Austin Jack,
> Stopped an' put the bloodhounds right on my track,
> 'Cause the hounds they couldn't catch my scent,
> You know they couldn't tell where Little Hat went –
>   'Cause I left so keen,
>   People, I was just like a submarine.
>
> Well here comes the Santa Fe just puffin' and flyin',
> Oughta seen me when I reached up and caught them blinds.
> They said "There's another Long Gone – from Kentucky,
> Long Gone – an' he got away lucky,
>   'Cause he's ever so keen,
>   He's just like a submarine." [43]

Little Hat Jones projected himself into the personality of Long John Dean and, in effect, replaced him. Not only did this make the song more entertaining for his listeners, it also permitted creative development for the singer. Songsters expanded their repertoires by changing tunes, by embellishing the stories and by developing new instrumental accompaniments.

Fluent as an accompanist to Texas Alexander, Little Hat Jones revealed in his guitar playing his songster–musicianer roots. Only occasionally were these evident in the vocals he made under his own name, which were mostly blues. Like many songsters he responded to changing tastes, satisfying the older generation while meeting the demands of the young dancers and the rapidly growing blues audience. In the process, transitional songs which mixed idioms were put together from differing components by able songsters. A conspicuous example is Henry Thomas's *Bob McKinney*, mentioned previously, which commences as a version of the ballad *Bad Lee Brown*. As the singer went down Johnson Street, "Bob McKinney come passing by":

> Bobby said to Marg'et "Come to me, I said
> If you don't come in a hurry, I'll put a .38 through your head",
>   Wasn't he bad, yes, wasn't he bad?
>
> Bobby said to Ben Ferris, "I'm bound to take your life
> You caused trouble, between me an' my wife"
>   Wasn't he bad, yes, wasn't he bad?
>
> Bobby says to the High Sheriff, "Needn't think I'm goin' to run
> If I had another load, me and you'd have some fun",
>   Wasn't he bad, yes, wasn't he bad –
>   Oh my babe, take me back
>   Why in the world don't take me back?
> Monday morning, won't be long,
> You gonna call me, I'll be gone.
> She turned around, two or three times.
> Make my bed and take me back.
>   Take me back, take me back
>   Make my bed and take me back.
> Oh make me a pallet on yo' floor . . .   (3)
> Won't you make it so your man never know.
> Yes, I'm looking for that bully laid me down,   (2)
> Eh, I'm looking for that bully, the bully can't be found,
> I'm looking for that bully laid me down.[44]

Within the same song he included snatches from *Oh My Babe, Take Me Back*, the early blues *Make Me a Pallet On the Floor* and *The Bully of the Town* already discussed. One of the popular themes of the ragtime era, *Take Me Back* relates to Barrett McMahon's 1898 composition *Take Me Back, Babe*, and the refrain to George "Honey Boy" Evans's *Standing On the Corner, Didn't Mean No Harm*: "Oh my baby, tell me true, do you love me, as I love you . . ." Thomas used a stanza or two in other compound songs he recorded, and it appears to have been widely known to songsters. Frank Stokes recorded it accompanied by Dan Sane, in an accelerating dance rhythm. He seems to have known few verses and not added any of his own:

> Now take me back, take me back,
> Take me back, I'll treat you right.
>   Now what I mean, by treatin' you right
>   I'll bring you money every Saturday night.
>
> Now that ole girl that stays in town
> Call me fool and turns me around.
>   Now take me back, take me back
>   Take me back babe, I'll treat you right . . .[45]

Also recorded by Blind Lemon Jefferson as *Beggin' Back*, the song was adapted by William Harris, a medicine show entertainer from the Mississippi Delta. On his *Hot Time Blues* he played a dance rhythm similar to that used by Stokes.

> Say it makes no difference what mama don't 'llow,
> We're gonna have a good time right anyhow,
>   Eeh, mama, won't have it here.
>
> Well just want to tell you this one time,
> Mama you'll see nothin' but to worry your mind,
>   Heh baby, won't you take me back?
>
> Oh come on Daddy, this ain't no joke,
> If you got a good cigarette just give me a smoke,
>   Eeh, babe, won't you take me back?
>
> Well it makes no difference what your mama don't allow,
> We gonna have a good time right anyhow,
>   Eeh, babe, won't you take me back?
>
> Well if you don't like my peaches don't shake my tree
> Just stay out of my orchard and let my peaches be –
>   Eehey won't you take me back? [46]

Just as Henry Thomas incorporated *Take Me Back* in his ballad *Bob McKinney*, so Harris had combined the theme with another tune, popular in Memphis, *Mister Crump*. According to George Lee, a former black lieutenant in the Memphis police, a three-cornered fight for mayor of Memphis took place in 1909. "Jim Mulcahy, political boss, hired Handy to play for Crump. Echford and Bynum were employed for the other two candidates. In order to outdo these two great bands Handy was spurred to creative efforts." W. C. Handy himself stated that he "had composed a special campaign tune for this purpose but without words. We had played it with success. Meanwhile I had heard various comments from the crowds around us, and even from our own men, which seemed to express their feelings about reform. Most of these comments had been sung, impromptu, to my music." According to Lee "the crowd in the streets literally went wild with it. They shouted until they were hoarse, demanding to hear it again and again. They whistled and danced with the rhythmic sway of the music, as the words floated out upon the air:

> Mr Crump don't 'llow no easy riders here,
> Mr Crump won't 'llow no easy riders here,
> I don't care what Mr Crump don't 'llow
> I'm gonna bar'lhouse anyhow,
> Mr Crump can go and catch hisself some air.

The words as quoted by Handy were essentially the same. Later, he claimed to have adapted the tune to *The Memphis Blues*,[47] but it would seem that Frank Stokes's *Mr Crump Don't Like It* kept closer to the original, with words of a character that might have been sung by the crowd:

> Mister Crump don't like it ain't gonna have it here,   (3)
> No barrelhouse women, God, drinkin' no beer
>   Mister Crump don't like it, ain't gonna have it here.
>
> I'm tol' the Baptist Sister jumped up, and began to shout,   (3)
> "Brother, I'm so glad that barrel whiskey put it out"
>   Mister Crump don't like it he ain't gonna have it here.
>
> I'm tol' the Presbyterian Sister turned around and begin to grin,   (3)
> Lord I believe they fell out to barrelhousin' agin
>   Mister Crump won't like it, ain't gonna have it here.
>
> I tol' the Deacon looked aroun' "Sister why in the world don't you
>   heard?   (3)
> I'd rather see you get drunk than wear a hobble skirt."
>   Mister Crump don't like it, ain't gonna have it here.
>
> If you don't like my peaches, don't shake my tree | (3)
> Don't like my fruits, let my orchards be,   ₒ
>   Mister Crump won't 'llow –[48]

A further step in the creative associations which the folk songsters made was taken by Papa Charlie Jackson, whose *Mama Don't Allow It* retained strong textual links with William Harris's *Hot Time Blues*:

> Came from the country the other day
> Some cool kind daddy stole my heart away,
>   'Cause mama don't allow it, ain't gonna have it here.
> Says we don't care what mama don't allow,
> Got a cool kind daddy, anyhow
>   'Cause mama don't allow it, ain't gonna have it here.
>
> Now give me another kiss and we'll have some fun,
> We'll break 'em down and then we'll run,
>   'Cause mama don't allow it, ain't gonna have it here.
> So come on daddy, it ain't no joke,
> If you got any cigarettes just give me a smoke,
>   'Cause mama don't allow it, she ain't gonna have it here.[49]

Any political associations had been eliminated, and the song was cheerfully uncommitted. The tune had been remodelled by Charlie Jackson – or William Henry Jackson, presumably a relative, to whom this and other songs were sometimes credited – or it may have been a prototype as heard originally by Handy. If *Mister Crump* was eventually to become *Memphis Blues* in Handy's version, it was also to have a long life among blues singers as *Mama Don't Allow No Easy Riders Here*, as adapted by pianist Cow Cow Davenport.

Many other songs were adapted from the ragtime era and the minstrel stage and incorporated in the repertoires of songsters and blues singers, by no means all of them by black composers. Pat Rooney was an Irish comic whose most famous song *Is That You, Mr Riley?* was a hit in 1883, but *I've Got a Gal for Ev'ry Day in the Week* was composed as a ragtime–coon song in 1900, with music by the extraordinarily successful white composer, Harry von Tilzer,

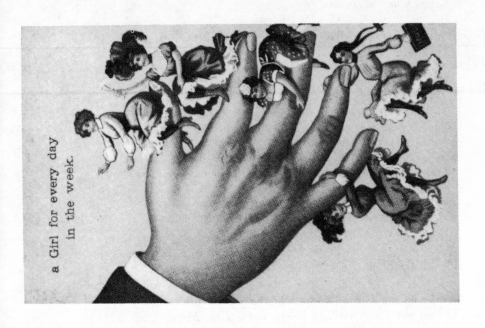

The words of Gus Cannon's 1927 record, *My Money Never Runs Out* remained close to Irving Jones's original lyrics. *Paul Oliver collection.*

The theme of "a girl for every day in the week" was popular enough to provide, with some erotic symbolism, the subject of a postcard, c. 1905. *Paul Oliver collection.*

who published more than 2000 songs and claimed to have composed four times that number. His hits, *A Bird in a Gilded Cage*, *Down Where the Wurzburger Flows* or *Alexander*, had no impact on black song, but he was the composer of a number of coon songs, including *What You Goin' To Do When the Rent Comes Round?* which slipped a phrase or two into black use – or returned them. Von Tilzer's tune doubtless helped popularize Rooney's song, but it was the lyrics which were adapted by the songsters: "I've got a Monday gal, by the name of Sal, I've got a Tuesday gal so sweet . . .

> I've got a Friday gal, I've got a Saturday gal
> Now you may call that lots of cheek,
> I've got a Sunday girl and she's a jet-black pearl,
> I've got a gal for ev'ry day in the week.[50]

The essential theme remained the same but the songsters used richer language. Papa Harvey Hull and Long Cleve Reed for example made a recording of *Gang of Brown Skin Women*: "Hang around boys, gon' tel you 'bout my brown skin gals . . ." said Reed:

> "Got a gang of brown skin sweet women, got a gang of high yellers too
> I got so many womens I don't know what to do.
>
> Got a Monday, Monday girl she works it on Broad and Main
> Got a Tuesday woman she gives me my spendin' change.
>
> Got a Wednesday, Wednesday girl, she works it on Broadway Square,
> Got a Thursday woman takes me each and everywhere.
>
> Got a Friday, Friday girl, she brings me a bottle of beer
> Got a Saturday one, well she better not catch me here . . .[51]

Jim Jackson, unquestionably the richest store of this material from the turn of the century, also sang a version:

> My Monday girl, she works twenty-two on Main
> When my Tuesday brown-skin brings me pocket change.
>
> My Wednesday girl loves whiskey, sometimes she do drink beer
> But my Thursday woman give me the devil if she catch me here.
>
> My Friday good girl, she read me the Mail and News
> But my Saturday high-brown buys my socks and shoes.
>
> My Sunday woman, she lays on my right arm and sleep
> You can know from that I got a woman for every day in the week.[52]

While it is evident that these boasting songs are related, they derive directly from Pat Rooney's composition. Of particular interest here is the resolution of the two versions of the song on record, Hull and Reed singing in harmony in a style that appears to relate to that of the quartets, and using a "scat", or wordless, nonsense-syllable chorus before concluding with the couplet:

> Well I love my sweet baby, I tell this world I do,
> And I hope someday she'll learn to love daddy too.

Long Cleve Reed, Sunny Wilson (guitars) and Little Harvey Hull were illustrated in a Black Patti advertisement for *Gang of Brown Skin Women*, published May 21, 1927, six weeks after recording. *Paul Oliver collection.*

Jackson similarly introduced an eight-bar blues theme, employing a bridging verse which related structurally to his *Kansas City Blues*, one of the biggest sellers of any Race issue in the first phase, and compressing a stanza that also appeared in Frank Stokes's *Mr Crump Don't Like It*.

> I got a gal in Georgia, one in Louisiana,
> Four in Chattanoogie, six in Alabama.
> Four or five women right here in Memphis, Tennessee;
> If you don't like my peaches, let my orchard be.
>
> I wish I was a jaybird in the air,
> I'd build my nest in some of you high-brown's hair.
>
> I'm jest from the country, you know I'm easy to rule,
> You can hitch me to your cart girl, and drive me for your mule.[53]

He had no difficulty in moulding the song into a blues, and probably saw little distinction between them. The use of ragtime era popular songs, the composer's adaptation of rural tunes, the textual and melodic remodellings, the medleys of different songs, all of which are to be found on the Race recordings, are firm indications of the interchange between the folk tradition, published sheet music and the inventiveness of the songsters themselves.

Songsters may have picked up the occasional song from the recordings of their contemporaries, but the date of publication of many of their songs, and the early collection of others suggest that most were in circulation long before recording. Professional black-face minstrel companies may sometimes have provided the songsters with employment, but the evidence is stronger that they were nurseries for ragtime and coon song composers and for vaudeville stage entertainers. For the Southern country singers the openings for making an erratic living from their music were more modest in scale. But they were important nevertheless, not only for the jobs they provided but for the opportunities they afforded for the sharing and dissemination of folk and popular secular traditions.

3

The Long-Tailed Blue

Songsters of the road shows

"100 Performers and Musicians WANTED. Both ladies and gentlemen for my 2 shows under canvas. A Rabbit's Foot Comedy & Funny Folks Comedy. 40 weeks engagement for the right parties", ran Pat Chapelle's advertisement for participants in his shows. He was a native of Jacksonville, Florida, where he was born in 1869, and as a boy performed in a string trio. By the time he was twenty he was an experienced performer on the black minstrel stage, working with his own touring company, the Imperial Colored Minstrels. Converting a local billiard hall into a concert hall, he became a promoter and by 1900 he was joint owner of two other Florida theaters and was planning a new road show, which featured a musical entertainment "A Rabbit's Foot". It opened in 1900 with a cast of fifty, a brass band and a railroad car for the assembly. Within five years the Rabbit Foot Minstrels, as the show became known, included a baseball team which competed with local players and a concert orchestra which played light classics.[1]

In 1911 Pat Chapelle's show was bought out by Fred S. Wolcott, promoter of the F. S. Wolcott Carnivals. Wolcott was white, but he followed Chapelle's policy in touring a black cast. He got the show on the road late the following year and was soon handling the rising performers who were destined to shape the "Classic Blues" on stage and record, the "Assassinators of the Blues" Ma Rainey and her husband Will, Ida Cox, Bessie Smith and, a little later, Ethel Waters, Bertha "Chippie" Hill and the team of Butterbeans and Susie. Wolcott's base was Port Gibson, Mississippi, located on the river half-way between Vicksburg and Natchez. Though the "Foot's" toured widely in the South playing under canvas, the company was especially popular in the Mississippi Valley region from which it drew many of its cast.

Initially the show included entertainments with a story line but, by the 1920s, a series of acts and entertainments augmented the "really high class musical comedy and beauty chorus" of "High Brown Chorus Girls" for which Wolcott was advertising. Members of the company traveled in the "Dan Emmett" railroad sleeping car and a dining-cum-baggage car, the "Southland", carried the equipment. It was the best-known of the later minstrel shows but it had many competitors, of which the most celebrated was "Silas Green from New Orleans". Originally mounted by the vaudeville showmen Salem Tutt Whitney and J. Homer Tutt, from the remains of a

78

circus owned by another pioneer in the field, Eph Williams, "Silas Green's" was destroyed in a storm in Hampton, Virginia in 1905. Williams kept Whitney to an agreement made at the time of the formation of the company and took over. Before Eph Williams died in 1921 a white promoter, Charles Collier purchased a half interest in the show and soon after was in full possession, employing as producer the veteran black entertainer Tim Owsley, who was formerly a companion of W. C. Handy in Mahara's Minstrels.[2]

"As an adolescent", wrote A. B. Spellman, black jazz historian, "I recall crawling under the canvas tents of 'Silas Green from New Orleans' to watch the semi-naked women do their dances and to hear the comedian's crude, but I thought then, hilariously funny jokes . . . Elizabeth City was a small enough town (approximately 13,000 population), but the Negroes who lived in it seldom attended Silas Green shows; the group drew its biggest revenue from the 'country people' who lined the city streets on weekends . . . and if a Silas Green group hit town during the summer potato season when the migrant workers were in Elizabeth City, the entire area would be off limits to us 'city' kids." He was writing of the 1930s but the show was substantially the same as it had been, when Gertrude "Ma" Rainey, Bessie Smith and Ida Cox performed in it in the 1920s, and in a similar company Pete Werley's Florida Cotton Blossoms Minstrels. These shows were on the road in 1929–30, when The Alabama Minstrels, Jordan's Swiftfoot Minstrels, Richard's and Pringle's Georgia Minstrels, J. F. Murphy's Georgia Minstrels, The Fashion Plate Minstrels, Warner and Moorman's Famous Brown Derby Minstrels and John Van Arnam's Minstrels were all playing the South and Midwest. Several of these black companies were using "autobus" transport by this time, including J. S. Lincoln's Minstrels, J. A. Coburn's, and the Royer Brothers' Great American Minstrels. Many featured celebrated show singers: Lizzie Miles with the Alabama Minstrels, Bessie Smith with Irving C. Miller's show, Butterbeans and Susie with the Cole Brothers' Carnival.[3]

In essence the carnivals were similar to the minstrel shows, working under canvas in a large tent, but including acts with animals and circus performers: Lizzie Miles worked with the Cole Brothers as an elephant rider. Tolliver's Circus and Musical Extravaganza also featured both Ma Rainey and Butterbeans and Susie Edwards. Ethel Waters worked with White's Greater Shows Carnival while the Mighty Wiggle Carnival had Billie Goodson (later, Billie Pierce) playing piano.[4] Leroy Carr, later to be famous as a blues singer, ran away from home and school to join a circus around 1916. In a version of a childhood song played to a compelling piano rhythm Carr described having to work and to share in the excitement of the circus and its menagerie:

> Circus come to town to the circus I went,
> Didn't have a ticket, didn't have a cent,
> Circus man said "To see the show without a cent,
> You got to carry water for the elephant.

Itinerant "High-pitch" salesman at Belzoni, Mississippi attracting a large crowd. On the wall, posters for Silas Green from New Orleans "showing under their Mammoth Tent Theater". Photograph by Marion Post Wolcott. *Library of Congress collection.*

I carried water for the elephant,
Back and forth to the well I went.
Arms got sore and my back got bent,
But I couldn't fill up the elephant.

I says to the man with the standin'-up collar,
"Bet you four bits that elephant's hollow".
He gave me a ticket, says "first you'll see,
The animals in the menagerie . . ." [5]

and the song continued with a list of the animals and imitations of the noises
that they made – the lion, wild cat, wild dogs and hyena among them.

Circuses and carnivals generally traveled by road in horse-drawn wagons.
But when they paraded in town to draw a crowd they displayed the animals
from the menagerie while the brass band, in the full splendour of its uniforms,
played from high up on the band-wagon. Behind the circus and tent show
came the canvasmen, the "roughnecks", who raised the big tent and
manhandled the seating – in his younger years the songster Jesse Fuller had
been one. In the shadow of the show were the "grifters", who set up booths,
tents or merely collapsible tables to operate "con" tricks, "shell games" and
other side events. And there were the "trailers" who operated small
concessions, selling pop-corn and soda, or who set up small independent
entertainments on payment of a fee or a percentage of their takings. Carnivals
often played principally for white audiences, and some of these ad-
junct sideshows were termed the "dirty shows", or "jig shows" with black
entertainers and playing for black audiences. Later they were more circum-
spectly called "No. 2" shows, or some similar name to differentiate them. [6]

Traveling minstrel, carnival and circus shows enabled people in even the
smallest townships and remoter rural areas to hear the current songs of the
day, as well as the older favorites of the minstrel tradition and from the
ragtime era. In particular, with a number of the major jazz-blues and
vaudeville-blues singers performing under canvas with traveling companies,
there would appear to have been many occasions when songsters were able to
hear them and to learn their numbers. Such singers had been recording for a
few years before the songsters made records, and these issues would have
offered additional opportunities for them to memorize the words and tunes.

By 1928 Newman I. White was deploring the fact that "the folk blues and
the factory product are today almost inextricably mixed" and that "most
blues sung by Negroes today have only a secondary folk origin; their primary
source is the phonograph". [7] If this observation was sufficiently true of the
blues, a comparatively new music in the rural South, it would seem that it
would be even more likely to be true of the wider range of songs chosen by the
songsters.

Sam Jones, or Stovepipe No. 1, the "one-man band" who played guitar,
harmonica and stovepipe and whose country dances, including *Sourwood
Mountain*, have already been discussed, had the characteristically varied

With both crutch and crucifix, a "grifter" performs a snake-eating act in a side-show at Donaldsonville, Louisiana. Photograph by Russell Lee. *Library of Congress collection.*

repertoire of the songster, ranging from barn dances to gospel songs. At his last recording session in 1927, he recorded *A Woman Gets Tired of the Same Man All the Time*:

> I mean, I mean my wife, I mean we don't of late,
> We don't get along so well,
> I mean the older she gets, I mean the more I do mean,
> I mean to – to change her ways,
> I mean she used to be, I mean so kind to me
> I didn't think a wife could be so kind,
> As I sit down, now I see,
> My wife don't pay me no mind.
> Ain't it funny how a woman can change?
> That wife of mine is bound to run me in a strain –
>> A woman gets tired, I mean real tired,
>> Of the same man, all the time.
>> Oh the way my wife been actin' of late
>> Bound to make me lose my mind;
>> When I'm out on my wagon trying to sell a little coal,
>> Oh well, she's round the corner "who wants sweet jelly-roll?"
>> Because a woman gets tired, I mean real tired
>> Of the same man all the time.[8]

A simple guitar accompaniment by David Crockett complemented Sam Jones's own tuba-like, serio-comic playing of the tune on stovepipe. It could have been convincing as his own composition, but it had been recorded a couple of times before: once by Edna Johnson, with piano accompaniment by the writer of the song, Charles Booker, in 1924; and the previous year by the vaudeville singer George Williams, who was accompanied by Fletcher Henderson on piano. It is evident from aural comparison that Sam Jones had based his record on one by George Williams, even to the unnecessary repetitions of "I mean". Its simple tune must have suited the pentatonic scale of the stovepipe, but it was perhaps because of its potential for humorous interpretation that the song appealed to Jones. George Williams's recording was issued on Columbia 14002 – one of the first batch of Columbia recordings on their newly initiated "Race" series – and it may therefore have had good promotion. As for the composer, he was partner in the Yancey and Booker artists agency on Beale Street, Memphis, and it is possible, in view of Sam Jones's fairly wide traveling, that he may have been directly influenced, or even managed, by Booker.

It is not an isolated example: a contemporary singer, Walter "Buddy Boy" Hawkins, reportedly from Blythesville, Arkansas, recorded *How Come Mama Blues*, sung in a pinched, high voice against an easy and relaxed guitar accompaniment. A number of his recordings were in rural blues form, like *Jailhouse Fire Blues*. Several mentioned railroads and one was unusual in describing the work of a section gang. Other recordings were guitar rags suitable for dancing, and even including Mexican fingering, while *Voice*

Throwin' Blues was a novelty number, on which he imitated a second voice in a manner that would have been most appropriate in a ventriloquist's act. Not only was he a country blues singer, Walter Hawkins was ragtime guitarist, ventriloquist and show singer too. Originally titled *Deeble Bum Blues*, his *How Come Mama Blues* followed the pattern of many popular vaudeville songs, using a couplet commencing with the title words, which acted as a bridge between the verses.

> How come you do me like you do baybay
> What makes you do me like you do?
> How come you try to make me feel so blue, mama
> You know I ain't done nothin' to you.
> Now you know you left home at seven,
> Came back at eight,
> You brought another big fat man,
> Slap up to my gate –
>> What make you treat me like you diddle last night
>> You know I ain't done nothin' to you, I said baby
>> I ain't done nothin' to you.

His other verses narrated her treatment and his own reactions:

> . . . You know you hugged and kissed him, and said,
> "Daddy you know you sure is fat",
> I stuck my head out the window
> And hollered "Who in the world is that?"
>> What makes you do me like you do, do, do,
>> What makes you do me like you do?
> . . . I bought a pistol, I bought it today,
> Now I got an undertaker with it just to haul you away.

and, recalling the Sam Jones song,

> You know a nickel is a nickel, a dime is a dime
> A woman get tired of one man all the time . . .
>> How come you do me like you do sweet baybay,
>> What makes you do me like you do?   (talkin' 'bout 'chu, mama . . .)
>> How come you do me like you do (now looka here)[9]

Hawkins had provided new couplets to fill out the song in a more personalized fashion, using current idioms that would appeal to his rural audience. But the song itself had been composed as *How Come You Do Me Like You Do* by Gene Austin and Roy Bergere and, after an undistinguished introduction on record by Marjorie Royce in March 1924, was recorded in the succeeding three months by Rosa Henderson, Viola McCoy and Edith Wilson. If he did not learn it from a show, it was doubtless one of these versions that Buddy Boy Hawkins had heard and reinterpreted. Both Rosa Henderson and Viola McCoy also recorded *West Indies Blues*, composed by Edgar Dowell with help from Spencer and Clarence Williams. So too, did Clara Smith, whose reputation was second only to that of Bessie Smith in the early 1920s. Her Columbia version had an accompaniment by Charlie Dixon on guitar and Fletcher Henderson in the unlikely role of ukelele player. Later the same year, in November 1924, a single record was issued of Ukelele Bob Williams who chose *West Indies Blues* (identified as a "Calipso" on the Viola McCoy version), for one of his sides. But whereas the slow if slightly jaunty Clara Smith recording used the ukelele for little more than a steady beat, Bob Williams displayed his skill by taking the tune at a breakneck tempo, the words of the vocal tumbling from the lips of the singer who obviously had performed the song many times:

> Got my trunk and grip all packed
> A big ship I'm gwinea take 'er;
> So goodbye dear ole New York town
> I'm gwine back to Jamaica.
> When I get on the other side
> I'll hang aroun' in de water,
> I'll make my livin', sure as you born.
> Divin' for a quarter.
>> I'm gwine home, won't be long
>> Gwine home, sure as you born,
>> Gwine home, won't be long
>> I got no time to lose   (2)[10]

The singer continued in mock West Indian accents to declare that he has "the bestest job, I run a hotel elevator". When he got back "to this great land" he was going to be "a big man, like my friend Marcus Garvey" and later when he had "plenty money now," he was "gwine back on the Black Star Line". The song was directly related to the trial the previous year of the black nationalist leader Marcus Garvey for offences related to the mailing of shares in his ill-fated Black Star Line – too topical to be of lasting influence in this form. Several years later the tune was to surface in a different guise, as the theme of the highly successful recording by Georgia Tom and Tampa Red, *Beedle-Um-Bum*, virtually the first to be issued under the name of "Hokum".[11]

Ukelele Bob Williams was one of the earliest folk singers to record – a few months after Stovepipe No. 1 and Papa Charlie Jackson. The latter eclipsed him, for Jackson had already had a runaway success with his second record, *Salty Dog*, and was even more successful with *Shake That Thing* in May the following year. The entertainer and, later, film actress Ethel Waters claimed to have been performing it on stage since 1921, but she did not record it until December 1925. By this time Jackson's record was an established hit, and Viola McCoy, Eva Taylor, and some months later, Viola Bartlette were among the vaudeville singers who "covered" it with their own versions. Here the influence was in all probability the other way – the folk song was taken up by the stage performers, as Clara Smith exploited Jackson's *Salty Dog*. Possibly though, Jackson may have acquired it from singers in his native New Orleans,

Papa Charlie Jackson playing banjo for a Hootchy-Kootchy dancer on the
fore-stage of a tent show, at the State Fair, Lexington, Kentucky. From an
advertisement for Paramount 12700. *Paul Oliver collection.*

like Lorenzo Stall, who sang it as a version of *Ballin' the Jack*.[12] In this, as in
many other songs, the folk tradition was assimilated into the theatrical
repertoire. Cross-fertilization between songsters and vaudeville singers occurred in both directions but, in spite of the examples quoted, this does not seem
to have been a particularly marked phenomenon. On recorded evidence
songsters in general did not derive many of their songs directly from the
vaudeville singers or from their records.

Undoubtedly the larger touring companies sometimes employed songsters
in their shows; Frank Stokes for instance played with the Ringling Brother's
Circus. Many songsters earned their living by their playing and singing, at
least for part of the year, and in this sense they were "professional". But they
remained folk artists and the shows in which they performed were popular
entertainments for audiences that gathered from the streets. These were the
"doctor shows" or "medicine shows" which were by far the most important
employers of the songsters and jug bands, and a major contributor to the
dissemination of their songs.

Medicine shows developed after the Civil War as entertainments designed
to attract clients for the vendors of patent pills and remedies that were of
dubious, if any, merit. Some "doctors" – they were seldom qualified – dressed
in Quaker clothes with typically wide-brimmed hats; others affected the beard

and mien of a Kentucky colonel, or sported broad Stetsons in Western style. Doctors who sold "Indian" herbal remedies were popular from the 1880s, with the Oregon Indian Medicine Company of Col. T. A. Edwards from Corry, Pennsylvania (its name notwithstanding) was highly successful with its Ka-Ton-Ka remedy, Nez Perce Cataarh Snuff and other supposed native American cures. It was challenged by Colonel John Healy's Kickapoo Indian Agency shows which varied from a few "Indians" and entertainers to large companies. Setting up their acts on street corners and vacant lots, performing for audiences of bystanders who did not pay for the amusement except through the pills and purgatives they were induced to buy, the medicine show entertainers had to be able to sing, dance, tell tales, crack jokes. [13] Sleepy John Estes and Hammie Nixon worked with "an old guy they called Dr. Grimm, traveled everywhere, he had a little old trailer with a stand on it. Sometimes we would just start something, just to get them coming in. Then he'd start to pass that medicine around . . ." They gave examples of their jokes: "Get people laughing and they going your way." [14]

It is possible from the Race recordings of singers who are known to have worked on the minstrel and medicine shows to piece together something of the repertoires of the road companies. Unfortunately, interest in this aspect of black song has been limited and recent, while the tradition was on the wane in the 1950s and had ended by 1975. Few songs were collected from hearing them on the show, but an exception was noted by Howard Odum before 1910, who described "a version of the once-popular song 'I Got Mine' [which] has been adapted by the Negro and is sung with hilarity". A few years later the same song was collected in Choctaw County, Alabama from "a Negro guitar picker", in Campbell County, Georgia as "sung by an old Negro cook (male)", in northern Alabama as "sung on a road working camp" between 1915 and 1916, and in Durham, North Carolina in 1919 from "a Negro minstrel show" – all examples published by Newman White. [15] To a staccato banjo accompaniment which must have been close to the sounds of an early minstrel banjo player, "Big Boy" George Owens recorded what he titled *The Coon Crap Game*:

> Well I went down to a coon crap game
> It certainly was against my will;
> The coons won all the money I had,
> But a green-back dollar bill.
> With a hundred dollar bet laying on the table,
> And the nigger's point was nine,
> Just then the cops come in the door, when
> – I got mine.
>> Yes, I got mine, boys, I got mine,
>> I grabbed all that hundred dollars, through the window, I did climb.
>> Ever since then I beware of coons,
>> I been livin' on chicken and wine –
>> I'm a leader of all society now, but –
>> I got mine. [16]

Writing in 1928, a couple of years after "Big Boy" Owens's record, Newman
White observed that it "was a popular vaudeville song about twenty years
ago, presumably not a Negro song at all. But the Negroes have taken it up
extensively", as the spread of his examples showed. In fact it was of a little
earlier date, having been composed by John Queen and Charlie Cartwell in
1901.[17] A white native of New Orleans, John Queen was himself a traveling
show entertainer, noted for his clog dancing. Recorded versions of *I Got Mine*
kept closely to Queen's lyrics, though they generally expanded the themes
using the original framework. Typically, Frank Stokes played it with a strong
dance beat, singing Queen and Cartwell's verse of the coon's turkey feast,
without using their terminology:

> Now when the turkey was brought in
> Tell me all the peoples began to grin;
> Now to think about the good times all would have,
> But they couldn't say exactly when –
> So the man got the turkey right by the leg
> But I clung on behind,
> He might have thought he had the whole fowl and gone –
> But – I got mine.
> > I got mine, boys, I got mine,
> > Round here trying to get some good eats,
> > All the time.
> > Ever since then I been livin' high,
> > I been livin' on chicken and wine.
> > Says, I belong to the crap society
> > But – I got mine.

The traditional verse of the crap game was slightly changed in his version:

> I went uptown to a little crap game,
> Ask some others ["please, might play?"]
> The man looked at me, never cracked a smile,
> I couldn't get that feller to lay.
> So he throwed the dice down on the floor,
> And I think that I'd fin'lly like nine,
> But just as the bully jumped in the back door,
> Lord – I got mine!
> > I got mine, I got mine,
> > Around here trying to get some good eats,
> > All the time.
> > Since then I've been living high,
> > I been living on chicken and wine.
> > I belong to that knock-down society,
> > But – I got mine.[18]

The point of most verses is that the singer wins, even if it is by beating a
hasty exit, by cheating or scooping up the stakes, or by making an undignified
departure through the window; he looks after his own interests first.
Retribution generally follows at least once and "I got mine" means a beating-

up or a sentence, dealt with humorously and ruefully. It was a song which used a familiar minstrel show situation but allowed for amusing variations, effective with both white and colored audiences, who doubtless interpreted the shades of meaning rather differently.

Though it was not one of the four titles that he recorded with Blind Simmie Dooley, the song was a favorite of Pink Anderson who spent a lifetime on the medicine shows. Learning much from Dooley, whom he met in 1916, in turn he taught Peg Leg Sam (Arthur Jackson) while working a couple of years later on Dr. Kerr's show. A minimum of three performers, apart from the "pitchman", and sometimes as many as ten musicians, dancers, singers, and comedians appeared in the shows in which they worked. They performed to both white and black audiences, wherever the doctor could make his sales pitch. A "low-pitch" show might have little more than a soap box from which to address the crowd: a "high-pitch" doctor toured with a large wagon sporting a platform at the rear which did duty as a stage. Mixed shows of both black and white members of the kind in which Pink Anderson played, were not uncommon. [19]

Many white entertainers of note got their basic training in the medicine shows, singing from the platform of the "physick wagon". The comedian of the silent movies, Buster Keaton, was born of medicine show parents, the Joe Keatons, who worked the Dr. Hill's California Concert Company selling Kickapoo Magic Snake Oil; their companions on the show were Bessie and Harry Houdini. Before his "white-face" act, Buster Keaton himself played in blackface in 1896. Even the smallest "Doctor Shows" employed an Indian and a blackface, or black singer, musician or comedian to attract a crowd. White country singers as various as Uncle Dave Macon, Fiddling John Carson, Roy Acuff, Dock Walsh, Bradley Kincaid, Clarence Ashley, Hank Williams and "Harmonica" Frank Floyd all "paid their dues" on the doctor shows. So too did Jimmie Rodgers who played both tent-rep shows and worked with the "pitchmen"; the shows of Doc Zip Hibler, Doc El Vino, Widow Robbins and Population Charlie have been mentioned in this connexion but it is not certain whether Rodgers worked with them. Made up in blackface, he traveled through Kentucky and Tennessee with, in his wife's words, "a shabby little medicine show", later to join a tent show, a Hawaiian group and a traveling carnival which broke up in a storm in Indiana. In places as far apart as Mississippi and Texas he is remembered playing on one medicine show in the company of the black songster, Frank Stokes. [20]

A bald, well-built, six-foot Memphis blacksmith, Stokes was a memorable figure, whose gritty voice and powerfully rhythmic guitar playing would have stood out in any show; with Jimmie Rodgers in the same company it is not surprising that they were easily recalled forty years after. [21] There can be little doubt that they learned from each other and exchanged items; perhaps under these circumstances Jimmie Rodgers picked up *In the Jailhouse Now*, one of the most popular songs among black medicine and minstrel show entertainers. It was not recorded by Frank Stokes it is true, but it was made by several other

I GOT MINE.

COON SONG.

Words by JOHN QUEEN.

Music by CHAS. CARTWELL.

Allegro Moderato.

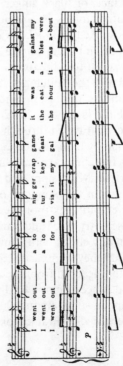

I went out — a to a nig-ger crap game it was a-gainst my

I went out — a to a tur-key feast the eat-a-bles were

I went out — for to vis-it my gal the hour it was a-bout

Copyright, MCMI, by Howley, Haviland & Dresser.
English Copyright Secured.

TELL ME DUSKY MAIDEN.

BY COLE & JOHNSON.

A travesty on the song from "Florodora," written in these composers' best vein.

John Queen's highly popular "coon song" *I Got Mine*, composed in 1901. *Paul Oliver collection.*

Blacksmith and songster Frank Stokes, from 1927 Victor catalog.

songsters, among them the veteran medicine show entertainer, Jim Jackson:

> I had a friend named Campbell,
> He used to steal and gamble,
> He made his living cheating all the while;
> He played a game they called euchre,
> Pinochle and poker,
> He thought he was the smartest dude in town.
> But I just found out Monday,
> That he got locked up Sunday,
> They got him in that jailhouse down in town.
> They got Campbell in the jail,
> No one to go his bail,
> The judge won't even accept him a fine.
> > He's in the jailhouse now   (2)
> > I told Campbell once or twice,
> > "Stop playing cards and shooting dice"
> > Yes they got him –
> > He's in the jailhouse now.[22]

He made the record in the fall of 1927 at his first recording session but it had been in general currency for some years before. A one-time white Atlanta journalist and stage performer, Ernest Rogers, claimed to have sung it over the radio as early as 1922; it's possible – by the end of that year there were over 500 licensed radio transmitters in the country. Within two years, in 1924, it had been recorded by the jug band leader Buford Threlkeld – "Whistler" – as *Jail House Blues*:

> I went out last Friday,
> I met a big brown gal named Idie,
> I told her I was the swellest coon layin' around in town,
> She started to call me "honey,"
> You know I got [hip?] and started to spend my money,
> We took in every cabaret and buffet in town.
> We were striking every minute,
> I made sure I was in it,
> I was buying Jamaica gin just by the gallon.
> But when I went to pay that man,
> I found that poor gal's hand
> In my pocket where my money was –
> > She's in the graveyard now
> > She's in the graveyard now.
> > I told the judge right to his face
> > That woman's hand was out of its place –
> > She's in a graveyard now.[23]

A version by Earl McDonald's Original Louisville Jug Band three years later had only slight changes in the words. This could have been the result of direct influence of Whistler's record, or of one group upon the other, but the persistence of the verses in the various recordings made of the song suggests that it had been composed and published. I have been unable to trace any such

sheet music, but the "coon" references in some of the earlier recordings are an
indication of its likely date. McDonald's version included the verse:

> Now up in New York City,
> Folks thought it was a pity,
> The landlord had to raise that rent so high;
> We hustled round that town,
> In all our hustlin' 'round,
> We could not raise that rent no way we tried.
> My mother took in washing,
> My sister done the ironing,
> I helped around the town by shining shoes;
> But my daddy walked around,
> Like he owned New York town,
> Spending all mama's money buyin' moonshine booze.
> > He's in the jailhouse now,   (2)
> > As that Moses get that rent,
> > Policy begin to pay –
> > He's in the jailhouse now.[24]

He too, sang of "a big fat gal named Ida" though after taking in every cabaret
he had been "buying Jamaica ginger by the pound". The verse also appeared
in Blind Blake's version, made in 1927 on which he was accompanied by the
medicine show banjo player, Gus Cannon. Blake opened with another
favorite verse, implying a carpetbagger politician's exploitation of black
political representation:

> I remember last election
> Everybody was in action
> Trying to find themselves a President.
> There was a man named Lawson
> From New York down to Boston
> Represent the Colored peoples we had sent.
> My brother was a voter,
> Also a great promoter
> Goin' around giving advice,
> Says "Go down to the poll and vote"
> Instead of voting once, he voted twice.
> > He's in the jailhouse now   (2)
> > We got him downtown in jail
> > No one to go his bail
> > He's in the jailhouse now![25]

It was the naive black "promoter" who put him in jail, the message being
conveyed that, however dubious the political operation, blacks should not
interfere. The point was made more explicit in a slightly different interpretation by the Memphis Sheiks – essentially the Memphis Jug Band with
Charlie Nickerson taking the vocal:

> I remember last election,
> Jim Jones got in action

Said he'd vote for the man who paid the biggest price.
Next day at the poll
He voted with heart and soul,
But instead of voting once, he voted twice –
   He's in the jailhouse now,   (2)
   Instead of staying at home
   And let those white folks business alone –
   He's in the jailhouse now.

In the Memphis Sheiks version "Son" was taking in every cabaret with a little chick, drinking lots of liquor and getting into trouble:

Now Son is jailhouse bound,
   He's in the jailhouse now,   (2)
   If he got a political friend,
   Judge says sentence he will suspend –
   He's in the jailhouse now.[26]

With a little manipulation of the words the song could be made to suit most occasions, and with a change of names could fit any audience. "Son is jailhouse bound" referred to "Son Brimmer", the name by which Will Shade the harmonica player on the Memphis Sheiks recording was known to his friends. Similarly, sly references to letting "the white folks' business alone" or getting "a political friend" to influence the judge could be worked in, making a bond between performers and audience.

A few months later Jimmie Rodgers recorded the song, which proved to be one of his most successful titles. He was often invited to perform it and even, somewhat incongruously, chose to sing it to a Men's Bible Class in Florida. It was credited to himself on the original record label, and on the remake a couple of years later.[27]

In the Jailhouse Now was a comic song of the kind which told a short narrative before making a point in the refrain: always the same point, but with good timing and the interpolation of a couplet into the chorus which extended the theme of the verse or a change of reference, like Stokes's "I belong to the crap society" or "I belong to the knock-down society", it could be very effective. Stokes's terms of course referred to gambling and fighting – belonging to a group which took its chances and looked after its own interests.

Somewhat similar in attitude, but with the central figure aided by supernatural powers, was the song of the *Traveling Man*. Odum and Johnson collected three versions – one from a quartet which came to Dayton, Tennessee; another by Kid Ellis, of Spartanburg, South Carolina, himself a professed traveling man; a third from a North Carolina Negro youth who had traveled through several states. Luke Jordan came from Appomatox, Virginia, where he was born in 1892, and lived for most of his life in Lynchburg.[28] He sang a version of *Traveling Coon*, in his high, clear voice to a poised and immaculately picked guitar accompaniment.

Folks, let me tell you about a Travelin' Coon,
His home was down in Tennessee,
He made his livin' stealin' people's chickens
And everything he seen.
Policeman got [straight] behind this coon
And certainly made him take the road.
There never was a passenger train run so fast,
That Shine didn't get on board.
    He was a travelin' man, he was a travelin' man,
    He was a travelin'est man, finest was in the land.
    He was a travelin' man, it's known for miles around –
    He never give up, no, he wouldn't give up
    Till the police shot him down.

They sent the Travelin' Coon to the spring one day
To fetch a pail of water,
I think the distance from the house to the spring,
Sixteen miles and a quarter.
The Coon went there and he got the water all right
Came back stubbed 'e toe and fell down.
He ran back home, he got another pail,
He caught the water 'fore it hit the ground.
    He was a travelin' man,[29]   etc.

Percy F. Dilling collected the song from "a traveling minstrel at King's Mountain, Cleveland County, N.C." in 1919. It was "obviously of vaudeville or street-singer origin", Newman White considered, noting that several years before – possibly before 1920 – it "circulated in Durham N.C. as a printed 'ballet'".[30] This could account for the marked similarity of all collected versions in the Eastern seaboard states, but Coley Jones, who led a string band in Dallas, Texas, was many hundreds of miles away, and it is more likely that he learned it from another singer. He added a couple of verses not in text collections:

That coon stole ten thousand dollars,
It was in the broad open day time;
Folks said the man was desperate,
For doin' such a dirty crime.
Police squad went 'n arrested
But he didn't have no fear,
They tied handcuffs around the darkey's arms
And the coon begin to disappear.
    He was a travelin' man, certainly was a travelin' man,   etc.

They sentenced this coon now to be hung,
He knowed his time was near,
Folks all ganged up for miles around
Because they didn't have no fear.
Tied a rope around this darkey's neck,
Everybody begin to sigh,
He crossed his legs, winked one eye

> Sailed up to them skies . . .
> He was a travelin' man,[31]   etc.

Inevitably, Jim Jackson also recorded the song. Including the "stealing chickens" and "pail of water" verses which are common to all versions, he added a variant of a favorite final verse:

> Well a policeman got right in after this man,
> He run and jumped on the Titanic ship,
> And started up that ocean blue,
> He looked out and spied that big iceberg
> And right overboard he flew;
> All the white ladies on the deck of that ship
> Says "that man certainly was a fool",
> But when the Titanic ship went down –
> He's shootin' craps in Liverpool.[32]

In his study of black oral culture, Lawrence Levine discusses the *Traveling Coon* (which he considers, for some reason, to be a *quasi*-minstrel song). He sees the 'Traveling Man' as trickster hero. Indeed he is, in the sense that he possesses superhuman powers, a characteristic which he shares with other trickster figures like Brother Bill or High John the Conqueror. Unlike Br'er Rabbit, the Traveling Man does not engineer the circumstances in which he plays his trick; instead he finds himself in situations from which he escapes by magic or his wits. But not indefinitely; the Traveling Man, who as a hero in Levine's account "is caught but not even the gallows can contain him", *does* succumb. Levine does not quote the chorus, but in every version "he never give up, till the police shot him down". He was not proof against bullets, and one gathers from the context, he was defenseless. For the Traveling Man wins through his cunning when the opportunity arises, and wins with his superior skill when he can use it. We never learn how the police shot him down, or under what circumstances. Newman White suggested that the song may relate to *The Derby Ram* and its refrain, "he rambled and he rambled, till the butchers cut him down".[33]

Traveling Man was not sung, or indeed recorded, solely by black singers; Henry Whitter and Doc Walsh were among the white country singers who recorded the item at much the same time. There was a considerable overlap of repertoires, which is scarcely surprising in view of the common availability of sources in records, sheet music or the radio, let alone the similar audiences for the medicine shows and their frequent mixed shows. In his pioneering study, *Blacks, Whites and Blues*, Tony Russell has posited a "common stock" of songs on which both blacks and whites drew. He pointed out that the songster Henry Thomas recorded *John Henry, Arkansas, The Fox and Hounds, Jonah In the Wilderness, Shanty Blues* and *When the Train Comes Along*, "all of which Macon recorded, virtually all earlier". Uncle Dave Macon was born in 1870, ran a Mule and Wagon Transportation Company until the First World

War and thereafter, until he died in 1952, was a "folk-vaudeville" entertainer, a mainstay of Grand Ole Opry. Born just four years after, in 1874, Henry Thomas from Upshur County, Texas was an inveterate hobo and wanderer whose shared songs with Uncle David Macon underline the spread of traditional material, much of which they had probably both learned before the turn of the century.[34]

Yet it is not merely the similarity of repertoires that is significant, though the subject demands further research with closer comparative study. As important is what the songs meant to their respective audiences when performed, for while the surface humor may have been much the same, the deeper meanings and symbolism may have been different. To white listeners such road show and street singer staples of the songsters as *I Got Mine*, *In the Jailhouse Now* and *Traveling Man* were reassuringly conventional images of standardized black figures; for black listeners these images were embraced in hero figures – the 'Traveling Man' or the singer himself – who are cunning, know how to play the system and "leave the white folks' business alone". They have a combination of native shrewdness and secret powers on their side: to the "white ladies" the Traveling Man was a fool, but he survived to play craps when they went down with the ship.

Both blacks and whites sang "Coon" songs, unpalatable though this has been to writers on black song; moreover, blacks chose to record them for a Race market. It is reasonable to assume, in view of the fact that record talent scouts merely asked for performances and made their own judgement on their suitability for recording, that singers offered the songs they knew and performed. Alec Johnson in Atlanta sang, among other songs from the minstrel show, *Next Week, Sometime*. It describes a visit to a fortune teller who tells him that he can get a pot of gold:

> He says "The way you got to get this gold,
> You got to listen while I tell –
> You got to go in a lonesome graveyard
> As the clock is striking twelve."
> I got myself a pick and a shovel
> I reached the graveyard, twelve that night,
> When I got in there, I do declare
> I found a form all dressed in white . . .

It is, of course, a ghost, or "ha'nt"

> This ha'nt said, "Don't be afraid,
> I wanna help you dig your gold."
>   I told him "Next week, sometime,
>   Brother – but not now!"
>
> I never did believe in digging gold,
> With a no-head man, in a graveyard, no-how.
> Now me an' this ha'nt run breast to breast,
> He says "Look-a here Brother, When are you goin' to rest?"

> I told him, "Next week, sometime –
> Brother, but not now!"

Though the comic scene of the graveyard ha'nt was familiar enough on the minstrel and vaudeville stage the song was unusual in one respect: it was composed by the entertainer Bert Williams with Chris Smith in 1905, and such songs from the New York stage seldom filtered through to the folk community.[35] It is not known who Alec Johnson was, but his accompanists on some titles came from Mississippi and may well have met up with him in a show. The violin player, who clearly knew the tunes at the session well, was Bo Carter who, with other members of the Chatmon family, worked minstrel and medicine shows, though he was to become a popular blues singer. Other accompanists at the session included Joe McCoy, who played with Jed Davenport's Jug Band and later organized the Harlem Hamfats, a jazz-blues band, and his younger brother, Charlie McCoy, only nineteen at this session, who accompanied such central blues figures as Tommy Johnson and Ishman Bracey. By such unexpected meetings of artists are the artificial boundaries of blues history confounded. The song situation was a stock one – as was the advent of the *Mysterious Coon*, also sung by Alec Johnson. Its origins are unknown though it fits with other songs of the 1890s including *New Coon in Town*, *Hypnotizing Coon* and *The Sensitive Coon*. It told of a strange and wealthy newcomer to Coontown:

> He's always dressed so neat and trim,
> He wears patent leather slippers, a high silk hat,
> He's got diamonds all over his silk cravat.
> He's got a face like a preacher, he don't ever smile,
> Always dressed in a gambler's style;
> He ain't tipped his hat since he's been in town,
> And the darkeys all crazy started mumblin' around
>   Saying, "I wonder what is that coon's game,
>   The way he spends his money is a sin and a shame,
>   Is he from Klondike or from Maine?
>   That's what I'd like to know.'

The coon makes an "awful hit" with the "yaller girls" and his money causes suspicion among the "darkeys":

> One went and told the police,
> "I think that darkey's stealin'."
> So they 'rested him on suspicion about nine one night,
> The darkeys held a meetin' with great delight.
> Every darkey was in court the next mornin' soon,
> To see what they were going to do with this mysterious coon.
> "One hundred dollars!" is what the Judge said.
> The darkey pulled a roll of money – big as your head
> And everybody in court began to look strange,
> When he gives the Judge a thousand dollars
> And says "Keep the change . . ."[36]

The doctor presents a sales spiel in a "low-pitch" medicine show at Huntingdon, Tennessee. A black performer in blackface and a white "Indian" await their turn. Photograph by Ben Shahn. *Library of Congress collection.*

This was a song which invited "blackface" and white glove treatment, and Alec Johnson, whose expressive vocal interpretation indicated that he was a singer with experience of the shows, may well have worn them. It would not have been unusual, as Walter "Furry" Lewis, a Memphis singer born in Greenwood, Mississippi in 1893 confirmed. He joined Jim Jackson on a medicine show as early as 1906 and worked such shows regularly for the next fifteen years, "selling Jack Rabbit medicine, pills and such as that, corn medicine too". They traveled in Model T. Fords and had a flat-bed truck for a stage where they did and wore "everything funny . . . something like a clown". In frock coats "we was all messed up" he said, "we work blackface comedian you know. Just take lamp black, some grease, put it all over your face, like in those vaudeville shows." Another singer, not known on record for his minstrel show songs, but celebrated as a blues singer, was Big Joe Williams, born in Crawford, Mississippi in 1903. He joined a minstrel–medicine show at the age of nine and stayed with it for six or seven years. "They had dancing, cracking jokes, blackface comedians – we all used to do that. Take flour and soot to make you dark; we had wigs we wore sometimes; we had them old high hats and them long coats and a walking cane and them button-type spats" – the typical minstrel show attire.[37]

Next Week, Sometime and *Mysterious Coon* represented some of the imagery which was present in the show songs: humor, self-preservation, supernatural powers, success through covert means. To the white audiences they probably confirmed the image of the fearful, superstitious, eye-rolling "darkey" and to some extent this would be shared by knowing and sophisticated blacks who would have the simple subject of fun to look down upon. But for black audiences on the sidewalk watching the medicine show it was possible to identify with the wealth-seeking Fred, who placed personal safety above risk. Or with the arrogant, expressionless coon who had success with the yellow girls; who was subject to police arrest for suspicion and then put down the judge. Fantasy, but important for morale.

These songs also contained other symbols and attitudes with which the audiences could sympathize: confident bragging, fondness for food and feasting, mild stealing and hustling, brushes with the police who always break up good times. These aspects of presumed black behavior were reflected in many songs. A popular favorite was *Chicken, You Can Roost Behind the Moon*, or simply, *Chicken*, which was related to W. J. Simons's *There Is No Chicken That Can Roost Too High For Me*, published in 1899. It was recorded with the former title by Frank Stokes.

> I got to thinkin' 'bout chicken late the other night,
> Man, I couldn't a-hardly rest,
> I jumped out of bed, grabbed up my old shoes,
> Gone to where those chickens was at.
> I grabbed up each bird, boys, tucked 'em under my arm
> Some I never let go,

> I don't think I'll rob your hen-house,
> Till I get you rooster chicken at all.
>   Now chicken, oh chicken, you can go up in a balloon, (dog-gone)
>   Chicken, you may hide behind the moon; (dog-gone you, now)
>   Now chicken, I never let a fowl be,
>   Ten thousand dollars reward, ain't no fowl on earth
>   They don't roost too high for me.
>
> Say that police 'rested me last Friday night
> They couldn't think what to look out;
> They goin' down the alley where I lived at,
> Another chicken tied in my house.
> Says "You may carry me to the penitentiary walls
> I'm gonna work out my time,
> Just as quick as you can put me on that L an' N track,
> I'll have chickens on my mind."
>   Now, chicken, oh chicken, you may go up in a balloon,[38]   etc.

To a lively stovepipe, harmonica and guitar accompaniment, Stovepipe No. 1 sang another version, with the bizarre title *A Chicken Can Waltz the Gravy Around*. He bragged that "in fifteen minutes by any man's watch I'll have chicken on my plate".

> Oh chicken, oh chicken, you can fry 'em nice and brown,
> Oh chicken, oh chicken, you can waltz the gravy around,
> Oh chicken, oh chicken, I don't mean no fault in that,
> Fine chickens grow in this town
> And they wings can't get too fat.
>   Oh when I come to this neighborhood,
>   Chickens knows just what I mean;
>   Chickens skippin' and dodgin',
>   No chicken can't be seen.
> The hen she said to the rooster,
> "There ain't no use to hide;
> Got a sharpshoot' gun
> And it hurts to run,
> And our wings can't roost too high."[39]

One of the attractions of a song like *Chicken* was that it could be adapted to a variety of circumstances and ascribed meanings best suited to the audiences to whom it was directed. Though the "chicken" hunting and stealing subject of the song could be taken at face value, it was relatively easy for a singer to sing "I got chickens on my mind" with an ogling eye to any young women in the audience. To a predominately white crowd he could "play nigger" and satisfy their delight in the chicken-stealing black simpleton; to a black audience he could lay more emphasis on harrassment by the police or the successful duping of white people. Often such sentiments were expressed in conventional verses. Jim Jackson, whose total output is one of the richest stores of traditional songs, used verses in *What a Time* that had been collected by Perrow in Mississippi in 1909 and several times around 1915 in Alabama:

Figures depicting stereotypes of black life on a torn wall poster; they include watermelon and chicken-stealing thieves, a razor-toting jealous husband, frock-coated banjo playing minstrel, washwoman, billy-wielding cop and kicking mule. *Library of Congress collection.*

I got a girl, just because
She works right over in the white folks' yard,
Brings me chicken, brings me pie,
I get some of everything the white folks buy.
    Ain't that a time, what a time, what a time, what a time,
    What a time, talkin' with angels, what a time. } (2)

I got another girl, just because
Works right over in the white folks' yard,

> Brings me chicken, brings me ham,
> If she don't bring me nothing' I don't give a –
> Oh, what a time,[40]   etc.

Overt comments on relations between the races were rare, and if there were many such songs they scarcely got on record. Few songsters would have performed them to a white or mixed Southern audience, except under the cover of a heavy screen of other associations. Jim Towel told a story of the spells cast by a girl he had refused to marry. Getting a rabbit's foot "She buried it with a frog, right in the holler of an old burnt log . . .

> Ever since then my head's been wrong
> My bones begin to ache, my teeth begin to chatter.
> I went to the doctor he couldn't tell the matter
> Says "old chile you are goin' up the spout."
> He looked at my hair and my hair fell out.
> Nobody knows how funny I feel
> Even the husk fell off-a my heel.
> I went to the doctor, doctor jumped in the river
> Looked at the water, my bones begin to quiver.
> Later on the doctor fell fast asleep
> Tried to wake up, my flesh begin to creep.
> Later on the doctor got a pain in the head
> When I woke up to tell the truth I found myself dead.
>   I been hoodooed, hoodooed,
>   Hoodooed, hoodooed by a doctor hoodoo . . .

Then, unexpectedly, the song changed as he sang forcefully;

> Put on your state, you children
> Listen to what I say,
> Don't disgrace, the colored race now,
> Don't be led astray.
> Put on your state, you children,
> There's a time to make your mark,
> If you can't come yeller, come the right color
> But for goodness sake, don't come dark,
>   'Cause I been hoodooed, hoodooed,
>   Hoodooed by a doctor sure as you're born.

Collected by Newman White without the concluding verse, the song had been composed in 1894 by a one-time black janitor Gussie Davis who, at the age of twenty-five in 1886, wrote *Irene, Goodnight.* Jim Jackson used the verse pointedly in *I'm a Bad, Bad Man,* already discussed. "Don't put on your slick, you children", he sang, "Now don't come yeller but come the right color; For God's sake don't come dark." To "come dark" was to "act nigger" and in his song the verse was related to the boast of a recalcitrant "bad man". But in the context of Jim Towel's version the implication seems inescapable that the "hoodoo doctor" is the white race, though he conveyed his message in the guise of a coon song.[41]

Similarly, at his first recording session Bo Chatman made *Good Old Turnip Greens*, which was apparently about the supposed passion of the poor blacks for boiled turnip top leaves, but which slipped in a reference or two to racial inequalities:

> When I was a little boy,
> I always wanted to fly,
> I flapped my wings like a seagull
> And I flew up to the sky.
> When I got up in Heaven,
> I seen somethin' I never have seen –
> There was a lot of burly coons
> Just a-scratchin' on the turnip greens.
>> He's a fool about his turnip greens
>> Oh yes, indeed he are,
>> Corn bread and buttermilk
>> And the good old turnip greens.
>
> Mister Spencer went to Chicago,
> And I went to New Orleans,
> I got mad and walked all the way back home,
> Just to get my greasy turnip greens.
> Oh the white man wears his broadcloth,
> And the Indian he wears jeans,
> But here comes the darkey with his over-alls on,
> Just a-scratchin' on the turnip greens.
>> He's a fool about his turnip greens   etc.
>
> White man goes to the college
> And the Negro to the fields,
> The white man will learn to read and write,
> And the Negro will learn to steal.
> Oh the white folks in their parlors,
> Just eatin' their cake and cream,
> But the darkey's back in the kitchen,
> Just a-scratchin' on the turnip greens.
>> He's a fool about his turnip greens[42]   etc.

As a member of the Mississippi Sheiks string band, and solo as Bo Carter, Bo Chatman became one of the most extensively recorded of blues singers, swiftly learning to adapt his repertoire to popular black demand. But *Good Old Turnip Greens* seems to have been older – another coon or minstrel song. Another title, his first, *The Yellow Coon Has No Race* was never issued; perhaps because the record producer felt that it would offend black sensibilities. As it happens, Bo Carter was very light-skinned and his features "Caucasian" so the unissued song may have had particular meaning for him. Often the butt of the songs were others of the singer's own race, especially those of a lighter hue, as was the case in *Goin' Round the Mountain Charmin' Betsy*. It was one of the first pieces which Gus Cannon learned to play, though he did not record it until many years later. An inoffensive version was made by Henry Thomas:

> Yellow gal rides in an automobile
> Brownskin does the same.
> Black gal rides in an old airship
> But she's ridin' just the same.

Color stratification was also used by Jim Jackson to introduce his version, but he worked in some sharper barbs as the song progressed:

> Well a yeller girl got this long sleek hair,
> Brownskin's got the same;
> Well a black gal buys hers at a ten cent store,
> But it's good hair just the same.
>> Sing, I'm goin' round the mountain, Charmin' Betsy
>> Going round the mountain, Pearlie Lee,
>> Now if I never see you again,
>> Do Lord, remember me.
>
> Well a yeller girl smells like sweet toilet soap
> Brownskin girl does the same.
> Well a poor black girl smells like a billy goat
> But she's smellin' just the same.
>> Sing, I'm goin' round the mountain,   etc.
>
> Well a white man gives his wife a ten-dollar bill,
> He thinks that's nothing strange,
> But a colored man give his wife a one-dollar bill
> And beat her to death 'bout the 90 cents change.
>> Sing, I'm goin' round the mountain,   etc.
>
> Well a white man lives in a fine brick house,
> He thinks that's nothin' strange,
> But we poor colored men lives in the county jail
> But it's a brick house just the same . . .

Versions with similar words were collected from "Negro actors in a small show" in Alabama in 1915, from a "street minstrel, King's Mountain, N.C. in 1911", and it was reported from a minstrel show in 1919 in Durham, North Carolina. [43] Collectors noted single stanzas which had a measure of protest in them which nevertheless retained, or were masked by, an element of humor. Some of these may well have been in currency for a century, relating to the songs of Ole Master, or Ole Mistis, which were sung by slaves and by ex-slaves following the Civil War. Many of these became part of the minstrel repertory and some fed back into oral tradition; others were collected later but have a form of verse and chorus, and content in the economical lyrics, that suggest nineteenth-century origins. This is the case with *Go 'Long Mule*, which was "sung with remarkable effect at the Dayton, Tennessee Scopes trial, with hundreds of whites and Negroes standing around the quartette of Negroes who came for the occasion", as Howard Odum reported. John Thomas Scopes, a young biology teacher, had defied the state law prohibiting the teaching of the theory of evolution and was tried, and found guilty, of the offense. The song was, wrote Odum in 1926, "the best illustration of the minstrel type in this volume". Ukelele Bob Williams's version was recorded a year before the Scopes trial, in 1924.

> I got a mule, he's a fool
> He never showed no heed,
> 'Till I built a fire beneath his tail
> And now he shows some speed.
> > Go 'long mule, don't you roll them eyes,
> > You can't change a fool, for a dog-gone mule
> > Is a mule until he dies.
>
> My mule refuse to work for me,
> I know the reason for that.
> He found out that I was a Re-publican
> And he's a Demo-crat.
> > Go 'long mule, don't you roll them eyes, etc.
>
> I bought some biscuits for my dog
> I laid 'em on the shelf,
> Times got hard, I shot my dog
> And ate them up myself.
> > Go 'long mule, don't you roll them eyes,   etc.

The song permitted the invention of new verses with ease; none of Ukelele Bob Williams's verses was as pointed as one collected by Odum which referred to a Ku Klux Klan gathering:

> They're gonna hold a meetin' there
> Of some society.
> There's 'leven sheets upon the line,
> That's ten too much for me.[44]

Travelers in the South and ex-slaves alike recollected that a black worker could sing comments about his master or boss to his mule, which he could not say to his boss's face.[45] Some traditional quatrains were more incisive than those in *Go 'Long Mule*. As early as 1876 Lafcadio Hearn had noted the words of *Limber Jim*:

> Nigger and a white man playing seven up
> White man played an ace; an' nigger feared to take it up,
> White man played ace an' nigger played a nine,
> White man died, an' nigger went blind.

Fifty years later Odum heard:

> Niggers plant the cotton,
> Niggers pick it out,
> White man pockets money,
> Niggers does without.

Another, widely collected, stanza ran:

> Nigger and a white man playing seven-up,
> Nigger won the money, scared to pick it up;

> Nigger made the motion, the white man fell;
> Nigger grabbed the money and he run like hell.[46]

To the tune of a folk song found among both white and black traditions, an obscure singer from the Carolinas, Julius Daniels, recorded the verse in association with a "mule" stanza, in which the stubborn animal is belabored with the pole which linked his harness to the wagon.

> I had old mule, the mule wouldn't "gee" this morning,   (2)
> I had old mule, the mule wouldn't "gee",
> I hit 'im on the head with a single tree,
> This morning, that's too soon for me.
>
> This old mule kep' a-cuttin' his food, this morning,   (2)
> This old mule kep' a-cuttin' his food,
> I can't put the bridle on this ole mule,
> This morning, that's too soon for me.
>
> I told that nigger with the black hat on this morning.   (2)
> I told that nigger with the black hat on,
> I'm gonna hit 'im in the head as sure as you're born,
> This morning, that's too soon for me.
>
> Oh nigger and the white man playing seven-up this morning,   (2)
> Nigger and the white man playing seven-up,
> Well nigger win the money, but he scared to pick it up,
> This morning, that's too soon for me.[47]

Threatening violence against the "mule" was one means whereby racial frustration could be vented safely; though the final verse explicitly stated a fear of whites, it also existed in an animal parallel as Dorothy Scarborough reported from New Orleans:

> The monkey and the baboon
> Playing seven-up.
> The monkey won the money
> And was scared to pick it up.

Substituting animals for members of the races had been popular among the tellers of tall tales and Br'er Rabbit stories. By this simple artifice, meanings could be applied to the stanzas that were the listener's own; challenged, the singer could feign innocence of any double meanings or word play. It was a device employed by a singer from Atlanta, Georgia, Barbecue Bob, who made a recording of the *Monkey and the Baboon*:

> Monkey and the Baboon shootin' crooked dice,
> Monkey throwed a seven and eleven, twice,
> Baboon grabbed a switch, swung it fas'
> Knocked the little monkey out in the grass.
>   Monkey's doodledoo, monkey's doodledoo,
>   If you try to make a monkey out o' me
>   I'll make a baboon out o' you.

blacks in blackface

> Monkey and the baboon sittin' on the fence
> Monkey called the baboon "Chocolate-haired trash",
> Baboon sittin' back in his class
> Knocked the little monkey on his yas-yas-yas.
>   Monkey's doodledoo,[48]   etc.

In such songs the monkey usually represented the black character while the baboon was the white. Though blacks often accepted and joked about alleged simian features, and sang "You're bound to look like a monkey when you grow old", or "he's in the ape-yard now", they saw in the long nose, lowered brow, brightly pigmented features and brown hair of the baboon parallels with whites which the baboon's aggressiveness and apparent stupidity supported.

Writing of the early minstrel show Constance Rourke observed that after the Civil War "if the Negro was set free, in a fashion his white impersonators were also liberated". Irish and German and eventually "the Jew emerged in blackface. Again in fantasy the American types seemed to be joining in a single semblance. But Negro music and Negro nonsense still prevailed; through years the old pattern was kept." [49] Black entertainers contributed to the process; on the surface, far from being liberated, they were entrapped by the clichés of the minstrel show. Blacks too, were wearing blackface, causing embarrassment to those race leaders who were seeking dignity and advancement for their people.

Yet this may be subject to a different interpretation: by adopting the image of the minstrel figure of ridicule, black entertainers defused the charge. When the butt of the joke participated in the joke much of its effect was extinguished. White minstrels were ready enough to turn to the new waves of immigrants from Central Europe with their folkways and struggles with the language of their new country for the focus of ridicule and crude humor. Meanwhile, blacks, dressed in minstrel garb of the "long-tailed blue", and their frock-coated successors made it clear by adopting the burnt cork or soot and flour make-up that the minstrel or medicine show was a vehicle for satire.

Songsters were expected to participate in the humor of the show and to perform songs which gathered a crowd around the pitch and kept it in a state of amusement and excitement. An entertainer who showed that he was a member of "the crap society" had the people on his side. His songs played on and reinforced shared beliefs in the capacity of the folk figure to use his native cunning to his own advantage. Given that the odds were half-way to being fair he could get himself out of a scrape until "the police shot him down" and the odds were hopelessly against him. That certain ragtime and coon songs of the turn of the century should be still sung thirty years and a world war later is evidence of their potency; many were still being sung after *two* world wars. They treated the behavior of the simpler blacks and their folkways with superiority, but in doing so helped to change attitudes. They laughed at black superstitions while acknowledging that they persisted, and then traded on white fears in turn; the crowds felt better.

Through fantasy heroes, "coon" figures, animal parallels and oblique satirical references, racial confidence was restored. True, much of the laughter was ironic and in a rural society where women's jobs and roles were more stable than those of the men, the humor was often chauvinistic. But the songs of the road shows were comments on life, not portraits of it. The medicine show entertainment was a comic strip with the songsters as its draughtsmen, delineating home truths with cartoon characters.

4

If Luck Don't Change

Fantasy, reality and parody

"We just go out and play, stand on the corners, on vacant lots – all different places – play all day. Play for medicine shows. That was right around World War 1, 1918 or so. We played on sidewalks, streets, in stores, anywhere." Carl Martin, a violin player with a string band who unfortunately recorded little at the time, recalled that he "played for both white and colored . . . traveled all over, went through Virginia and West Virginia, Kentucky and all down South". They played "anything they want – if it was weddings, dances, breakdowns, churches, anything they sent for me to come and play. That's why I learnt to play so well."[1] Scores of other songsters could have made similar claims. Shows, especially the medicine shows, may have been the most specific vehicles for the distribution of songs through various parts of the country. They were the most institutionalized means by which songsters from different regions could meet, work together and exchange items from their repertoires. But songsters worked in a variety of other milieux.

Unlike many songsters Carl Martin could justifiably call himself a professional musician. He even taught himself to read music sufficiently well to "get it off the sheet". In spite of the evidence of sheet music sources for many songs, very few songsters could read music and few were exclusively employed as musicians. In the 1910 census over a quarter of a million black men, and nearly as many women over the age of ten were employed in agriculture in Mississippi alone. There were 12,000 black laborers in the saw and planing mills, over 600 barbers and even more blacksmiths; more than 1000 black clergymen were listed but scarcely more than 100 musicians and teachers of music, of whom more than half were women. In Georgia 60 men gave their occupations as "Musician", while the number of women was double; nearly as many were engaged in agriculture as in Mississippi, and other figures were comparable. In the country as a whole fewer than 6000 black musicians and teachers of music were listed, of whom two-thirds were women. There were 1000 showmen, virtually all male, but over half a million servants.[2]

Exhaustive though the census data were, the figures did not reveal the numbers of workers who were musicians for part of the year – who were gainfully employed in, say, agriculture, but who were well known for their music ability. At a time when the total black population was nearly ten

A string band of fiddle, guitar and bass could bring in extra money for a large rural family, Hammond, Louisiana, early in the century.

THE KODAK SHOP, PHILA.

million, of whom nine-tenths lived in the South, the number of professional musicians and showmen was remarkably small relative to their influence and reputation. Songsters, string band and dance musicians in the South were, for the most part, farm and plantation workers during the week and musicians on Saturday night. Music doubtless meant more to them than jobs in service or agriculture, but it was a leisure-time activity for most songsters. In the summer and fall lay-off period, many traveled, touring with the shows if they could get employment or simply by making their own way, to sing, play or perform when and wherever they had the opportunity.

This was also the time when the picnics and country suppers were held in the wooded areas close to the river or in the backlands of the hills; it was the period of the year when fish-fries and barbecues could last all night and the songsters played till their strings or their strength gave out. In the warm fall evenings when the full blaze of the summer heat was over, travelers passing through the South heard the music – at a distance – saw the cheerful, tired dancers returning and reinforced their picture of happy black folk enjoying a life free of serious cares. If it was a colorful, false and sentimental picture, it was one that some blacks, at any rate, seem also to have believed in and sang about. Archie Lewis was one. He was not a gifted musician when he recorded, but songsters had to learn their craft and not all were good musicians. He had a rich voice, if a lugubrious delivery, but his guitar-playing was as simple as Stokes's was rhythmically complex. He also appears not to have noticed the incongruity in the third line of *Miss Handy Hanks*:

> Miss Mandy [sic] Hanks and old Bill Jones
> Went to a swell party one day,
> With a four-wheeled horse and a bob-tailed buggy,
> Certainly was looking gay.
> Miss Mandy said to ol' Bill Jones
> "Honey what we gonna do?"
> Says "Sit still honey, we got no money,
> But chittlins – we got a few.
> > Hot chittlins red hot, that's the dish for me
> > Hot chittlins red hot, oh can't you see?
> > I got bread [in markets] from North to South,
> > Seepin' tastes good right in your mouth   (hey, what?)
> > Hot chittlin's, red hot."

The song continued with a visit to a turkey feast where "the colored people act like a pack of wild geese" before the melody changed, and a dialogue from another song was introduced.

> "Oh mammy, pray tell me where Daddy ⎫
> Where my Daddy, oh Daddlee-do?"   ⎬ (2)
>   ⎭
> "He's way down South among the fields of cotton,
> Way down South among the clover and the bees;
> Way down South among the fields of cotton,
> I'll take you back . . . way down home."[3]

nostalgia

Nostalgic and idealized pictures of the South, so redolent of Stephen Foster's songs and other sentimental ballads of the late nineteenth century, occurred in unlikely circumstances. The gruff-voiced Tennessee singer Hambone Willie Newbern, mentor of the blues singers, Sleepy John Estes and Yank Rachell, is best known for his influential *Roll and Tumble Blues*. Of his six recorded titles half were minstrel or ragtime songs, and though he served time in a Southern prison he had no hesitation, apparently, in singing a pretty song about Arkansas:

> Way down yonder in old Arkansas,
> Where you find the turkey in the straw,
> You can hear the roosters crowin' 'bout the break of day,
> Old hens are a-layerin' in the new-born hay [sic],
> That's where my great grand-ma
> Was married up with my great grand-pa;
> Well, they settled down together,
> How they loved each other,
> Way down in Arkansas.
>   I can hear the donkey moanin' at the old barn do' – yeah
>   See the ladies tippin' cross the kitchen flo'.
>   When you get your coffee it'll be 'fore day,
>   See the turkeys slippin' out through the hay . . .[4]

It is Newbern's gritty delivery and his sour-toned finger-picking that give the record its quality; not the words, which are as mundane as any of an aged couple dreaming of the South. Yet it is not certain how it was interpreted by its hearers in the twenties in Tennessee. It may have been accepted nostalgically at its face value – or it may have been sung satirically and enjoyed as such by Newbern's audience. Some who listened must have turned to the reality of life in the South for poor blacks on the threshold of the Depression and, regarding the sagging cabins, the dirt patches round them littered with discarded utensils, the skinny children with swollen bellies, smiled ironically at the comforting domesticity that the song portrayed.

There's nothing in Willie Newbern's performance on record to suggest that satire was in his mind; the song appears to have been purely escapist, describing an Arkansas that existed only in the romantic imagination. A very different view of the state appears briefly in Henry Thomas's *Arkansas*, a medley already discussed in connexion with the Irving Jones song *Let Me Bring My Clothes Back Home*, in which a verse from *The Roving Gambler* is fused with *The State of Arkansas*:

> I am a rambling, gambling man,
> I gambled in many towns,
> I rambled this wide world over,
> I rambled this world around.
> I had my ups and downs through life
> And bitter times I saw;

But I never knew what mis'ry was –
Till I lit on old Arkansas.

I started out one morning
To meet that early train,
He said "You better work with me
I have some land to drain;
I'll give you fifty cents a day,
Your washing, board and all,
And you shall be a different man
In the state of old Arkansas."

I worked six months for the rascal,
Johanna was his name.
He fed me on corn-dodgers,
They was hard as any rock;
My tooth is all got loosened,
And my knee-bone 'gin to raw,
That was the kind of hash I got –
In the state of Arkansas . . .[5]

While Newbern's song appears to have come from the ragtime era, Thomas's derived from the nineteenth-century white minstrel tradition, recorded by Gid Tanner, Uncle Dave Macon and many others. *Arkansas* took a more jaundiced view of life in the South, but though the one was sentimental fantasy and the other realist narrative they were both generalized rather than specific comments on the state and its inhabitants. As the poorest of Southern states, Arkansas became a symbol of mean conditions and meanness of spirit in the Thomas song, while in Newbern's it was on the surface, an idealized image of the state.

Fictionalized places where life was easy existed in local black folklore, and belief in them was exploited by labor contractors, according to an ex-slave from Alabama, Henry Green. They "brung that hundred head of folks the time us come. They told us that in Arkansas the hogs just laying around already baked with the knives and the forks sticking in them ready to be et, . . . and that there was money trees where all you had to do was to pick the money offen 'em like picking cotton offen the stalk, and us was sure put out when us git here and find that the onliest meat to be had was that what was in the store . . . and that there wa'n't no money trees a-tall."[6]

This land of Cockaigne had many parallels, among them "Ginny Gall", and the "largest and best known of the Negro mythical places", Diddy-Wah-Diddy. "Its geography is that it is 'way off somewhere'. It is reached by a road that curves so much that a mule pulling a wagon-load of fodder can eat off the back of the wagon as he goes", wrote Zora Neale Hurston when recording folklore in Florida. A place of no work and no worries, it was where the hungry traveler was met by "a big baked chicken . . . with a knife and fork stuck in its sides" and a sweet potato pie that "no matter how much you eat it grows just that much faster. It is said 'Everybody would live in Diddy-Wah-

Blind Arthur Blake, songster from Florida, was one of Paramount's most popular singers.   *Paul Oliver collection.*

Diddy if it wasn't so hard to find and so hard to get to after you even know the way'." [7] Blind Blake, though he came from Jacksonville, Florida, claimed not to know the term.

> There's a great big mystery,
> And it sure is worryin' me,
>   This Diddie Wa Diddie,
>   This Diddie Wa Diddie;

> I wish somebody would tell me
> What Diddie Wa Diddie means.
>
> Went to church, put my hat on the seat,
> Lady sat on the seat, said "Daddy you sure is sweet."
>   Mister Diddie Wa Diddie,   etc.
>
> I said "Sister I'll soon be gone,
> Just give me that thing you sittin' on"
>   My Diddie Wa Diddie,   etc.
>
> Then I got put out of church
> 'Cause I talk 'bout Diddie Wa Diddie too much.
>   Mister Diddie Wa Diddie . . .[8]   etc.

The mythical location where dreams of food and comfort become realities had been transformed into a sexual fantasy. A year later, in 1930, having "just found out what Diddie Wa Diddie means" Blind Blake recorded a second version in which he was no longer the center of the story. Now wiser, he sang of "Two-gun Jim" who had been "carried away" by the police:

> They took him to jail, he began to shout,
> The judge said, "That won't get you out,
>   Mister Diddie Wa Diddie,
>   Mister Diddie Wa Diddie,
>   I just found out what Diddie Wa Diddie means."
>
> The gangster said, "Now that ain't right,
> I shot that guy about my wife,
>   My Diddie Wa Diddie"   etc.
>
> He told the judge, "You better set me free,
> You'll see some day you'll be [needin' me,]
>   Mister Diddie Wa Diddie"   etc.
>
> The Judge say, "Don't you give me no sass,
> I'm gonna lock up your yas, yas yas,
>   Mister Diddie Wa Diddie"   etc.
>
> The gangster's wife went in her door,
> Said, "Judge, let me get me some diddie, some more
>   Of this Diddie Wa Diddie"[9]   etc.

In Blind Blake's later song the irony lay in the fact that the gangster's luck had run out. He was Mr Diddie Wa Diddie no longer, and the fantasy world was at odds with the real one. This transition from dream to reality seems to have applied to other symbolic locations "way off somewhere", including Alabama, in the song *Alabama Bound*, which was, the Texas collector Gates Thomas noted in a paper written in 1926, "a psychic state, rather than a place". *Alabama Bound* was one of a song cluster which included *Don't You Leave Me Here* and *Elder Green's In Town*. Many versions of the song were collected in the early part of the century throughout the South. In Texas, W. H. Thomas of College Station included *Don't You Leave Me Here* in "some current folk songs" which in 1912 he presented as a paper to the Folk-lore

Society of Texas. Some years later his brother, Gates Thomas, published his own, fuller collection that included an *Alabama Boun'* with Elder Green verses, which he dated from 1908. Several others were collected before or during the First World War in Georgia, Florida, Louisiana, Tennessee and in Alabama itself.[10] Its widespread distribution suggests its early date as a folk song. Though it was described as a dance, a song with the title of *Alabama Bound* had been published as early as 1910 by Ed Rogers and Saul Aaronson which showed clear links with the chorus of the folk song. A recording of *I'm Alabama Bound* by Papa Charlie Jackson made in May 1925 showed the relationship of the traditional verses:

> Says the preacher in the pulpit
> Bible in his hand,
> Sister's way back in the Amen Corner
> Hollerin' "That's my man."
>   Alabama Bound, Alabama Bound,
>   If you want me to love you babe
>   Got to leave this town.
>
> Now the boat's up the river,
> And it's rollin' down,
> And if you need to go South, my darlin' babe,
> Alabama Bound.
>
> Elder Green's in town,
> And he turned around,
> And he tell all the sisters and the brothers he meets,
> "I'm Alabama Bound."
>   Don't you leave me here,   (2)
>   Jest before you and your partner get ready to go,
>   Leave a dime for beer.[11]

In several collected versions the singer will get to his destination come what may: "If the train don't run, I got a mule to ride, I'm Alabama Bound." This is reflected in a version by Papa Harvey Hull and Long Cleve Reed, songsters who sang of a riverboat of the Lee Line out of Memphis. The phrase "and the Stack don't drown" referred to the celebrated captain of one of the boats, "Stack" Lee.

> Alabama Bound, Alabama Bound,
> If the boat don't sink and the Stack don't drown,
> I'm Alabama Bound.
>
> Boats up the river, runnin' side by side,
> When you got my lovin', kind sweet babe,
> You'll be satisfied.
>
> Don't you leave me here, don't you leave me here,
> Well I don't mind you goin' sweet lovin' babe –
> Leave a dollar for beer.   (hey, hey, let's go boys)

> Katy Adams got ways, just like a man,
> Well she steals a woman, sweet lovin' babe,
> Everywhere she lands.[12]

Though the boats "side by side" could refer to riverboat racing, as it did in other songs, in this context the practice of tying two boats together to form a floating brothel for roustabouts may have been the subject. For the *Katy Adams* was of similar kind; known as "a woman's boat on the water" it was a mail boat on the Mississippi which leased out cabins to prostitutes for fifty cents fare between Memphis and Rosedale, Mississippi.[13] If the meaning of *Alabama Bound* was a determination to leave for another state where, presumably, conditions were thought to be better, then Harvey Hull's position is one of philosophical cynicism, willing to exchange his "sweet lovin' babe" for the pimp's dues. A similar irony exists in Charley Patton's *Elder Greene Blues* which has close affinities to the version of *Alabama Bound* collected by Gates Thomas. In both, the wayward elder sheds his religious obligations to indulge in more worldly pleasures.

> (Elder) Greene is (gone), Elder Greene is gone,
> Gone way down in the country,
> With his long coat on,
>   With his long coat on,   (2)
> Gone way down the country with his long coat on.

> Elder Greene told the Deacon "Let's go down in prayer,
> There's a big stone station in New Orleans,
> Come and let's go there,"
>   Come and let's go there,   etc.

> I like to fuss and fight, I like to fuss and fight,
> Lord and get sloppy drunk on a bottle in bond
> And walk the streets all night.
>   And walk the streets all night[14]   etc.

Another recording of *Don't Leave Me Here*, linking with *Alabama Bound*, was made by the songster Henry Thomas, who used the tune of *Don't Ease Me In*, a sexual song, though his version was carefully bowdlerized.

When W. H. Thomas, who was a Professor at the Texas Agricultural and Mechanical College, presented his collection of black songs in 1912 he offered an "economic interpretation" of "negro class lore". Though some of his attitudes read uncomfortably today, Thomas had witnessed major changes in the rural economy in the previous twenty years, and was of the opinion that the black man had been the victim of the competition of immigrant Europeans "whose staying qualities are much greater than his", and of developments in agriculture, which had moved "from a feudalistic to a capitalistic basis, which requires a greater technical ability than the negro possesses. The result is that he is being steadily pushed into the less inviting and secure occupations." He concluded that "the negro, then, sings because he is losing his economic

foothold. This economic insecurity has interfered most seriously with those
two primal necessities – work and love", and he noted that the songs he had
collected "cluster round these two ideas". In fact, songs specifically about
work were seldom recorded, but there were many that were about avoiding
work, or of living off "a gal who works in the white folk's yard", which might
be subject to Thomas's economic interpretation.[15]

Similarly, ballads of romantic love or affection were rarely recorded by folk
songsters. They were far more frequent in the recordings of the vaudeville and
jazz-blues singers, as will be illustrated in a subsequent study, but songsters
seem to have been awkward with such material. Recordings like Troy
Ferguson's *Good Night* with its conventional sentiment:

> Good night, good night, good night little girl,
> How I miss you tonight all alone,
> Baby may die, like his mother, may cry
> But tonight how I miss you, sweetheart all alone . . .[16]

or Spark Plug Smith's somewhat abashed version of *New Blue Heaven* or
Sweet Evening Breeze ("she was my blushing bride . . . please blow my loved
one back to me") are unusual and, when they do occur, are almost always
unsatisfactory. There was no lack of such songs in the sheet music of the
ragtime era, which dreamed of dusky, dark-eyed girls in Southern cotton
fields. Nor were they wanting in lullabyes, songs to or about children and
paeans to faithful domesticity, but though many other songs of the same
period entered the songsters' repertoires these did not do so, or did not survive
to be recorded.

Some songs on personal relationships, like William Moore's *Tillie Lee* seem
to denigrate the partner while professing affection, as if the singer was too
embarrassed or too nervous to acknowledge his emotions.

> Tillie Lee, Tillie Lee, I love my Tillie Lee,
> There's something very peculiar 'bout my Tillie Lee
> Funny as it can be,
> Tillie Lee, Tillie Lee, my yellow honey bee,
> She's bow-legged and lazy, cross-eyed and crazy,
> But I love my Tillie Lee.
>
> She got great big nose, she got crooked toes,
> I love my Tillie Lee.
> She got big thick lips, she got [bottle ham] hips,
> Nice as she could be.

Moore continued to describe her lack of physical charms but praised her
faithfulness and her value as a provider:

> She treats me right, she stays home at night,
> I love my Tillie Lee.
> She got poor eye-sight, she can't read or write,
> Sweet as she can be,

Originally from New Orleans, Papa Charlie Jackson played an unusually large, six-string banjo. *Paul Oliver collection.*

concluding by stating that "she calls me honey, she gives me money . . . she buys me clothes; everybody knows she sweet as she can be."[17] Such backhanded compliments were not uncommon. Papa Charlie Jackson, for example, performed a simple eight-bar song of couplets and refrain with a similar acceptance of his subject's shortcomings:

> Got a knock-kneed mama down in Tennessee,
> She's short and squatty, she's all right with me,
>   Don't you think I know?
>   Mama don't you think I know?

Now knock-kneed mama, what you gonna cook tonight?
Whatever you cook, jus' cook it right,
   Don't you think I know?   etc.

She got a face like a washboard, mouth like a tub,
Teach my mama that washboard rub,
   Don't you think I know?   etc.

Takes a long-tailed monkey, short-tailed dog,
Do that dance they called 'Fallin' off a log',
   Don't you think I know? [18]   etc.

A cheerful realism, even opportunism, characterizes many of Charlie
Jackson's songs, echoing the age-old themes of the cuckold and the amorous
wife, or the male lover seeking an accommodating female companion. On his
I'm Looking For a Woman, "who knows how to treat me right", he added,
slyly, "I'm a man with a family" complaining that she gave him "Turnip
greens, turnip greens, that's somethin' that I don't eat". His songs were
frequently humorous and drew their material from the feckless instability of
the "rounder", and the advantages of casual relationships. Sometimes these
were expressed in somewhat contradictory terms, like *I Got What It Takes*,
which continues "but it breaks my heart to give it away, ain't goin' to give it
away".

Now baby the stuff I got is the stuff that makes
The fiddler play, makes the fiddler play.
I've saved it up since the Lord knows when,
I ain't gonna save it for any of you men.
I've had it so long, I hate to lose it,
'Cause if I get broke, I'll be able to use it –
Now this little thing is what the whole wide world
Is trying to get, oh dying to get,
This wise baby she ain't goin' to part – from it yet . . .[19]

A song, in fact, which should obviously have been sung by a woman, even if
Jackson nowhere makes this explicit by a comment. But though such sexual
allusions are common in black song on Race records, they were of a suggestive
rather than an erotic nature, many having been bowdlerized before being
acceptable for recording. Though employment as such did not figure in them,
the use of farmyard metaphors and animal transpositions was common.[20]

Such animal parallels could be made humorous by their incongruity, as in
the Memphis Jug Band's *Move That Thing*, on which Charlie Nickerson sang
the vocal:

I got a job as a teamster, and I was out of my place,
The mule backed up, in my face,
   I said "Move that thing, be-ba-de-bum,
   You got to move that thing,
   If you want me to stay here –
   You have to move that thing."

Horse and a flea and two little mice,
Were down in the cellar shootin' dice,
　They moved that thing　etc.

Then the horse he slipped, fell on the flea,
Flea said "Police! – there's a horse on me."
　You got to move　etc.

Said the little red rooster to the little red hen
"You haven't laid an egg since I don't know when"
　You got to move　etc.

Walter Prescott Webb, who collected the penultimate verse before 1923 noted that in the dice game "if one darkey is a point ahead he says: 'I'm a hoss on you'; if behind 'that's a hoss on me'". Time ran out before the customary follow up to the last couplet could be made, in which the hen says to the rooster "You don't come around as often as you useter" or "That's all right, meet me round the barn tomorrow night." [21] Structurally the song was similar to *Shake That Thing* and *Tight Like That*, two of the most popular forms of the blues song in the 1920s. Though comprising stanzas of couplets followed by a four-line refrain, the verses were to a twelve-bar blues sequence and such songs could be considered technically as blues. The extraordinary success of the original recording of *It's Tight Like That* by Georgia Tom and Tampa Red in 1928 made the tune virtually obligatory for popular singers to record. [22]

Sometimes used to convey a measure of social comment, animal symbolism was more frequently employed as a device for conveying sexual or scatological allusions. Rufus and Ben Quillian, two clothes pressers in an Atlanta cleaning plant who came from Gainesville, Georgia, recorded a number of songs of a suggestive nature which they composed for performing on radio, but which drew from traditional sources and employed the familiar *Tight Like That* form.

The rabbit and the terrapin had a race,
The terrapin put it in the rabbit's face.
　Just workin' it slow,
　Just workin' it slow,
　You don't have to hurry,
　Just keep on workin' it slow.

I know a girl called Orang-Utang,
She got more men than the County Gang,
　Just workin' it slow,　etc.

I've got a model without any speed,
But I got all the speed she needs,
　Just workin' it slow　etc.

On some records they were joined by James McCrary whose songs were in similar vein – *Shove It Up In There* used the familiar baking parallel to make a suggestive association. He played guitar, but the guitarist on *Working It Slow* was a white musician, possibly Perry Bechtel, "The man with a Thousand Fingers". Louisa Quillian remembered that she had a lot of their records but "my mama made me get rid of them . . . she said they were too suggestive and a girl had no business listening to that kind of mess."[23] On the shows, such songs, including traditional sexual songs, were popular. When Speckled Red, who worked on the Red Rose Minstrel Show, first recorded *The Dirty Dozen*, he "had to clean it up for the record". Another singer who worked on the shows was Ben Covington, whose habit of soliciting from time to time by pretending to be blind, earned him the name of "Bogus Ben" among his associates. He was almost certainly the Ben Curry who recorded a less well-known version than Speckled Red's, accompanying himself with a clattering banjo-mandoline and, between verses, on harmonica:

> Papa killed a turkey, he thought it was a geese,
> Sister took a long time, to get a little grease;
> Brother tried to show her, she was so fast
> Dug all the fat from his yas, yas, yas.
> > Now he's a diggin' mistreater,
> > Robber and a cheater,
> > Slipped her in the dozen,
> > Father and her cousin,
> > Mama done the – Lawdy, lawd.
>
> Bill and Arther shootin' dice the other night,
> Arthur win the money and he started a fight;
> Bill tried to hit him, but he was too fast,
> Took his knife and juked him on his yas, yas, yas.
> > Now he's a jukin' mistreater,   etc.
>
> Charles the deacon come to our town,
> Preached to everybody who had a little brown.
> Old woman got out, little too fast,
> Caught the rheumatism on her yas, yas, yas.
> > Now she's a catchin' mistreater,   etc.

As the last line of each verse was open to various interpretations the humor of the song and its implications resided largely in the mind of the listeners.[24] The imagery was old and persistent, even when more modern allusions were introduced, as in the refrain to Charley Jordan's *Keep It Clean*. Jordan, who was born about 1890 in Mabelville, Arkansas, served in the First World War and subsequently hoboed and worked the shows, before a bullet wound in the leg, following an argument over his manufacture of illegal liquor, confined his movements to St. Louis.

> If you want to hear that elephant grunt,
> You can take him down to the river and then wash his trunk – now –
> > Got him over, give 'im a Co-Cola,
> > Lemon soda, saucer of ice cream,
> > Take soap and water, for to keep it clean.

If you keeps it dirty and I keeps it clean,
We don't know what keepin' it dirty means, now
   You go over, get a bottle of Co-Cola, etc.

The terriblest sight that I ever seen,
Was the cook cookin' business and his hands wasn't clean, now
   You go over, get a bottle of Co-Cola, etc.

You got a head like an owl, mouth like a goat,
Every time you see me, lookin' for some soap,
   Now you go over, get a bottle of Co-Cola,[25] etc.

"We don't know what keepin' it dirty means" sang Jordan, and the statement, embracing both himself and the listeners to the record, emphasized both his identification with the group and its familiarity with such songs. There were many which were widely known to songsters and blues singers, for their bawdy vigor. They included *Dirty Mother Fuyer*, "first cousin to the Dozens", *Sweet Patuni, Shave 'Em Dry, Stavin' Chain, The Ma Grinder, Just a Spoonful* or *Shake It and Break It.* All songs which were in general currency and, in several instances recorded, even if "cleaned up a little bit", they have been discussed at length in *Screening The Blues.*[26]

Fantasizing and escape through dreams of affluence or sex may have been one way in which the effects of social change were conveyed. But they were also expressed through a certain realism, which contrasted fading hopes with hard realities. Gus Cannon, who was chopping cotton at the age of twelve in 1895 near Hushpukena, Mississippi, had worked through the period at a variety of jobs, playing banjo at every opportunity and picking up songs from older musicians. His *Feather Bed* included one verse that referred to the expectations of blacks after the Civil War:

I 'member the time, just before the War
Colored man used to talk 'bout chips and straw,
But now, bless God, ole Master dead,
Colored man plumb fool 'bout feather bed,
Ee-wee, my dear [Nancy], Oh Lord I'm bound to go.[27]

But there was no feather-bedding for blacks during or after Reconstruction.

In the critical period of a score of years spanning the turn of the century, blacks in the South suffered from the conciliatory attitude of many of their leaders and most notably of Booker T. Washington. Invited to speak at the Atlanta Exposition of 1895, he declared a policy of conciliation and accommodation along with the principle of self-help and participation in the mechanization of the South. "Cast down your bucket where you are", he declared to both blacks and whites, "no race can prosper till it learns that there is as much dignity in tilling a field as in writing a poem. It is at the bottom of life we must begin, and not the top."[28]

When Theodore Roosevelt took office as President in succession to McKinley in September 1901, he invited Booker T. Washington to the White

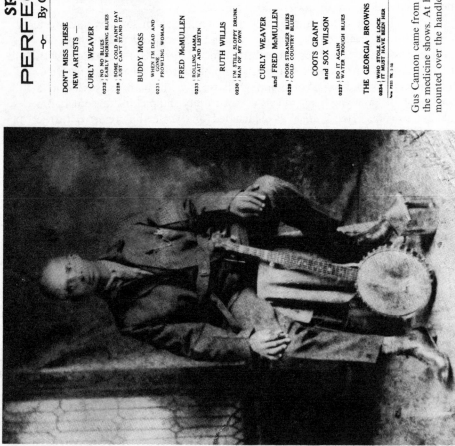

Gus Cannon came from Mississippi but used Memphis as his base while working the medicine shows. At his feet are his banjo and kerosene can "jug" with kazoo mounted over the handle. *Paul Oliver collection.*

A Perfect Race record fly-sheet in the Depression year 1933 illustrated the optimistic features of Spark Plug Smith. *Paul Oliver collection.*

House to discuss political appointments in the South. Roosevelt declared his intention to appoint fewer blacks to office but those that were appointed would be "not only of ability but of character". It was a long discussion and Washington was invited to join the family for dinner. The unprecedented invitation of a black man to dinner with the president, though largely ignored at first, soon created a furore in the South (a black gunman was hired by whites to assassinate Washington at Tuskogee University, but the attempt was thwarted when he injured himself while jumping from the train as it reached the station).[29] The event, and its political implications, left an impression even in the recordings of Gus Cannon three decades later:

> Now Booker T, he left Tuskogee
> To the White House he went one day,
> He was goin' to call on the President,
> In a quiet and a sociable way –
> He was in his car, he was feelin' fine.

> Now when Booker knocked on the President's door,
> Old Booker he began to grin;
> Now he almost changed his color,
> When Roosevelt said to "Come in,
> And we'll have some dinner, in a little while."
>   Now could you blame the colored man
>   For making them goo-goo eyes?
>   And when he sat down at the President's table
>   He begin to smile.
>   Eatin' lamb, ham, chicken roast,
>   Chicken, turkey, quail on toast.
>   Now could you blame the colored man for makin' –   etc.

> Now Booker was so delighted
> At the social was given to him;
> Well he hired him a horse and carriage
> And he taken the whole town in;
> He's drunk on wine; he was a-feelin' fine.
>   Now could you blame the colored man –[30]   etc.

According to Gus Cannon his source for the song was an older musician, Alec Lee whom he met in the Delta around 1900 and who was about thirty years of age at that time. The reference to "goo-goo eyes" indicates that it was probably composed very shortly after the event it described; John Queen, the writer of *I Got Mine*, had published *Just Because She Made Dem Goo-Goo Eyes* in 1901.[31] Both the topicality of the song and the "quail on toast" line suggest the composition of Irving Jones, but to date no source has been traced. Not surprisingly the song ridicules Washington, very effectively, by implying that his behavior with Roosevelt was, in the stereotype of the times, that of the chicken-loving coon. Any political significance was implicit rather than explicit in the satire; whether such levels would have been appreciated by the audiences that Alec Lee and, later, Gus Cannon played for, it is impossible to

say. But Booker T. Washington received an icy critique of his policies from
W. E. Burghardt Du Bois. During the years of Washington's leadership the
South had seen "the disenfranchisement of the Negro; the legal creation of a
distinct status of civil inferiority"; and "the steady withdrawal of aid from
institutions for the higher training".[32]

A great deal more had happened: segregation laws were enacted throughout
the South with established "Jim Crow" cars on the railroads and eventually,
segregated facilities of every kind, from eating houses to drinking fountains,
schools to Bibles in courts. Lynching as a means of repression and
intimidation resulted in the deaths of nearly 400 persons in the last decade of
the century, of whom by far the majority of victims were Southern blacks. The
boll weevil ravaged the cotton fields in 1905, and the economic depression that
affected the nation in the years before the First World War inevitably hit
blacks worst. Wages dropped below subsistence level and untold thousands
lost their jobs. Poorly educated, disenfranchised, subjected to segregation,
intimidated by police and state, subject to the pressures brought about by
economic and natural forces beyond their control, blacks must have felt that
they were being victimized on all sides.[33] Geeshie Wiley and Elvie Thomas,
unusual in that they were two women guitarists, possessed a strong rhythmic
sense and rural accents. They recorded a version of *Pick Poor Robin Clean* in
eloquent symbolism:

> I pick poor robin clean, pick poor robin clean,
> I picked his head, picked his feet,
> I would've picked his body, but it wasn't fit to eat.
> But I picked poor robin clean, picked poor robin clean,
> Then I'll be satisfied having a family.
> > Oh didn't that jaybird laugh, when I picked poor robin clean,
> > Picked poor robin, clean, picked poor robin clean,
> > Oh didn't that jaybird laugh, when I picked poor robin clean,
> > Then I'll be satisfied having a family.
>
> Get off my money, and don't get funny,
> For I'm a nigger, don't cut no figure.
> Well it's for my Sadie, she is my baby,
> And I'm a hustlin' coon, that's just what I am,
> > You better pick poor robin clean,[34]   etc.

Though Wiley and Thomas are recalled in both Mississippi and Texas their
origins are uncertain; "Geechie" means an inhabitant of the Georgia Sea
Islands. The song was earlier recorded by the Virginia songster Luke Jordan,
and was also popular as far west as Kansas City where it was heard by the
black writer Ralph Ellison: "Poor robin was picked again and again and his
pluckers were ever unnamed and mysterious. Yet the tune was inevitably
productive of laughter – even when we ourselves were its object. For each of us
recognized that his fate was somehow our own. Our defeats and failures – even
our final defeat by death – were loaded upon his back and given ironic

significance and thus made more bearable."[35] Though its origins are unknown, its wide diffusion and "nigger" and "coon" references suggest that this was yet another song dating from early in the century, when the "jaybird laughed" at the subjugation of blacks.

Those that picked the bones of black labor were largely political and out of reach; or they were employers and plantation owners on whom workers and their families were forced to depend, even as the wages dipped or the screws of the sharecropping system tightened on them. More evident were the debt collectors, the pawnbrokers and the recovery men for the stores that sold goods on credit.[36] Sang Lil McClintock:

> What insurance has the poor man got, with the furniture man?
> If he's got no dough, he's got no show,
> Right back there the wagon gonna stand.
> He'll take everything, that you possess,
> From a bed-tick to a frying pan,
> If there ever was a devil born without horns
> It must have been a furniture man.
>> So take your time, Mister Brown, take-a your time,
>> All o' this furniture am mine.
>> Well-a this pi-anner and everything –
>> Mister Cooper had it written down in-a ma name,
>> So take your time, Mister Brown, take-a your time –
>
> Now the furniture man come to my house,
> I told him that my wife was sick.
> He looked all around, rummaged through the house
> He even down-turned up the bed-tick.
> He went in the kitchen, he looked on the stove,
> He grabbed a frying pan –
> If there ever was a devil, born without horns
> It must've been a furniture man.
>> So take your time, Mister Brown, take-a your time,   etc.[37]

The song appears to have had some currency; a related stanza occurs in a song by Luke Jordan which combined both traditional and ragtime era verses to express the attitude of a "hustler" who lives on his woman's earnings and what she can purloin, and, having only a passive response to the recovery of his furniture, has recourse to his "good cocaine".

> Now go on gal, don't you take me for no fool,
> I'm not gonna quit you, pretty mama, while the weather's cool,
> Around your back door, says honey, I'm gonna creep,
> As long as you make those two-and-a-half a week.
>
> Now I got a girl she works in the white folk's yard,
> She brings me meal and I can swear she brings some lard,
> She brings me meat, she brings me lard,
> She brings me everything, I swear that she can steal . . .
>> I call my Cora "Hey, Hey"
>> She come on sniffin' with her nose all sore,

The doctor [says he] won't sell it no more.
Says "Run doctor, Ring the bell", the woman in the alley –
I sniffed a while upon my good cocaine.

Now the furniture man he come to my house, it was last Sunday morn,
He asked me was my wife at home, I told him she had long gone,
He backed his wagon up to my door, took everything I had,
He carried it back to the furniture store and I swear I did feel sad.

What in the world has anyone got
To deal with the furniture man?
If you got no dough certain for sho'
He certainly won't back your plan.
He will take everything from an ugly plant,
From a skillet to a frying pan,
If there ever was a devil born without any horns,
It must have been the furniture man.
  I called my Cora, "Hey, Hey"
She come on sniffin' with her nose all sore.
The doctor [say he] won't sell it no more,
Says "Coke's for horses, not for women and men"
The doctor say it'll kill you but he didn't say when –
I sniffed a while upon my good cocaine.[38]

One of the cornerstones of Booker T. Washington's policy for black advancement was the acquisition of wealth through agriculture: blacks should remain in the South to gain both property and recognition through their efforts. By 1910 there had been a net gain of some 30,000 farms owned over the figure a decade before, but even so only a quarter of those operated by blacks were owned by them; the remaining black farmers worked the land for others as tenants, or sharecroppers. Home ownership by blacks in the South at this time was also disproportionate: of nearly two million black homes only a sixth were owned free of "encumbrances". Outside of the South blacks occupied half a million homes, but, again, only one in five was owned, wholly or in part, by them. These were low figures bearing in mind the vast numbers of two-room cabins and small frame buildings which constituted a high proportion of the occupancies.[39] Many black males were not interested in such ownership, and valued their mobility more. Housing plays a minimal part in black song; Will Bennett, recorded in Knoxville, declared that all he wanted was "a new pair of shoes" and that, in a popular phrase, "any-old-where I hangs my hat is home sweet home to me".

I don't need no real estate and neither no bonds and loans
All I want is a place to stay I can call my home.
  I say Good-bye Hard Luck, Hello Joy, here I comfort Thee,
  For I didn't bring nothing to this old world
  And I can't carry nothing away.
Some people wants a lot of real estate and some wants bonds and loans
Then when they die, they leave it behind for someone to enjoy.

> Then when you're dead, lyin' in your grave
> They'll pass by you and smile –
> And say, yes indeed, don't you see,
> It's gonna come in there in [time] [40]

Bennett's song is open to more than one interpretation: it may be seen as a moral tract, condemning acquisition of land for its own sake; it can be viewed as accommodation to relative poverty, and acceptance of his condition, like Charles S. Johnson's interviewee: "Ain't make nothin', don't speck nothin' til' I die." [41] Or it may be regarded as the song of a rambler, a hustler, who is unburdened by property and merely seeks a base for a while. Probably it is a combination of some or all of these, but in any event it is moralist in tone.

Such admonitions in secular song were extremely unusual, but Spark Plug Smith, who was one of the last to record before the Depression virtually terminated the first phase of Race discs, did have some homilies for the married men who purchased the favors of the *Vampire Woman*: she was

> Causing all these married men to go astray.
> You can see them standing each and every day
> Waiting for some vamp to come their way.
> She'll ask for five, he'll give her ten,
> Says "If that ain't enough mama, call around again."
> Now he'll go stone crazy and he'll go stone wild,
> Go home and mistreat his wife and his child.
> Now married men that's not right –
> Go home and treat you own wife right:
> > Cause if you dress your wife
> > Like you do the women in the street,
> > Believe me you'll have a vampire too;
> > Running round here messin' with
> > Ev'ry single woman you meet –
> > That will never do . . . [42]

If moralizing was rare in other than religious songs, so too were expressions of remorse. *Rounders Lament* by Winston Holmes opened with an uncharacteristic declaration: "What a fool I've been to have left such a wonderful woman. Ah, it tears my very soul to think of it. Why, her love was like a mother's love. She loved me, she fed me, she clothed me. She took care of me when I was sick. Why she even gave me money. And to think I was crazy enough to leave her. The old saying has proven true, and now I'm reaping the whirlwind." By the time he is declaring "what a low, contemptible rounder I have been", any suspicions that he might have meant what he said are dispelled; the record continues with a song containing rather surreal words:

> See that song bird flying in the air?
> Mister Pilot, take me back down there,
> To my Dixie Mama
> Because she knows I'm here . . .

and concludes with bird calls and a dance tune to Charlie Turner's slide playing on his twelve-string guitar.[43]

The fragility of personal relationships and the structure of the black family was the subject of a number of studies in the period and were synthesized by E. Franklin Frazier. He maintained that there was a threat to the integrity of the family created by migration to the major Southern cities and particularly to the overcrowded black sectors of the cities in the North. Desertions by black men of their families were more frequent than, in some cases double, the rate among whites. Some of Frazier's conclusions have been questioned by Herbert Gutman but his data for the period 1905–25 are scattered, with a concentration on New York City which may not be representative of other black communities. Whereas Gutman's conclusions are drawn from Bureau of Census figures, both Frazier and Charles S. Johnson (who wrote of folk values in rural Alabama), illustrated their theses with interviews and case studies in support of their examinations of values within the poorest sectors. These correspond in many respects with those expressed by the songsters.[44]

"You will brand me as a shameless woman when you read this", wrote Mrs Tom Bartlett, a genteel lady from Marlin, Texas who was nonetheless an assiduous collector of black folk songs and one of Dorothy Scarborough's best informants. "I write it without a blush, however, and say that I have read as bad or worse in classic verse and fiction." The words of the song hardly merited her shy qualifications, but her transcription corresponded closely to *Honey Won't You Allow Me One More Chance?*, recorded by Henry Thomas some years later. Also recorded by Handy Archie Lewis, it may have been widely known, though it is possible that Mrs Bartlett obtained it from Thomas himself.

> I went home last night, the moon was shinin' bright,
> Drinkin', feelin' dizzy 'bout my head.
> Well I rapped on the door, I heard my baby roar
> "Honey I'm gone to bed."
> "Get up and let me in",
> "Oh what was that you said?
> You know you haven't treated me right,
> I've paid all this rent, you haven't got a cent –
> You'll have to hunt your new home tonight."
>   "Honey allow me-a-one more chance
>   I allus will treat you right.
>   Honey won't you allow me one more chance,
>   I won't stay out all night,
>   Honey won't you allow me one more chance,
>   I'll take you to the ball in France,
>   One kind of favor I ask of you
>   Just allow me just-a one more chance."
> "Well [Dandy Ben] been lettin' me in"
> I set down beside of her bed
> Says, "Honey dear, will you have some beer?"

She shook her head and said:
"I [often] wonder, you business could be bigger,
You know you haven't treated me right.
I paid all this rent, you haven't got a cent
You'll have to hunt your new home tonight . . .
 "Honey, allow me one more chance . . ."[45] etc.

In a verse quoted by Mrs Bartlett but not sung by Thomas, "this coon begin to grin" and pulled out of his pocket a ten dollar note. "Then her eyes begin to dance" and she allows him his "chance", a neat conclusion which confirmed its likely coon song origin.

Another Texas collector, the historian Walter Prescott Webb, published a number of song fragments "obtained from a Gatesville negro named 'Rags'". They included a verse of *If You Go Fishing* which was virtually identical to Henry Thomas's *Fishing Blues*. Gatesville lies some fifty miles to the west of Marlin and it is tempting to think that "Rags" was none other than "Ragtime Texas" – Henry Thomas. His song employed the "fishing" sexual metaphor but Thomas, who probably sang often to whites, was a careful editor of his songs for the record:

Says you been fishing all the time,
I'm a-goin' fishing too.
I bet your life your lovin' wife
Catch more fish 'n you.
Any fish bite, 'n' you got good bait
Here's a little something I would like to relate.
Any fish bite, you got good bait,
I'm a-goin' fishin', yes I'm goin' fishin',
I'm a-goin' fishin' too.[46]

Though the songs were in themselves unexceptionable, they reflected the casualness in personal affairs which promoted Mrs Bartlett's words. Thus, sexual promiscuity among the transient men and an acceptance of short-term liaisons without marriage among the women, which Frazier described, do not seem incompatible with the attitudes conveyed in the songs.

"As these men and women wander about, they slough off the traditional attitudes and beliefs that provided a philosophy of life in the world of the folk", Frazier wrote. "What is important in regard to these 'tribeless' men and women is that they have become purely individuated and have developed a purely 'rational' attitude not only toward the physical environment but also toward men and women."[47] When money became tighter with the advent of the Depression, this was still more evident – as in the song of the street hustler's lean times, *Tricks Ain't Walkin' No More*. Kid Coley, recorded in Louisville, Kentucky in the summer of 1931, sang of Katy Lee, who ran a "house on Front Street by the light of the silv'ry moon":

Now the officer called around one day,
Reproached her in a nice decent way.

> He said "Katy ain't you got no dough today?"
> You could hear little Katy Lee say,
> So she yells like this, from her lips Katy Lee did hiss:
>   "Tricks ain't walkin' no more,
>   Tricks ain't walkin' no more –
>   I been up ever since the rise of the sun,
>   Thirty went by and I ain't even caught a one."
>   The landlord's singing the blues,
>   Cause the gals ain't sellin' no more booze,
>   She says "They comes around every night with that same old stuff,
>   About 'Tricks ain't walkin' no more',
>   I say, tricks ain't walkin' no more." [48]

Strong and somewhat grating, Kid Coley's delivery was that of a man who sang to audiences, but it was lacking in vaudeville timing and was performed neither as a "point" number nor as censure. Like Smith's *Vampire Woman* which had earlier been recorded by Whistler as *The Vamps of "28"*, it was not Kid Coley's own song, though his version of *Tricks Ain't Walkin' No More* was unlike any other. It had been recorded twice in blues form by Lucille Bogan the previous year, and it remained popular with blues singers like Curley Weaver and Buddy Moss during the 1930s. The angry tone that was present in Kid Coley's version was to be heard to some extent in *The Panic Is On*, sung by Hezekiah Jenkins. If Coley's song was about one sector of the community that was both "scuffling" and hit by the Depression, Jenkins's was broader in its sweep. Not for the first time the phrase "the panic is on" was a catch-phrase for economic failure and resultant Depression: earlier it had applied to the "Panic" of 1893 when Jacob S. Coxey's "Army" of unemployed marched on Washington. Newman White quoted four "Panic is on" fragments from 1915 and related these to the Panic of 1908–9, [49] but it was the Panic of 1929, which had profound effects on the whole nation, that moved Jenkins to record his song.

> What this country is coming to
> I sure would like to know,
> If they don't do somethin' bye and bye,
> The rich will live and the poor will die:
>   Dog-gone, I mean the panic is on.
>
> Can't get no work, can't draw no pay,
> Unemployment gettin' worser every day.
> Nothin' to eat, no place to sleep,
> All night long folks walkin' the street.
>   Dog-gone, I mean the panic is on.
>
> All the landlords done raised the rents,
> Folks that ain't broke is badly bent,
> Where they got dough from, goodness knows,
> But if they don't produce it, in the street they goes.
>   Dog-gone, I mean the panic is on.

Some play the numbers, some read your mind;
They all got a racket of some kind –
Some trimmin' corns off of people's feet,
They got to do somethin' to make ends meet.
    Dog-gone, I mean the panic is on.

Some women are sellin' apples, some sellin' pies,
Some sellin' gin and rye,
Some sellin' socks to support they man,
In fact, some are sellin' everything they can.
    Dog-gone, I mean the panic is on.

I pawned my clothes and everything,
Pawned my jewelry, watch and my ring,
Pawned my razor and my gun,
So if luck don't change – there'll be some stealin' done,
    Dog-gone, I mean the panic is on.[50]

Frustration is communicated in a large proportion of the songs on Race records, sometimes directly expressed, sometimes conveyed through the theme of disharmony in personal relations. Much of the latter was exacerbated by poverty, want, lack of opportunity. W. E. B. Du Bois was a powerful voice in the fight for equality and political rights but even he advocated that blacks "forget our present grievances" when the United States entered the First World War: "if this is our country, then this is our war". Thousands of blacks responded to the call to arms, and the valor of the " Black Buffaloes", the 369th Regiment, became legendary. Yet the songs published by John Jacob Niles which he collected from black soldiers in various theaters of war, revealed little patriotism. None of the songs of "the natural-born singers, usually from rural districts, who, prompted by hunger, wounds, homesickness, and the reaction to so many generations of suppression", were recorded, at least, in the form in which he transcribed them.[51] Something of their indifference to the national fervor and their concern for self-preservation rather than the destruction of the enemy came across in a Coley Jones recording, *Army Mule In No Man's Land.*

Deacon Jones left his congregation about two years ago,
Gwine to help his country fight.
Says he didn't mind gwine out in No Man's Land,
He knowed that Uncle Sam was right.
They put him on that mule that pulled that cannon round,
Captain told him "right there you must ride".
He looked at the captain, said "That mules all right in its place
But let me tell you what I've got on my mind:
    When I get out in No-Man's Land
    They'll soon find out I'm no fool,
    I don't mind fightin' for my Uncle Sam –
    But in partnership with nobody's mile,
    Now suppose that mule would balk on the firin' line,
    That's where I'd leave him about a thousand miles behin'.

> When I get out in No Man's Land,
> I can't be bothered with nobody's mule – not even my pappy's."

When the captain said:

> "The healthy men must go right straight to the front"
> Because they was goin' to be just fine.
> There was me and that mule, we did dream done have a bad cold,
> Right there we had the first choice of the firin' line . . .[52]

Coley Jones's monologue – it was scarcely a song – was put in the mouth of "Deacon Jones", traditionally the butt of much black humorous song – though in this case, it was the singer's own surname. It is possible that he was using the Deacon Jones pseudonym to screen his disinclination to put himself in danger for Uncle Sam, an attitude which many of his listeners must have shared. This is suggested by a later verse in which the captain hollered "Boooy", with Coley Jones suspending the timing to emphasize the offensive form of address. But he may simply have been reflecting the common theme of the preacher's duplicity which was the point of the Mississippi Sheiks' *He Calls That Religion*, Hambone Willie Newbern's *Nobody Knows What the Good Deacon Does* or Frank Stokes's *You Shall*, which I have already discussed in "Preaching the Blues".[53] It was not the only item among Coley Jones's recordings which parodied the church: *The Elder's He's My Man* in which Sister Fullbosom "let all them secrets leak out" in the course of a service, was another.

Parodies of the black church, or of the spirituals sung in it, were an early element in minstrel entertainment, and this in turn may have reflected a popular secular theme. As the black church often aspired to white codes of behavior and respectability, and as a policy of accommodation had been preached from many a pulpit, more rebellious blacks resented its meekness, even if subconsciously. A parody of the spiritual *These Bones Goin' To Rise Again* was associated obliquely with the hardships of the Depression in *G. Burns Gonna Rise Again*, by a group comprising T. C. Johnson, "Blue Coat" Tom Nelson (whose nick-name suggests a minstrel association) and one known as Porkchop. A brief dialogue between the participants placed its reference to the present:

> "Look here Tom, what you-all doin' layin' round here in Memphis?" . . .
> "Well we just thinkin' about goin' down to the 'one-minute house' to
>   get a feed",
> "Yeah I thought you'all had the Miss Meal Cramps . . ."

Yet the song included stanzas that pre-dated the Civil War:

> Went to the River and I couldn't get across,
>   (*G. Burns gonna rise again*)
> Jumped on the alligator, thought he was a horse,
>   (*G. Burns gonna rise again*)
> Alligator settin', he was settin' on the sand,
>   (*G. Burns gonna rise again*)

He took me off to the Promis' Land.
   (*G. Burns gonna rise again,*
   I know, I know, I know   (Ha! ha! ha!)
   G. Burns gonna rise again)
My old Mistress promised me,
   (*G. Burns gonna rise again*)
When she died she gonna set me free.
   (*G. Burns gonna rise again*)
She lived so long till her head got bald,
   (*G. Burns gonna rise again*)
She grabbed a notion not dyin' at all,
   (*G. Burns gonna rise again*).[54]

Another humorous song which made an irreverent connexion between a hymn and poverty was *I Heard The Voice of a Pork Chop*, which parodied *I Heard A Voice from Heaven Say*. It was more of a jogging narrative than a song, except for the chorus, and was made in different versions by both Jim Jackson and Ben Covington. To his own rather primitive banjo and harmonica accompaniment, Bogus Ben Covington sang with bizarre imagery:

I was walking down the street today
Just as hungry as I could be;
I walked right in a swell cafe
This is what they said to me:
"Hey, want to have some chicken?"
"Oh no, I'll have some beef"
"Every time a man refuse chicken,
He has to pay for forty weeks."
   I heard the voice of a pork chop say
   "Come unto me and rest",
   You talk about liver, stew and beans
   But I know what's the best.
   That's pork chop, veal chop, ham and eggs,
   Turkey stuffed and dressed,
   I heard the voice of a pork chop say
   "Come unto me and rest."

Well I walked, and I walked, and I walked, and I walked
And I stopped to rest my feet,
I set down beside a great big tree
And I soon was asleep.
I dreamed I was sittin' in a swell cafe
Just as hungry as a bear,
My stomach sent a telegram to my throat
"There's a wreck on the road somewhere"
   I heard the voice of a pork chop,[55]   etc.

Though these songs assumed a knowledge of the traditional hymn or spiritual on the listener's part, they did not constitute a parody of the church service itself, or maintain the association with the church in the content. Winston Holmes, a Kansas City dancer, entertainer and modest music promoter was

Charlie Turner and Winston Holmes' *The Death of Holmes' Mule* was a parody; authentic religious recordings advertised with it included *Religion Is Something Within You* by Blind Joe Taggart.   *Paul Oliver collection.*

joined by a highly accomplished guitarist, Charlie Turner, on a number of recordings of evident relationship to the shows. They included a two-part parody, *The Death of Holmes' Mule* in which the "mule" – presumably an association with moonshine liquor was intended – was "buried" to the simulation of "one of them long Moody numbers":

> Hark from the tomb, the long-eared coon
> I hope my dog will catch him soon . . .

After playing the guitar with a slide in simulation of the mourners' crying and the moaning of Sankey and Moody's *Hark from the Tomb a Doleful Sound*, Turner imitates the utterances of the preacher by using the slide on the bass strings. After further business, the first side of the record concluded with a parody of an early and familiar "Dr Watts' hymn, *I Do Believe*. The original stanza by Isaac Watts asked:

> Am I a soldier of the Cross,
> A follower of the Lamb
> And shall I fear to own his cause,
> Or blush to speak His name?

Clearly there were no blushes on Holmes and Turner's cheeks when they sang in parody:

> Am I a shoulder of a horse
> A foreleg of a lamb?
> Shall I shave my moustache off
> Or go just as I am?[56]

They seem to have been more than usually skillful in their choice of verses. Reverend T. O. Fuller, pastor of the First Baptist Church of Memphis, published a history of black churches in Tennessee. He noted that a "most remarkable thing that characterized the worship of old-time Christians was the selection of suitable songs for the different services and occasions". *Am I a Soldier of the Cross?* was sung "when candidates were fellowshiped into the church", and "when administering the Lord's supper they would sing:

> Dark was the night and cold the ground
> On which the Lord was laid,
> His sweat, like drops of blood, ran down
> In agony he prayed.

Again, "at burials they sang 'Hark from the tomb a doleful sound'". As all three songs had been employed by Winston Holmes, his irreverent humor must have struck home to many Baptists; good parody requires sufficient accuracy in the portrayal. Holmes, who first recorded Reverend J. C. Burnett, was certainly familiar with preachers; so too were the Memphis songsters, whose haunts on Beale Street were virtually in the shadow of the immense Beale Street Baptist Church near Fourth, located on the site of former "brush arbor" or open air meetings. The fame of rural preachers was also known to the songsters; Reverend Fuller wrote of the "gifted and enthusiastic exhorter", the lay preacher George Willitt in Haywood County, Tennessee and the "patriarchal type" and pastor of the First Baptist church at Brownsville, Reverend Martin Winfield, whose name was given to the street where Sleepy John Estes was "schooled". Both would have been known to his father, Daniel Estes and to Hambone Willie Newbern.[57]

It was only a step to parodies of the preacher himself, and if these singers did not take it on record, others did. Preacher parodies had been a feature of the

minstrel stage, had even been published in song sheet form. They were part of
the stage act for white audiences of the celebrated black comedian Bert
Williams, and a number had been released in general catalogs for similar
purchasers. As early as 1924, The Three Deacons and Sister Lowdown, an
otherwise unidentified group, made a two-part Race record of *John Jasper's
Camp Meeting*. A rather pedestrian example, it made its points slowly and did
not attempt to create, or satirize, the fervor of the rural Camp meeting, but
used stock minstrel jokes, as when the imitation John Jasper announced:
"Now members as I have the collection in advance the exits are at your
disposal; use them as you see fit." There were echoes of other parody routines
– even a passing reference to "I heard the voice of a pork chop" and an
admonition: "never let your mouth start somethin' that your head can't
stand". But it was poor as humor and weak as parody, interesting only in its
assumption that the name of John Jasper meant something to the prospective
audience.[58]

More incisive was *Morning Prayer* by Philip "Jazz Baby" Moore, in which
the "preacher" called upon "Brother Fullbosom" to explain where he had
been, to which the pastor responded: "How in the world did the judge know
you had dice and crooked cards in your pocket when you know we don't 'llow
no brother to carry crooked cards in church?" – with the inference that
gambling otherwise was acceptable. The service concluded with a mock
prayer, delivered in a fair imitation of a Baptist preacher:

> Oh Lord, give thy servant this morning,
> The eye of the eagle and the wisdom of the owl.
> Connect my soul with the Gospel telephone to the Central in the sky,
> Illuminate my brow with the sunshine of Heaven . . .
> . . . Circumcize my imagination, and grease my lips with possum oil,
> Loosen my tongue with the sledge-hammer of Thy power
> 'lectrify my brains with the lightnin' of Thy word,
> Put perpetual motion in my arms,
> Fill me plumb full with the dynamite of Thy glory,
> And knock me all over with the kerosene oil of Thy salvation – Amen.[59]

The extravagance of language of Baptist and Sanctified preachers and their
concern with contemporary references was sharply observed in Moore's
mimicry. A few years later, when the Depression was biting hard, Brother
Fullbosom (not necessarily the character in Moore's parody) preached
A Sermon on a Silver Dollar, in which God was replaced by money.

"Dear Brothers and Sisters I take my chapter in the first chapter of St.
Louis, 'He that set down on a red hot stove shall rise again'" – incidently, the
theme of a circus roustabout's song. "I want all of you to know how nice a
Silver Dollar has been to me:

> Without you, Silver Dollar, I wouldn't have nowhere to go,
> Without you, Silver Dollar, none of my friends I wouldn't know.
> Without you, Silver Dollar, everybody would ignore me . . .

When I got you in my pocket, I get a friend 'most everywhere.
But when you gone, Silver Dollar, my friends want to give me some
      air. . . .
God Bless you Silver Dollar.
The Eagle on you says "In God we Trust",
Well I trust everybody, but please give me that Silver Dollar first . . .[60]

As a theme it was not new – the Three Deacons and Sister Lowdown had briefly hinted at it on the recording of *John Jasper's Camp Meeting* – though it was given a cutting edge by the accuracy of the mimicry of the preacher's vocal style. But it was hardly fair. The fantasizing, the cynicism, the bitter humor, the satire and the parodies were all responses to the encroaching reality of Jim Crow laws, discrimination, loss of employment and political powerlessness. In the face of these the black church in its many forms was neither ineffectual nor wholly acquiescent. Church leaders confronted the pressures that were exerted on black society by endeavoring to embrace the black poor.

Seeing the fragmentation of many black families, the willful loss of earnings in gambling and liquor, the incidence of petty crime and the pleasures which the more strict among the churches could not condone, they developed their ministry with evangelical fervor. In doing so, they employed the new medium of the Race record to create a remarkable corpus of hundreds of sermons and songs, which have been undeservedly overlooked.

5

As the Eagle Stirreth Her Nest

Baptist preachers and their congregations

To the scholar and polemicist W.E. Burghardt Du Bois, "the Preacher is the most unique personality developed by the Negro on American soil. A leader, a politician, an orator, a 'boss', an intriguer, an idealist – all these he is, and ever, too, the center of a group of men, now twenty, now a thousand in number." [1] Perhaps it was fear of the considerable power exerted by the preacher, or doubt as to his potential to influence through the media rather than through direct exposure to his words, that caused the recording companies to be slow in bringing him to the studio. Calvin P. Dixon, the first preacher to be recorded, appeared in the Columbia Race series in February 1925, but though he was labeled as the 'Black Billy Sunday' after the popular white revivalist and baseball player, Calvin Dixon did not stir the record buyers *"As An Eagle Stirreth Up Her Nest"* – his first title.

There was more in Du Bois's description of the characteristics of black religion than the preacher, though he was one part of a triumvirate: "the Preacher, the Music, and the Frenzy". Preaching was present in Dixon's records but of music there was little in his voice and of frenzy there was none. The following year a unit designed for recording in the field was sent by Columbia to the South, and in Atlanta, Georgia it made a few titles by a popular preacher, Reverend J. M. Gates. They were marketed cautiously; a mere 3,650 copies were ordered for the initial release of *Death's Black Train Is Coming*, but it proved so successful that Gates's second record, *I'm Gonna Die With the Staff in My Hand* had a first order of nearly ten times that amount. But probably the most popular of early sermons was *The Downfall of Nebuchadnezzar* by a Kansas City preacher, Reverend J. C. Burnett, which had an initial order of 66,750 and a supplementary order of 20,000. It opened with a long meter spiritual sung by Sisters Lucille Smith and Fannie Cox, who also shouted responses to Burnett's fierce preaching. He took his text from Daniel 4:14 "Hew down the tree" and spoke of the King of Babylon "whose fame went from the frozen Lapland of the North" and whose "heart was lifted up in pride my friends. *God* got angry with him; *God* brought a vision before him" which Daniel correctly interpreted. His voice became progressively more strained, the stressed words below hoarsely emphasized:

> And when Nebuchadnezzar had went out and eat grass seven long years,
> Finger*nails* growing out like birds claws,

140

Hair like eagles feathers
And his body washed with the dew of Heaven,
Lo-rd when seven *years* passed over him
He lifted up his eyes and declared: "The Heaven do Rule" (Yes sir!)
Now friends let me tell you, *God rules* in his *kingdom of men*
And he can take the kingdom from whomsoever he *will.*
And give it to the one he want to give it to.
Now you liars, *now* you backsliders, *now* you rich men –
Let me tell you that *God* is able to bring you down, my friends . . .[2]

He drew a forceful moral from his free, condensed version of the story, and in this he was representative of a long tradition. Through his growls, gasps and constricted utterances he communicated much of his message by the techniques that had often been noted in the past.

Black preachers have attracted the attention of writers for generations, and the services held in Southern churches have been the subject of numerous detailed descriptions. That many of the early black preachers were respected by whites even in the eighteenth century is evident from the accounts of the Virginia-born slave George Liele, who, before the War of Independence was a minister in Georgia. He baptized Andrew Bryan, the founder of the First African Baptist Church of Savannah, a celebrated exhorter and plantation preacher who had formed his black church in Georgia well before his death in 1812. There are reports of the "small, very black, keen-eyed" Black Harry Hoosier who possessed "great volubility of tongue" and who preached to both blacks and whites among the Methodist congregations before the end of the eighteenth century. And there are many descriptions of the sermons of John Jasper of Virginia – whose name, at least, was recalled in The Three Deacons and Sister Lowdown's parody. His celebrated sermon "De Sun Do Move an' De Earth Am Square" was delivered with such power and conviction that it swayed even those who came to laugh. John Jasper was born the year that Andrew Bryan died, and when he himself died in 1893 the black churches were well established in the United States.[3]

Though many black churches existed before the Civil War, their growth was considerable following Emancipation. Black as well as white missionaries worked in the South, urging congregations to unite in religious organizations of either Methodist or Baptist persuasion. In ten years the African Methodist Episcopal Zion Church increased its membership eightfold to 200,000 in 1870; yet within a decade the African Methodist Episcopal Church, the other principal black Methodist organization, had secured twice as many members. Among the Baptist churches, whose lack of doctrinal stipulations made them more attractive to blacks, the Reconstruction years saw marked consolidation. A number of Baptist groups combined to form the National Baptist Convention in 1893 and by the outbreak of World War I it was claiming three million members; half a century later this number had more than doubled, though the membership was now split between two major Conventions.[4]

These membership figures are impressive, but they are also deceptive. They

seem to imply united policies and consistent theology within the denominations whereas, in the majority of instances, the Conventions provided
association with a larger body which interfered little with the structure and
worship of the local churches. At the time when the Conventions were being
established the membership of each was predominately rural; only with the
massive migrations of blacks to the North that commenced shortly before
World War I, did the balance of rural to urban churches shift. Throughout the
South, black churches in localized communities were focussed on the
preacher, whose persuasive abilities and power to influence and shape
attitudes was not challenged by any other in the community. He was the one
member of the group who could command respect from the whites, and who
spoke for the blacks within his society.

"By the end of the Civil War", Eric C. Lincoln has observed, "the role of
the black preacher included the offices of educator, liberator, political leader,
and sometimes physician (or healer) as well as that of advocate and spiritual
leader." But, he argued, his "peculiar genius . . . derives from the fact that he
has never been far from the people". Most preachers came not from outside
the community but from within, their gifts and calling respected and rewarded
by the congregation. A preacher was "more than leader and pastor, he was the
projection of the people themselves, coping with adversity, symbolizing their
success, denouncing their oppressors in clever metaphor and spiritual
selection, and moving them on toward that day of Jubilee which would be
their liberation".[5] This image of the gifted, skillful and subtly militant church
leader has not been perceived by every writer on his role. While accepting that
the "preacher stood out as the acknowledged leader of the Negroes" Gunnar
Myrdal and his team considered that his "function became to transmit the
whites' wishes to the Negroes and to beg the whites for favours for his people".
So emerged "the typical accommodating Negro leader. To this degree the
Negro church perpetuated the traditions of slavery."[6] It was the preacher in
this mold that was most subject to ridicule and parody.

Many descriptions of black preachers can be found to fit either perception,
and the shades of ability and strength that lay between. E. Franklin Frazier
saw the church as an "arena of political life" as blacks were forced out of the
political life of the American community as a whole in the post-
Reconstruction years. Offering power to those who rose in its ministry, it
provided an organized social structure for the black masses in which they
could play a part. In this it offered hope and realization, but also a "refuge in a
hostile white world". For, as Myrdal observed, "The strength and the
weakness of the Negro church as a power agency for the Negro people is
related to the facts that the Negro church is a segregated church and that there
is astonishingly little cooperation between white and Negro churches."[7] It
was this separation from the white church which permitted the black churches
to assert their individuality, and the looseness of the denominational
structures which permitted the individualizing of the specific churches under
the leadership of their local ministers.

The charismatic preacher, Reverend John Jasper who founded the Sixth Mount Zion Baptist Church of Richmond.   *Valentine Museum, Richmond, Virginia.*

In such conditions the unfettered interpretations of the Biblical messages, the elaborations and improvisations of texts and stories were developed by the black preachers. Separation fostered a closer bond between preacher and congregation, and means of delivery and expression that were distinct and often awe-inspiring. If, in the view of Benjamin E. Mays and J. W. Nicholson, the hundred sermons that they analyzed were "characterized by poor logic, poor grammar and pronunciation and an excessive display of oratorical tricks" [8] the singularity of black preaching was still recognized. Theirs was an opinion that was based on preconceptions of what was grammatically, verbally and rhetorically correct according to standards that were more appropriate to a different cultural context. Others, less concerned with the argument and more with the substance, often recognized the poetic truth of many sermons, and the magnetic power of the preachers who delivered them, while acknowledging their skills at rhetoric. James Weldon Johnson wrote of a celebrated preacher in Southern Georgia early in this century, John Brown, who "possessed magnetism and an imagination so free and daring that he was able to carry through what other preachers would not attempt. He knew all the arts and tricks of oratory, the modulation of the voice to almost a whisper, the pause for effect, the rise through light, rapid-fire sentences to the terrific, thundering outburst of an electrifying climax." Brown's "heavenly march" involved the whole congregation and, wrote Johnson, "the torrent of the preacher's words, moving with the rhythm and glowing with the eloquence of primitive poetry, swept me along, and I, too, felt like joining in the shouts of 'Amen! Hallelujah!'" [9]

Another black writer, Zora Neale Hurston, was herself the daughter of a preacher in Eatonville, Florida. She recalled the revival meetings of her childhood when "sinners lined the mourner's bench . . . The pressure on the unconverted was stepped up by music and high drama. For instance, I have seen my father stop preaching suddenly and walk down to the front edge of the pulpit and breathe into a whispering song. One of his most effective ones was:

> Run! Run! Run to the City of Refuge, children!
> Run! Oh, Run! Or else you'll be consumed.

The "congregation, working like a Greek chorus behind him, would take up the song and the mood and hold it over for a while even after he had gone back into the sermon at high altitude". She described the effect of the sermon and congregation on the sinners. "The more susceptible would be swept away on the tide and 'come through' shouting, and the most reluctant would begin to waver." [10] In these, and many other descriptions of black services in Southern rural churches, the volatile chemistry of the preacher, the music and the frenzy is discernible.

Both James Weldon Johnson and Zora Neale Hurston, in *God's Trombones* and *Jonah's Gourd Vine* respectively, sought to recreate the form or the ambience of the preacher's art. But though Johnson's seven sermons conveys something of the poetry and, in his use of dialect transcription, a little of the quality of expression, neither these nor any other of the many attempts at transcriptions of sermons that have been published since the end of Reconstruction could capture the sound or the fervor of the originals.[11] In essence this is a problem of the medium, but the use of dialect transliterations frequently hindered rather than assisted in capturing vocal characteristics, while the problems of transcription from direct utterance during a sermon which is not repeated inevitably led, at least, to approximations of their form and content. It is ironic, nevertheless, that in 1928 at the very time when Marc Connelly's *The Green Pastures*, based on Roark Bradford's *Old Man Adam and His Chillun*, was being produced on Broadway, and *God's Trombones, Seven Negro Sermons in Verse* was receiving wide acclaim, the recordings of a score of preachers were available in the catalogues. They received no literary attention then, and have not since. What the recordings could provide, as no other medium could, was the opportunity to hear, and to hear again, the words spoken by the preacher and the responses of his congregation.

With the success of Reverend Burnett's *The Downfall of Nebuchadnezzar*, the record companies sought out many preachers, both in the cities and on location trips in the South. Assisted by members of their congregations, they were induced to create, or recreate, the essences of their sermons before the microphone. In 1926 half a dozen preachers were on record; as a result of intensive activity this was increased to thirty by the end of 1927, and a number of others had been recorded, though their sermons remained unissued. Eventually, in the space of approximately a dozen years, 750 sermons by some seventy preachers were released including field recordings in Memphis, Birmingham, Atlanta, Hattiesburg (Mississippi), New Orleans, Dallas and Rock Hill (South Carolina), in addition to many in Chicago and New York. Together they constitute a remarkable, yet still virtually untapped resource of black religious folklore.[12]

Experiencing a record is different from experiencing a live sermon within the church; a live sermon is an event, which is lived through by the congregation. Once over, the message and the spirit remain with the hearer; the details of the words do not. But a record is to be played, not once but many times. The condition of many recorded sermons is such as to suggest innumerable playings, though the circumstances under which they were played in the 1920s – in the home, in church meetings or in the homes of preachers – are unresearched and information probably now largely irrecoverable. Whatever the circumstances, replaying would lead to learning by the purchaser and this may have demanded some coherence in the sermon to stand the test of repeated listening.

Whether this was a consideration on the part of the preachers is conjectural, but it may well have been a factor which conditioned the recording and rerecording of particular preachers, and the issue of their sermons. The problem that faced a preacher when confronted by recording equipment was that of being able to say what he wished to say, and to make the points that were essential to the message of the sermon within three minutes. In the only detailed study of black sermons, *The Art of the American Folk Preacher*, Bruce A. Rosenberg does not give the duration of the sermons, nor have those he analyzed been issued on record. At one point he refers to "six to nine minutes" and an experimental recitation of selected sermons suggests that six or seven minutes – much shorter than the "hour-long" sermons often mentioned in the literature – was common for Reverend Rubin Lacy and the other preachers whose sermons he analyzed. The recorded preachers on Race records may not have had to condense too much or be draconian in the cuts that they made.[13]

Recorded in Memphis in 1928, the Reverend Sutton Griggs commenced his sermon *A Hero Closes a War* with the text (Micah 4: 3): "they shall beat their swords into plowshares . . ." He told the story of an incident in Chesapeake Bay one night during the First World War: "An open boat was carrying a crew composed of white and Negro men. The boat capsized, throwing the entire crew into the water. There was now a scramble for the bottom of the upturned boat and some white men gained possession." Seeing them knock any black sailor off the boat, "one Negro swam away and secured a white man struggling in the water and took him to the boat handing him to his white comrades". After rescuing two white men he brought a black sailor to the boat:

> Some of the men sought to deny asylum, but they were made to desist by other white men and the Negro was taken aboard. From that time on the swimmer could bring white or colored indiscriminately. The Race war was over . . . With us it is day, not night. We are safe ashore, not threatened with drowning. Under these circumstances, far superior to those of this Negro hero, come what will or may, let us have the vision and the courage to go forth helping the various races of mankind to tolerate one another on the bottom of the upturned boat in the troubled, tempestuous sea of life.

At this point a soprano voice led a small congregation into a sweetly performed verse of *Down By the Riverside*, to solemnly placed chords on the piano.[14]

Reverend Sutton Griggs's sermon was not lacking in conviction; on the contrary, its controlled emotion was itself arresting. But his carefully told narrative, measured phrases and pointed, even platitudinous, moral set it apart from the kind of sermon which sold in numbers to rival those of any blues singer. It was also almost alone among recorded sermons in making any specific reference to racial tension. The congregation, silent until they sang their brief spiritual, showed no response to his sermon, nor supported him in its delivery. It is possible that Reverend Griggs was Methodist, for this denomination rejected the emotional techniques of Baptist preachers. It was his sole recording, and it is likely that he was too "straight" for the record-buying black church members. But it is also possible that he had made a career in a literary field, if he was also the Sutton Griggs who wrote the novels on Race themes, *Overshadowed*, *Unfettered* and *Pointing The Way*, published between 1901 and 1908. On the evidence of this recording Reverend Sutton Griggs appears to have been committed, intellectual, literary in inclination. He managed the limitation of time with ease, and was capable of completing his sermon comfortably in the three minutes. But his preaching was not dramatic and his congregation unresponsive. An emotional delivery needed time to be developed to the pitch that black congregations admired, and the record did not allow much time to enlarge on the theme and project this degree of excitement. One way of doing so was to speak rapidly as did Reverend Jim Beal from Coldwater, Mississippi, who was heard by recording executive Jack Kapp, preaching on the streets of Chicago. In a relatively high-pitched voice he addressed his congregation with a verbal torrent, placing contrasting emphasis on particular words by drawing out the syllables. These are italicized below:

I find my text in the 37th Chapter Ezekiel and about the 37th verse and way it reads like this: "The Hand of the Lord was upon me, and I went out in the spirit."
My friends, Ezekiel went out in the spirit for Almighty God.
Ezekiel was ready to go forward for Almighty God at any time,
Ezekiel, my friends, was a prophet of Almighty God –
In way back yonder.
After a while Ezekiel looked,
And he saw a *whee-eel* movin' in a wheel,
Wheel movin' in-a middle of a wheel.
And after a while – that *wheeel* represents the spirit of Almighty God,
Someday gonna move in our hearts
That *whheeel* represents God movin' sometimes in our hearts . . .
After a while Ezekiel was willing to go forward for Almighty God
And God carried him through the valley down there
Where a great many dry bones layin' in the valley
The bones represent the Children of Is'l (Israel)
That was slain in the battlefield of freedom. . . .

His utterances nevertheless were repetitious, the narrative moving in parallel phrases, stated, and then reinforced. Certain words – "the wheel" – would be emphasized by holding on to the syllable and singing them as when Ezekiel "walked into the Valley by his lonely self . . ."

By-y his *lone* -ly self,
Nooo -body was with Ezekiel but God Almighty,
Some*ti-mes* when you are lonely, by yourself,
You ain't lonely, lone – But *Goood* is with you all the time . . ."

The Congregation responded with rumbling moans and occasional exclamations as Reverend Beal described the Valley of Dry Bones and Ezekiel's prophesying:

They commenced to walkin' out of the valley, knit together my friends,
And some of those joints was kneebones,
Some had hands my friends, layin' in the valley,

> And Ezekiel prophesied to those old dry bones,
> And after a *whiiile*, after a while, my friends,
> After a while the bones commence to walkin' 'bout in the valley,
> And God told Ezekiel, "I know Ezekiel,
> They ain't got no breath in their body,
> I want you to go out this mornin',
> I want you to call the wind from the East"
> When Ezekiel commenced to call the wind from the East –
> I *heeearrd* the *wi--ind* blowing from the Eas'
> When the *wi-ind* commenced a blowin' from the East
> *Goood* suffered breath to come upon these bones my friends . . .

As the sermon neared the climax he held on to more syllables, emphasizing:

> *Looord* gonna open our graves some of these days
> And we is gonna walk out of our *graves*,
> Just like Ezekiel did with the dry bones in the valley one day,
> *Am-men* (Hallelujah!) [15]

In spite of the rapid utterance he preferred to keep to a simple narrative, underlining his message of assurance that God's spirit is within men's hearts, that he accompanies those who are alone, and that there is a promise of a personal resurrection. The story of Ezekiel was one of the most popular of themes, as it had been since slavery. Writing of the spirituals, an ex-slave, Robert Anderson, observed that they "make an anthology of Biblical heroes and tales from Genesis where Adam and Eve are in the garden, picking up leaves, to John's calling the roll in Revelations. There are numerous gaps of course, and many repetitions. Certain figures are seen in an unusual light. Paul, for instance, is generally bound in jail with Silas, to the exclusion of the rest of his busy career. Favored heroes are Noah, chosen of God to ride down the flood, Samson, who tore the buildings down, Joshua who caused the walls of Jericho to fall", Jonah, and Job.[16] Such stories offered free range for the imagination of the preacher to interpret them, and captured their congregations by their vivid imagery.

Particularly favored among sermons were themes drawn from the Revelation of St. John the Divine, providing the subject for Reverend Gipson's *John Done Saw That Holy Number*, Reverend McGee's *A City of Pure Gold*, and Reverend Burnett's *The Great Day of His Wrath Has Come*. Unlike the previously cited preachers, Reverend Burnett was called back to the studio several times. He had settled in New York, where he was still preaching and recording in the 1950s. An extremely powerful preacher, with a deep and forceful voice, he gathered his congregation to him with the evident effort in his delivery. At the commencement of *The Great Day of His Wrath Has Come* he led Sisters Ethel Grainger and Odette Jackson in singing a concluding verse of a spiritual, lining out the words before beginning to preach:

> Oh the hour of his Judgment has come,   (2)
> He's tellin' every Nation, in the Book of Revelation,

> Well the hour of his Judgment has come.
> I find my text this evening at the 6th Chapter,
> And 17th verse of the Book of Revelation:
> The words of this text "the Great day of His Wrath is come;
> And who shall be able to stand?"
> These words were spoken by John, who was exiled from Ephesus,
> And kept on the Isle of Patmon, by the word of God,
> And er – he prayed while he was on the Isle of Patmon;
> He prayed all day Saturday, and soon Sunday morning . . . (yes sir!)

From the level statement at the beginning, his sermon became a chant, the phrases shorter, punctuated with the urging cries of "Oh yeah . . . tell it . . ." from the two sisters. He described how Jesus Christ, dressed up in the glory of his eternal majesty, commanded John,

> "Ooooh John, I want you to write
> And tell the churches John, about me whilst you're on the island."
> And John began to write my friends,
> He saw, my friends, the four beasts, and he saw the red horse and the
>   pale,
> And the white horse, my friends,
> He had opened the sixth seal
> John said he saw the heavens a-parting
> As a scroll when it's rolled together,
> Every mountain and island were moved out of their places
> And he saw the rich men running,
> Ooooh – rich men . . . ooooh, mighty men . . .
> Ooooh gamblers . . . running to the rocks on the mountains . . .

At this stage his voice becomes so hoarse and constricted as to be virtually unintelligible: the ends of syllables become barking gasps, the narrative becomes a violent address to the Sisters and the unseen congregation:

> For the great day of his wrath has come –
> And who shall be able to stand?
> I warn you – hah –
> Do you know you be able to stand – hah
> No-ow – if you have made your peace with God – huh
> Ohhh Loord with your Heavenly goodness – Amen.[17]

Like many of his contemporaries Reverend Burnett chose to keep mainly to the Biblical stories, but later in September 1927 he recorded *The Gambler's Doom* which, too, made reference to the Book of Revelation in which Jesus says "that he's comin', with his reward, and reward simply means the Pay-off. And he's gonna pay off the world; every gambler, and every drunken liar":

> I have seen that the gambler standin' with his cards in his hand
> And the fifty-two cards in the deck represent the fifty-two weeks in the
>   year,
> And the 365 spots on the cards, represent the 365 days in the year,

> And the highest cards, my friends is the Ace, represents One God high
> over all,
> And the deuce represents Jesus' law – "one of you could sic me and then
> you would find me".
> And the trey represents the three Godheads of the Trinity,
> God the Father, God the Son and Holy Ghost.
> And the four-spot represents the four gospel writers, oooh-
> Matthew, Mark, Luke and John,
> And the five-spot represents his five bleeding wounds on Mount
> Calvary . . ."

and so on until the "ten represents the ten virgins".

> And five was foolish and five was wise – aaaah Lord,
> And the Jack represents – Jesus rode a jack from Bethany to Jerusalem,
> And the King, oooh represents Jesus – it says in Revelations
> He was King of Kings and he was Lord of Lords, . . . Aah, Lord I
> heard him say . . .
> And the Four Queens: the first one represents Mary, the Mother of
> Jesus,
> And the Second represents Queen Esther because she saved a nation of
> people,
> And the Third represents the Queen of Sheba comin' because she was the
> most popular with Solomon,
> And the Fourth . . ."

But here time is running out, and with a brief, hoarse reference to pay-day he is obliged to bring the sermon to a close.[18]

Departing from the usual format of Biblical story and moral, Reverend Burnett may have based his sermon on a published model. Texts like *One Hundred Illustrated Sermons* by Evangelist Cal Ogburn had been published for many years and such books as *Master Sermon Outlines* and *Sermons in a Nutshell* were still popular among black preachers in the 1960s. His theme was an old one, known in the Spanish dominions since the eighteenth century and popular in the English folk tradition as *The Soldier's Bible*, *The Religious Card Player* and *The Gentleman Soldier's Prayer Book*. Reverend Burnett was the first to record it, though T. Texas Tyler's post-World War II hit, *The Deck of Cards*, inspired many later versions, including, Bruce Rosenberg noted, one by Reverend Rubin Lacy.[19] Whatever his source it is likely that Burnett employed the theme as a direct response to the challenge of the new issues by Reverend A. W. Nix.

A native of Birmingham, Alabama, Reverend A. W. Nix was a miner and piano player who was "called" to preach shortly before the First World War. As a Baptist minister he participated in the National Baptist Convention held in Chicago in 1921, and electrified the vast congregation with his singing of a C. A. Tindley composition *I Do, Don't You?*, incidentally inspiring Thomas A. Dorsey to compose religious songs in the process. He was brought to New York to record in May 1927 and between then and October was engaged in four recording sessions. *Black Diamond Express To Hell,* solved the problem of the short sermon by being developed in two parts over six minutes; it was a great success.[20] Reverend Nix's sermons were those of a practical man with considerable wisdom, if little formal education: he was the "Power in Jehovah's Quiver," the advertisements proclaimed. He used contemporary themes, or, as on *After The Ball Is Over* gave a modern title to an old one. In this sermon he painted a vivid picture of Herod's palace which:

> . . . was all lighted up with glittering and sparkling lights.
> The peoples were coming in from everywhere to take part in this lustrous
>   occasion
> They all are sitting down around the table.
> They are drinking strong wine and strong drink.
> They're not satisfied. The King cries out:
> "Turn on the lights!
> Pour out more wine and let the music sound.
> Call in Salome! the dancing girl."
> Salome comes in, runnin' and skippin' and whirlin' on tiptoes
> Salome's all dressed in low neck and short tight skirts,
> And now she's dancin' before the king,
> They all are spellbound.
> "Stand back!" cries the dancefloor master,
> "Make more room on the ballroom floor."
> Salome is dancin' now
> The king's eyes are placed on her fascination.

He described how, when the ball is over, the king made a promise to Salome who called for the head of John the Baptist. He drew the conclusion:

> Just as the ball is over, so many bad promises are made,
> When troubles start, jealousy arises
> Then comes fightin' and killin', just after the ball is over,
> And then comes hell, hell in your home.
> A great many people are livin' in hell today,
> That started on the ballroom floor . . .[21]

In style and delivery Reverend Nix was similar to Burnett, though his voice was consistently more deep and hoarse, with his exhortations to the congregation and the listener roared in leonine tones. Though his sermons were humorless they were more imaginative, the two-part *The White Flyer to Heaven* having surreal elements in the images he evoked. A sacred counterpart to *The Black Diamond Express To Hell, The White Flyer* was a train, on which

> God is the engineer,
> The Holy Ghost is the headlight, and Jesus is the conductor.
> It departs when Jesus cries, "All aboard for Heaven!"

The train, on which there are no liars, no gamblers, stops at Mount Calvary and proceeds on its way to the First Heaven, the Heaven of clouds:

Advertisement for Reverend A. W. Nix's popular *Black Diamond Express To Hell* in *The Chicago Defender*, July 2, 1927. The Sam Collins display also listed titles by Reverend J. W. Gates. News items and ads. were for J. M. Murphy's Georgia Minstrels, Wolcott's Rabbit Foot Company, The World's Medicine Show, The Fashion Plate Minstrels, and many other shows. *Paul Oliver collection.*

Higher and higher! Higher and higher!
We'll pass on to the Second Heaven,
The starry big Heaven, and view the flying stars and dashing meteors
And then pass on by Mars and Mercury, and Jupiter and Venus
And Saturn and Uranus, and Neptune with her four glittering moons.

On to the Rock of Ages, higher and higher, "beyond the sun, moon and stars, back behind God's Eternal Word", until

We'll go dashing through the Pearly Gates into God's Heavenly
    Kingdom
And when we get there I'm gonna sit down and chat with the Father,
And chat with the Son,
And talk about the world I just come from . . .[22]

It was a sermon remarkable for its use of dynamics, of sustained notes and declamations set against the long-meter soprano singing of one of the accompanying sisters, and the responses and shouting of the congregation. In *After the Ball Is Over*, Reverend Nix employed the dance of Salome as symbolic of contemporary wickedness: in *The White Flyer To Heaven* he made the vision real by projecting himself into the scene and carrying his congregation with him on the Heavenly train. As one preacher, Henry H. Mitchell, wrote, defending the "black climax" in sermons: "the Black preacher has shifted from objective fact to subjective testimony – from 'he said' and 'it happened' to 'I feel' and 'I believe'. While middle-class white preachers are admonished to avoid what Henry Sloan Coffin called 'ecclesiastical nudism' in the pulpit, Black preachers, in climax, lay bare their souls in symbolic and contagiously free affirmation", a process which "affirms the preacher's personhood in a positive, healing catharsis" and "in which the whole congregation participates and from which it benefits both vicariously and directly".[23]

Typically, the black sermon on record is introduced by the preacher with a statement of his chosen Biblical text and verse; a quotation, sometimes quite brief, from that text, and the "subject" or title of the sermon itself. So consistent is this pattern as to suggest that it was a formula required by the recording companies which accorded with common practice. The preacher develops his subject, often speaking in a direct address at first and moving to a singing tone as he warms to his theme. Frequently the sentences are chanted rhythmically, broken up in short phrases of six or eight beats and given accents or stresses as the sermon proceeds. Towards the latter part of the sermon the phrases are likely to be shorter, terminated with gasps or exhalations and with emphasized words uttered in falsetto or with a harsh, forced rasp. The congregations liked their preachers to give evidence of their convictions and their authority; to be, as Louis E. Lomax stated, "what we used to call a 'hard preacher'" who "preaches as if Heaven and Hell were coming together and only he, sustained by the God-given power of oratory, could keep them apart". Urged on by the murmurs, cries, shouts of approval

CAMPBELL, REV. E. D.—Sermons

Sermon	No.
Come Let Us Eat Together	35824
Daniel Prayed Three Times	20546
Faith	20810
Hell Under the Water	20810
Hem of His Garment	21535
In Hell He Lifted Up His Eyes	20767
It's Gonna Rain	21535
I Will Arise and Go To My Father	35824
Pharaoh Said "Who is the Lord?"	20767
Prayer	21283
Preach the Word	21283
Saul of Tarsus	21642
Take Me to the Water	20546
Wait Until	21642

Rev. E. D. Campbell

G

GATES, REV. J. M.—Sermons

Rev. Gates

Sermon	No.
Adam and Eve in Garden	20365
Amazing Grace	20216
Bank That Never Fails	21414
Building That Never Gives Away	21414
Do It Yourself	21523
Dry Bones in the Valley	35810
Dying Mother and Child	20216
First Born	21125
From the Pit to the Throne	V-38016
Funeral Train	20217

Sermon	No.	Sermon	No.
Hebrew Children	20421	Kidnapping	21281
He Was Born in a Manger	21030	Moses in Wilderness	20421
If You Say You Got Religion	V-38016	Samson and the Woman	21125
I Know I Got Religion	20217	Somebody's Been Stealing	21281
Jesus Rose from the Dead	35810	Sure-Enough Soldier	21523
Just As Soon	20365	You May Be Alive	21030

Reverend J. C. Burnett, Reverend A. W. Nix, Reverend E. D.
Campbell and Reverend J. M. Gates, portraits from contemporary
catalogs. *Paul Oliver collection.*

and encouragement from the congregation, he might struggle for the right words, "straining" with constricted throat or "using a musical tone or chant . . . variously referred to as 'moaning,' 'mourning,' 'whooping,' 'tuning,' 'zooning', each with a slightly different shade of meaning". Swept on by the flow of his words, the sermon would often conclude with a spiritual or hymn sung by the entire congregation, the preacher leading them into the appropriate verse.[24]

There were, however, many variants of this form among the Baptist ministers on record. Some would open with a spiritual that brought the congregation – or those of their number in the studio or location – together, before citing his text. Occasionally a preacher might intersperse verses with sermon fragments, or alternate them so that the role of the congregation was not that of a passive audience but of active participants. Part of the preacher's function was to engage the church members in the total religious experience, and this quality of involvement came over so strongly as to embrace the unknown listener to the record as well.

In the black Baptist Church the lack of prescribed structure permitted the congregations to elect their minister from a number of applicants who may preach to demonstrate their abilities. "The only requirement is that it be announced three Sundays 'hand running' from the pulpit, that on a given date there will be a special church meeting for the purpose of 'calling' a pastor", Louis Lomax explained, observing that the "calling" of the pastor engendered such excitement and competition as to require the police to "preside over the election in the interest of community peace and security".[25] Committing to memory the *Baptist Discipline* and *Roberts' Rules of Order*, the minister had also to know his Bible thoroughly and to be able to draw lessons and morals from its texts. He needed in particular to be familiar with the more colorful and symbolic stories and parables, and to apply them to the needs of his congregation as he perceived them. Stories of patience, fortitude, trials of faith and ultimate justice, narratives of suffering and eventual reward were popular themes. Both Reverend Beaumont and Reverend E. D. Campbell preached on the theme of *In Hell He Lifted Up His Eyes* which told the story of Lazarus and the Rich Man, their descent into Hell and the torments that the rich man endured – a story of great appeal to working-class blacks on the edge of the Depression. In *He Sinned Against Heaven* Reverend W. M. Mosley told the familiar story of the Prodigal Son, which offered some hope to those wit' errant members in their families; it was a popular subject, retold by Reverend C. F. Thornton, Reverend S. J. Worell and others. Stories that had significance in slavery times could still be found to have meaning, like Reverend E. D. Campbell's *Pharaoh Said "Who Is the Lord?"*, based on the story of Moses.

It was not the mere subject itself that was important but the manner of its telling and interpretation. Single verses, even single lines in the Bible, could be rich with symbolic meaning. Verse 11 in Deuteronomy 32, "As an eagle stirreth up her nest, fluttereth over her young, spreadeth abroad her wings, taketh them, beareth them on her wings", was a subject "so, loved in the Black church", wrote Professor Henry Mitchell. Himself a minister, he discussed its demand on the preacher. "Faced with the generation gap in the ghetto family [he] must emphasize the awesome wisdom of the eagle, who knows when to insist that the eaglet fly on his own." From his words "men will indeed glorify God in response, for parents will see their problems as they have never seen them in secular terms. Youth too will be grateful for having the rites of passage eased by seeing themselves in a new relation to the eagle's nest." [26]

This theme was sufficiently popular to permit a comparison between versions by different preachers. *As An Eagle Stirreth Up Her Nest* was the subject of Calvin P. Dixon's first title, and the first sermon on Race record. He wasted no words in getting to the lessons to be drawn from his theme: "All the apostles had their nests stirred . . . all the great evangelists":

> And the great religious leaders had their nests stirred
> Until they were willing to emigrate to the new quarters,
> Or to the ends of the earth,
> Or change their localities or change their religious relationships,
> Or change their traditional theology,
> Or move into new walks for prayer or walks of experience.
> We can never move into any new locality,
> Without breaking our relationship with the present locality;
> We can never go into a better climate,
> Without disrupting those in the climate we are now in . . .

He developed his theme, emphasizing the contrasts that have to be recognized and the problems overcome in making changes in life. "We can never step towards Holiness without breaking with Unholiness", he argued, explaining that "If God did not stir up our nests we would be unwilling to move out to new quarters."

> "When God allows trouble, and sorrow, and sickness,
> And poverty, and bereavement, and desolation to come to us,
> And we weep, and cry, and murmur and get sad and blue
> And look around us for something to lean upon,
> And hunt for comfortsome creatures
> And find none but sharp barbs and [get entangled] –
> God watches over us
> And we hear the sound of His wings

After urging his listeners to look away from earthly property and human comforts, he appealed directly to them: "Are you an orphan?"

> Are you poor? Is your husband dead, or your wife dead?
> Are you criticized or perplexed? Are you hated or cast down?
> Are you barefooted, hungry, homeless, a beggar in the streets?
> Or are you on your way to the Poorhouse?
> If you are in such a condition, in Good Faith

> God will spread His wings around you
> And unfurl the blue skies of his attributes upon you and around
> you . . .[27]

A complex sermon, it was delivered with firmness and conviction with the rolling syllables, rhythms and repetitions employed by many Baptist preachers which, years later, were made widely known through the sermons of Reverend Martin Luther King. But he did not exploit the vivid image of his original text, nor summon a picture in the minds of his listeners, as did Reverend Isaiah Shelton.

Misquoting the "Twenty-Second Deuteronometry at Eleventh verse", he compared "this bird is the greatest bird of all birds, and the greatest of all fowls of the world" with Christ who watched "over you while you sleep and slumber". As he developed his theme, he gradually moved into song-sermon:

> If any man hear my voice, harden not your hearts.
> He stirred up the nest
> And he stirred the whole world,
> And he stirred it through the war.
> During the War he stirred the world,
> All the soldiers in the camps –
> He stirred it through disease among the camps of the soldiers
> Till he stirred – ummmmm – every nation – under the sun – mmmmuh
> And said "My word – mmmuh – is the word of Peace – mmmmuh"[28]

In this powerful version he clearly had symbolic associations in mind, though he left them largely to his congregation to visualize. This technique was dramatically demonstrated by the popular Reverend J. M. Gates, who drew a graphic picture of "the eagle bird":

> So his home is not here,
> His home is over the oceans, on the other side
> And he's here in Glory land – like a child of God
> We're here in a little old foreign land.
> He can fly, and watch the sun,
> He's the only bird that can view the sun in the morning
> And read the message written in the sun.
> And if he sees that sign in the sun,
> Or in the moon, through the sun,
> He gets up on the wings of the morning –
> And gets up higher and higher –
> And gets above the dark clouds
> Up where the rain is not . . .

But then he recalled the image of the eagle stirring the nest, and compared it with God, "always stirrin' up the people",

> As he stirred them up in Egypt in Moses' time,
> Talking with Moses – out of the burning bush,
> "Oooooh Moses – Oooooh Moses

> I want you to go down in Egypt's land –
> Tell Pharaoh, I said 'Let my people go . . .'"
> Eagle's stirring – my Lord stirring – my Lord

and as he held the notes, half shouting, half humming, the congregation which
had been urging him on with cries of "Come oooon!", joined him in a verse of
the old spiritual, *Go Down Moses.*[29]

It is uncertain what Reverend Gates's intentions were, but the references to
the stirring of the nest, to taking flight, to Moses leading the Children of Israel
and the fragment of the spiritual are consistent associations for a demand for
freedom.

The stream of consciousness expressed in the sermon makes interesting
comparison with the transcription made by Rosenberg of Reverend Rubin
Lacy's sermon on the same theme, almost forty years later, in which he leaves
the image of the eagle stirring for "the four beasts of the apocalypse, comes
back to dreams, then reverts to Daniel's dream that he had used earlier;
Daniel's function reminds Lacy of the functions of various members of the
clergy . . . and on that note he closes. As in few other sermons can we so
clearly observe the preacher's mind traveling from idea to idea and phrase to
phrase through association." But Lacy admitted to him, "he had forgotten to
come back to the main point of the image of the eagle stirring in her nest", a
lapse which does not occur in Reverend Gates's shorter sermon.[30]

Though the possibilities of interpretation of Biblical texts were almost
limitless, many preachers began to make greater use of contemporary
references through which to convey their religious messages. Parallels were
drawn with familiar phenomena, like Reverend B. L. Wrightman, who made a
comparison between the sick in a modern hospital and the "sickness" of the
world which could be cured by Jesus, *The Soul's Physician.* After describing
the rooms in a hospital where the inmates were wasting away with
consumption or were mentally ill, not only sick but prisoners as well, he
included his hearers:

> Yes, even though some are sicker than others in this hospital,
> All needed a doctor because all was sick,
> For that matter, this whole world is a hospital,
> Ev-ery-body in it needs to be cured of sickness,
> Jesus is the Soul's Physician – yeah . . .

His sermon laid less importance on the nature of worldly sickness than on
Christ as healer, but he sustained the metaphor by comparing the soul's
physician with the general medical practitioner:

> Jesus is always in his office, too
> Day and night, never sleeps, never slumbers
> Never tired; always on the job. Yeah –
> Not only that but he can attend to all who come to him [and are sick].
> Always ready – no waiting room is needed.
> When you open your hearts . . .[31]

The generalized contemporary context of an unspecified hospital provided a vehicle for comparison with Christ's unfailing, eternal presence. But more specific phenomena could be employed to emphasize human weaknesses, as Reverend Milton sought to do in his sermon *Silk Worms and Boll Weevils*:

> Oh the silk worm is very productive to China and all Eastern Countries.
> Silk worms keeps the mills running, yes, and keep the silk-mills yarning,
> Preparing – yes, to send silk to America
> American market, that is making demands for it,

American boys wanted five-dollar shirts and girls six-dollar stockings.

> And that's very productive to the Eastern Market, doncha see?
> Comin' over here, they get a little speculative interest over here,
> But our destruction comes with the boll weevil –
> Ooh he's a very little thing, but he brings all sorrow in the home,
> He cause the great commerce of the South
> To have to leave here and the general business of the South went down,
> Just because of our greatest commercial interest aah – was the cotton.

From this he drew the parallel that:

> And so the wickedness of the world and the sins of man is like the boll
>   weevils,
> Is a eatin' cancer; sin is an eatin' cancer to the mind.
> And that eats up your lives and eat up your thoughts,
> And eats up good feelin's,
> And uh-eats up the good desires you would do,
> And like the boll weevil eats up the cotton boll – Ah,
> So Sin eats up the lives of the good man or good woman.[32]

Instead of using stories retold from the Bible to serve moral judgments on current behavior, preachers increasingly directed their sermons against the sinful ways of the times without recourse to such examples. Sermons that condemned "drinking shine", dancing, women's fashions, or gambling were frequent. "Fast living" was often directly equated with fast cars – perhaps because they were associated with the wealthier blacks. In another sermon, Reverend J. M. Milton, for example, spoke of *The Black Camel of Death* which awaited the reckless.

> The fast driver of a car – autocar –
> Sees the curves, and the signals, and fails to understand the danger,
> And he rides on, in a hurry – he's in such a hurry
> The faster he goes, the faster he wants to go,
> mmmmm Till he meets another fast-goin' car, right round the curve,
> And he goes – a head on collision,
> And the Black Camel of Death meets him in the path of
> Misunderstanding, and on to Judgment he goes . . .[33]

It was a popular theme: "Speed on. I want you speedin' people to know one thing: you'll never be able to carry your body as fast as you can carry your mind", warned Reverend Gates, quoting a newspaper report that a "Mister Lee was killed while he was speeding at a rate of 202 miles an hour with a car having 36 cylinders on Dayton Beach, Florida. Death beat him drivin' yes he did", adding that "James Hanley, a colored undertaker in Atlanta, Georgia, has just moved in a new two-storey building on 21 Beryl Street. He has plenty room for your dead body, plenty coffins waitin' for you . . . drive on, you joy-makers, drive on . . ."[34]

That a number of Baptist preachers were recorded only once, or over a brief span of years, may reflect to some extent the precarious tenure of pastors who might be ousted at the next specially convened meeting of their churches. It says much for Reverend J. M. Gates that he was in a position to be recorded for some fifteen years; as well as the fact that the sales of his records must have been on a scale to warrant his frequent recall to the studio or the field recording unit. Between April 1926 and October 1941 Reverend Gates recorded two hundred sides which were issued on some twenty labels. His recorded output was over a quarter of all the sermons released during the period and it offers a unique, but as yet untapped, opportunity to study the ideas and imagery of a black preacher in depth. Though he recorded principally in his native Atlanta, Gates was also recorded in Chicago and New York, and by field units in Memphis, New Orleans and South Carolina, which suggests that he also traveled as a preacher on occasion. Born about 1885, he commenced preaching in 1910, probably spent a period as a young pastor in Alabama, and in 1914 took up the ministry of Mount Calvary Church, Rock Dale Park, Atlanta, where he was still pastor when America entered World War II.

Reverend Gates was signed up for an exclusive contract with the talent scout Polk Brockman, for whom he cut over seventy titles between August 1926 and the end of that year.[35] Inevitably, this prolific output involved some repetition, especially of popular themes like *Baptize Me, Amazing Grace, The Dying Gambler* and *Death's Black Train is Coming*. Nevertheless, the recordings even at this period are remarkable for their variety. Reverend Gates had a clearer and somewhat higher voice than many of his contemporaries, so that while he employed a straining technique it seldom interfered with the message. Possessing a good singing voice, he led the members of his congregation present – sometimes merely two voices, sometimes possibly a dozen – in long-meter spirituals on such titles as *Sit Down Servant, and Rest a Little While, You Belong to that Funeral Train* or *I'm Trampin' to Make Heaven My Home* – recordings with very little preaching. The first seventy or so titles on which he preached he drew from Biblical texts, though there was a foretaste of his later sermons in *Yonder Comes My Lord With a Bible in His Hand*, made in 1926. "I believe my Lord is comin'", he preached,

> . . . He's comin' to judge the world; He's comin' – to separate the right from the wrong.

Reverend Gates, seated on a throne, Bible in hand. He preached on current issues and used arresting titles as in the examples listed in this Okeh advertisement for September 21, 1929. *Paul Oliver collection.*

> And I believe that people should live in the expectation –
> They should expect my Lord's Second Coming.

And he turned his attention to targets that were to become familiar:

> Many women should live – uh – expectin' Jesus,
> You should not be doin' what you wouldn't desire to be doin' when my
>   Lord come,
> You slick fingered gamblers . . . you oughta throw your cards away,
> You all-night dancin' girls oughta leave the dancin' floor.[36]

In the fall of 1927 his preaching changed. Though he still used Biblical texts and parables for many of his records, Reverend Gates turned with increasing directness to issues and the examples of the day. Wishing to preach on the subject of "God's Anger" he referred his congregation to the Book of Nahum, "where he says, in the First Chapter, and the Third verse, 'He hath his way in the whirlwind and in the storm, and the clouds are the dust of his feet . . .'" and drew his moral from the recent catastrophe:

> "Not only did he ride – through St. Louis in the Cyclone,
> But he rode – Glory to God –
> He rode through Memphis;
> And he rode, through Sodom and Gomorrah,
> And all of them mothers, brothers and sisters, they lost their lives.
> But he rode, God knows he rode,
> God not only rode through St. Louis in the Cyclone,
> But he passed through Louisiana, and Arkansas, Mississippi and
>   Tennessee,
> In the flood of water, he rode through Miami, Florida in a storm,
> And in a flame of fire he rode through Atlanta, Georgia,
> And a long time ago he rode through Chicago, Illinois
> In a flame of fire . . .

To the shouts of "Oh yes," from the congregation, he asked, "Are you ready now for him to ride, through your city, and through your land?" and led them into singing, "*Be ready, when he comes again*".[37] Though he did not discard the traditional approach to the sermon – most of his recording sessions included one or two of this type – Reverend Gates made use of current events for themes after 1927. He drew from the media, as he commented on *Hell is in God's Jail House* – "when I begin to read the newspapers and begin to think over the matter and see where mens are breakin' jail, and chain gangs, even breakin' out of the penitentiary, it makes me think of this subject: Hell is God's jailhouse; it's a place where you can't break out; it's a place where you live as long as God lives . . ."[38]

Late in February the following year he recorded three sessions in Memphis which found him in fine form on *A Sure-Enough Soldier*, gathering an "army" with the stomping feet of a "shouting" congregation which recalled John Brown's Heavenly March. On *Do It Yourself* he also developed the form of sermon which offered advice without the basic foundation of a Biblical text, on the theme that "things that you can do don't ask God to do for you". In the course of the sermon he addressed a member of his church:

> G: "Deacon Davis, you drive a coal wagon.
> And in the morning, when you get up
> And get ready to catch your mules.
> Do you ask God to catch your mules?"   D: "No."
> G: "What do you do about it?"
> D: "I catch 'em myself."
> G: "And do you ask God to hitch 'em to your wagon?"   D: "No"
> G: "What do you do about it?"   D: "I hitch 'em myself."
> G: "And when you drive down the streets humpin' coal –
> And when you get ready to take a sack of coal off,
> Do you ask God to take the coal?"   D: "No"
> G: "What do you do about it?"
> D: "I carry it myself."
> G: "And when they hand you the money,
> Do you ask God to take the money?"   D: "No"
> G: "What do you do about it?"
> D: "I take it myself . . ."[39]

Humor is an essential ingredient in the mixture that makes for successful preaching in the black church. Rapport between preacher and congregation is all-important; the preacher uses every tactic to project his message; histrionics, dramatic gesture, native wit and in-group humor. Though the Baptist church can be strict in its demands on its members, the preacher also has to recognize, condone even, some of the frailties of his flock while being dedicated to converting them. In some of his sermons of 1930, Reverend Gates employed humor which appeared to owe more to the minstrel show than the ministry. "They tell me God taken a bone out of man and made a woman; I wonder sometimes whether a man ever had a bone in his tongue or not. If a man ever had a bone in his tongue, I believe that he made woman out of that bone", he began in *The Woman and the Snake*, by no means the only chauvinistic sermon he recorded. Members of the congregation chipped in with their own comments and Gates concluded with an attack on cosmetics. "You take fifty cents and go down here to one of these chain stores, and buy a whole lot of that stuff, and make yourself up with powder, creams, and make yourself over, and look like an angel" he criticized, and added unreasonably, "got a razor in your stocking or a pistol somewhere, or dirk, ready to take somebody's life. A woman and a snake; I don't like a snake no-how." [40]

In this, as in *Clean The Corners of Your Mind* or *Meeting the Judge on Monday Morning*, the attitudes of both preacher and church members seem spurious and the exchanges crudely staged. Today they do not convince but at the time they may have been more readily accepted – bearing in mind that motion pictures of the time were convincing enough to their audiences even though they often seem naive and artificial now.

For, though the focus of the church is its ministry, much of the life of the black church is involved in other activities besides "preaching Sundays".

Total immersion Baptism "by the pool of Siloam", in Virginia at the turn of the century. A small group of whites watch from beneath the trees in the center; umbrellas shade church members on the bank. *Valentine Museum, Richmond, Virginia.*

Some of these are fundamentally secular, such as means for raising funds, running burial societies, assisting with welfare and even, in the cities, playing a significant part in housing. But the religious life also involves a calendar of events arranged by the Deacons, the Sisters and Brethren, or the Elders of the church, which include prayer meetings and meetings of the officials of the church for the transaction of current business. A number of pastors sought to reflect such aspects of the world of their churches in their recordings, perhaps to remind members of other churches of their responsibilities, and to reassure them of the value placed upon their roles.

As might be expected from his extensive output, Reverend Gates recorded a number of these occasions, delegating a substantial part of a recording to an officiating member. On *Praying for the Mourners* he declared that they had "men and women, boys and girls, on bended knees" who were seeking to know what they should do to gain Eternal Life. "I'm gonna ask Deacon Davis to come down to the altar tonight and carry their case to the throne of Grace." Deacon Davis then took over, praying for the sinners who, by tradition, sat on the "mourner's bench" on such occasions. He indicated that the struggle was not an easy one, and that there would be regressions as there had been in his own life; "You got to plow with your hands; you know you got to weep and moan." Recalling his own conversion he said, "Ever since that morning, I been a-runnin'; I been a-fallin'; I been baptized twice. Sometimes turning in the middle of the road" but eventually, "coming to Jesus". His prayer was half-sung in a husky voice while the moans and humming of the congregation rose above him.[41]

Backing this title was a *Sister's Prayer Meeting*, in which Sisters Jordan and Norman thanked God for watching over them. Both these services were convincing; the two-part *Deacon Board Meeting*, which censured the same sisters for staying out late at night, seemed less so. Leon Davis, the officiating Deacon, was a preacher in his own right and, with the assistance of Sisters Norman and Jordan, recorded in 1927 a simulated *Deacon's Prayer Service* and an *Experience Meeting*. The latter was an occasion when church members would give accounts of their conversion or personal religious experiences. Less sophisticated than Reverend Gates, the Deacon ingenuously revealed the circumstances of the recreated event.

> Sisters and brothers, I'm glad to be in your midst this mornin',
> And see as many faces as I see.
> And I have decided that we will have
> What you call a genuine-uh experience meetin'.
> What you know-uh-I'm talkin' about,
> Like, round the fireside.
> You know, an experience meetin', sure 'nough (oh, yes)
> I want you to talk like you talk
> When you went into church,
> I want you to tell the same thing;
> And I'm going' to see who is able

> To walk out on the world this mornin'
> And let the world know you is born again.

The transparent honesty of his appeal seems to have prompted Sister Jordan to a quick and excited response:

> Sisters and brothers, I have been born again
> I went up to the mourners bench about five years,
> And I got tired and I stopped.
> And my sister Mary got down one night and was prayin' for me,
> I knowed I was older than she was, and I started from then out, prayin',
> And then I was converted, Heavenly Father,
> And I didn't have a dress to wear in church and I had to borrow
>   one . . .[42]

Central to the calendar and the tenets of the Baptist church was the rite of baptism itself. Pastor of the Roger William Baptist Church in Birmingham, Alabama, Reverend J. F. Forest preached a *Sermon on Baptism* to the shrill cries and enthusiastic responses of his congregation. He quoted Isaiah 1, verse 16:

> The words of the text read like this:
> "Wash you and make you clean,
> And put away the evil of your doings
> mmm – before my eyes, and cease to do it."
> And our text teaches us that we oughta wash
> Before we can be clean.
> And we have the word 'wash' twelve times in the Bible,
> And it means immersion in water:
> Go to Jordan as Jesus did.
> And we have the word 'Baptism' four hundred and ninety-three times –
>   in God's Bible;
> And it means immersion in water.[43]

His sermon continued with statistics on the incidence of words in the Bible to support his argument as if their repetition generated a particular authority for the ritual.

Conducted before all the members of the congregation at the river (usually called Jordan for the purpose) or at a local pool, the total immersion of the candidate seeking admission to the church was required at the ceremony. "These 'baptisms' attract large crowds of onlookers", Julia Peterkin observed, "The candidates all arrive at the 'pool' dressed in long white robes, which are carefully put away after the ceremony to serve as their shrouds some day." Each candidate was led to the water and dipped three times, leaving his sins behind.[44] Several such baptisms were recorded, of which one by Reverend R. M. Massey from Itta Bena, Mississippi cut in 1928 is the most authentic. Against the slow, measured singing of the congregation he called upon each candidate to state whether he or she was willing for baptism, and prepared to abide by the regulations of his church. Then, calling upon those in favor of

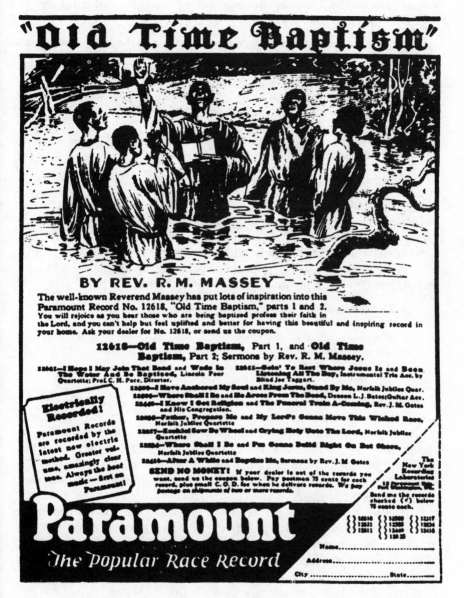

The advertisement for Reverend R. M. Massey's *Old Time Baptism* also lists titles by Blind Joe Taggart, Reverend J. M. Gates, and blues singer Blind Lemon Jefferson under the pseudonym of Deacon L. J. Bates. *Paul Oliver collection.*

"the motion" to baptize them to say "Aye" he proceeded with the ceremony. Voice hoarse and broken from shouting, he took each in turn, dipping him or her three times with the words:

> "I baptize you my sister in the name of our Faith, in the name of the Father,
> In the name of the Son, and in the name of the Holy Ghost; Amen.
> Now my dear brothers and sisters, and to those candidates
> Who have gone down to the elected place
> And have put on the whole armour of faith by receiving Baptism –
> You all follow me back to the church of God.
> And given the right hand of fellowship,
> So that they can enjoy the Golden Privilege
> Of our Lord and Savior Jesus Christ,
> And can be saved among the Lord's children
> Through Christ's sake, Amen.[45]

The importance of the baptism, not only as a sign of admittance to the Christian faith but also as a rite of passage into the community of believers within the church itself, is indicated further in another baptism on record, *Take Me To the Water*, by Reverend E. D. Campbell, made in Memphis in 1927. After a similar ritual of baptism he enjoined the congregation of new and old members with a straining declaration of faith:

> He's a ball of fire – mmmm-mmm burnin' in my soul –
> I want to see you at the church tonight;
> Meet me there at seven o'clock.
> We gonna fellowship these candidates,
> We want to shake glad hands –
> Everybody be at the church tonight – Amen.[46]

Total immersion baptism is undertaken as a result of the candidate's deliberate choice, and not, as in infant baptism through a ritual in which he or she has no conscious decision to make. As a basic tenet of faith in the Baptist church the baptism itself symbolizes the washing away of the sins of the candidate and the burying of an old way of life. From total immersion the Christian is born anew, cleansed in spirit and ready to take his part in the way of life demanded of him.

Whatever the teachings of the Bible, the lessons to be learned from contemporary failings spelled out by the preacher, the exchanges with the members of the church and the responses of the congregation, this was at the heart of Baptist belief and observance. But it was challenged, on record as well as in the church, by a new denomination of declared power and undeniable emotional appeal to working-class blacks in the 1920s.

6

Three Ways to Praise

Saints of the Sanctified churches

Barely two months after Reverend J. F. Forest gave his *Sermon On Baptism*, a sermon was recorded in Atlanta, Georgia, that made a direct challenge to conventional Baptist belief. Quoting Matthew 3, verse 11, Elder J. E. Burch, in a voice trembling with a marked vibrato, spoke of "the difference between the two baptisms:

> Some claiming that John's baptism is more essential
> Than the baptism of the Holy Ghost;
> But we find that John himself declared that he indeed
> Baptized with water unto repentance,
> But there is one coming greater than I,
> Whose shoes I am not worthy to wear.
> He will baptize you with the Holy Ghost and with fire . . .
>
> I want to say to you that the baptism of the Holy Ghost
> Is a baptism that is essential that each and every man might have,
> That he might have power to live in this world above sin,
> But the water baptism will not give you any power at all;
> – Bless his great name –
> It is just a sign before God approvin' to you, – Glory to God – Amen –
> Of the inward purity, but without the baptism of the Holy Ghost
> You have not got power to live in this world above sin." [1]

Elder Burch was not disregarding the symbolic importance of cleanliness, his sermons were, in fact, almost obsessed with the subject. "Know ye not that ye are the Temple of the Living God, and that the spirit of God dwell in you; Halleluyah! And if God Almighty is calling for a clean temple that He might dwell in He wants you to clean up your lives, He wants you to put away lying and every unclean thing", he preached in *God's Dwelling Place*. In *The Church and The Kingdom*, he envisaged "a clean church without spot or wrinkle, it's not a stone church built somewhere, but it's the body of baptized believers". More prosaically he declared on *Wash You, Make You Clean*, that the subject for his sermon "is *wash*; all of you wash-ladies understand the necessary need of every garment being perfectly clean. And *you* is a garment for God".[2]

All Elder Burch's nine titles were recorded at a single session, and his apparent fixation on cleanliness may have been the result of a preoccupation with the theme on the occasion of recording a sermon on baptism. The session can be considered virtually as a single, extended recording of a service, broken at three minute intervals and then reshuffled when issued on record, out of matrix sequence. Thus the preaching of *Life and Death* (He is not the God of death; He is the God of life) excites the congregation, one woman breaking into the singing of *He is the Lily of the Valley*, which is instantly taken up by other members. The same woman slows the hymn to half the tempo for a chorus before breaking into fast time, while the congregation shouts and sings, and breaks into syncopated hand-clapping. Snare and bass drums beat, tambourine and guitar can be heard in the exuberant din. With barely a disjunction in the flow of the meeting the next track opens with strong, if simple, gospel song, *I Sing So God Can Use Me* – "right down here in this land". After a few choruses, as vivid as a field recording, Reverend Burch calls to the congregation: "Let's all stand in prayer, Glory be to God, Hallelujah! Amen." As *The Prayer Service* proceeds the shouts of "Glory" and moans from the congregation of "Ooooh Lord, Bless thy name!" act as a counterpoint to the gravelly monotone of the preacher. At the conclusion of the prayer and the end of this recording he opens another, *Love Is My Wonderful Song*, providing an energetic lead to the singing of the repetitive but joyous gospel melody. Drums, tambourine, stamping and "shouting" accompany the singing until it concludes with cries of "Praise the Lord!" and "Glory!" The service concludes with a female lead to a slower, unaccompanied hymn, with the responses of the congregation joining in on

> My heart keeps – (*singing, singing, singing, all the time,*)
> I'm sanctified – (*I'm sanctified*)
> With the Holy Ghost – (*with the Holy Ghost*)
> My heart – (*keeps singing, singing, all the time . . .*)

Reverend Burch's sermon was indubitably sincere in its content and convictions, yet not only was it a direct confrontation with the fundamental observance of the Baptist church, it was also a service which was based on certain premises that were directly opposed to Baptist practice. Most immediately evident of these was the use of music on the record, but the emphasis in the sermon on Sanctification and being imbued with the Spirit of the Holy Ghost was contrary to Baptist belief. In fact, Reverend Burch's was a Sanctified church, a representative of the smaller but increasingly significant churches that arose with the Holiness movement of the late nineteenth century.

Holiness sects arose in the rural South during the nineteenth century as a fundamentalist reversion to the doctrine of perfection through a conversion experience, as taught by John Wesley. Their origins were Methodist but, as the way to entire sanctification through a "Second Blessing" became increasingly the objective of the rural churches, Holiness groups consolidated. Their religion was emotional, their services highly charged, their preachers firebrands. Placing himself in the hands of God, the supplicant sought possession by the Holy Spirit. He alone knew when he had received the Spirit in his heart, when he was "sanctified", but he testified to his fellow members of the Holiness congregation of his conversion experience. The marks of the Holiness sects, Joseph Washington has summarized, "are set in affirmation of an emotional experience of conversion, the experience of a second blessing, or sanctification, the need to strive for perfection, the guidance of the Holy Spirit in all events of life through visions or dreams, the fundamentalism of their faith, the practice of revival techniques, the expectation of the Second Coming of Christ, and a strict Puritan morality." [4]

It was a morality whose strictures differed from those of the fundamentalist Baptist churches in a number of ways, including "holy dancing" (though dancing without "crossing the feet" was permissible in many Baptist churches), musical accompaniment and "speaking in tongues". Glossalia, or uttering unintelligible syllables believed to be the language of the Holy Ghost, was evidence to many that the speaker was possessed by the Holy Spirit, and among the Pentecostal churches which grew out of the Holiness movement, this was an essential part of the process of sanctification. Persons possessed of the Spirit in church might "fall out" in a trance and might even require to be forcibly held down or controlled until they came round. The heat, excitement and infectious enthusiasm of the churches, heightened by the fierce exhortations of the preachers, the "shouting" of holy dancers and the accompaniment of musical instruments provoked profound emotional experiences which were evidence that they were joining the congregation of Saints.

In the two score of years following the Reconstruction era, when the white back-lash isolated blacks and the Jim Crow laws were enacted, various Holiness and Sanctified, Pentecostal and related sectarian churches were established. They appealed particularly to the poorer blacks and their independence of the well-structured Methodist churches and the long-established Baptist ones encouraged loyalty among their small congregations. Between 1895 and 1905 a large number of "Churches of God" were formed in the South. [5]

Statistical evidence of the relative membership of the Sanctified black churches once they had been established is difficult to ascertain. The United States Census for Religious Bodies recorded a figure of 5,660,618 members of black churches. Of these the Baptist churches claimed 68.8 per cent and the Methodist churches 24.65 per cent of the total. After the Roman Catholic, Protestant Episcopal, Congregational, Lutheran, Presbyterian and Christian Science churches had been deducted, all "other" churches represented 2.83 per cent, with a membership for all Holiness churches of a mere 7,379. As Gunnar Myrdal remarked, "Obviously there is something seriously wrong with these figures." [6] Yet a study of 570 churches and the families occupying 1,542 Negro homes in the rural South made by Ralph A. Felton and published in 1950, based on research in seventeen counties in eight states, produced correspondingly low figures: 76.9 per cent of church members were Baptist; the A.M.E. churches represented 6.1 per cent, the Holiness churches 1.2 per cent, and Church of God in Christ only 0.4 per cent. To some extent this may reflect the shift of the Holiness churches from the South to the Northern cities, where they flourished; nevertheless the proportion is surprisingly low bearing in mind how influential they were on the style of worship in churches of the lower class among all denominations. [7]

Of the Sanctified churches, the Church of God in Christ was, in terms of music and song, the most influential. It was also to become the largest of the non-Baptist independent churches, claiming 425,000 members by 1970. It was founded by a black minister from Memphis, Tennessee, Charles H. Mason, in 1895, who had trained as a minister in the Missionary Baptist Church, but who now established his new Church of God in Christ in a disused gymnasium in Lexington, Mississippi on the eastern edge of the Yazoo-Mississippi Delta. In this musically rich area the appeal of a church which encouraged playing instruments in church was considerable, and the new denomination spread rapidly. Within a year "chapters", as the first subsidiary churches were termed, opened in Oklahoma, Arkansas, Kansas and Tennessee. Not only did the new church encourage music, it also placed great importance on being "called" to preach, rather than on ordination. This meant that even the totally uneducated in a mainly illiterate and poor Southern community could become pastors of the church, if they had been "sanctified" and had the call to preach to others that they too, might be possessed by the Holy Spirit.

With his connexions in Memphis still strong, Reverend C. H. Mason held a Convention, or "big congregation", every Thanksgiving which lasted three weeks and which attracted more than 5000 people annually in the 1920s. Though the Church of God in Christ was to have great appeal in the North, its roots were in the South at a time when fewer than one black church in ten was in the North. Memphis remained a focus for the Southern Church of God in Christ and a number of Sanctified sermons were recorded there. [8] On the same field trip which resulted in the recording of the straight and unaccompanied sermon by Reverend Sutton Griggs, a Victor field unit recorded *The Solemn Warning* by Reverend E. S. (Shy) Moore. In a hoarse and forceful voice he quoted Joel 2, verse 1:

> "Blow you the trumpet on Zion and sound alarm in the Holy Mountain,
> Let all the inhabitants of the earth tremble" – Amen –
> "For the day of the Lord cometh, for it is nigh on hand" – yea
> Subject is – "the solemn warning".
> I'm gonna sermon my brothers and sisters.
> It is the duty of the minister of the gospel
> To stand on the walls of Zion,
> And warn men of their coming danger.
> And it is the duty of the minister of the gospel
> Is to warn mother's daughters that's on the Hell-bound train,
> It is the duty of the Minister of the Gospel
> To preach until all the gamblers are purified in the fire,
> Until they cry "I can hold out no longer" – eeeh[9]

Empathizing with his theme as the sermon progressed, his voice becoming more urgent, he told of "Norah" building the Ark and warning the people of their coming danger, while the congregation responded with moans sustained on a high note. Reverend Moore's preaching, which led to the congregation joining him in singing, to the sound of a piano, guitar and jug, *Get Right With God* was poetic rather than consistent as argument; the text forgotten and replaced by another in which the verses were distorted to fit his overall theme. But the sermon was compelling and the message expressively conveyed.

Reverend Moore had just one record issued; Elder Bryant, who also recorded in Memphis a year later, had several. They underscored the essentially emotional appeal of the rural Sanctified service. Quoting from John 11, verse 28, on his first title, *The Master Came and Called To Me*, he told the story of the Resurrection in loosely hoarse, fragmented sentences:

> Now Jesus loved Mary and Marthy, And Jesus was the son of Mary
> And Marthy, she was the sister of Mary – Thank God, Amen!
> Now Mary lived down – thank God! Hallelujah! Amen, thank God.
> Thank God for Jesus and the Holy Ghost Aaaameen –
> Glory, we thank God, Amen, Jesus, Amen, Thank God,
> Amen he loved Mary and he loved Marthy,
> And he loved Lazarus, Thank God for Jesus, Amen, Thank God
> And Mary and Marthy bein' at home, Thank God, Amen,
> And Brother Lazarus got sick,
> And Mary began to rush Marthy, Thank God, where Jesus was . . .[10]

While the sermon, which drew no moral from its confused narrative, was virtually inchoate, the repetition of the words of praise excited the congregation to loud and exultant cries, responses and released energy as he led them into song. Perhaps because his sermons were so unclear Okeh chose to record him singing only, with his Sanctified singers, three weeks later. Relatively simple tunes which underscored their largely secular character, they included *Come Over Here*, a version of a popular gospel song also known as *Ananias*, and the song which became a popular jazz vehicle, *Lord, Lord, He Sure Is Good To Me*. These recordings were notable for the vigorous accompaniment by unknown players of harmonica, guitar and mandolin, to the booming bass of a jug and crisp washboard playing close to the microphone. The exuberant, relaxed, ragged and remarkably spontaneous singing captures the spirit of the Holiness service, of the kind that Elder Bryant was leading in his churches in Hollandale and Moorehead in the Mississippi Delta. A last session later in the year probably involved the members of one of the other of his congregations, accompanied by jug and a guitar, perhaps played by himself, and with a cornet lead in New Orleans jazz style. The tune of *He Shut the Lion's Mouth* was based on a children's song, *The Farmer Takes a Wife*, while *Everybody Was There* was to the tune of the jazz-hokum song *Keep a-Knockin' and You Cain't Come In*.[11]

The annual Conventions at Memphis of the Church of God in Christ made this city a natural focus, and much of the finest Sanctified singing was recorded there. Memphis after World War I was ravaged by influenza, which was probably further transmitted by the Conventions where Arizona Dranes appears to have contracted it. *Memphis Flu* was the subject of one of the recordings by Elder Curry, who was directly influenced by Reverend Mason, and joined the denomination in 1915. Made in Jackson, Mississippi, where he had his church, he had the support of a strong, ragtime-styled piano accompaniment by Elder Charles Beck. Elder Curry's own guitar playing provided the rhythmic impetus for the song, which was led by Jo-Ann Williams to the tune of *With His Stripes We Are Healed*:

> Nineteen hundred and twenty-nine
> Men and women, you were dyin',   (Glory!)
> If they couldn't see a doctor,
> For their flu-u,
> People dyin' everywhere,
> Death was creepin' through the air.
> [What they got, for their sins,] you were saved
> God's almighty hand,
> He has journeyed this old land,
> North and South, East and West yes, he's been
> Yes he gives to rich and poor,
> And [when he calls] you can't go,
> If you don't turn away from your shame.[12]   (Praise the Lord!)

Joyous but untutored, spontaneous and uninhibited, the Saints of the Sanctified Church provoked the derision of many Methodists and Baptists. In his sermon *Prove All Things*, Elder Curry confirmed their faith and their belief in music and dance as vehicles for praise.

"Thank God for Jesus, he come to us to prove all things – and we are his people – saints. People try to condemn us everywhere; they all say we are wrong. We dance you know, in service, we can talk in service. We praise God on stringed inst'ments in service, now it's got to be proven tonight." He drew his proof from "'the 149th Division of the Psalms' and Mark, chapter 16, verse 16, 'Make a joyful noise unto the Lord' – now some people they don't like that noise –" but his vociferous congregation responded with the gospel song "when the Bible's right, somebody's wrong".[13]

Familiar in the South still, is the small, clap-boarded frame church, with wooden towers flanking its simple facade, standing white-painted in or near the rural community. As late as 1936 the Bureau of Census figures on religious bodies, though not wholly reliable, indicated that nine out of ten black churches were in the South. Of these latter, three-quarters were located in the cities, and of them the Pentecostal, Holiness and Sanctified churches still represented a minority.[14] They, however, changed the balance of urban worship and accounted, in particular, for a large proportion of the store-front churches. While there were large and imposing black churches in the cities, generally dating from early in the century and of Methodist or Baptist persuasion, the majority of the churches were installed in converted premises. Sometimes a private room acted as a meeting-house, but, frequently, disused garages, vacant shops, gaming and pool halls, even abandoned theaters were bought and converted into churches. By far the largest number of these were in empty commercial premises, which gave them the general name of "store-fronts". They were numerous in Southern towns and in Chicago they constituted well over half of all black churches both Baptist and Sanctified.

Membership of the churches was fairly evenly distributed in the class categories used at the time, with Baptist churches in the lower-class "worst areas" constituting half and Holiness churches a quarter of those in Chicago, where a third of the 100,000 lower-class black adults were affiliated to the churches. The size of congregations varied greatly; in scores of store-front churches the number of worshippers would be less than fifty. [15]

Why did the store-fronts not combine to gain in strength and purchasing power? Why, for that matter, were they so numerous? It would seem that the lack of an overall organization encouraged the smaller Baptist churches to exist independently, while the Holiness churches responded to the "call" of their preacher founders with small, but significant differences in worship or welfare. Though Chicago's Olivet Baptist Church had clubs for boys and girls,

Southern country churches played an important part in society providing welfare, and often, as in this school at Gee's Bend, Alabama, education. Photograph by Russell Lee. *Library of Congress collection.*

athletics, a literary society and an unemployed relief program as early as 1908, and others like the Quinn Chapel had similar facilities, the established Northern churches were not able to cope with the vast influx of migrants during and after World War I. Olivet in fact, did establish a migrants' center in 1917 but in general the migrants were seen as a threat to the older residents, and the churches chose to disregard them. This lack of interest was matched by that of the Southern churches that did not facilitate entry into Northern churches by the members once they had left the South. For the members themselves on the other hand, the stresses of urban living, the sinful environment that they perceived around them in the cities, and their need for comfort, friendship and solace in alien surroundings, made the membership of a new and small church very appealing. [16]

Perhaps it was because the recording studios were often in makeshift premises themselves (Gennett's was in a converted garage by a railroad track, for example) that the preachers and their congregations seemed to adapt so readily to them when they recorded. Most of those on record worshiped in buildings not greatly dissimilar and were used to improvising in their churches. What mattered was the manner of worship, not the setting. For the members of the Sanctified churches, that manner took its guidance from the last words of the Book of Psalms: "Praise him with the sound of the trumpet; praise him with the psaltery and harp; praise him with the timbrel and dance; praise him with stringed instruments and organs . . . let everything that hath breath praise the Lord." [17] It was a direction which they followed to the letter. "We find our text in the Book of Ephesians, in the Fifth Chapter and the nineteenth verse and it reads as follows: 'Speaking to yourselves in psalms, and hymns, and spiritual songs, singing and making melody in your heart to the Lord'", declared Reverend F. W. McGee on *Three Ways*. "I don't want any to get confused when I speak of three ways when I'm tellin' you all the time there is but one way . . ." but, he added, "I think of the songs that we often sing when we gather together. I am reminded of our privilege to sing spiritual songs." Such songs, and the up-tempo gospel songs featured prominently on his recordings. [18]

Though he was born in Tennessee in 1890, Ford Washington McGee was raised in farming communities in Texas. His parents sent him to college in Oklahoma where he trained as a teacher, leaving this profession for evangelism and practicing faith healing, until he joined the Church of God in Christ. The blind pianist Arizona Dranes helped him build up his congregation in Oklahoma City, while he successfully evangelized in Iowa and elsewhere. In 1925 he established a church under canvas at 33rd Street on Chicago's South Side, and three years later laid the foundation stone of his "Temple" on Vincennes. His first recording under his own name and with his Church of God in Christ Jubilee Singers was a single title for Okeh, *Lion of the Tribe of Judah*, a shouting spiritual with stomping piano by Arizona Dranes. It ensured him over forty titles with Victor, of which a number were sung

The First Baptist Church, Beale Avenue (Beale Street), Memphis, Tennessee.
Photograph by Paul Oliver.

The Church of the Living God Jesus Christ and the Trinity Church of God in
Christ sharing the same store-front premises at 403 Beale Street, Memphis. A
Cola advertisement brings a little revenue. Photograph by Paul Oliver.

throughout, to the accompaniment of Reverend D. C. Williams on piano, and
a variety of horn, string and rhythm instruments. They included the spiritual
You Got To Walk That Lonesome Valley, a dirge-like *Rock of Ages* which
included the recitation of a Psalm, and his last recording, the extraordinary,
dynamic *Fifty Miles of Elbow Room*. McGee's own singing gave some quality
to an otherwise rather dire gospel song, *Jesus the Lord Is a Savior*, and Sister
Elsa Henry Reid took the lead on an oddly dated hymn, *Sin Is To Blame For It
All*, sung in waltz time. [19]

As a preacher Reverend McGee was more deliberate than many; instead of
the rapid enunciation and rasping voice of a Sanctified preacher like Reverend
Gipson, who also led his congregation into song on *John Done Saw That Holy
Number* or *God Will Protect His Own*, McGee made greater use of verbal
dynamics and, generally, preached slowly. His voice was musical, though rich,
and he employed it to great effect on such a sermon as *Jonah In the Belly of the
Whale*. After introducing his subject he explained that Jonah found a ship
going to Tarshish,

> And while he was on that ship, the Lord
> Mooved – upon the waa-a-ters –
> And the sea got tempestuous, and the seamen got afraid
> And they cast lots to see what was the matter,
> So they found out that Brother Jonah was the trouble.

After finding Jonah in the bottom of the ship they brought him up,

> And Brother Jonah told them the fault was in him,
> And he told them to cast him overboard – eeee – heeh
> And the Lord had prepared a great fish,
> And they cast him over
> And the fish swallowed him up – Glory – Amen.

And immediately McGee led his congregation into song:

> Oh they stopped that ship in the middle of the sea,
> Jonah cried out "the fault is in me!
>   Throw me overboard, (*I've got the fault in me*)
>   Throw me overboard." (*I've got the fault in me*)
> If you want to get to Heaven like anybody else,
> Treat your neighbours like you treat yourself –
>   Overboard . . .[20] (*I've got the fault in me*)

The message of the sermon was somewhat truncated by McGee's relatively
slow delivery and desire to lead into song. Many of his sermons were on
traditional themes, as he said himself on *A Dog Shall Not Move His Tongue*:
"We have heard so much about Daniel in the lion's den, and the three Hebrew
boys in the fiery furnace, and the fish tail, or the whale tale (or whatever you
may want to call it) and you have also heard about the wall-fall at Jericho and
how Joshuay fit the battle of Jericho. All these wonders of the Bible. And yet I
have another wonder in the language of our text." His eventual message was

however, "don't be a dog, if you do you might get your tongue so you cain't move it", and the concluding verse of the brief gospel song warned that:

> The Devil is in the churches,
> Drinking, preachin' and lyin',
> Trying to teach the people
> It's no harm to brew moonshine.[21]

On this, as on *The Crooked Made Straight*, he used the text to drive home a contemporary message by making a pun on the theme, telling the story from Luke 13, "on the Sabbath day Jesus was in a synagogue beholding a poor crooked woman; eighteen long years she had been bent over and could not in anywise straighten herself up. Jesus called her to him and laid his hands on her, and immediately she became straight and glorified God. All straight folks will glorify the Lord. When I find someone who won't glorify God I know he is a crook . . .", and after testifying to his own conversion he continued, "I would say to all you crooks, 'Let Jesus lay his hands on you and he'll straighten you out. You lyin' crooks; you moonshine crooks; you midnight ramblers – God can straighten you out.'"[22]

There was a marked tendency towards secularized content in McGee's recordings from the fall of 1929 with the recording of *Shine-Drinking* and *Women's Clothes*, two familiar targets from the pulpit. "I tell you I thought the women had done bad enough when they hacked their dresses off, up to and above their knees, but after raising them from the bottom they lowered them from the top till it's a disgrace to some of the men, and of course it's a pleasure to others – ain't that right brothers?" he asked. "And not only that, they've discontinued them altogether along the other line. It's hard for men to stay sane, with women dressin' as they do. All kinds of fine underwear – And I tell you, they don't buy it to hide it either; some of these dresses so short they can't hide."[23]

It appears that he was reflecting a general trend. Early in 1930 a record was issued which dramatically challenged the attitudes of most preachers in that it acknowledged the existence of secular music in terms that were not disapproving. *Is There Harm In Singing The Blues?* backed by a *Sermon on "Tight Like That"* was made by a Chicago Baptist preacher, Reverend Emmett Dickinson. He had a curious style of preaching, in short bursts, declaiming high, and dropping his voice at the ends of phrases rather as if he were selling in the streets. It was the content of his sermons rather than his manner of delivery that was arresting. On his first title he spoke of how the Israelites "crossed the Red Sea on dry land and landed on the other side. I'm told they sang a new song. I don't know what they sang, but I call that *The Israelite Blues.*" And again, "when Paul and Silas was in the Philistine jail, Paul said 'Silas, do you feel like prayin'?' Silas said 'I never felt so much like prayin' before in all my life'. I call that *The Jailhouse Blues.*"[24]

In some respects his message was conventional even if the context was not.

"He that is not with me is against me, says the Lord – you must be pig or pup",
he argued in another sermon, castigating the "two-face-ed" man. But it was
his testimony to the blues singer Blind Lemon Jefferson when that singer died
in a snowstorm which must have seemed shocking to Baptists.

> Let us pause for a moment
> And look at the life of our beloved Blind Lemon Jefferson who was born
>   blind.
> It is in many respects like that of our Lord, Jesus Christ.
> Like Him, unto the age of thirty he was unknown,
> And also like Him in a short space of a little over three years
> His name and his works were known in every home.[25]

At much the same time as Dickinson first recorded, Reverend McGee made
Holes In Your Pockets. In this title, which drew from the unusual source of the
Book of Haggai (1:6), he clearly showed an awareness of blues. After singing
the text in a beautifully executed slow chant he addressed his sermon to
wayward husbands in a very direct manner, chiding them with:

> Spend what you have left
> When you leave Miss Susan James' house, on moonshine,
> Talkin' about "Michigan water tastes like cherry wine –
> If water was whisky I'd stay drunk all the time –"
> – No wonder you got holes in your pockets![26]

The shift in emphasis in sermon content was not made by Reverend D. C.
Rice, whose thirty issued titles made him the fourth most recorded preacher of
the period. Jack Kapp, the Vocalion repertoire director, had attempted to
induce Reverend Rice to record sermons on themes similar to those made by
Dickinson, but he refused, considering the style of preaching unsuited to
himself. Rice was born around 1888 in Barbour County, Alabama and
attended his father's Baptist church there. During the war he moved to
Chicago and was "saved" when he joined Bishop Hill's Church of the Living
God, Pentecostal on the East Side.[27] After Hill's death in 1920 he took over a
small Sanctified church which expanded through the appeal of his leadership,
and the attraction of the eight- or nine-piece bands which he often used. In
1928 having heard recordings by Reverend McGee and Reverend Gates he
sought a recording session with Kapp, who told him to "preach like you are
preaching to the whole world out there". Though scared, "I just let myself go
and preached like the Lord told me to save all the sinners in the world".[28] His
sermon, based on Luke 24:2, "and they found the stone rolled away from the
sepulchre", was a forceful but very condensed summary of the Resurrection.
It was more for his singing and music than for his preaching that Rice's
records are notable. The Sanctified congregation which he brought to record
I'm In the Battlefield For My Lord was accompanied by trumpet (possibly
Punch Miller from New Orleans), Louis Hooper on piano and his father on
string bass, a trombonist named Hunter, tambourine and drums. The

congregation, well used to lusty singing and with a strong female lead, created an exciting, infectious sound on a recording that was entirely song and accompaniment.[29]

A large proportion of Reverend Rice's recordings were songs without sermons, including *Who Do You Call That Wonderful Counsellor, Were You There When They Crucified My Lord?* and a version of the same song, *Sin Is To Blame*, that Reverend McGee had recorded earlier. When he preached, his sermons were brief, as on *I Will Arise and Go To My Father*, stating a text and describing it before leading his congregation into song. He was a firm, clear preacher with a full voice, but he did not match this with an interpretative skill; his sermons pointed no morals, drew no conclusions. Clearly he was aware of other preachers, particularly Reverend McGee, and recorded a version of *Shall Not a Dog Move His Tongue*, quoting Exodus 11:7. "When I use the word 'dog', I do not mean the natural dog, but you that have a dog-like spirit. You bark at the pastors, you snap at the deacons . . .", he explained. But he did not develop the theme, undoubtedly derived from McGee, nor did he refer to it again in his short sermon, which continued the story of Moses before Pharaoh.[30]

Most original of Reverend D. C. Rice's recordings was the fifth to be issued, though it was made at his second session, *Come and See*. Drawing from the sixth chapter of Revelations it described the opening of the Seven Seals, with the title as a sung refrain:

Pure Gospel Mission, store-front church, West Lake Street, Chicago. The signs on the windows echo the themes of recorded sermons. Photograph by Paul Oliver.

> And I saw when the Lamb had opened one of the seals
> And I heard the first beast saying –
>   Come and see; come and see; come and see.
>
> And there went forth a white horse and he that sat upon him
> Had a bow and a crown.
> And he went forth conquering and to conquer,
> And I heard the second beast saying –
>   Come and see, come and see, come and see . . .

So he continued through the opening of the seals in turn, with the congregation singing the refrain in slow harmony, the trombone playing majestically with them. Reverend Rice, with his talent for condensing the scriptures continued:

> I looked under the altar and I saw the souls
> That were slain for the word of God,
> And for the testament of Jesus,
> And they looked out and cried with a loud voice,
> 'How Long, Oh Lord, dost thou judge and avenge our blood?'
> White robes were given to each of them,
> That they might rest for a season.
> And I heard the sixth beast saying –
>   Come and see, come and see, come and see . . .[31]

Alternating sermon with song throughout a recording was rare, although one Sanctified preacher, Deacon Gallamore, had recorded a fine example, *Just Had To Tell It*, in Atlanta the previous year. One aspect of the Sanctified worship demanded it however, and this was the Testifying Meeting, which was as important in Holiness and Pentecostal churches as total immersion baptism was to the Baptists. As Baptism by the Holy Ghost was a personal experience, testifying to being saved to the other members of the congregation was important. It was shared with rejoicing and singing and usually took the form of the repetition of a "Testify"gospel song, interspersed with calls on members to testify to their conversion. Reverend Mose Doolittle's *Testimonial Meeting*, Reverend P. M. Williams's *Testifying Meeting* and Reverend McGee's *Testifyin' Meetin'* were all of this type. Reverend Rice's *Testify – For My Lord is Coming Back Again* was, however, devoted entirely to the gospel song, sang in responsorial form by Rice and his congregation to the boom of a brass bass, piano and clattering tambourine:

> Testify (*Testify!*) Don't be sad (*don't be sad!*)
> Tell the truth (*tell the truth!*) Don't you add (*don't you add*)
> For no adder – can't go in,
> For my Lord is coming back again.
>
> Sanctified father, sanctified son,
> Sanctified people, all are one
> If you're not sanctified – can't go in –
> For my Lord is Coming Back again.[32]

We Got the Same Kinda Power Over Here, made at Reverend Rice's last session in mid-1930, was to the customary form of a Testifying meeting. Reverend Rice's wife was called upon to testify:

> I'm saved and I'm sanctified, baptized with the Holy Ghost and power,
> Speaking with tongues as the spirit give up.
> I thank God today for that same power,
> That raised up Jesus from the dead,
> Has also [quit] my mortal body
> And today I'm running up the King's Highway – pray for me!

"Hallelujah!" responded Rice, "It's a wonderful power in the blood." [33]

Unlike the other denominations and the dominant Baptist and Methodist churches, the Pentecostal, Sanctified and Holiness churches permitted women to preach. Though relatively few women preachers were recorded, Evangelist R. H. Harris of the Pentecostal Mission, "The Lady Preacher", was one who made a couple of sides in Chicago in March 1927 with her Pentecostal Sisters. Her voice was measured and a little nervous, but if she was no "fire and brimstone preacher" she spoke of it, taking as her subject *Jesus Is Coming Soon*. The sinful, she warned, were risking "sudden destruction" and "they shall not escape":

> Like the destruction of Sodom and Gomorrah,
> The same day that Lot went out of Sodom
> It rained fire and brimstone from heaven
> And destroyed them all . . .
> Be not like the foolish virgins did
> Which took their lamps with no oil;
> Went to buy oil;
> The Bridegroom came
> And they that were ready went with him,
> And the door was shut: Too late – too late.
> The foolish things said "Lord, Ooh Lord open to us."
> He answered and said "Verily, verily I say unto you I know you not.
> Take heed, watch and pray
> For you know not when the time comes,
> Neither the hour or the day.
> When the Son of Man comes, therefore be ready . . ."

The Pentecostal Sisters moaning in the background joined in with a warning of sinful behavior:

> Be ready when he comes again –   (3)
> He's comin' again so soon.
>
> Don't let him catch you on the ballroom floor   (3)
> He's comin' again so soon. [34]

A stronger preacher was Reverend Leora Ross of the Church of the Living God, who recorded in Chicago the same year with a number of women

NEW ORTHOPHONIC VICTOR RECORDS

		Number	Size	List prc.
Love of God / City of Pure Gold	Sermons with Singing — Rev. F. W. McGee / *Rev. F. W. McGee* }	V— 38005	10	.75
Loving Talking Blues / *Dark Night Blues* — with Guitar	Blind Willie McTell / *Blind Willie McTell* }	V— 38032	10	.75
Lucky "3-6-9" / *Jungle Crawl*	"Tiny" Parham and His Musicians / *"Tiny" Parham and His Musicians* }	V— 38082	10	.75

M

MACK, IDA MAY—with Piano

	Number
Elm Street Blues	V—38030
Good-Bye, Rider	V—38030
Mr. Forty-Nine Blues	V—38532
Wrong Doin' Daddy	V—38532

		Number	Size	List prc.
Madison Street Rag — Cannon's Jug Stompers / *Cannon's Jug Stompers* / *Minglewood Blues*		21267	10	.75
Maggie Campbell Blues — with Guitar — Tommy Johnson / *Tommy Johnson* / *Bye Bye Blues*		21409	10	.75
Make a Country Bird Fly Wild—Fox Trot — Allen's N. Y. Orch. / *Pleasing Paul—Fox Trot* — Henry Allen and His New York Orchestra		V— 38107	10	.75
Mamma, 'Tain't Long Fo' Day — with Guitar — Blind Willie McTell / *Blind Willie McTell* / *Writing Paper Blues*		21474	10	.75
March of the Hoodlums—Fox Trot — Ellington's Cotton Club Orch. / *Ellington's Cotton Club Orchestra* / *Breakfast Dance—Fox Trot*		38115	10	.75
Market Street Stomp—Stomp — The Missourians / *The Missourians* / *Missouri Moan—Fox Trot*		38067	10	.75
Mary Bowed So Low — Taskiana Four / *Taskiana Four* / *Hallelujah Side*		V— 38520	10	.75
Mary Lee—Fox Trot — Bennie Moten's Kansas City Orchestra / *Bennie Moten's Kansas City Orch.* / *Sweetheart of Yesterday—Fox Trot*		V— 38114	10	.75

McGEE, REV. F. W.—Sermons

	Number
Babylon Is Falling Down	21090
City of Pure Gold	V—38005
Crooked Made Straight	21090
Crucifixion of Jesus	V—38028
Dead Cat on the Line	38579
Death May Be Your...	21656
Fifty Miles of Elbow...	38328
Half Ain't Never Been Told	21492
He Is a Saviour for Me	20858
He's Got the World	V—38513
Holes in Your Pockets	V—38583
Holy City	21205
I Looked Down the Line	38561
I've Seen the Devil	V—38583
Jesus in the Fire	V—38574
Jesus, the Light	V—38513
Jesus the Lord...	38561
Jonah in the Whale	V—38574
Love of God	v—38005

Ida May Mack

Rev. F. W. McGee

23

singers. Her voice was nearer to that of the male preachers, though higher pitched, and she closed her phrases with similar exclamations. While *God's Mercy To Colonel Lindbergh* was an example of the Sanctified preacher's use of current events on which to build a sermon, it illustrated the partial confusion in the minds of many who obtained news at second-hand. In her sermon the hero–aviator's 3,735 mile non-stop flight from Roosevelt Field to Le Bourget in May, was combined with his goodwill mission to Mexico City also that year. She took her text from Job 5, verse 19, "He shall deliver thee in six troubles; yea in seven there shall no evil touch thee; subject: God's mercy to Lindbergh," who she said, was "a great man", a "wonderful man":

> . . . He made up in his mind, "I'm goin' way 'cross the oceans
> With the Spirit with me." Rich men, high men
> And men of many nations, have tried and failed – uh
> So he named his plane the "Spirit of St. Louis".
> Colonel Lindbergh realized God's eyes upon the ways of men
> And sees all things goin' – uh
> So he started out across the mighty waters – uh
> With all nation's prayers. He realized that God said
> "Let not your heart be troubled, and neither let it be afraid!"

The women broke into song, "He will answer prayer", and then Sister Leora Ross returned to her theme, singing her sermon with her voice rising at the end of the lines.

> . . . and the rain begin to fall
> And Lindbergh was way beyond the sun –
> And he remembered what God said:
> "I'll be a rock in a weary land.
> A shelter in a time of storm" and,
> Oh, Lord, he guided him to the City of Mexico . . .[35]

If some women preachers, like Sister Erna Mae Cunningham, did not seem to have the command or the power of their male counterparts to move a congregation, others were spirited in their attack. Missionary Josephine Miles's preaching on *God's Warning To the Church* with her interpolated exclamations of "Thank God", "Bless God, Amen", strongly recalled the style of Elder Richard Bryant. Of the women preachers she was the most uninhibited, telling the story of Moses and the Israelites in a condensed but dramatic sermon. *You Have Lost Jesus* and the two-part *Holiness*, on which Sister Elizabeth Cooper playing a ragtime-influenced piano that would not have shamed Arizona Dranes, testified to her part in the Sanctified church.

> You have *lost* Him to go to the pool-hall,
> You have *lost* Him to go to the dance-hall,
> You have *lost* Him to go to the drinking stand,

she shouted accusingly to her congregation, but then declared,

> The day I come in contact with him,
> Not knowing the power of God I lost Jesus too . . .

then, recognizing her condition he,

> Sanctified me, Baptized me, with the Holy Ghost and his fire![36]

Missionary Josephine Miles has been identified as the vaudeville singer Josie Miles, who is known to have joined the church in Kansas City in the 1920s. There is however, little to suggest in her effete vocals that Josie Miles was capable of the Sanctified preaching of her near namesake.

A woman preacher with a voice of uncompromising forcefulness, who employed the harsh utterances and growls of the male preachers, was Reverend Sister Mary Nelson, whose sermon *Isaiah*, "calling you to make preparations" was a singularly powerful example of the idiom. It concluded with entreaties of grating rawness, calling on all, "regardless to your sins, come on – if you be a murderer, come on . . ." while the congregation members present urged her on. Her preaching had its own momentum and, while she did not have any musical accompaniment, the rough quality of her voice, evident on all her four recordings, was made more marked by the contrast of the near-children's voices of the chorus.[37]

Perhaps because they were more of a challenge to traditional roles for women in the South, there were no female preachers recorded on location. Rural communities were often too small to support more than one or two churches, whereas the density of populations in the expanding black belts of the urban North could support a great many. Women played a significant part in the founding of the churches that sprang up to meet the needs of the immigrants from the South. Mattie L. Thornton formed her Holy Nazarene Tabernacle Apostolic Church in Chicago as early as 1908, and held camp meetings annually. During World War I an uneducated but warm and humane woman from a Georgia plantation, Elder Lucy Smith, opened a meeting-room in her Chicago home, and within a decade she had begun work on the building of her All Nations Pentecostal Church, which was famous in Chicago throughout the thirties. Built on a "fashionable boulevard" it was much resented by wealthier blacks who objected to its lower-class approach to religion. Still another successful church leader was Bishop Ida Robinson, also raised in Georgia, who founded her Mt. Sinai Holy Church in Philadelphia in 1924, and who had branches of her church in a number of cities.[38]

But though some committed women were able to take advantage of the less restrictive attitudes to their role in religion found in the Sanctified and related churches, the majority of the pastors and Elders were male, even if the membership was generally two-thirds female.

Often the strong voice of an elder or sister could be detected rising out of the group sound of the congregation. Women increasingly demonstrated their superiority as solo performers in the Sanctified churches, though the record companies were slow to recognize them. There were one or two exceptions: perhaps the first was Madam Hurd Fairfax who as early as April 1923 recorded for Paramount. But the carefully trained voice of Madam Fairfax, and the stiff piano accompaniments by Porter Grainger to Odette Jackson and Ethel Grainger, (The Baptist Duet) or to "The Two Baptist Sisters", Albertina and Victoria, appear to have had limited appeal.

These Baptist duets were recorded in New York, but only a few days before Albertina and Victoria recorded, a field unit in Atlanta had cut a couple of spirituals sung by Sister Sallie Sanders with the Shady Grove Quartet, and two songs by Matthew and Mark, "the Nugrape Twins". Both at this brief session and on a return trip in March the next year the Twins were accompanied by a pianist who played an introduction, paused for the singers to commence, and carefully followed them through their songs:

> Pray Children, if you want to go to Heaven,   (3)
> If you want to go to Heaven when you die.
> > Your brother is gone, he prayed mighty hard
> > Down on his knees at the midnight hour,
> > The Lord heard a prayer, and he saved his soul –
> > Don't you wanna see your brother when you die?[39]

Their nasal voices and use of minors gave them a rural sound but it is evident that they had been "arranged", with a *sotto voce* final chorus such as might have been heard in a concert version of a spiritual. Concert approaches to solo spiritual singing and accompaniment, never common on Race records, became rarer still in the next year or so. The harmonium or small church organ provided a sonorous background to one or two recordings, like those of Homer Quincy Smith, a singer with a remarkable range but a smooth and studied approach to *Go Down Moses* or *Pilgrim's Journey*. It was played too, by another deliberate and rather dreary performer, Blind Connie Rosemond, and only seemed to come to life with the addition of a tambourine as on Luther Magby's *Blessed Are the Poor In Spirit*:

> If you cannot – pray like Daniel
> If you cannot – moan like John,
> Brother, you will know the love of Jesus
> 'Cause when I say He died for us all.
> > Blessed are the poor in spirit
> > Children of the heavenly king,
> > We shall all wear a crown in glory
> > Oh when on earth – our work is done.
>
> If you cannot give a million,
> You can give – a widow's mite
> For the least you do – on earth for Jesus
> It is precious in his sight.[40]

His barely comprehensible voice with its strong rural accents was as artless as Homer Smith's was self-consciously modulated, and, textually, his song had a

The blind singer and pianist Arizona Dranes, from an Oken advertisement.
It's All Right Now, recorded by Arizona Dranes, was written by Benjamin
Franklin Butts in 1909, and was still in print in *Gospel Hymns* of 1925.
Paul Oliver collection.

more contemporary flavor than had the well-loved but old spirituals. It was
his use of the organ as a percussive instrument against which the tambourine
rhythms were placed, which distinguished his musical approach from that of
other accompanists.

Already the way to a more dynamic instrumental support to the modern
church soloist had been indicated by a young blind girl from Fort Worth,
Texas–Arizona Juanita Dranes. Born in Dallas about 1905 she was playing
piano in the Fort Worth church of Reverend Samuel Crouch when she was
heard by the pianist and talent scout, Richard M. Jones. He invited her to
Chicago to record for Okeh, and with Sara Martin, joined her on *My Soul Is a*

Witness For The Lord. Their role was distinctly subordinate, limited to simple responses, while the young pianist cried out the words in a high, firm voice. Her piano playing was quite unlike that of the pianists on previous sacred recordings: a mixture of ragtime and barrelhouse techniques, with considerable rhythmic drive.[41] The blues guitarist Aaron "T-Bone" Walker, who was some five years her junior, recalled that "the blues comes a lot from the church, too. The first time I ever heard a boogie-woogie piano was the first time I went to church. That was the Holy Ghost Church in Dallas, Texas."[42] It could have been Arizona Dranes that he heard. Her pronounced use of ostinato reflected the Texas barrelhouse tradition and imparted a remarkable thrust to her recordings on her vocals and in the instrumental choruses between verses:

> My heart is now rejoicing,
> Filled with the Savior's love,
> I'm in the narrow pathway
> That leads to life above.
> I'll follow him forever
> To die on Calvary's brow,
> For he's my loving Savior
> It's all right now –
> > It's all right now   (2)   ⎫
> > For Jesus is my Savior ⎬ (2)
> > It's all right now.[43]   ⎭

It was not only in her performance that Arizona Dranes had drive; she had been instrumental in getting Reverend McGee to record, and before he made his first titles under his own name he brought his Jubilee singers to Chicago to make four titles with her in November 1926. She immediately took the lead; McGee's voice was scarcely to be distinguished from the rest of the group, who enthusiastically cried the responses to her shouted lines on *Bye and Bye We're Going To See the King* (a version of *Wouldn't Mind Dying, If Dying Was All*) and *Lamb's Blood Has Washed Me Clean*:

> Lord Lord (*Lord Lord*) Ain't gonna live in this world no longer ⎫ (2)
> Lord Lord (*Lord Lord*) Lamb's blood has washed me clean   ⎭
> > Jesus knew what I needed most,
> > (*Lamb's blood has washed me clean*)
> > Filled my soul with the Holy Ghost,
> > (*Lamb's blood has washed me clean*)
> > Lord Lord,   etc.
>
> > Reason I praise His Holy name –
> > (*Lamb's blood has washed me clean*)
> > He brought me out of sin and shame.
> > (*Lamb's blood has washed me clean*)
> > Lord Lord,   etc.
>
> > Jesus done just what he said,
> > (*Lamb's blood has washed me clean*)

> Healed the sick and raised the dead –
> (*Lamb's blood has washed me clean*)
> Lord Lord (*Lord Lord*) Ain't gonna live in this world no longer . . .[44]

She performed in many churches in Texas, Tennessee and Chicago and was heard by hundreds of thousands through the popularity of her records. Though she was apparently subject to recurrent bouts of influenza, she recorded again in 1928, accompanied by a group of exuberant women singers and a mandolin player who had clearly learned from Coley Jones, if he wasn't Jones himself. Arizona liked shouting short lines that invited quick, loud responses which she made more ragged by slightly anticipating them:

> Just look (*just look*!) just look (*just look*!)
> If you want to read it [the Bible], just look,
>   You can shout and dance about the power
>   It don't amount a single thing;
>   You got to be pure and holy
>   If you want to hear the joybells ring –
> Bells ring! (*Bells ring*!), Bells ring! (*Bells ring*!)
> If you want to hear the joybells ring;
> Bells ring! (*Bells ring*!) Bells ring! (*Bells ring*!)
> If you wanna hear the joybells ring![45]

It was her last recording session though she continued to perform in Holiness churches during the 1930s. Undoubtedly her influence was considerable, and it is directly traceable in the work of other singers of her times. Perhaps the closest was Jessie Mae Hill, who recorded for Okeh between Arizona's Chicago visits. Her voice was even harder, if somewhat less shrill, and she was given to falling notes on many of her syllables. Accompanied by her Sisters of Congregation, though as instrumentalists rather than as singers, she made half a dozen titles, two of them, *The Crucifixion of Christ* and *God Rode In the Windstorm* being sacred ballads. The former had a strong piano which recalled that of Arizona Dranes, who recorded a non-vocal version of it. Two guitars filled out the rhythm as she sang:

> What do you think of dyin'? Hallelu!
> I think it's mighty fine! Hallelu![46]

Earth Is No Resting Place had a hopeful vision of the after-life which was expressed in its swinging waltz time.

> Earth is no resting place, earth is not home
> As I wander alone,
> Singing sweet songs as I journey along
> I'm trying to reach my home.
> Sadly I wonder if ever there will be
> Home Sweet Home for me,
> Where there'll be Glory, yes, Glory for me
> Through eternity.

Oh, that'll be Glory for me,
Lord, through eternity.
Staying our path, I'm home at last
Singing in joy for Thee.
All we know, sweet rest there will be –
Over on that shore,
Where we can stay, and we never will say,
"Goodbye", any more.[47]

Jessie May Hill was a member of the Church of God in Christ which was certainly more tolerant of worldly dance; nevertheless this lilting song is surprising.

Arizona Dranes had set a model for lusty, committed singing, and her own clear, sharp vocals were reflected in those of another Texas woman who briefly recorded in Dallas and Kansas City, Laura Henton. Her voice was remarkable for its clarity and its range, which was especially evident on *Heavenly Sunshine*. The song was composed by Lucie Eddie Campbell, from Duck Hill, Mississippi, who taught for forty years at the Booker T. Washington High School in Memphis. For much of that time she was an active member of the National Baptist Convention and she held many positions in the world of Baptist music and education.[48] Nevertheless her songs were popular with the Sanctified church and Laura Henton's version was typical of its bright, optimistic approach:

When my heart is – bowed in sorrow
And it seems all – help is gone,
Jesus whispers "Do not falter
I will leave you not alone",
There's a power in Mount Zion
How it is I cannot see,
Till I hear a voice from Heaven
"Come to Zion and follow me".
    There is sunshine – in the shadows,
    There is sunshine in the rain,
    There is sunshine in our sorrows
    When our hearts are filled with pain.
    There is sunshine when we are burdened,
    There is sunshine when we pray,
    There is sunshine, Heavenly sunshine,
    Blessed sunshine all the way.[49]

Other recordings by Laura Henton included *Lord, You've Sure Been Good To Me*, a theme popular with New Orleans marching bands, and the fine *I Can Tell the World About This*. *Plenty Good Room In My Father's Kingdom* was less varied as a tune and offered little instrumentally to the accompanying musicians, but its words were characteristic of the oddly practical elements in the imagery of the new churches, as well as the free movement of verses from

one song to another – the first verse quoted has already appeared in Arizona
Dranes's *The Lamb's Blood Has Washed Me Clean*:

> My Lord done just what He said –
>   Way up in the kingdom,
> He healed the sick and He raised the dead –
>   Way up in the kingdom.
>
> There's plenty good room, plenty good room,
> Plenty good room in my Father's kingdom;
> There's plenty good room, plenty good room,
> Choose a seat and then sit down.
>
> One of these mornings bright and fair,
>   Way up in the kingdom,
> Gon' hitch on my wings and seize the air –
>   Way up in the kingdom . . .[50]

The combination of a good tune, a structure which permitted the easy
addition of new stanzas, a lyric sequence which related strongly to contemporary issues and which enabled the singers to express censure or reproof,
and a content which implied direct knowledge of God's values combined to
make many popular gospel songs acceptable to the different religious
denominations. Many of these characteristics were to be found in the songs of
other soloists, like Mother McCollum's, who recorded in Chicago with the
unlikely accompaniment of banjo and guitar (the banjo having virtually disap-
peared by this time; it certainly would have seemed outdated in Chicago). The
assurance of a place in a heaven that was an image of an idealized earth, and
an awareness of responsibilities to be met and duties to be fulfilled was evident
in her version of *When I Take My Vacation In Heaven*, sung in a lilting waltz-
time with a smooth and confident expression:

> When I take my vacation in Heaven,
> What a wonderful time it must be.
> Givin' comfort [in the Vale of sweet sorrow]
> And the face of my Savior I'll see
> Sitting down on the bank of the River
> 'neath the shade of the Heavenly tree –
> I shall rest from my burdens for ever –
> Won't you spend your vacation with me?
>
> There's many are taking vacation,
> To the mountain, the lake and the sea,
> To rest from their cares and their worries,
> What a wonderful time it must be.
> But it seems if I want to be like him,
> I must start in the heat and the cold,
> Seeking out all the sheep on the mountains,
> Bringing wanderers back to the fold.[51]

Original perhaps to the singer, was the naive but disarming *Jesus Is My Air-O-
Plane*. The symbol of the gospel train had been overworked by preachers and

singers alike, generally with the members of the congregation seen as ticket-purchasing travelers on a Heaven-bound train. The airplane image had been seen in this way by John Byrd in his recording of *The Heavenly Airplane*, and less favorably by Reverend Gates in his sermon *The Devil In the Flying Machine*. But to Mother McCollum it was Jesus who was pilot:

> Oh Jesus is my air-o-plane,
> He holds this world in His hand.
> He rides over all, He don't never fall,
> Jesus is my air-o-plane.
> You can run to the East, run to the West,
> You can't find a soul at rest,
> Some of these mornings, He's comin' again,
> Comin' through in an air-o-plane,
> Jesus is my air-o-plane,[52]   etc.

Hers was not a God of retribution, and the devastating potential of the airplane, which was still much in the minds of Americans a decade after the war, had been offset by the success of Colonel Lindbergh's flights. Yet it was a period of dramatic events and disasters that seemed to discriminate against blacks. Between 1928 and 1930 there was an unaccountable increase in tornadoes, averaging almost two hundred a year for the three years, twice the average of the previous decade. Among them was the St. Louis Cyclone, while in Florida, between 1,500 and 2,000 people lost their lives when a hurricane struck the state in September 1928.[53] With the memory of these events it was not surprising that Sister Cally Fancy of the Sanctified church in Chicago should use the disasters to make her religious points. But she was aware too, of the political events of the time, and the potential of a religious message in them. On *Everybody Get Your Business Right* she related God's wrath to man's misdemeanors, and to his laziness:

> Men's robbin', lyin' and killin',
> It brought in cursin' and swearin',
> Death's black train is on her way
> She's rumblin' through the land,
>> Everybody – get your business right,   (3)
>> God told me to tell you "Get your business right"
>
> While standin' all day idle,
> When there is work to do
> Go forth into the harvest field,
> The laborers of you –
>> Everybody   etc.
>
> God's warning you in tornadoes,
> Earthquakes and windstorms too.
> He's sending high water overflowing your land,
> Friends what are you going to do?
> Everybody get your business right,   (3)
> God told me to tell you "Get your business right"

Marooned refugees from the Mississippi floods wait for the waters to subside. Natural disasters provided subjects which could point up a moral in sermons and the new gospel songs. Unknown photographer. *Library of Congress collection.*

God's riding on the windstorm
On sea and on the land,
When God get angry with the Nation
The righteous alone can stand.
    Everybody   etc.[54]

On *I'm Gonna Tell My Jesus Howdy* with its harmonica and slide guitar accompaniment, she looked forward to a familiar relationship with her Lord, a seat at the Welcome Table and feasting on milk and honey. Its sentiments contrasted with her foreboding catalogue of disasters, of which the 1927 floods in Mississippi were the most devastating.[55]

The Mississippi floods were powerfully summarized by Elder Lonnie McIntorsh, who probably originally came from the state, though he seems to have spent most of his active life in Memphis. A member of the Church of God in Christ, dark-skinned but with brilliant blue eyes, McIntorsh was born about 1890. His *The 1927 Flood* was made with Elder Edwards, assisted by Sisters Johnson and Taylor. Sung in forced accents, his own voice being highish and somewhat strained, it had a simple guitar accompaniment:

It was in nineteen twenty-seven
It was an awful time to know,
Through many storms and thunderin',
God let the water flow.
The people worked in vain
But God wouldn't stop the rain –
For he poured down his flood on the land.

Well it poured through the land
And it killed poor beasts and man.
For the people had got so wicked,
They wouldn't hear God's command –
They had prayed for a deal,
But the Lord didn't have no deal –
Well he poured out his flood upon the land.[56]

One senses a note of reproach in the song, and justification for God's retribution on the sinful, and on the animals too, is barely stated. The recording that immediately followed was *The Latter Rain Is Fall*, apparently inspired by the same catastrophe. After the "early rain" on the day of Pentecost a prolonged drought ensued, which, to the Pentecostal churches, would be broken by the "latter rain" that, in the words of James, Book 5, verse 7, would reward the husbandman who "waiteth for the precious fruit of the earth, being patient over it". Textually it was of minimal content, but as a performance it was remarkable, with the guitar accompaniment slowly accelerating, the voices forced in growling tones, and the singing punctuated by hand-claps and cross-rhythms. It is probably the nearest to a ring-shout issued on a commercial record.

The latter rain is fallin', (*fallin' from on high*)
The latter rain is fallin', (*fallin' from on high*)
Make you just like Jesus, (*fallin' from on high*)
Make you just like Jesus, (*fallin' from on high*)[57]

Credit for the extraordinary dynamism of these recordings must be largely
due to the singing of the Mississippi lay preacher Sister Bessie Johnson and
Sister Melinda Taylor. While Melinda's was a deep and rounded contralto,
Bessie Johnson's was remarkable for its growling falsetto. Hers was clearly a
deliberate false voice for on some songs, like *He Got Better Things For You*,
she commenced by singing in a deep, full voice, before changing to the forced
one emitted from the back of the throat in a loud, heavy rasp. This growl was
of the kind imitated by New Orleans musicians on trumpet and trombone with
the use of the mute, and was often affected for short phrases or single words by
singers wishing to emphasize a line. Bessie Johnson's technique was notable
for its sustained strength and, in spite of its roughness, for its musicality,
qualities that were particularly evident on the restrained song by the Memphis
Sanctified Singers (Johnson, Taylor and Sally Sumler) on which they were
accompanied economically by Will Shade of the Memphis Jug Band, on
guitar. The verse was sung by Bessie Johnson, and her use of the vibrato rasp is
underscored thus: _____

Kind friends I want to tell you
Because I love your soul,
No doubt you been converted
But the half ain't never been told.
Some people they'll try to fool you,
There's nothing else to do
But Jesus Christ my Savior –
He got better things for you.[58]

An out-of-tune guitarist and a dragging beat marred the recordings made with
her Sanctified Singers under her own name but with McIntorsh and Edwards
providing the rhythmic propulsion and joining their voices with those of
Johnson and Taylor the combined effect was extremely compelling. McIntorsh and Edwards's use of accelerando, the responses and cries of "Glory!"
and the vigorous hand-clapping and cross-rhythms on tambourines all
contributed to make *What Kind of Man Jesus Is* among the finest of Sanctified
recordings.

"Oh, Ananias – (*Ananias*)
Ananias, (*Ananias*) tell me what kind of man, Jesus is?"
"Healed the sick – (*Healed the sick*) ⎫
Raised the dead – (*Raised the dead*) ⎬ (2)
Tell me what kind of man Jesus is.   ⎭
    Ananias – (*Ananias*)
    Ananias – (*Ananias*), tell me what kind of man Jesus is?" (Glory!)

"Talked to the wind – (*Talked to the wind*) ⎫
The wind obeyed – (*The wind obeyed*) ⎬ (2)
Tell me what kind of man Jesus is.[59] ⎭

Either certain songs and tunes enjoyed a period of popularity or, as seems more likely, the need to create new songs appropriate to the spirit of the Sanctified church led to a focus on particular items. Their popularity acted as a bond between the churches and the Sanctified singing groups. *What Kind of Man Jesus Is* was clearly one of these, while its gospel tune was the basis of Elder Bryant's *Come Over Here,* and *Within My Mind* by Eddie Head and his family.

Joined by his wife and children, with one playing tambourine, Eddie Head sang in an easy, integrated manner somewhat different from the tension of the Bessie Johnson groups. His songs emphasized the symbols of a rigorous life with its ultimate rewards in Heaven familiar in Sanctified song, as well as the slight persecution complex which was far from uncommon: "My road is rough and rocky", "I'm gonna wade into deep water" on *Tryin' To Get Home* or *Down On Me*:

Down on me, down on me,
Seems like everybody in the whole round world is down on me,
    If I could, I surely would
    Stand on the rock where Moses stood,
Seems like everybody in the whole round world is down on me.
Down on me, down on me,
Seems like everybody in the whole round world is down on me.
    I ain't been to Heaven but I've been told
    The streets are [pearly] and the Gates are gold,
Seems like everybody   etc.[60]

Down On Me was notable for the fluent guitar playing which imparted an easy swing to the recording, and for Eddie Head's skillful harmonizing to his family's singing.

Sanctified singers seem to have taken exception neither to the use of instruments normally associated with secular music, nor to the presence of secular instrumentalists on their recordings. Reverend Rice used New Orleans style jazz instrumentation on many of his records while Elder Bryant employed a jug band to accompany him. Jug band support, perhaps Will Shade's, was also to be heard on the four titles of the Holy Ghost Sanctified Singers who recorded in Memphis in February 1930. Their songs were uncomplicated, with repeated phrases and generally only a single lead line changing in each stanza. On *Thou Carest Lord, For Me* was a sprightly harmonica player who interpolated solos between the verses and with unison singing and hand-clapping to the jig-like tune, the overall sound was not dissimilar to that of a children's ring game:

Thou carest Lord, Thou carest Lord,
Thou carest Lord, only for me,

> Why should I fear, when Thou art near
> Thou carest Lord for me.[61]

Other Sanctified groups using jug band accompaniments included Brother Williams' Sanctified Singers, who also employed a cornet player on the old song *I Will Meet You At the Station*. Somewhat inexpert and faltering, the Louisville Sanctified Singers were among the last of the groups to record before the Depression, the nine members singing with spirit on *God Give Me Light* to the beat of guitar and tambourines.

With many melodies and rhythms derived from country dance music and jigs, instrumentation that came from secular sources, even extending to that of the jug bands and juke joints; with words and subjects that related to events or phenomena of the day and vocal techniques which matched those developed by the blues singers, the secularization of black sacred song had become marked in the Sanctified churches.

The very worldliness of some of the Holiness sects, even while the focus of their devotions was on another world, may have made them more ready to use contemporary devices, like recording, to spread their gospel and may also account for their substantial representation on record. Accustomed to singing in store-fronts and make-shift churches, they found the recording studio less inhibiting, while the fact that they represented a minority church with considerable zeal, infectious enthusiasm and an evangelical spirit meant that they would have welcomed the media as a means of reaching a larger congregation. At the sales counter, purchasers of Race records, notwithstanding their costliness, were largely working class, and the Pentecostal churches were representative of a genuinely working-class religious revival. For them, the issue of gospel records by Sanctified singers inspired a sense of solidarity in a period of uncertainty.

Honey In the Rock

Jack-leg preachers and evangelists

I want to tell you the natural fact,
Every man don't understan' the Bible alike,
   But that's all now, I tell you that's all;
   But you better have Jesus now, I tell you that's all.

Now the A. M. E. Methodists they believe
Sprinkle the head and not to wash the feet,
   But that's all,   etc.

Now the African Methodists they believe the same,
Cause you know denominations ain't a thing but a name,
   But that's all,   etc.

Now the Church of God have it in their mind
That they can get to Heaven without the sacrament n' wine,
   But that's all,   etc.

To the accompaniment of a home-made instrument with the quality of sound of a music-box, Washington Phillips recorded his *Denomination Blues* for a field unit in Dallas, Texas in December 1927. Played, it seems, like a lightly hammered dulcimer, the rippling notes of the instrument contrasted with the nasal, rather "white" sound of his voice and his reproachful intonation. Clearly, he did not like preachers in conventional churches:

Lot of preachers is preachin' and think they're doin' well
An' all they want is your money and you can go to hell,
   And that's all   etc.

There's another kind of preachers is high on speech,
They have to go to college to learn how to preach,
   And that's all   etc.

That kind of man he's hard to convince,
A man cain't preach unless 'n he's sense,
   And that's all   etc.

When people jump from church to church
You know their conversion don't amount to much,
   And that's all   etc.

When Jesus come in at Dividing Day
From the colored sheep he turned the goats away,
   But that's all   etc.

> It's right to stand together, it's wrong to stand apart,
> Cause none don't enter but the clean in heart,
>   But that's all[1]   etc.

Probably born in Freestone County, Texas around 1891, Washington Phillips earned his living as a farmer. His antipathy to education and to trained preachers was evident, but so was his commitment to his own calling, as he declared on *I Am Born To Preach the Gospel*:

> I have-a never been to no College
> And I didn't get a chance in school,
> But when Jesus Christ anointed me to preach the Gospel
> He sure didn't leave me no fool, oh yes –
>   I am born to preach the Gospel   (3)
>   And I sure do love my job.
>
> Well we have-a lots of educated preachers
> That are fixed it up in the head,
> And got their hearts un-fixed with God
> And walkin' round spiritual' [ly] dead, oh yes . . .[2]

More than once Phillips stated his mission in life: "What are they doing in Heaven today? I don't know boys but it's my business to stay here and sing about it." He had a strong drive to "lecture" as he termed his addresses on *Jesus Is My Friend*, or *Train Your Child*. There were "lots of people in the world, of course you cannot blame them. God has given them children and they don't know what to train them. When you educate an untrained child that's brought up full of sin, it just only got sense enough to poison notes and go to the pen." He criticized the "little womanish girls" and "little mannish boys" acting beyond their years and concluded "Education is all right, I will tell you before you start: before you educate the head, try to educate the heart." [3]

Simple though the rhyme schemes and doggerel rhythms were they were offset by his quiet sincerity and delicate playing. Though some of his songs told Biblical stories, like *Paul and Silas in Jail* or "old Daniel in the lion's den" the roots of his faith seem to have been in the teachings of his parents, themselves the subject of three songs. "I had a good father and mother", he sang, "they laid an example for me, they taught me how to pray; now I'm truly converted and I'm walking in the narrow way." [4] From his records we can deduce that Washington Phillips was a "jack-leg", without education or a regular church but a strong call to preach.

Jack-leg preachers were an important feature of religious life in the lower economic groups. Generally associated with the Sanctified movement they sometimes attended regular services of the churches, seeking a chance to preach. More often they addressed spontaneous congregations in the streets, or endeavored to start small store-front churches of their own. Ordination was not important; the call to preach was. In the late 1930s, when Savannah, Georgia had a black population of 43,000 there were ninety black churches, a

hundred regular preachers and as many more jack-legs. Jack-leg preachers
were not popular with "high-status" blacks, according to a poll made in
Chicago by Drake and Cayton, who found that only three per cent of their
sample liked them, whereas nearly half of the store-front church members
polled voted in their favor. Drake and Cayton quoted a denunciation from a
Baptist conference: "Brothers, the day is past for untrained preachers. You
can't hop around, whoop and holler and spit-at-a-bubble these days. You
have to deliver the goods. Some of these preachers are ordained for a mere
five-dollar bill." [5] This contempt was expressed more than once on record,
with the jack-leg preachers the subject of attacks by their ordained brethren.
Reverend W. M. Mosley from Atlanta, Georgia indulged in character
assassination in one recorded sermon, to the "A-men" chants of his
congregation:

> You jack-legged preachers – stay out of widow's houses.
> Some of these mornings – some of these nights,
> You goin' to some widow's house,
> Some grass widow, that you ain't got no business there.
> They gonna find your body there –
> But you won't find yo' head.
> Preacher – stay out of widow's houses . . .

And he condemned

> You drunken preachers, you ungodly preachers,
> You preachers . . . who preach lies
> Who preach false doctrine . . . stay out of widow's houses. [6]

There is no reliable indication as to which recorded ministers were jack-legs
and "chair-backers", for many of them may have been recorded with studio
participants acting as congregation. If Washington Phillips by the evidence of
his records was one, others who recorded songs similar to his might be better
classified as evangelists, who preached in the streets or in the churches when
opportunities arose, and who sang for coins outside the churches of Southern
towns. A familiar sight in the courthouse squares of the South throughout
the first half of the century, their potential appeal to the Race market did not
immediately occur to the record companies, and it was only through the
religious recordings made by blues singers and songsters that attention was
drawn to the singing black evangelists.

Sam Jones, the earliest of the songsters to record, was also the first to record
religious songs, his *Lord Don't You Know I Have No Friend Like You?* being
made in August 1924. To his own guitar accompaniment and with harmonica
choruses played between the simple verses it was a fragmentary, rather
melancholy song, issued in a general series before the Race series began:

> Lord don't you know, I have no friend like you
> If Heaven is not my home. Oh Lord what shall I do? . . .
> Some have forsaken me, Heaven when I die
> I'm on my way, back to the Promised land . . . [7]

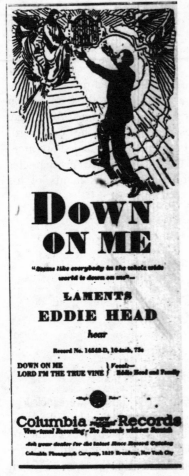

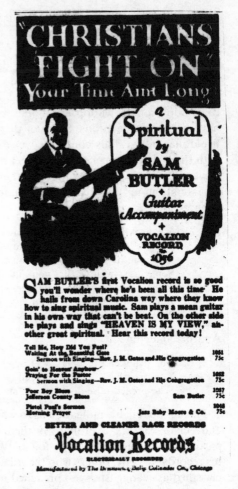

A Welcome at the Pearly Gates for Eddie Head. September 13, 1930. *The Chicago Defender. Paul Oliver collection.*

Stating that he "plays a mean guitar" the Vocalion 1926 announcement of Sam Butler's *Christians Fight On* also listed two of his blues, sermons by Reverend J. M. Gates, and Jazz Baby Moore's sermon parody. *Paul Oliver collection.*

At the end of the following year, Christmas 1925, the blues singer Blind Lemon Jefferson recorded for his first title a rather repetitive *I Want to be Like Jesus in My Heart* and *All I Want is that Pure Religion*. Retained to be the fourth issued disc by the singer, it was released under the pseudonym of Deacon L. J. Bates. Probably other singers detected the bluesman in the recording; Sam Collins, whose "crying" voice was a selling point for the Gennett company, made another version of *I Want to be Like Jesus in My Heart* to the whining sounds of his bottleneck guitar playing. That was in

September 1927, by which time a number of other songsters had cut religious songs. Among them was the Carolina singer Julius Daniels who sang, in February,

> Don't you hear them horses's feet   (2)
> Slippin' and slidin' up the Golden Street,
>   Taken my Lord away – way, oh Lord away,
>   Taken my Lord away,
>   Go an' tell 'em where to find Him.
>
> Eve and Adam was the first,   (3)
> Lord, God created from the dust,
>   Taken my Lord away   etc.
>
> Mother and father, 'member well   (3)
> Your daughter 'Lizabeth ringin' in Hell,
>   Taken my Lord away   etc.
>
> Mind my sister how you wanted to cross,   (3)
> Says your life is slippin' and your soul get lost,
>   Taken my Lord away   etc.
>
> I wonder what ole Satan's grumblin' 'bout,   (3)
> Says, he locked up in Hell and can't get out.
>   Taken my Lord away[8]   etc.

More than a dozen blues singers and songsters made religious titles, though in the majority of instances only a couple were issued by each – token items by Bessie Smith, Sara Martin, Clara Smith, Barbecue Bob, Sam Butler and others. Several were of markedly secularized gospel songs, like *When the Saints Go Marching In* or *Get On Board*. Of the earlier generation of blues-songsters to make spiritual recordings only Charley Patton, whose titles included *Oh Death, I Shall Not Be Moved* and *Jesue is a Dying-Bed Maker* (sic) recorded a significant number – ten issued, in his case. His two-part *Prayer of Death*, issued under the name of Elder J. J. Hadley, *Lord I'm Discouraged* and *I'm Going Home*, though including in the first instance in particular snatches of a few religious songs, had the theme of *Take A Stand* common to them all. *Lord I'm Discouraged* was sung at a slower tempo with occasional words carried by the guitar:

> Sometime I get discouraged, I believe my work is in vain,
> But the Holy Spirit whispers, and revive my mind again,
>   There'll be glory, what a glory, when we reach that other shore,
>   There'll be glory, what a glory, praying to Jesus evermore.
> I'm on my way to glory, to that happy land so fair,
> I'll soon reside with God's army, with the Saints of God up there.
>   There'll be glory, what a glory,   etc.[9]

When singing and accompanying his common-law wife, Bertha Lee, on spirituals like *Troubled 'Bout My Mother*, Patton was extremely convincing. He had a reputation as an occasional preacher himself, and on *You're Gonna Need Somebody When You Die* he included a sermon fragment: " Well friends,

I want to tell you – they tell me when He come down his hair gonna be like lamb's wool. And his eyes like flames of fire, And every man gonna know he's the son of the true living God; round his shoulders gonna be a rainbow, and his feet like fine brass. And, my friends, I want you to know again, He says that he's going to have a ol' river o' water that's flowing through the garden, 'clared the preacher . . ." The sermon continued but the statement "'clared the preacher" suggests that it may have been a remembered quotation rather than his own sermon. [10]

How sincere then, were the recordings of religious songs by songsters and blues singers? The question is not easily answered, but it is known that Blind Lemon Jefferson would not play blues on a Sunday, and that Charley Patton's step-father, Bill Patton, was a part-time preacher. [11]

Some blues singers appear to have recorded gospel songs simply in response to the suggestions of record promoters. Lucien Duckett and "Peg-Leg" (or "Pig") Sam Norwood from Mississippi made titles that were "all sacred and not blues because Speir was looking for some religious material", according to Duckett's step-son, the blues singer Johnnie Temple. [12] Though the two singers were known to have worked with Tommy Johnson, Ishman Bracey and Charlie McCoy, their few recordings, like *When the Saints Go Marching In* or *I Want to Go Where Jesus Is*, a version of the old hymn *Amazing Grace*, suggest some association with white styles of religious singing and playing. There is no evidence that Duckett and Norwood played in churches or even habitually sang sacred songs, though their ease with these few items make this a possibility.

Occasionally the "separation line" between sacred and secular became somewhat blurred: as sacred singers might use blues instrumentation and intonation, blues singers just as readily employed the expressive devices of the evangelists. But the blues did not influence the form of sacred songs to any great extent. A rare exception is the case of Leola Manning, who was recorded in the relatively unusual location of Knoxville, Tennessee in September 1929. Her title *He Fans Me* appears to have been intended to exploit the success of *Fan It*, a suggestive song recorded by Frankie "Half-Pint" Jaxon the year before. Its tune, too, linked strongly with blues like Lillian Glinn's *Dogging Me*, though Leola Manning's song was taken at a faster pace.

> My mother's she's a Christian
> Been washed in the Blood of the Lamb,
> She caused me to be a Soldier,
> And I want her to know I am.
>   Caused he fanned me, God knows he fanned me,
>   He fanned me and fired me,
>   Until I come home.
>
> If it takes six months to study
> Don't reject the call,
> Read Matthew 3 and 11,
> How He's come to fan 'em all

> Cause he's fanning, God knows he's fanning,
> Cause he's fanning and firin'
> Till the faith' come home.[13]

The text of Matthew 3: 11 and 12: "He shall baptize you with the Holy Ghost and with fire; whose fan is in his hand, and he will thoroughly purge his floor and gather his wheat into the garner, but he will burn up the chaff with unquenchable fire", was one of the key texts of the Pentecostal churches. Leola Manning's other records were all blues or ballads based on one form or another: *The Blues Is All Wrong* was based on Blind Blake's rag *Too Tight* but she was at pains to point out that it was "set to a blues tune but the words 'all right, all right – this song's all right'". Even *Laying In the Graveyard*, a twelve-bar blues had as its theme "when I'm laying in the grave, I will hear God when he calls", and depicted in blues lyrics the favorite heavenly encounter described in gospel song, by re-phrasing a standard blues verse:

> Good morning, Judgment, Mother how do you do?   (2)
> I been so lonesome in this world without you.[14]

It seems likely that Leola Manning was a blues singer who had recently undergone an experience of conversion, just as Lillian Glinn herself at this very time was experiencing the revelations that ended her career as a blues singer and brought her to a life-long commitment to the church. For Leola Manning if "the words' all right" neither the secular tune nor the barrelhouse piano accompaniment detracted from its religious intent.

One songster who made several religious titles was Blind Roosevelt Graves, who, with his half-blind brother Uaroy Graves playing tambourine, recorded in Chicago in 1929. Their religious titles, like *I Shall Not Be Moved* and *When I Lay My Burdens Down* were made at the same session as such secular titles as *Crazy About My Baby* and *Staggerin' Blues*. Their gospel songs were drawn from a recently developing repertoire rather than from the traditional spirituals. One in particular, *Telephone To Glory*, was representative of the new trend to find images that related to contemporary society and linked the familiar with the holy. It had been recorded in 1927 in a fiery version by Sister Mary Nelson, and in a rather colorless one by Blind Connie Rosemond. With the driving rhythm and marked syncopation of their guitar and tambourine theirs was an exhilarating performance backed up by cornet and piano:

> There will be no charges, telephone is free,
> It was built for service, just for you and me.
> There will be no waiting on this royal line,
> Telephone to Glory, he'll answer just in time.
>   Telephone to Glory, oh, what joy divine,
>   I can feel the current movin' on the line.
>   If we get the buzzin' from his lovin' arms,
>   We may talk to Jesus on his royal telephone.
> If your line is grounded and connexions thru'
> Have been lost to Jesus, I'll tell you what to do;

> Prayer, Faith and Promise mends a broken wire
> And leaves your soul a-burnin' with that Pentecostal fire –
> Telephone to Glory,   etc. [15]

Such familiarity with a personal God and a 'direct line' to Jesus strongly appealed to working-class worshipers who had little access to theological abstractions. That they were not on the point of "changing" or being converted is evident from the fact that they recorded some years later in their home town of Hattiesburg, Mississippi, with the pianist Cooney Vaughn, as the Mississippi Jook Band. On this occasion, in July 1936, they again made a couple of powerful gospel titles.

Religious titles by Roosevelt and Uaroy Graves were issued under their own name, as by Blind Willie Jackson and Brother, as Blind Arthur Groom and Brother, even as by the Jubilee Male *Quartet*! Such pseudonyms were partly devices employed by different record companies (in these instances Paramount, Broadway, Herwin, Crown, Varsity) to screen the fact that they were all issuing identical titles; partly a means of separating religious from secular issues in the lists. Often this would have been a matter of labeling at the time of issue, but probably not always: another songster, John Byrd, who made a singing sermon *The White Mule of Sin*, clearly connived in the pseudonym of Reverend George Jones, for it was used in the recording itself. More frequently it was a device to hide the fact that some religious recordings were by secular songsters and blues singers.

There would be no more reason to remark upon blues singers and songsters performing religious songs than there would be to comment upon members of an English parish church singing *Lily of Laguna* or *You Are My Sunshine* at a church social, except for the fact that the black churches were, as has been shown, extremely strict in their attitudes to singing, music and dancing. Even the Sanctified church seems to have condoned music and song only in its function of praising the Lord. For the devout church member it was probably extremely difficult to bring himself to sing blues or blues-songs; for the player of the Devil's music on the other hand, the inhibitions against playing religious items may have been rather fewer. Attitudes to the church, its preachers and deacons and its doctrines were for many blues singers humorous, even contemptuous, but many more were uneasy or ambiguous. As I have shown in *Screening the Blues*, these attitudes and conflicts were often resolved in maturity, and many blues singers, accustomed both to singing and addressing in public eventually became gospel singers, preachers and devoted church members. [16]

One of the first street singers to record and the one whose issues as by "The Guitar Evangelist" gave the name to the genre was Reverend Clayborn. He made some thirty titles for Vocalion. No information has been uncovered concerning Clayborn, whose recording career was relatively brief. He shared a Chicago session with Hound Head Henry and Charles Davenport and this lends slight support to the speculation that he may have come from Alabama, where Davenport had strong links. His voice was quite strong, if parched, its dryness offset by the clarity of his slide guitar work. A certain sameness pervades his records, which are marked by the use of a two-beat rhythm on the bass strings behind the vocals, and smooth, singing tones in the instrumental choruses. His guitar complemented his singing, and on a title like *Death Is Only a Dream* the slide frequently replaced the sung words in a manner favored by many blues guitarists, the guitar notes being themselves expressive of the voice.

> Only a dream, only a dream
> Of Glory beyond the dark stream,
> How peaceful the slumber,
> How happy the waking –
> For Death is only a dream.
>> Mother was dark
>> But the light came at last
>> And flooded my soul with its gleam;
>> True, that this life, is like clouds o'ercast
>> For death is only a dream.[17]

Though his work lacked rhythmic variety, Edward Clayborn appears to have been secure in his knowledge of the life to come and in the dependability of Jesus Christ to support the failing. *In Time of Trouble Jesus Will Never Say Goodbye* was a song which appears to have been his own composition:

> When you go before judge for trial
> Employ [as] your lawyer, Jesus Christ.
>> He will never say goodbye   (3)
>> When you havin' ups and downs
>> With your relations and child,
>> He will never say goodbye.
> When your mortal doctor gives you up to die
> Employ Heaven's doctor – Jesus Christ.
>> He will never say goodbye[18]   etc.

A bullet-headed man of stern countenance, he offered this as advice to the listener, for Clayborn's songs were frequently of this kind: as *Everybody Ought To Treat Their Mother Right, Men Don't Forget Your Wives For Your Sweethearts, The Wrong Way To Celebrate Christmas.* But he also seems to have been disillusioned in personal relationships which might account for his detachment; certainly *Your Enemy Cannot Harm You (But Watch Your Best Friend), You Never Will Know Who Is Your Friend* and *Let That Lie (Liar) Alone* were not the songs of a contented man.

> Don't want to get in trouble,   (3)
>> You better let that liar alone.
> Just let me tell you how a liar will do,
> He's always comin' with something new.
> Steal your wives as fast as he can,

Making all out he's your bosom friend.
Then you'll find out you believe what he says,
Then that liar goes his errant ways,
He will bring you news 'bout women and men,
He'll make you fall out with your dearest friend.
    Don't want to get in trouble[19]   etc.

Clayborn was sighted, confident and probably sufficiently independent to survive without companions. This was not always the case for the sightless singer. As is evident from the names of musicians already cited, many songsters were blind, probably from congenital syphilis. With other routes to employment closed to them some young blind persons became adept musicians who played at picnics and Saturday night jukes, sang for coins in the streets, or, like Willie McTell, held down regular tavern jobs. McTell, who recorded gospel songs only after 1935, was well known for his uncanny ability to find his way around even in strange cities, and Lemon Jefferson, who eventually had a chauffeur-driven car, certainly needed no guide in his home city of Dallas. Some were strictly religious singers, street evangelists who worked singly or in pairs. Others were primarily songsters or blues singers who were, in effect, competing for the same small change on the street corners, and who sang gospel songs when it was expedient to do so. Many singers, especially those who worked the streets, needed a child guide as their "eyes". As a boy, Josh White earned three or four dollars a week guiding street singers, mainly religious performers. "I was seven years old when I left home in Greenville to help support myself and my family", Josh White recalled many years later, "my job was to lead a blind man while playing the tambourine". "Man Arnold was the first, and then I think came Joel Taggart, Joe Walker and Blind Willie Walker, then Archie Jackson and Columbus Williams . . . and, around that same time, Blind Blake, a very good guitar player, – about the best for my money." Blind Joe Walker, he recalled, made finger picks from tin cans, while Blind Man (John Henry) Arnold was "mean but honest" and "owned several race horses".[20]

Blind Blake recorded no religious tunes, Joe Walker and Archie Jackson did not record, and Willie Walker made a couple of sides only. But Blind Joel Taggart made thirty titles, including some, in 1928, with the youthful Josh White playing second guitar and singing in his still unbroken voice. On *There's a Hand Writing On the Wall*, Taggart took the opening chorus solo, after which Josh joined him on the second half of the lines as responses: (italicized)

There's a hand writing on the wall,   (2)
Come and read and see what it say,
There's a hand writing on the wall.
Nobody could read it Lord – (*Hand writing on the wall*)
Nobody could read it Lord – (*Hand writing on the wall*)
Come and read it, see what it say, there's a –
Hand writing on the wall.

My Jesus wrote it Lord – (*Hand writing on the wall*)   etc.
Old Daniel could read it Lord – (*Hand writing on the wall*)[21]   etc.

White claimed that he "managed to get on those recordings because I could play better guitar than Joe Taggart". It is true that his single string work provided a filigree that complemented Taggart's rhythmic strum, much as his piping tones acted as a foil to the older man's rougher voice. Taggart often recorded with other accompanists or singers, including members of his own family, his wife and daughter, Emma and Bertha Taggart, and his son James, who joined him on a simple version of *The Half Ain't Never Been Told*. At his first session in November 1926, a few weeks before Reverend Clayborn's, he recorded *I Wish My Mother Was On That Train*. Emma Taggart joined him in concert rather than in responsorial fashion, her thinner voice backing him up on the chorus after the first line. With a good range and slightly abrasive quality, Taggart's own voice was strong and he led the singing confidently, with no guitar accompaniment:

> Oh Lord, I wonder will my mother be on that train,   *duet*
> Wonder will my mother be on that train?
> The train I'm talkin' about
> She's a movin' through the land,
> Good Lord I wonder will my mother be in on that train.
>
> Oh some of us have mothers, Lord they left us here below,
> They gone to live with Jesus, and rest for evermo'.
> Expect to meet her there, in the home beyond the sky,
> Oh Lord, I wonder will my mother be on that train   etc.
>   Wonder will my mother   etc.
>
> Oh Christian you better be ready, and standing in one band,
> For the gospel train is coming, she's a-movin' through the land,
> Make the station (sic) blow, Lord you better be ready to go,
> Good Lord I wonder will my mother be on that train,   etc.
>   Wonder will my mother   etc.
>
> Oh sinner your train is coming, I know she goin' to flag,
> I know her by her rumbling, for she's always draped in black,
> I bid you fare you well, for you made your bed in Hell,
> Oh Lord I wonder will my mother be on that train   etc.
>   Wonder will my mother[22]   etc.

The slightly surprising implication of the last verse may not have been intentional; the train his mother was on was still presumably, the Gospel train.

The chorus acted as both the introduction, the conclusion and the link between stanzas creating a continuous song. This formula also permitted stanzas ranging from a couplet to four or six lines to be introduced. The form was clearly one that he had made his own, and some months later Taggart made a solo version of *God's Gonna Separate the Wheat From the Tares*, one of his most forceful records, essentially to the same tune:

God's gonna separate the wheat from the tares, now didn't he say?
Separate the wheat from the tares now, didn't he say?
    Then I will stand with our mate
    Till that great harvest day,
God's gonna separate the wheat from the tares didn't he say.
    Up on the mountain Hobab spoke,
    Out of his mouth came fire and smoke,
For God's gonna separate the wheat from the tares,   etc.
    Read in the Bible, you'll understand
    Samson was the strongest man.
    Lived in favor with the Lord,
    God given him strength, over all.
God's gonna separate the wheat from the tares now,[23]   etc.

A vein of anxiety ran through Blind Joel Taggart's songs which was not
present in Reverend Clayborn's: if Clayborn sang *In Time of Trouble Jesus
Will Never Say Goodbye* – Taggart felt it necessary to appeal, *Lord Don't Drive
Me Away*. Frequently Blind Joel Taggart's songs reflected his personal
dilemmas and intimations of mortality – *I'll Be Satisfied, I've Crossed the
Separation Line, I Ain't No Sinner Now, When I Stand Before the King* and,
perhaps most expressive of this philosophy, *Religion Is Something Within You*:

    Yes religion is something within,
    Lord religion is something within you,
    Yes religion is something within.
      It will take you home to Heaven
      When on earth your work is done,
      There you'll see your blessed savior,
      God the Father, Holy Son.
    For religion is something within you,[24]   etc.

It was the closest he came to offering advice. Taggart's guitar playing was
highly rhythmic, if not complex, and provided the compelling movement that
the song demanded. On one occasion he was accompanied by an unknown
fiddle player and a second guitar, producing, with harmonized nasal singing
and swooping syllables, a sound somewhat reminiscent of Ernest Phipp's
white Holiness Quartet. It is just possible that the accompanists were white,
but the experimental coupling was not repeated in the Paramount Race series
and it seems likely that the white character of the singing and gospel hymns did
not appeal to the black record buying public.[25]

In roughly the span of Taggart's period of recording, several other blind
evangelists were also recorded, a number while units were on location in the
South. Perhaps it was the success of singers like Taggart and Clayborn that
encouraged the companies to seek them, or possibly the desire to find singers
of rival appeal; whatever the reason, these interesting singers were well
represented, even if few made many sides. One or two were also accompanied
by their wives, like Blind Benny Paris who was recorded in Atlanta in 1928,

probably at the instigation of Blind Willie McTell. Both he and his wife were blind, and used a guide dog in the streets. David Evans reports that they came from Woodcliff in Screven County, Georgia, traveled with an unrecorded singer, Blind Log, and lived with their children in Savannah.[26] Paris announced his recording with the words "I'm goin' sing a song, and the subject of this song is *Hide Me In the Blood of Jesus*." Nevertheless his wife led him into the song and provided the antiphonal responses in the chorus and refrain lines of the verses (italicised).

> Oh sinner man you better pray,
>   Hide me in the blood of (*Jesus.*)
> You gotta stand for trial on the Judgment Day,
>   Hide me in the blood (*of Jesus.*)
>
>   Oh hide (*me in the the blood*) – (*hide me in the blood*)   (2)
>   While the storm is ragin' high (*storm is ragin' high*)
>   Hide me in the blood (*hide me in the blood*)
>   Till the danger passes by.[27]

It was a simple and artless performance, the singers' nasal voices and high pitch imparting a somewhat hillbilly sound to the song. In the case of A. C. Forehand and his wife Mamie, who recorded in February 1927 in Memphis, where they were street singers, it was the wife who was blind, though both recorded a couple of songs each under their own names. On *I'm So Glad Today, Today*, A. C. Forehand sang with the quavering, rather weak voice of an old man, following his verses with a solo on harmonica, presumably rack-held as he continued to play a steady guitar accompaniment. A slight hint of a jig in the guitar and harmonica linked his approach with that of Sam Jones.

> Well I'm so glad, so glad today,
> That Jesus taken my sins away,
> He's my all – all in all,
> Well I will answer to his call.
>
> Well I'm so glad I'm saved from sin,
> Jesus so sweetlified within.
> Well you – to him I will come in,
> For he'll go with you to the end.[28]

Faintly audible behind the vocal were Blind Mamie Forehand's bells or hand-cymbals, with which she accompanied herself on her own songs. On *Honey In the Rock* her husband played slide guitar, gently holding the notes. Though they recorded a year before Blind Willie Johnson, there was a similar approach in the use of the slide at times, though vocally Blind Mamie Forehand was even shakier than her husband. Theirs was an affecting performance, Mamie freely adapting a song that had been composed by F. A. Graves, a white gospel song writer, in 1895.

> Mother, mother, can't you see,
> Oh what the Lord – has did for me?

> There is no evil – ever been tried,
> While I'm walkin' by my – Savior's side,
> Honey i' the rock – honey i' the rock,
> All well it tastes jus' like honey –
> Taste and see –
> Oh Lord it's good,
> Oh well it tastes jus' like honey in the rock . . .[29]

Not all the blind singers would appear to have been street evangelists and not all were equally interesting. Blind Willie Davis who is believed to have come from Bude, in Lincoln County, South Mississippi, recorded popular gospel songs like *When the Saints Go Marchin In, Rock of Ages* and *I've Got a Key To the Kingdom.* Nevertheless he seems to have been almost the archetypical street singer. According to the talent scout H. C. Speir he was fearful that he should have to record blues. Edward Clayborn's *Your Enemy Cannot Harm You* may have had special meaning for him.

> People I just want to tell you
> Just how your friends will do,
> They will wait and guess your secrets
> And turn their backs on you.
>   Your close friends, your close friends,
>   Your enemies cannot harm you, but watch – your close friends.[30]

Certain of his songs seem to have been almost totally improvised around a theme. *I Believe I'll Go Back Home*, for instance, was a sung monologue apparently based on the white song, *Where Is my Wandering Boy Tonight?*

> I saw my old mother,
> An' I was sittin' at the winder,
> And a house full of sobbin'
> And a house full of moanin' too,
> Goin' down the street,
> She wonderin' "Where is my boy tonight?"
> And I wonder where he's gone –   (2)
> Go and see if you can find him.[31]

On these songs he played a steel guitar tuned to a chord, strumming a forceful rhythm and drawing a slide along the treble strings. Willie Davis's voice was reminiscent of that of the blues singer Hi Henry Brown, and his loosely structured sacred songs were at times close to blues. *Trust In God and Do the Right* included verses on which he again soliloquized about his mother:

> Don't think he has forsaken you,
> Trust in God and do the right –   (3)
> If you want to go to Heaven when you die –
> Trust in God and do the right.
>
> I stood by the bedside and I saw my mother die,
> It hurt me to my heart when she said good-bye,

> I'm goin' to leave you in the hands of the Lord,
> Trust in God and do the right . . .[32] etc.

Of other blind evangelists recorded before the Depression mention should
be made of two who recorded in New Orleans. Blind Willie Harris had a voice
somewhat similar to that of the New Orleans songster Richard "Rabbit"
Brown. He played elementary guitar to his obviously sincere singing on *Does
Jesus Care*, a somewhat maudlin song that recalled the white singer Jimmy
Rodgers in his performance of his more sentimental songs. *Where He Leads
Me I Will Follow*, Harris's only other title, related to W. A. Ogden's *Where
He Leads I'll Follow* composed in the 1890s.

> I have watched [thee, growing] weary
> In the desert ways of sin,
> I have yearned to have thee near me
> And have tried thy heart to win.
> "I would give thee peace and comfort,
> Rest from all the sins and strife,
> Follow me and I will guide thee,
> I'm the Way, the Truth, the Life."
>   Where He leads me, I will follow   (3)
>   I'll go with him, with him, all the way.[33]

Another evangelist who made only two titles was Blind Roger Hays,
recorded in New Orleans the previous year and, like Harris, from the evidence
of his recorded voice, not a young man. *On My Way To Heaven* was a simple
song of single lines repeated in couplets, but *I Must Be Blind, I Cannot See* was
a touching song whose jig-like tune and jaunty harmonica solos contrasted
with the poignant words:

> I must be blind I cannot see, } (2)
> I never will see you no more. }
>
> He cast his eyes up in the skies, } (2)
> He never will see you no more. }
>
> His eyes is green, they's awful white, } (2)
> I never will see you no more. }
>
> I'm walking in the light, I'm walking in the light,
> I'm walking in the light, the beautiful light,
> The beautiful light of God.[34]

Though blind singers rarely made reference to their affliction in their songs,
there are some that emphasize the comfort that the sufferer, or the bereaved,
may gain through Christ. This is the theme of Blind Gussie Nesbit's *Pure
Religion*, already recorded in a version by Blind Lemon Jefferson. Nesbit was
born in Spartanburg, South Carolina in 1902, and in 1930 he recorded, at his
own request, in Atlanta.

> Deep is Jordan, you cain't go round, hallelu, hallelu,   (2)
> Deep is Jordan you cain't go round,

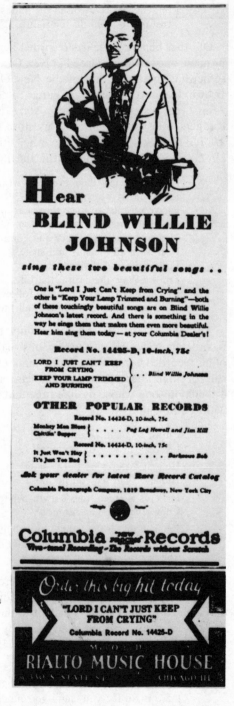

Edward W. Clayborn, "The Guitar
Evangelist" and Blind Joe Taggart, from a
Vocalion record sleeve. *Paul Oliver
collection.*

Blind Willie Johnson, illustrated with tin
cup on his guitar. The June 15, 1929
advertisement included *Chittlin' Supper* by
Peg Leg Howell. *Paul Oliver collection.*

Ain't got religion you sure to drown,
Then you're gonna need that pure religion, hallelu, hallelu.

Doctors standing lookin' said, hallelu, hallelu, (2)
"Hardest case I ever had",
Then you'll need that pure religion, hallelu, hallelu.

Mother and Father round the bed cryin', hallelu, hallelu, (2)
"Lord have mercy, my child is dyin'",
Then you're gonna need that pure religion, hallelu, hallelu.

Forty years later he was still an active religious singer though he had recently given up the guitar.[35] As a young man his guitar playing was strong with fine slide work, while his half-hummed "Oh Lord" suggested an awareness of the recordings of Blind Willie Johnson.

Exactly three years before Blind Nesbit was recorded, a Columbia field unit for the first time visited Dallas, Texas. The unit had the good fortune to find not only Washington Phillips but also Blind Willie Johnson. One of the most dramatic religious singers on record, he was the son of a Texas farmer, born about 1902 near Marlin. Blinded at the age of seven by his stepmother, who in a fit of jealousy threw lye water in his face, by the time he was recorded at the age of twenty-six, he was a well-known street singer with a remarkable technique and a wide range of songs.[36] At his first session his versatility as a guitarist was evident in his sensitive slide imitation of the moaning of a Baptist congregation humming, *Dark Was The Night – Cold Was The Ground*. At this first session he performed solo and used his guitar on *I Know His Blood Can Make Me Whole* virtually as a second voice. Johnson was a master of slide guitar playing and this recording demonstrated as well as any, the vocal character of the instrument. It was a song with few lines – "I know his blood can make me whole" or "I was sick and couldn't get well", which he rarely sang in full, the slide notes carrying the omitted vocal parts.[37] On subsequent sessions he was generally joined by his young wife Angeline Johnson, and this need to provide a voice through the instrument became less marked. Nevertheless there were other songs on which he used slide, such as *You'll Need Somebody On Your Bond* which he recorded twice. The second version was very close to the first, opening with a slide guitar solo, and introducing another during the song, with a bass string rhythm. The light swing and syncopated character of this song was further enhanced by a vocal contrast, often created by Angeline (italics) singing the second half of a line while he sang the first, and sometimes the reverse, or by both singing together (broken line).

Well, you gonna need *somebody on your bond*,
You gonna need somebody on your bond,
Now it's way, at midnight,
When Death comes slippin' in your room
You gonna need – aah – somebody on your bond.[38]

In the second version he used marked contrasts of rasps and softer singing,
even employing both in the same line. Johnson had a naturally growling voice
– no other word describes its quality better – but he clearly employed the effect
deliberately. *Praise God I'm Satisfied*, for example, is sung entirely in this deep
rasp, offset by Angeline's higher and thinner voice which follows the tune and
his vocal line closely. In only a few instances did they repeat a performance,
though *Go With Me To That Land* and *God Don't Never Change*, on which
Johnson again sang without excessive use of rasp, were basically the same
tune.

Rhythmically his work was varied, the simple song *Let Your Light Shine On
Me*, which had a basic rhythmic accompaniment similar to that on *Praise God
I'm Satisfied*, being given interest by the use of a slow verse at the outset
followed by double-time verses and choruses; the latter were further enlivened
by a secondary rhythm produced by tapping on the body of the guitar.
Though this device was exploited by Charley Patton and other blues singers,
who also sometimes used slide techniques, only occasionally did Blind Willie
Johnson's instrumental approach come near to blues. Nonetheless he has been
appropriated by blues writers and enthusiasts and hence he is among the best
known of the guitar evangelists.

Angeline Johnson's vocals accompanying Johnson have been used re-
peatedly to illustrate antiphonal singing, although she did not sing solely in this
manner. On *If It Had Not Been For Jesus* she sang the verses, and took the lead
in the choruses, using a tune which was close to Gussie Davis's *Irene,
Goodnight*, performed in waltz time:

> One night I went to a meeting
> Just to hear them sing and shout,
> But there I got salvation
> And I found their secrets out.
>   If it had not a-been for Jesus,
>   I would not have been here tonight,
>   But he has fully saved me,
>   And he washed my black heart white.
>
> Oh once I was a deep-down sinner
> Just as vile as I could be.
> I was on my way to destruction
> And deep down misery.[39]

Blind Willie Johnson joined her in the refrain on this, and on *Go With Me To
That Land* he sang the responses to her simple stanzas:

> Oh we'll see Jesus – (*in that land*)   (3)
> Where I'm bound.
> Ain't no dying (*in that land*)   (3)
> Where I'm bound
> Don't you want to go – (*in that land*) . . .

On *John the Revelator* their roles reversed, with Angeline answering, literally, his one-line questions in similar fashion:

> Well who's that a-writing? – (*John the Revelator*) (3)
> Eh, Book of the Seven *Seals* . . .[40]

But she was more at ease in the songs where Willie took the lead, and in her responses varied the point of entry where she came in on the verse. Often she overlapped with him, singing one or two words at the point of overlap, or coming in fractionally before he had completed a phrase. The technique added great musical interest to songs which were textually often very simple. Among the several songs which they performed in this responsorial manner were *Church I'm Fully Saved Today, Can't Nobody Hide From God* and *The Rain Don't Fall On Me* – another song on the Pentecostal theme of the "Latter Rain": it was performed as a duet, but with Angeline singing solo the italicized words.

> . . . Oh the rain, *latter rain*,
> Latter rain – *done* fell on me
> Oh the rain, latter rain done – fell on me
> *Don't you know*, promised it true,
> It was sent from heaven to you,
> It was sent, dearly beloved – *from above*
> Oh the rain latter rain.[41]   etc.

Blind Willie Johnson elaborated his technique when the content of the song was a simple message, and kept his accompaniment to a forceful rhythm when the text was fuller, with several verses developing a theme. He seems not to have been assailed by any doubts, or to have withdrawn from the world; on the contrary, there is a fierce conviction in his singing and more than a note of censure in many of his songs. Clearly he wished to convert others and, like the fire and brimstone preachers whose delivery was similar to his, he aimed to do so by fear if not by persuasion. His recording career was short, a little over two years, but he remained a well-known and influential singer in Beaumont, Texas.[42]

It has been assumed in the past that Johnson's songs were all his own composition, but this was not so. *Sweeter As the Years Go By*, for example, was composed and published by Mrs. C. H. Morris in 1912. Two years later Thoro Harris and Howard B. Smith published a *Jesus Is Coming Soon* while the white collector, publisher and composer Homer Rodeheaver published in 1923, in sheet music form at 25 cents per copy, *You Better Run* and *Shine On Me*, both recorded by Johnson. C. A. Tindley's composition *Leave It There*, copyrighted in 1916, had entered the folk tradition as *Take Your Burdens To the Lord*, to be recorded by Blind Willie Johnson as well as by Blind Joel Taggart, Roosevelt Graves and Washington Phillips. This absorption of published song sheets was to be found in the recordings of a number of singers.[43]

Mrs. C. H. Morris's *Sweeter as the Years Go By* of 1912, and Charles A. Tindley Jr.'s popular 1916 composition, *Leave It There. Paul Oliver collection.*

Many other songs by gospel performers and evangelists on record were derived from previously published compositions. In some cases oral transmission must have already taken place – Arizona Dranes was blind, but she recorded *It's All Right Now* composed by Benjamin Franklin Butts in 1909 (subtitled as "Jerry McAuley's dying words") in a version very close to the original. Blind Mamie Forehand similarly recorded F. A. Graves's *Honey In the Rock* (1895). The sources of a great many of the songs have not been traced, but it is interesting to note that Blind Joel Taggart, Edward Clayborn, Charley Patton and Roosevelt Graves all recorded *I Will Not Be* [Re]*Moved*; Clayborn, Graves and Lonnie McIntorsh all made versions of *When I Lay My Burden Down*; while Reverend Clayborn's *Death Is Only a Dream* had been published in the first edition of the hymnal *Gospel Pearls* which was distributed at the National Baptist Convention in 1921.

Gospel Pearls became one of the best-known and most widely used of the gospel song books, but there were many others, like Henry Date's *Pentecostal Hymns*, "A Winnowed Collection for Evangelistic Services", published as early as 1895, which claimed only three years later to have "found its way into nearly every town and hamlet in the land". Later collections included Thoro Harris's *Full Gospel Songs*, with a cover motif bearing the legend "Baptism with the Holy Ghost" which clearly emphasized its intention to reach Sanctified congregations. [44] Some of the songs may have been composed originally by the members of those congregations: Homer Rodeheaver, who published some fifty other titles in a paperbound collection in 1923, admitted that a large number of the songs had been "discovered" by him when the Billy Sunday evangelistic campaign was held in Columbia, South Carolina. When they were transcribed there by Dr. J. B. Herbert he had the "invaluable aid" of Reverend Dr. T. H. Wiseman, "now of Detroit, formerly a leading colored divine of Columbia, South Carolina". [45]

It is likely therefore that at least some of the songs were already in the tradition before transcription, arrangement and publication, while the conventions were obviously important in the process, attracting evangelists and church singers, when songs were exchanged. Published song sheets were available to both black and white, while the conventions frequently had tented churches for both. Songs therefore entered into the traditions of each group, and blind singers, in particular, with only their ears to depend on, appear on occasion to have assimilated white mannerisms in both song and accompaniment.

As the century advanced the various currents in religious song gained in strength through a confluence of streams. Significant among these was the change in the nature of the Jubilee quartets as they moved towards gospel singing, a phenomenon which must be discussed in a subsequent study. The literacy of the clergy, and that of many elders and deacons in the churches meant that new songs published in the collections of gospel songs compiled, for example, by the Fillmore Brothers in Cincinnati, or later, Stamps-Baxter in

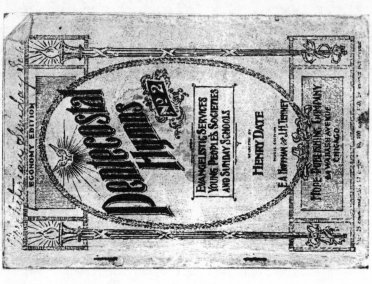

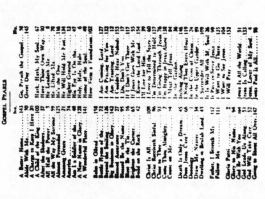

CONTENTS

Gospel Pearls, published in 1921 by the National Baptist Convention, included *Death Is Only a Dream*, later recorded by Edward W. Clayborn. *Paul Oliver collection.*

Henry Date's "winnowed collections" published in 1895 and 1898 helped to bring the new gospel songs to all denominations. In spite of the "Pentecostal" associations this copy was owned by a Presbyterian Sunday School. *Paul Oliver collection.*

Dallas or Alfred B. Smith in Wheaton, Illinois, were introduced into services. Though intended mainly for use in white churches, the collections were readily available to black communities. Frequently, spirituals and popular hymns from the nineteenth century were reprinted alongside songs composed in the previous two or three decades and new compositions, with the effect that there was both continuity and change in gospel hymnals.[46]

Large numbers of ballets were nonetheless printed. Street musicians who composed their own songs could narrate them to jobbing printers and subsequently sell the ballet sheets to interested passers-by.[47] Emmett Kennedy noted ballets "in miniature broadsheet form" were published and "recomposed by the Missionary Reverend F. J. Montgomery of New Orleans, La., better known as the 'World's Battle Ax'". One of these ballets, *Samson Tore the Building Down* was reminiscent in some respects of *Wasn't That a Witness For My Lord* as in the Calhoun collection.[48] Under a similar title it was first recorded as early as 1923 by the Paramount Jubilee Singers, with a piping vocal by a young girl. As *If I Had My Way* it was made by Reverend T. T. Rose in 1927 in another version, suggesting that the ballet was in wide circulation. And under this title it was also recorded by Blind Willie Johnson in one of the most powerful discs made by any religious singer. Delivering the words with alarming ferocity Johnson used his bass falsetto, forcing his syllables in leonine tones ideally suited to the theme:

> Delilah was a woman fine and fair:
> Her pleasant looks, her coal black hair.
> Delilah gained ole Sampson's mind,
> When he first see the woman that looked so fine.
> When he went to Timothy – I cain't tell
> Daughter of Timothy pleased him well.
> Sampson told his father "Go an . . .
>   If I had my way,
>   Well if had-a wicked wife,
>   If I had-a –
>   I would tear this old building down."   (Well –)
>
> Sampson's mother replied to him,
> "Can't find a woman of your kind and kin
> Sampson, though it grieves your mother's mind
> Go and marry that Philistine."
> Let me tell you what ole Sampson done:
> He broke at the lion, the lion run,
> Sampson was the first man the lion attack,
> Sampson caught the lion and got on his back.
> Written that the lion had killed a man with his paw –
> But Sampson had his hand in the lion's jaws.
>   If I had my way, etc.

The epic narrative sung to a throbbing rhythm, told fragments of further stories in the legendary wit and strength of the hero, from the riddle at the feast:

> – out of the strong come forth the sweet?
> Well I killed a lion; after he's dead
> The bees made honey in the lion's head.

to the slaying of the Philistines:

> – Looked on the ground, found an ole jawbone.
> Moved his arms, rope popped like thread;
> When he got through slayin', three thousand was dead.

and the cunning of Delilah:

> Sampson's wife she talked so fair;
> Told his wife to cut off his hair.
> Shaved his head, clean as your hand,
> So he become a nach'l man.
>   If I had my way,[49]   etc.

Which black ballads were the first to follow the traditional Anglo-Scots secular form of eight- or sixteen-bar stanzas, but were developed on religious themes, must remain conjectural. It is possible that they were about the exemplary Biblical figures – Noah, Jonah, Joshua, Moses – whose stories were so dramatically used by the preachers. The Texas singer, Henry Thomas, often thought to be representative of the earliest generation of songsters on record, told of Jonah, but, perhaps because of time limitations, omitted his being swallowed by the whale:

> Lord told Jonah, said to "go and preach"
> Jonah declared that he would not go;
> Hid himself in the bottom of the ship.
> Searched that ship from bottom to top –
> Held Brother Jonah, said "Overboard";
> Cast him a bird and dropped the seed,
> Dropped the seed, [strong came the] root,
> From that root, that strong vine,
> From the vine, that strong shade,
> Under that shade brother Jonah laid . . .[50]

Again, it was more chanted epic narrative than ballad, seldom fitting the ballad stanza form. But it was sufficiently close to the Samson and Delilah theme as sung by Blind Willie Johnson as to suggest that it was based on a similar source, perhaps another printed ballet.

Though some ballets were on Biblical figures there was a clear incentive to compose new songs on current events from which a moral might be drawn. One such incident occurred in 1912 which had international implications and was met around the world with horror, the *Titanic* disaster. Its loss following a collision with an iceberg in a calm sea, made a deep impression on the folk memory, to be recorded not only in ballads but in other forms of popular music, like William Baltzell's "Descriptive Composition for Piano Solo", *The*

Wreck of the Titanic. It was probably also circulated as a ballet at the time.
Richard Brown's account of the tragic circumstances was a doleful, if
straightforward, ballad of how "the Titanic left Southhamilton" when,

> Everyone was calm and silent,
> Ask' each other what the trouble may be;
> Not thinking that Death was lurking
> There upon that Northern sea.

> The *Carpathia* received a wireless,
> "S. O. S." in distress,
> "Come at once, we are sinking,
> Make [up late] and do your best;
> Get your lifeboats all in readiness,
> Cause we are goin' down very fast.
> We have saved the women and the children,
> And try and hold out to the last."

> You know at last they called all the passengers,
> Told them to hurry to the decks,
> Then they realized that the mighty *Titanic*
> Would undoubtedly be a wreck.
> They lowered the lifeboats one by one,
> Saving the women and children from the start;
> The poor men was left to take care for themselves
> But they sure played a hero's part.

> They stood out on that sinking deck
> And they was all in great despair;
> You know accidents may happen most any time
> And we know not when and where.
> The music played as they went down
> On that dark blue sea,
> And you could hear the sound of that familiar hymn
> Playin' "Oh Nearer my God to Thee".
>> Oh nearer my God to Thee   (3)
>> Nearer to Thee,
>> Almighty, wondrous, as the sun goes down
>> Darkness be over me,
>> Just then the Titanic went down.

The final verses were adapted from Edith M. Lessing's song, *Just As The
Ship Went Down.*[51]

For whites the scale of the disaster and its cruel involvement of the weak and
innocent could only be accounted for in human error or folly; for blacks, the
sinking assumed a somewhat different significance, indicating the inevitability
of God's judgment on the arrogance of those who believed themselves
invincible. The moral issues that the loss of the ship symbolized were
expressed by a number of singers. Blind Willie Johnson in *God Moves On the
Water* emphasized that the passengers sought help in prayer, but presumably,
only in this hour of disaster:

Year of nineteen hundred and twelve,
April the fourteenth day,
Great Titanic struck an iceberg,
People had to run and pray.
  God moves – moves – Ah know-ah
  An' the people had to run and pray.

Many had t'leave a happy home,
All that they possess.
"Oh Jesus will you hear us now?
Help us in our distress."
  God moves – God moves –   etc.

Women had to leave they lovin' ones,
People had to save their –
When they heard their loved ones moans
Hearts did almost break.
  God moves – God moves –   etc.

Johnson's song corresponds closely to a version published by Dorothy
Scarborough in 1919. It is likely that this was in general circulation for a
typescript of a seven-stanza *God Moved On the Waters* is included in the Frank
C. Brown collection held at Duke University. Its first verse is close to that of
Blind Willie Johnson's and though the others differ it is clearly the same song,
while the attempt at dialect transcription indicates that it was collected from a
black singer. The second verse stated that "de rich dey had decided dat they
would not ridah wid de pore", but that "dey place de pore on de deck of de
ship and de pore was de first to go".[52] A widely held belief that the
heavyweight boxer Jack Johnson had been refused a berth on the *Titanic*
because of his color may have been apocryphal, but the separation of the
"poor" from the wealthy on the ship was well known. This verse, slightly
adapted, appeared in another recording by William and Versey Smith, *When
That Great Ship Went Down*:

On a Monday morning, just about nine o'clock,
Great Titanic, begin to reel and rock,
Children screamin' and cryin', some were goin' to die,
Wasn't it sad when that great ship went down?
  Sad when that great ship went down –   (2)
  Husbands and wives, children lost their lives,
  Wasn't it sad when that great ship went down.

When that ship left England, makin' for that shore,
The rich had declared, would not ride with the poor,
Pushed the poor below, well, first they had to go –
– Wasn't it sad when that great ship went down,   etc.

People on that ship, long ways from home,
Friends all around they – knew their time had come.
Death come a-ridin' by, fifteen hundred had to die,
– Wasn't it sad when that great ship went down,[53]   etc.

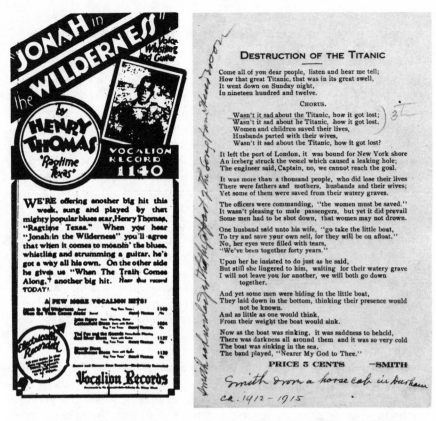

Though *Jonah in the Wilderness* was a parable of salvation, Vocalion's 1927 announcement of Henry Thomas's recording referred to his "moanin' the blues". *Paul Oliver collection.*

A broadside or "ballit" *Destruction of the Titanic* collected from Bill Smith who sold copies for 5 cents each. *Frank C. Brown Collection, Manuscript Dept. William R. Perkins Library, Duke University, Durham N.C.*

Their song was similar in several respects to *Destruction of the Titanic*, a printed broadside or ballet, also in the collection, obtained from its composer on May 26, 1920. It was credited only to Smith, bore no printer's name and sold for five cents. Notes at the time indicated that it was "made by W.O. Smith and Irma Smith", Bill Smith having driven "a horse cab in Durham c. 1912–15". It is tempting to reflect that William and Irma Smith may have been the same singers as William and Versey Smith. If so, they changed the key line of the chorus from the somewhat awkward "Wasn't it sad about the Titanic, how it got lost", to the smoother "Wasn't it sad when that great ship went down". One would expect them to have produced a polished version fifteen years after the event, but in fact the Smiths repeated each verse thus reducing the chances of development of the song, while the last verse which referred to the intention to "build a ship that water can't come through" was garbled and incomplete; a verse, incidentally, that was included in the collected version of *God Moved On the Waters.*

Another song, *The Great Titanic*, bearing the date November 30, 1920, was contributed by Miss Fanny Grogan to the Brown collection; it was even closer to the text of the Smiths' record, but the source was not identified. Still another, also called *The Destruction of the Titanic* was printed "as it appeared in a broadside published by the Reformer Publishing Company, a Negro Press. It was printed for the 'Rev. J.H. Brown' who sold copies at 5 cents each". The close relationship of these songs, the overlapping and exchange of verses and their eventual wide distribution – Blind Willie Johnson was recorded in New Orleans on this occasion – are instructive of the folk creative process and the part that printed broadsheets may have played in it.

On this evidence the Titanic broadsides constitute the fullest documentation we have of ballets on one theme. The editors of the Frank C. Brown collection quoted the observation of A. E. Perkins that only a week after the loss of the ship he saw "a blind preacher selling a ballad he had composed on the disaster", adding that one broadside in the collection bore the date April 13, 1912 – a day *before* the tragedy. This was composed by S. C. Martin who was white, though, perhaps significantly, he was known in Durham as "Coon Martin".[54]

If the fate of the *Titanic* was appalling, it was one that was imaginable and about which the rural singer could summon a mental picture which he could translate into song. Within a few years, the scale of events as America entered the First World War, was such that for the evangelist it was too great to comprehend or embrace its lessons within a few verses. The opposition of governments, the confusion of conflicts and the loss of hundreds of thousands of lives on decisions of generals were beyond their imaginings. But with the retrospect of a decade both Blind Willie Johnson and William and Versey Smith were able to record a post-war theme, *Everybody Help the Boys Come Home*, from which they could draw a clearer moral of unity and co-operation. With harsh, constricted tones and marked cadences, they sang:

> Taxes heavy, but we must pay
> Helping the boys over 'cross the sea,
> In the muddy water up to their knees
> Facing the Kaiser for you and me.
>   Everybody help the boys come home,   (3)
>   We'll [rest], everybody, when the war [was on]
>
> Three cents on a letter we had to pay,
> Two cents on a postal card going first class,
> Eight cents on the dollar just to ride the train,
> Helpin' the government with our might and main.
>   Everybody help the boys come home,   etc.
>
> President Wilson was on his throne
> Making laws for everyone,

> Raising the rich and raising the poor,
> Raising up the taxes from everybody's door.
>> Everybody help the boys come home,   etc.
>
> President Wilson came from France
> Meeting the doctor now, face to face,
> All he wanted was a prodigal's chance,
> We got to go to Germany now to settle the case.
>> Everybody help the boys come home,[55]   etc.

Blind Willie Johnson's *When the War Was On* was clearly from the same source, presumably a printed ballet, with the stanzas slightly altered. Rationing measures of "half a pound of sugar a person a week; folks didn't like it they blamed Uncle Sam; got to save the sugar for the boys in France", had a stringent note in Johnson's version and he pointedly censored one stanza by omitting an offending line and beating its rhythm on his guitar instead: "President Wilson sittin' on his throne, Makin' the laws for everyone; Didn't call the black men, called their wives, ... (instrumental line) . . . . .[56]

The Spanish influenza epidemic followed the cessation of the War in 1919 and its effect killed more people than did the battles of the war itself. With Angeline Johnson accompanying him with a lighter, but complementary voice, Blind Willie sang the words of *Jesus Is Coming Soon* to a throbbing guitar rhythm on the theme of the "Spanishin' 'flu."

> In the year of Nineteen and Eighteen,
> God sent a mighty disease,
> It killed a-many a-thousands
> On land and on the seas.
>> When I die, God done warned me, } (2)
>> Jesus coming soon.
>
> Read the Book of Zachariah,
> Bible plainly say,
> Said the people in the cities dyin',
> Account of their wicked ways.

The impact of the influenza epidemic was also evident in his song *God Don't Never Change*: "God in the time of sickness, God in the doctor too; In the time of the influenza, he truly was a God to you."[57] It is possible that this also had been printed in ballet form. One of Newman White's examples was a 32-page pamphlet, *The Golden Trumpet Jubilee Hymns*, "compiled by Rev. W. M. Jones, Richmond, Va., Price 25 cents"which included *That Influenza Train*, an eleven-stanza song which, while not the same as Johnson's, suggests a similar origin.[58]

With the war and the influenza epidemic over, the natural disasters of the 1920s formed the basis of some songs of warning among the Sanctified singers as has already been noted. Sister Cally Fancy followed her admonition to "Everybody" to "get their business right" with a two-part recording made two years later. If the war was over its terrors were not forgotten and in the aftermath, the League of Nations was formed to prevent such a conflagration recurring. Any complacency that hopes for the success of the League may have inspired in her hearers was rapidly dispelled by Cally Fancy in her uneasy reminders that *Death Is Riding Through the Land*, sung to the vigorous playing of a pianist in the mold of Arizona Dranes:

> Death is bringing down your great aeroplanes,
> Overturning automobiles,
> He's wreckin' trains, causin' hearts to pain,
> Oh nations, don't you feel –
>   Death is riding through the land   (3)
>   He's bringing dangers on sea and land.
>
> You mothers who claim you know God,
> God is giving you a chance;
> Some of you haven't prayed a heartfelt prayer,
> Since your son returned from France.
>   Death is riding through the land,   etc.
>
> The saddest moment ever you felt –
> You can't forget that day
> When Death's pale horse rode down in France,
> And stole your son away.
>   Death is riding through the land,   etc.
>
> You think the War is over,
> Because the U. S. A.
> Has joined the League of Nations
> But the War is on her way –
>   Death is riding through the land,   etc.
>
> You depended on your navy
> And your grey submarines,
> You had better plan should War break out
> To bring Jesus on the scene.
>   Death is riding through the land,[59]   etc.

Whether Sister Cally Fancy published her song as a ballet is not known, nor even whether she practiced as a street evangelist as her strong voice suggests she may. Like a number of soloists in the Sanctified church she showed an aptitude in using current events to point her moral. In this respect Blind Willie Johnson was unlike his other frequently recorded contemporaries, Washington Phillips, Blind Joel Taggart or Edward Clayborn in showing a readiness to draw from recent experience to emphasize that man's follies and misdemeanors will lead to Divine retribution. Nevertheless, though they picked up new songs the street singers were basically conservative in their approach – a fact which makes recordings of their vigorous folk music an important documentation of a vanished Southern tradition, but which also accounts for their declining appeal to the recording units and talent scouts.

8

Natural-Born Men

Survivors of the ballad tradition

Of all the forms of black secular song, the genre which attracted the most attention and which was discussed at greatest length before the advent of concentrated writing on the blues, was the ballad. Judging by their prevalence in early collections, black ballads were widely sung at the beginning of the century. But they were also probably easier for collectors to identify: the form was clearly derived from the British/American ballad tradition, the songs often told sequential stories which invited comparison, and the subjects were usually focused around a single incident or the depredations of a single individual. These aspects made the naming of the songs easier, and hence the requests for specific ballads could be made by the collector. Nevertheless, they could not be obtained if they were not known to the singers, and the large number of ballads and their variants which were collected indicates that they formed a significant part of the songster's repertory.

In view of the popularity of the ballads as a form it is surprising that the traditional Anglo-Scots ballads do not feature more markedly in the songs of black performers, many of them having entertained white audiences. Versions of *The Maid Freed From the Gallows, Lady Isabel and the Elf Knight, The Jew's Daughter* and *Lord Lovel*, among other British ballads, were collected in the first quarter of the century.[1] Several of these came from the lips of black mammies and others in service whose contact with whites and role in the raising of children had influenced their knowledge of traditional songs. In total they were still few, and in later years only a scattering of traditional ballads were recovered from black singers. John A. Lomax, field collecting in Texas for the Library of Congress in 1933, recorded "Iron-Head" Baker, "this Negro singer of English ballads" who had been born in 1870 and his companion Moses "Clear Rock" Platt, born 1862, in the Ramsey State Convict Farm, Texas. Baker sang *Young Maid Freed From the Gallows, The Farmer's Curst Wife* and *The Rich Old Lady*, while Platt obliged with "'Bobby Allen', as he called the old English ballad, true to tune, but hopelessly mixed up with a famous cowboy song entitled 'The Streets of Laredo'", as Lomax recalled.[2] There were few other examples recorded for the Library of Congress or on commercial issues which could be compared with any of the three hundred ballads in the great collection made by Francis James Child.

There are just one or two exceptions, like *Drunkard's Special*, recorded by a

Dallas singer and leader of a string and jug band, Coley Jones. A troubadour song which was popular in Europe, translated into German and published in Germany as a broadside in the late eighteenth century, it was known as *Le Jaloux* in France and as *Our Goodman* (*Gudeman*) or *The Merry Cuckold* and *The Kind Wife* in Britain.[3] To a simple guitar accompaniment Jones sang *Drunkard's Special* in a voice that emphasized his own ingenuousness:

> First night when I went home, drunk as I could be,
> There's another mule in the stable, where my mule ought to be.
> "Come here honey, explain yourself to me:
> How come another mule in the stable where my mule ought to be?"
>   "Oh crazy, oh silly, can't you plainly see?
>   That's nothing but a milk cow where your mule ought to be."
> I've traveled this world over, a million times or more,
> A saddle on a milk cow's back I've never seen before.

On the second night he discovered another coat on the coat-rack but his wife explained that it was nothing but a bed-quilt, to which the singer observed that "Pockets in a bed-quilt I've never seen before".

> Third night when I went home, drunk as I could be,
> There's another head on the pillow where my head ought to be.
> "Come here honey, come here, explain this thing to me.
> How come another head on the pillow where my head oughta be?"
>   "Oh crazy, oh silly, can't you plainly see?
>   That's nothin' but a cabbage head that your grandmaw sent to me."
> "I've traveled this world over a million times or more,
> Hair on a cabbage head I never seen before . . .[4]"

With its potential for ribald extension and the delayed action of its final punch lines (one example quoted by Child had twenty-eight verses) the song was understandably popular among black singers. Their penchant for animal songs and stories might also lead one to expect that some animal ballads might have been recorded. But there were no variants of *A Moste Strange Weddinge of the Frogge and Mouse* on record, though one or two were collected from oral tradition. Of the ballads of British origin which gained some popularity among black singers, only one, the Irish ballad of *The Unfortunate Rake*, gained some currency. Though it passed into the American ballad tradition as *The Dying Cowboy*, it was sung in black communities as *St. James Infirmary*, *The John Sealy Hospital* or *The Dying Gambler*. As such it was recorded by Emmett Matthews, and by Rob Robinson with the Hokum Boys, but these were jazz or hokum performances which owed much to Louis Armstrong's version. Publication in Wayman's Song Sheets undoubtedly encouraged its circulation as a jazz song rather than as a ballad. In this it is comparable to *The Derby Ram*, which survived as the jazz song *Oh Didn't He Ramble* in which "The habits of the ram, sir" had their gargantuan appeal.[5]

In general, the songsters were more interested in the narratives of black heroes with whom they, and their audiences, could identify. Biblical figures like Samson or Jonah have already been discussed, but such personalities, though they were made real in song and sermon, still lived in mythical time; most secular heroes of black balladry are more specifically tied to believable events. Perhaps the earliest of these was *John Henry*. No figure in the tradition has been more written about than "the steel-drivin' man"; he has been the subject of novels by Roark Bradford and James Cloyd Bowman, and of serious investigations by Guy B. Johnson and Louis W. Chappell into his origins and the ballads that have told of his legendary exploits. Most recently summarized by Norm Cohen, these researches have examined the authenticity of the hero, but have not substantiated the legend.[6]

It was one that was widely believed nevertheless, and could have had a basis in fact. Frequently told at length, it can be described, in essence, as the competition between a black worker and the machine that threatened to replace him. John Henry "drove steel", hammering a drill held by his "shaker" into the living rock so that dynamite charges could be placed in the drill holes to blast away a tunnel through a mountain. A location in the Big Bend tunnel on the Chesapeake and Ohio (C & O) Railroad in the Allegheny Mountains, West Virginia, is most frequently identified. Mechanical steam drills were introduced there to do the work of the rock-drilling crews between 1870 and 1872. Competitions with steam drills are known to have taken place and even to have been won by the steel-driver. In most versions of *John Henry* collected by folklorists, he wins the contest but dies in the attempt, fulfilling a prophecy made when he was "at his mama's knee".[7]

A version sung by "The Two Poor Boys", as they were termed on the record label, Joe Evans and Arthur McClain, though somewhat truncated, refers to this premonition. They situated the action in the Big Bend tunnel, but did not sing of the contest. Little is known of Evans and McClain, who were recalled in Tennessee, but their musical approach, with beautifully matched guitar and mandolin accompaniment, affirms an Eastern or Border states origin.

> John Henry he was a li'l baby boy
> Sittin' on his mama's knee,
> Had a nine-pound hammer, holdin' in his arms
> "Goin' be the death of me – "   (4)   (mm-mmm)

> John Henry went to that Big Bend tunnel
> Hammer in his hand,
> John Henry was so small and that rock was so tall –
> Laid down his hammer and he cried.   (4)   (oh, pardner)

> John Henry asked his shaker,
> "Shaker did you ever pray?
> Cause if I miss that piece of steel
> T'morrow be your buryin' day."   (4)

> "Who's gonna shoe your pretty little feet,
> Who's gonna glove your li'l hand?
> Baby who's gonna kiss your rosy cheeks, when
> I'm in a differ'nt land?"   (2)

> John Henry took sick and went to bed,
> Sent for the doctor and in he come.
> Turned down the side of John Henry's bed,
> "Sick and can't get well – oh pardner,
> Sick and can't get well"[8]

Only one record gave adequate space for the narration of the story – Walter Furry Lewis's two-part *John Henry*. A native of Greenwood, Mississippi, where he was born in 1893, Furry Lewis had worked as a medicine show entertainer for many years, using Memphis, Tennessee as his base for most of his active life as a singer and musician. He had obviously picked up a very full version of the ballad, but was somewhat vague about its narrative order. The action was placed in the "Big Bend tunnel on the Y. M. V." – the Yazoo and Mississippi Valley railroad which in his youth ran from his home town via Tutwiler to Clarksdale and beyond: a line without a tunnel, or a mountain:

> John Henry said to his captain
> "Lord, a man ain't nothin' but a man,
> Before 'be beaten by the steel driving gang,
> Lord, I'll die with this hammer in my hand."   (3)
>
> Lord they taken poor John Henry,
> For to help hew the mountain down,
> Lord the mountain was so tall, John Henry so small,
> 'Till Lord he laid down his hammer Lord and he cried, cried.   (2)
>
> John Henry had a li'l baby,
> Which he sit in the palm of his hand.
> Cryin' "Baby, baby, take your daddy's advice,
> Don't you never be a steel-drivin' man, man."   (2)
>
> John Henry hammered in the mountain,
> Says the head of the hammer caught a-fire,
> Cryin' "Pick 'em up boys and let 'em down again,
> One cool drink of water before I die, die."   (2)

Other verses described his woman's devotion, and a ring which he gave her so that "when I'm dead and buried poor gal, you can give it to your other man". At one point Lewis dropped in a verse which was of the kind sung by railroad crews who used the John Henry theme as a work song: "I can set your track, and I can line your jack, I can pick and shovel too". On hearing of John Henry's death the women, "some dressed in white, some dressed in red", went to where he fell:

> Lord they buried poor John Henry
> And they buried him in the pits of the sand.
> And the people they gathered ten thousand miles around,
> For that leader of that steel driving gang.[9]

Furry Lewis seems not to have understood the nature of the contest, for in the first verse it is a steel driving gang which threatens to beat him, and in the last he is himself the leader of a gang.

Even less clear was the five-verse example sung by the Texas singer Henry Thomas, which opened with a verse declaring that "Henry got a letter, said his mother was dead; put his children on a passenger train, he gonna ride the blind". Far removed from the traditional location of the action, the likely source of the song in Virginia and from any tunneling activities, the song had little meaning for Texas singers. Yet Thomas included one verse which may have referred to the mechanical drilling machine, unlike any other version recorded by a black singer in this period:

> Henry looked up the railroad track,
> Fast steel driver coming down;
> Before I let that steel driver beat me down,
> Die with that hammer in my hand,
> Gonna die with that hammer in my hand.

But there is little sense in the subsequent verse:

> Henry went on the mountain top,
> Give his horn a blow,
> Last words the captain said,
> "John Henry was a natural man,
> John Henry was a natural man."

The remaining verses find his woman, dressed in red, going where John Henry fell dead and his baby boy declaring in his *last* words "I'm gonna learn to be a steel-driving man." [10]

A particularly vigorous and rural recording was made in Atlanta by the Birmingham Jug Band. Joe Williams claimed that he, the harmonica player Jaybird Coleman, and the fake blind musician Bogus Ben Covington were among the musicians on the record. Be that as it may, it is clear that the song was no longer associated with the steel driller but with "Bill Wilson", apparently a wagoner.

> Bill Wilson had a baby,
> You could hold in the palm of your hand,
> Says the last words I heard the baby cry,
> "Goin' be your wagon-drivin' man, Lord."
>
> Bill Wilson went to the mountain,
> It was so solid high.
> "If I cain't climb this mountain Lord,
> I'm gonna lay at this seat and I die – hey"
>
> Bill Wilson had a li'l woman,
> Couldn't read or write,
> Bill Wilson said "Old [gal] again
> You better not slip out tonight – hey" [11]

The vocal was rasping, the harmonica forceful. Once or twice the harmonica playing was elaborated with whoops in the manner of *The Fox Chase*, and it is of some interest to note that both *The Fox Chase* and *John*

Henry were recorded as harmonica soli by De Ford Bailey. Though black, Bailey performed from 1925 on Grand Ole Opry, the Nashville show on which all the other entertainers were white. When Bailey recorded his non-vocal version of *John Henry* it was released on the Victor hillbilly series and not as a Race record. The sole remaining black version of *John Henry* from the period was a harmonica duet by William Francis and Richard Sowell on their only record. *John Henry* was recorded in the 1920s by many white country singers, among them Fiddlin' John Carson, Riley Puckett, Gid Tanner and Uncle Dave Macon. Norm Cohen lists (literally) hundreds of versions of the ballad, mainly by white singers, and the majority recorded after – in most cases long after – the 1920s. He notes that in spite of the fact that the contest is reputed to have taken place in the 1870s, no versions are known from before 1900, the presumed date of a white ballet circulated in Georgia and authorized by one W. T. Blankenship.

So it seems that the most popular, most widely noted and written about of all ballads was not prominent on Race record. Those songsters who chose to perform it frequently forgot salient verses and placed them in almost random order; the contest with the steam drill was hardly mentioned. Of most interest to the singers were the verses which stated either that "John Henry was a li'l boy" or "John Henry had a li'l baby" which you could "hold in the palm of your hands"and the verses that spoke of his woman who was "goin' where John Henry fell dead". It would seem that the traditional John Henry was no longer the kind of folk hero with whom singers wished to identify. To Richard Dorson the story "carried its overtones of social protest . . . John Henry pitted his massive strength with only a hammer and his bare hands against the white man's drill." Many other writers have made the same point, emphasizing John Henry's stature, his sexual prowess, and his heroic fight against the steam drill, which kills him: "In the fashion of so many legendary heroes it is the glory of his victory not the tragedy of his demise that dominates the songs", wrote Lawrence Levine. "He is the representative figure whose life and struggle are symbolic of the struggle of worker against machine, individual against society, the lowly against the powerful, black against white . . . it is this representative quality that gives his struggle epic proportions and makes John Henry the most important folk hero in Afro-American lore." [13] But the black singers on record seem not to have viewed him in that way. In Evans and McClain's version John Henry is a failed hero; one who was dwarfed by the task and "laid down his hammer and he cried". Rather than dying in a contest with a steam drill he "took sick" and "went to bed". Even allowing for the reduction of the ballad necessitated by the limitations of recording time, which accounts for the shift from addressing the shaker to John Henry's wife (traditionally named Polly Ann), this is an unheroic interpretation.

What happened to the heroic symbolism? Levine states that John Henry was a moral figure, whose life provided "models for action and emulation for other black people". But by the late twenties, and probably very much earlier, the model of moral living according to white society's values seems to have lost its appeal. John Henry as both hero and song came into being after the failure of Reconstruction, when the white South closed its ranks, the Jim Crow laws were enacted and lynchings rose to over a hundred a year. It was not a period when moral examples were likely to impress; on the contrary the examples were ones of brutality and summary punishment. Blacks found other heroes about whom to sing in this period, heroes – and heroines – that broke away from the accepted roles. John Henry's wife was one. Traditionally known as Polly Ann, she "drove steel like a man" when John Henry "took sick in the bed". As for John Henry, in Mississippi John Hurt's *Spike Driver Blues*, he left his hammer "layin' side the road" and simply walked off the job.[14] In taking up John Henry's hammer Polly Ann assumed a male role, challenging the norm. Similarly, the heroine of *Frankie and Albert*, one of the older and best-known of late nineteenth-century black ballads, took the law into her own hands. Three hundred versions were collected in text form by Robert W. Gordon, first curator of the Archive of folk music of the Library of Congress, and they probably refer to a number of incidents, some apocryphal. Though the identity of the participants, or even the locale, have never been established beyond doubt, the crime is generally associated with St. Louis. Some informants claimed to have heard the song as early as 1850, but the most authenticated story was reported by the *St. Louis Post-Dispatch* for October 20, 1899, when "an ebony-hued cake-walker", Frankie Baker, was locked up for stabbing her lover, the seventeen year old Allen Britt, "also colored", at their quarters in the rear of 212 Targee Street.[15] In most versions, however, Frankie shot her lover, Albert – as in Mississippi John Hurt's well-known *Frankie*, which followed the customary story closely. A "good girl", she paid a hundred dollars to buy her lover a suit of clothes. Later, looking through the keyhole of the "corner saloon" she spied Albert in "Alice's arms". She shot him three or four times but the judge ambiguously told her "You gonna be justified": it is not clear whether she was to be cleared on the grounds of justifiable homicide, or punished for her crime.

> Dark was the night, cold was on the ground,
> The last word I heard Frankie say, "I done laid ole Albert down"
> He was my man and he done me wrong.[16]

A farmer and occasional laborer from Teoc, Mississippi, John Hurt taught himself to play guitar at the age of ten in 1903. For some sixty years he played mainly for local dances, parties and picnics. His fellow Mississippian Charley Patton also recorded *Frankie and Albert* but in a confused version which suggests that both Albert and Frankie had committed a murder, and which concludes with Frankie's mother crying that her son is dying:

> Well Frankie went down to Albert's house, "How late Albert been here?"

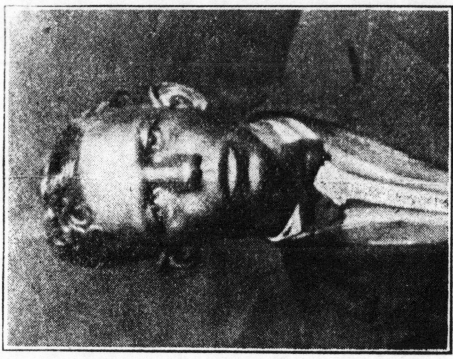

The Mississippi songster, lay preacher and blues singer, Charley Patton.

Walter "Furry" Lewis as he appeared in the 1927 Victor catalog.
Paul Oliver collection.

"Oh Albert's sittin' down in some cheap gal's lap, buyin' some cheap gal
    beer"
Say, he was my man but he done me wrong.

Well, Frankie went down to the courthouse, to hear little Albert's trial,
Oh, Albert was convicted, Frankie hung her head and cried,
Say, he was my man, but he done me wrong.

"Say you remember on last Sunday, twentieth day of May,
You 'buked me and you cursed me, Oh baby all that day"
Say, he was my man but he done me wrong.

Tell you, it's some gonna give you a nickel and it's some gonna give you
    a dime,
But I'm gonna [kill your scoulin'] face, for I know you was a man of
    mine.
Kill 'er man – go kill 'er man.

Well Frankie went to the cemetery, fell down on her knees,
"Oh Lord, will you forgive me, and give my poor heart ease?
Say, he was my man, but he done me wrong."

Well Frankie's mother come runnin', come a whoopin', screamin' and
    cryin'
"Oh Lord, oh Lord, my only son is dyin',
She kill' er man, Judge, she kill' 'er man."[17]

By the more popular title of *Frankie and Johnny* the song was recorded by
Nick Nichols; made in Dallas with, probably, Alex Moore playing piano and
Blind Norris McHenry guitar, it gave a fuller account presented in two
"scenes". As befits a Texan interpretation, there are hints of *The Dying
Cowboy* in the words, which also overlap with *St. James Infirmary*. The
thirteen-verse song ended with a cheerfully amoral note and a glimpse of a
Frankie notably lacking in contrition. After hearing at the bootlegger's shop
on Second Avenue that Johnny had "a brand new gal",

Frankie went over to the pawnshop, she got herself a brand new .44,
Walked right up to the bar of the bootlegger's shop, shot her man right
    in the door,
He was her man but he done her wrong.

Says now "Roll me over Frankie, roll me over slow,
Roll me over honey, for them bullets hurt me so,
I was your man but I done you wrong."

Says six big rubber-tired carriages and one great big long black hack,
Took ol' Johnny to the graveyard but they never brought him back.
He was her man but he done her wrong.

An exultant Frankie bought herself some gin "'cause I done killed that so-
and-so man of mine. I'm gonna shimmy some shim-shim", and, drunk and
shimmying on the floor, she called "Let that music professor let that shimmy
go on." Unfortunately,

A great big six-foot policeman came down, and brought her by the hand,
Says, "The county jail wants to see you about shootin' your lovin' man,
He was your man why did he do you wrong."

Says the Judge looked right at Frankie, says "Gal what have you done?
Do you know you been drinkin' that doggone gin, you done killed your
        lovin' man?"
He was your man, why did he do you wrong?"

But after explaining to the judge that her man "had another woman named
Nellie Fry",

Frankie, she started to shimmy, and the judge begin to smile,
Says "My Golly, she's a pippin, oh, she's my angel chile,
I'll be her man and I won't do her wrong."

With different lyrics *Frankie and Albert* had been published in 1912 as
Frankie and Johnny, by the vaudeville entertainers Ren Fields and the
Leighton Brothers.[18] Undoubtedly its popularity in this form was greatly
enhanced by their performances and sheet music, at least among whites, but
Nick Nicholls's version was independent of theirs. Its tongue-in-cheek
amorality would have appealed at a time when blacks believed that they had
little justice in the courts and had often found that pretending naiveté, or
repentance (or in this case shimmying before the judge) was as likely to turn
the case in their favor, as any attorney's pleading.

If there was an excuse for Frankie's committing her crime, and implicit
sympathy for her, the depredations of Stack O'Lee (Stackolee, Stagolee,
Stack-O-Lee) did not receive the same amused tolerance. But neither were
they censured; Stack O'Lee was a bad man, a ruthless killer, but in the songs he
was regarded with awe, and a certain detachment. The origins of the Stack
O'Lee narratives and ballads are unclear, and Richard Buehler's inquiry did
not precisely identify the source of them. The original Stacker Lee was the son
of Jim Lee, founder in 1866 of the celebrated Lee Line of riverboats on the
Mississippi. Jim Lee named his boats after his sons, so that Stacker Lee was
also the name of the third of a fleet that eventually, by the turn of the century,
numbered fourteen. Stacker Lee had been a cavalryman in the Confederate
Army who fathered several sons of young black women, of whom one,
according to Shields McIlwaine, was "a short black fellow, a cabin boy on the
Anchor Line . . . a black with a bad eye" and a killer, Stack Lee. Though
credited with a number of killings including one reportedly in San Francisco in
April 1906, it was the shooting of one Billy Lyons which is normally recounted
in the ballads. *Stackolee* ballads are recalled from before 1900 and by 1911
Howard Odum had published variants collected not only in the Mississippi
Valley but also in Alabama and Georgia.[19] Papa Harvey Hull and Long Cleve
Reed were singers who may have come from the Alabama/Mississippi border;
Reed played guitar, accompanied also on guitar in a well-integrated and
accomplished version of the song, *Original Stack O'Lee Blues*. Though the

names of the participants at one point clearly should have been reversed, the song indicates the fear with which the "bully" was held, without bringing him to account.

> Stack O'Lee was a bully, he bullied all his life,
> He bullied two, three coppers down with a ten-cent pocket knife,
>   Well it's cruel Stack O'Lee.

> Stack said to Billy, 'How can it be, you arrest a man as bad as me, (oh,
>   bad man)
> But you won't 'rest Stack O'Lee.
>   Well it's cruel Stack O'Lee   (oh, bad man)

> Stack said to Billy, "Don't you take my life,
> Well I ain't got but two li'l children and a darlin' lovin' wife,"
>   Well it's cruel Stack O'Lee.

> "One is a boy and the other is a girl",
> "You may see your children again but it'll be in another world."
>   Well it's cruel Stack O'Lee.

> Standing on the corner, well I didn't mean no harm.
> Well a policeman caught me, well he grabbed me by my arm
>   Well, it's cruel Stack O'Lee.

> Stack O'Lee and Billy had an awful fight,
> Well Stack O'Lee killed Billy Lyons one cold dark stormy night.
>   Well it's cruel Stack O'Lee.

> Standing on the hill-top, the dogs begin to bark,
> Well it wasn't nothin' but Stack O'Lee come creepin' in the dark
>   Well it's cruel Stack O'Lee.[20]

In this version Billy appears to have been a policeman, but Furry Lewis identified the cause of the killing as a dispute over a gambling loss, which occurred "one September, on one Friday night" when,

> Billy Lyons shot six bits, Stack O'Lee bet, he passed –
> Stack O'Lee out with his forty-five, says "You done shot your last,
>   When you lose your money, learn to lose"[21]   (refrain)

In another version by John Hurt, though several verses are similar to those sung by Reed and Hull, the cause of the shooting was the theft of the bad man's hat. To the entreaties of Billy "the Lion", he answered,

> "What do I care about your two little babies, your darlin' lovin' wife?
> You done stole my Stetson hat, I'm bound to take your life"
>   That bad man, cruel Stack O'Lee.

Only in John Hurt's narrative does Stack O'Lee suffer retribution for his killings when

> Standin' on the gallows, head way up high,
> At twelve o'clock they killed him, they's all glad to see him die.
>   That bad man, cruel Stack O'Lee.

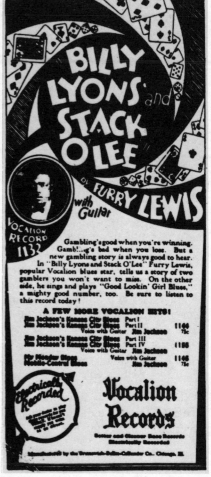

The display for *John Henry* by Henry Thomas also advertized popular records by
Reverend A. W. Nix and Reverend Edward W. Clayborn.

Billy Lyons and Stack O'Lee by Furry Lewis was advertized in *The Chicago
Defender* for April 21, 1928. Jim Jackson's *My Monday Blues* was also listed.
Paul Oliver collection.

"Gentlemen's of the jury, what do you think of that?
Stack O'Lee killed Billy the Lyon about a 5 dollar Stetson hat.
    That bad, oh cruel, Stack O'Lee."[22]

Like the recordings by Furry Lewis and Hull/Reed his had extremely fluent
and practiced playing, developed, one suspects, many years before and
repeated on innumerable occasions. The smoothness of these performances
suggests that they were virtually second nature to the songsters, while the slips
of verse order and sometimes of sense, as in the transposition of names, may

have arisen from their ceasing to regard the ballads as logical narratives.

Other singers, notably Gertrude "Ma" Rainey, and the lesser-known Evelyn Thompson, both recorded versions of *Stack O'Lee* as it was performed on the vaudeville stage, Ma Rainey's being sung to the tune of *Frankie and Albert* and the lyrics confused with it:

> Stack O'Lee wept all night, turned his face to the wall,
> Dirty women and raw corn whiskey was the cause of it all,
>   He was her man, and he doin' her wrong.[23]

In these, however, the awe with which the callousness of the killer was held was tempered by justifying his criminal activities.

If Stack O'Lee remained a shadowy and uncertain figure, the subject of *Railroad Bill* was an authentic historic character. Morris Slater, a native of Escambia County, Alabama, was a turpentine worker in the pine forests. Carrying a gun in town one day in 1893 he was challenged by a policeman, whom he shot before making his escape by hopping a freight train. During the next couple of years he was credited with many daring raids on trains on the L & N and other lines, and several killings. Traced to a house near Bluff Springs in July 1895, he was fired on by Sheriff E. S. McMillan and two deputies; "Railroad Bill", as he was now known, suffered no injury but Sheriff McMillan fell with a bullet through the heart. Many hold-ups and shootings were attributed to Railroad Bill during the ensuing months. Then in March 1897 he was ambushed at Tidmore and Ward's General Store, Atmore by two white men, who blasted half his head away and collected $1250 for their prize. As Norm Cohen has indicated the stories are conflicting and justification for the murder of Railroad Bill may have been sought by exaggerating his villainy.[24]

Railroad Bill was the bad man/hero who was admired and feared by the black community; the outlaw on whom could be projected the challenge to the dominant whites which, in a troubled time, they were too frightened to make themselves. Over thirty years after Morris Slater's death an unknown songster, Will Bennett, was recorded in Knoxville, Tennessee. His version of *Railroad Bill* unconsciously transfers the narrative from the outlaw as the subject of the ballad to a fixation on the weapons he amassed and an image of himself as the outlaw hero.

> Railroad Bill, ought to be killed,
> Never worked and he never will,
>   Now I'm gonna ride my Railroad Bill.
>
> Railroad Bill done took my wife,
> That don't mean that he would take my life.
>   Now I'm gonna ride   etc.
>
> Goin' up on the mountain, take my chance,
> .41 Derringer in my right and left hand.
>   Now I'm gonna ride   etc.

Goin' up on the mountain, goin' out West,
.41 gun just stickin' in my breast.
    Now I'm gonna ride   etc.

Buy me a gun just as long as my arm,
Kill everybody ever done me wrong.
    Now I'm gonna ride   etc.

Buy me a gun with a shiny barrel,
Kill somebody 'bout my good lookin' gal.
    Now I'm gonna ride   etc.

Got a .38 Special on a .44 frame,
How in the world can I miss him when I got dead aim.
    Now I'm gonna ride   etc.

Will Bennett's interpretation of the song has several more verses, but these are dissociated from the main theme. In his concluding stanza he stated "I'm goin' to the World in the Natchez Queen," making an oblique reference to the World's Fair, held in St. Louis in 1904; an indication at least, of the age of some of the verses he was using, and very probably the relatively advanced age of the singer himself.[25]

Many ballads that survived emphasized the exploits of a personality with whom singer and listener alike could feel some bond. There was undoubtedly a considerable measure of admiration for the outlaws and bullies who challenged the established white social mores at a time when these were so markedly to the disadvantage of the black population.

Publication of ballads may have played some part in shaping those performed on disc but they seldom directly derived from them. Sheet music of traditional songs got into general circulation quickly and could have fixed their form. Instead, they appear to have aided their persistence as popular themes which were remodeled to suit the taste of individual songsters, and which were adapted to local conditions or events. Mention has been made of the Leighton Brothers who, with Ren Fields, found a lucrative occupation in copyrighting folk ballads or writing in the same idiom. These included a pseudo ballad, *Steamboat Bill*, in 1910 and *Frankie and Johnny* two years later. Even earlier, in 1909, they featured on stage *Casey Jones (The Brave Engineer)* which told the story of the death of its hero railroader, modestly claimed by the composers T. Lawrence Siebert and Eddie Newton to be the "Greatest. Comedy Hit in Years; The Only Comedy Railroad Song".[26] Already it had been the subject of some debate as a ballad, being published in *Railroad Man's Magazine* the year before. Within the next couple of years many versions, and many conflicting accounts, both as to the identity of the original engineer and the accident in which he lost his life, were published. An exhaustive examination by Norm Cohen revealed two major lineages for the song though many others were related to it. Nevertheless, for a period it was extremely popular. "During the winter of 1908–9", wrote Perrow, "I found the State of Mississippi full of versions of a song, very popular then, called Casey Jones." But Howard Odum, who had published a version in 1911, writing again in 1926 published a version "somewhat below par", remarking that "Casey Jones is still heard occasionally"[27] with the obvious implication that its one-time popularity was fast waning.

The original ballad of *Casey Jones* is most frequently attributed to a black roundhouse cleaner at Canton, Mississippi, named Wallace Saunders. He it was who cleaned the Engine 382 after John Luther "Cayce" (or Casey) Jones ploughed his great "Cannonball Express" into the back of a freight train on the double curve at Vaughan, a dozen miles from Canton. Jones told his fireman, Sim Webb, who survived the crash, to jump clear, but was himself killed in the wreck.[28] Though it was recorded by white singers including Fiddling John Carson, Riley Puckett and Uncle Dave Macon, only one black singer in the 1920s – Furry Lewis – recorded it. *Kassie Jones*, a two-part ballad, drew on *I'm a Natu'al Bohn Eastman* (as collected by Odum before 1911) and made an oblique reference to a more obscure ballad, *Stavin' Chain*.

I woke up this morning, four o'clock,
Mr. Kassie tol' his fireman get his boiler hot;
"Put on your water, put on your coal,
Put your head out the window, see my drivers roll –
   See my drivers roll,
   Put your head out the window, see my drivers roll."

Lord some people said Mr. Kassie couldn't run,
Let me tell you what Mr. Kassie done,
He left Memphis, was a quarter to nine,
Got to Newport News, it was dinner time,
   It was dinner time,
   Got to Newport News, it was dinner time.

Lord people said to Kassie "You're runnin' over time
You'll have another loser with the 1.0.9."
Mr. Kassie said, "Ain't in mind,
If I run any closer, I'll make my time."
Said "All the passengers better keep themselves hid,
I'm nach'al gon' shake it like Chainey did,
   Like Chainey did,
   I'm nat'al gon' shake it like Chainey did.

Mrs. Kassie said she dreamt a dream,
The night she bought a sewing machine,
The needle got broke and she could not sew.
She loved Mr. Kassie 'cause she told me so,
   Told me so,
   She loved Mr. Kassie 'cause she told me so.

Kassie looked at his water, the water was low,
Looked at his watch, the watch was slow,
   On the road again,
   Nach'al born Eastman, on the road again.

Lord the people tell by the throttle moans,
The man at the fire, Mr. Kassie Jones –
   Mr. Kassie Jones.

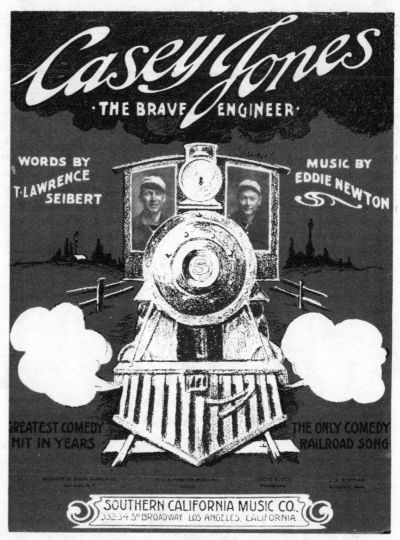

T. Lawrence Siebert and Eddie Newton Popularized several ballads, including *Casey Jones*, published in California in 1909.   *Paul Oliver collection.*

An exchange between Mrs. Kassie and her children somewhat cynically concluded with "Children, children, won't you hold your breath, draw another pension from your father's death". Lewis ended with a verse that brought himself back into the story and which declared his own independence from the values of the "good old engineer".

> I left Memphis to spread the news –
> Memphis women don't wear no shoes.
> Had it written on the back of my shirt

"Nach'al born Eastmen, don't have to work"
Don't have to work,
Nach'al born Eastmen, don't have to work.[29]

The Eastman, or "easeman" was a hustler who lived by his wits and most often, as a pimp. Perhaps because the principal figure was white, perhaps because he died at the throttle straining to make up time, Casey Jones seems not to have been an enduring hero-figure in black ballads compared with the popularity of the engineer in white songs. If the moral of the story to some white singers was a reckless attention to duty, Furry Lewis's insouciant final stanza made it quite clear where he stood.

There were others who were less than enamoured with the values that Casey Jones's death was seen to represent. An Atlanta singer, Waymon "Sloppy" Henry made a *Hobo Blues* which placed himself rather than Casey Jones in the center of the picture. His song was closely related to Gus Horsley's *J. C. Holmes Blues* – an obvious pun on "Casey Jones" – recorded some years before by Bessie Smith. Several parodies of *Casey Jones* were composed like *Casey Jones Went Down On the Robert E. Lee* written by Marvin Lee and Clarence Jones in 1912. One was recorded by the Louisville Jug Band leader and street entertainer, Earl McDonald. It bore a slender relationship to the Lee–Jones composition, but effectively parodied two songs by the Leighton Brothers and Ren Fields and made a socio-political comment of its own. *Casey Bill* was an amusing combination of the two stories describing a race when:

Now, down the river came Steamboat Bill,
Spied Casey Jones comin' over the hill,
The engine was puffin' and the boiler was hot,
While the coons on board done the Turkey Trot.
Railroad run alongside the bank,
Casey crawled out from behind the tank.
Bill said to Casey "If you're a racin' man,
Get up your steam, an' go as fast as you can."
Now Casey 'n' Bill, down the Mississippi,
Casey 'n' Bill, all full of glee
Casey 'n' Bill, down the Mississippi,
Tryin' to break the record of the Robert E. Lee.

Inevitably, before them was a bridge which Casey's train had to cross. When the riverboat collided with it: "the race was over, and it was a tie".

Now in the wreck, it was a shame, was no one that knew their name.
When their wives got the message their husbands was dead,
They both raised the river with the tears they shed.
The little kids didn't seem to bother
When someone told they had lost their father,
One said to the other "don't cry and fret,
We don't need no daddy, Ma's a suffragette . . ."[30]

Specific events, known or believed to have taken place, were the source for most of the earlier ballads, but as the first decades of the present century unfolded ballad-making declined even though the nature of current events was dramatic. What was significant to the society at large was not necessarily perceived by the songster in the same way; if he did compose a ballad he was more likely to use a local happening for his theme. But, in fact, very few original ballads appeared on Race records and these were mainly fragmentary: like Henry Thomas's *Bob McKinney* or Mississippi John Hurt's *Louis Collins* which recounted that "Bob shot once and Louis shot two, they shot poor Collins, shot him through and through" but did not identify who Bob was, nor the reason for their duel, nor when or where the incident occurred.[31]

One ballad among those recorded stands apart, *Mystery of the Dunbar's Child* performed by Richard "Rabbit" Brown, a songster born before 1890, in the James Alley turpentine distillery district of New Orleans. To a resonant guitar accompaniment he described in his deep and gritty voice a kidnapping which took place at a country picnic on a local lake resort at Opelousas, Louisiana in August 1912. Two local children, Bobby and Conrad Dunbar wandered away from the function, Conrad eventually returning alone:

> Y' know they searched and searched for miles around
> Almost the whole night long,
> No one couldn't imagine
> Where poor Bobby Dunbar's gone.
> So they drag the lake and they dynamite
> Almost the whole next day,
> Until someone had suspicion
> Some kidnapper taken Bobby away.

The Dunbar parents were agonized by the loss of their child –

> For months and months they looked and listened
> To hear something of their boy,
> And at last they heard about Walter's child
> That he called his pride and joy.
> They were summoned to Hub, Mississippi,
> You know that little country town,
> And everyone shouted out with joy
> So glad that Bobby had been found.

Walter was taken to Opelousas jail, protesting his innocence: "If I could see the Governor face to face I'm sure he would set me free." He hoped to find his erst-while wife to prove the child was hers, "I pray she's not dead; you can picture their resemblance, from his feet up to his head." But,

> The jurymen found him guilty
> And the clerk he wrote it down.
> The judge passed the sentence,
> Penitentiary he was bound.
> He was brought for safe keeping

To dear old New Orleans.
There he appealed for a new trial
Through the Court of Supreme.

Eventually, sang Rabbit Brown, fifteen years later, "I'm glad to tell you all that Walter is now a free man"; one whom, it may be assumed from the transfer to New Orleans for "safe keeping", was fortunate to escape a lynching.[32]

Mystery of the Dunbar's Child was singular in that no other ballad on the subject has been collected either in the field or recorded by another singer. Structured on traditional ballad lines, it had clearly marked stanzas. More significantly, the events were described in a sequential narrative. Compared with many ballads by songsters both black and white, this adherence to the traditional form was already somewhat unusual at the time of recording. A number of songs have been identified as "blues ballads" by D. K. Wilgus, Marina Bokelman and others. As summarized by Norm Cohen, a blues ballad is one "with little or no evidence for coherent and complete antecedent narrative ballads" which are "persistent among both whites and blacks". They "tell a story in a very loose, subjective manner", David Evans has observed, and "tend to 'celebrate' events rather than relate them chronologically and objectively in the manner of other American folk ballads".[33]

Hence, the blues ballad in these terms does not bear a relation to the blues form but to the tendency in some blues to use the single stanza as the thematic core and to couple a number of other stanzas sometimes, but not always, loosely related to it. Blues verses are often sung as a succession of discrete, encapsulated comments on a situation rather than as a narrative. The singer perceives the theme less as a linear progression and more as a nodal point, on or around any aspect of which he may make observations in any verse order.

In view of the structural differences from the blues and the fact that the nodal approach may not have been influenced by (or have influenced) the methods of blues composition, the term is rather misleading; "nodal ballad" as distinct from "sequential ballad" is probably more appropriate.

An example of this form of nodal ballad is *The Midnight Special*, a prison song known in penitentiaries in many parts of the South. One stanza fragment which relates to the song was noted by Howard Odum about 1905 and published in his 1911 collection. Others were gathered by Robert Gordon from various informants around 1923, the date of a Houston jail-break which was the focus of versions sung in Texas. A detailed *dramatis personae* of the Texas song, especially as it was sung later by Leadbelly, was compiled by Mack McCormick.

Other explanations of the song include the widespread belief that prisoners were permitted conjugal visits in Southern penitentiaries: "Convicts who had been outstanding during the week were rewarded on Sunday by a visit from Memphis prostitutes who boarded a train in Memphis at Midnight Saturday; hence the title of the song."[34] This theme was reflected in Sam Collins's

Midnight Special Blues which included a verse that related to Odum's collected stanza. In his shrill, crying voice he referred to the blazing headlight of the engine as it illuminated the dormitories of the penitentiary and made succinct comments on the monotony of penitentiary confinement and the visit of "Miss Norah":

> Let the Midnight Special
> Shine its lights on me,
> Let the Midnight Special
> Shine its ever-lovin' lights on me.
>
> When you get up in the mornin'
> When the ding-dong ring – Lordy
> You make it to the table,
> See the same old thing.
> Ain't nothin' on the table,
> But the pots and the pans – Lordy
> Say anything about it,
> Have trouble with the Man.
>   Let the Midnight Special,   etc.
>
> Yonder comes Miss Norah
> "How do you know?"
> "I know her by her apron,
> And the dress she wear,"
> Umbrella on her shoulder
> Piece of paper in her hand
> Gonna ask some sergeant,
> To release her man.[35]

Though *The Midnight Special* was a nodal ballad, which in this form did not describe a specific incident, its basis was firmly in the reality of twentieth-century life, at least as perceived by a particular sector of the community. Such realities were not necessarily the stuff of heroic ballads, nor of songs of suffering or the endurance of the harsh conditions of plantation or penitentiary. Sometimes they reflected the qualities perceived in aspects of rural experience, such as those vicariously enjoyed in the free spirit of a hunting dog like the half-mythical "Tige", "Rattler" or "Blue". Another nodal ballad, *Come On Blue*, was collected in Mississippi by one of E. C. Perrow's informants, W. P. Cassedy in 1909 and in the Carolinas, subsequently, by Frank C. Brown.[36] Jim Jackson's praise-song to the hunting dog included stanzas that were identical to those collected in the field:

> Old Blue's feet was big and round,   (2)
> Never 'llowed a possum to tetch the ground.
>
> Me and Blue went out on a hunt,
> Blue treed a possum in a holler stump.
> You know Blue was a good old dog.
> Blue treed a possum in a holler log,
> You know from that he's a good old dog.

Songster Jim Jackson. His recordings comprise the fullest documentation of black song from early in the century. *Paul Oliver collection.*

When Old Blue died and I dug his grave,
I dug his grave with a silver spade,
I let him down with a golden chain.
And every link I called his name,
Go on Blue, you good dog you. (2)

Blue laid down and died like a man, (2)
Now he's treein' possum in the Promis' Land.

I'm goin' to tell you this to let you know
Old Blue's gone where the good dogs go . . .[37]

One of the most important black nodal ballads was not about a human hero, nor an event, nor even a pet animal but about an unremarkable brownish-black beetle a mere quarter-inch long, the boll weevil. After ravaging cotton in Mexico the weevil entered Texas in 1892, soon damaging crops there. Settling on the cotton "square", or bud, it deposited its larva which hatched to consume the boll from within. By 1903 the weevil had reached Louisiana where the crop was reduced by three-quarters in 1908. That year it entered Mississippi where the crop was halved for the next ten years; the effects were even more disastrous in Alabama and Georgia. In the latter state the impact on the black farm population was severe, as a quarter of a million sharecroppers and members of their families quit during the next ten years.[38] It was a small, brown, ubiquitous insect; a pest, but one with which blacks in the many collected versions of *The Ballad of the Boll Weevil* appear to have identified. Its indestructibility, its covert behavior, attacking the white crop from within had its symbolic appeal, even if the losses the farmers suffered were transmitted to their 'croppers.

The date of the ballad is uncertain; Gates Thomas claimed to have noted it in Texas as early as 1907 and it was collected by John A. Lomax as *The Ballit of the Boll Weevil* from transported Mississippi workers on the Brazos River in Texas in 1908; but Newman White quoted half a dozen versions collected in Alabama between 1915 and 1916. Dorothy Scarborough also quoted one in her autobiography *From A Southern Porch*, published in 1919, and in 1925 quoted others. Lizzie Coleman, a Greenville Mississippi teacher in a black school wrote that "*The Boll Weevil* was composed by a man in Merivale, I believe. It is like many other ballads written by men in this state. The tune is made, the writer sings it and sells his song. His hearers catch the sound – and on it goes."[39] This was doubtless true for one version, but there were *Boll Weevil* ballads in every Southern state. Yet it seems there were virtually no versions in ballad form on Race records; perhaps the nearest was Charley Patton's succession of two-line stanzas, *Mississippi Boweavil Blues*, in which "the square" referred to the cotton "boll"; the "forty" was a forty-acre farm plot;

> It's a little bo weevil she's movin' in the [air] Lordy –
> You can plant your cotton and you won't get half a bale, Lordy –
>
> "Bo weevil, bo weevil where's your native home?" Lordy –
> "A-Louisiana, live in Texas, is a-where I was bred and born", Lordy
>
> Well I saw the bo weevil Lord, a-circle, Lordy, in the air, Lordy
> The next time I seed him Lord, he had his family there, Lordy
>
> Bo weevil left Texas, Lord he bid me "Fare ye well", Lordy (where you
>   goin' now?)
> "I'm goin' down in Mississippi, gonna give Loosiana hell", Lordy
>
> Bo weevil said to the farmer, "Ain't gotta treat you fair", Lordy (How
>   is that, boy?)
> "Suck all the blossom and leave, you have the square", Lordy

Next time I see you, you had your family there, Lordy.

Bo weevil met his wife "We can sit down on the hill", Lordy
Bo weevil told his wife "Let's take this forty in", Lordy

Bo weevil told his wife says "I believe I may go north", Lordy (Boy,
    I'm gonna tell all about that)
"Let's leave Loosiana, we can go to Arkansas" Lordy[40]

Probably as a result of the interest of folk song collectors like the Lomaxes, the *Ballad of the Boll Weevil* was recorded more frequently in later years in the sixteen-bar ballad form, but the words of the ballad were readily assimilated in the blues. A somewhat colorless version was recorded by Charlie "Dad" Nelson, believed to be a Texas singer, who played twelve-string guitar and kazoo, with which he introduced the theme;

"Bo weevil, bo weevil, where did you come from?" (2)
"From Beaumont, Texas, I'm just over here on a farm."

Farmer says to the bo weevil, "Don't you know you done me
    wrong? (2)
Eat up all my cotton and eat up all my corn?"

Says "I'm goin' to town, buy me a lil gasoline, (2)
He's the worst bo weevil b'lieve that I ever seen."[41]

Here, at least, the term blues-ballad might be accurately applied, for the blues had a ballad theme, and was clearly adapted from the ballad. In the sense employed by Wilgus it was also non-narrative, focussed on a dialogue with the weevil rather than a sequence of events related to the damage caused by its voracious appetite.

Yet there are several examples on record of ballad themes, narrating a story line which are in the twelve-bar, three-line structure of the established blues idiom. A remarkable example is *Old Timbrook Blues* recorded by John Byrd, an associate of Walter Taylor, the leader of a washboard band. It was a ballad blues about a horse race; an actual event which, however, took place over fifty years before. On July 4, 1878, the last four-mile heat race was held at Louisville, Kentucky when the mare Miss Mollie McCarthy lost to Ten Broeck, ridden by the jockey Billy Walker, who was black. Before a crowd of 40,000 Ten Broeck won in 8 minutes, 19 seconds in sweltering heat. Years after the race, in 1884, the ballad of Mollie and Ten Broeck was apparently in circulation in Kentucky. Occasionally thereafter, collectors noted the ballad of *Ten Broeck*, the "race horse, slick as any mole; diamond in the forehead, shines like a diamond and gold".[42] John Byrd's *Old Timbrook Blues* was in twelve-bar form, but it kept to the story,

Ol' Timbrook was a black horse, black as any crow, (2)
Had a white ring round his forepaws, white as any snow.

Yes Old Timbrook he come dartin' like a bullet from a gun, (2)
And Old Mollie she come a creepin' like a prisoner to be hung.

"Johnny Walker, Johnny Walker, Johnny Walker my dear son,   (2)
Hold tight rein on Timbrook so that horse could run."

Oh the cuckoo was a fine bird, hollers when he flies,   (2)
But he never hollers "cuckoo" till the fourth day of July.

Oh the race track it was dusty and the wind was high,   (2)
Well you couldn't see old Timbrook as he come dartin' by.

Oh, the children they did holler and the old folks squalled,   (2)
But Old Timbrook he beat Mollie to the Hole in the Wall.

I love my race horse I like to have my fun,   (2)
Old Missus went to the racetrack and lost all her mon'.[43]

Louisville, Kentucky was the recording location of another ballad of possible local origin, recorded by Kid Coley with, probably, the Louisville jug band leader Clifford Hayes playing violin. *Clair and Pearley Blues* might have been based on the murder in Cincinnati of Pearl Bryan by her lover Scott Jackson and his accomplice Alonzo Walling in 1896. The girl was beheaded, though her head was never found.[44] Jilson Setters, a white Kentucky singer, composed a ballad on *The Murder of Pearl Bryan*, but its eight-line stanzas bear no relation to Kid Coley's song which, Coley claimed on the record, was his own:

Now come listen people, while I sing one song, so lonesome and so blue,
Now come listen people while I sing one sad song
'Bout two girls I really knowed well and I haven't composed it wrong.

It was on one Friday between midnight and day, so lonesome and so
          blue,   (2)
That Clair and Peal, Matthew Kelly laid these two girls away.

Now Clair and Pearl lay down to go to sleep in their lonesome bed I
          mean,   (2)
Matthew Kelly walked up, and through their back door did creep.

But she had a butcher knife some dirty work to do, so lonesome and so
          blue,   (2)
He's glad he had the hatchet, said "I swear I'm gonna fix both of you too."

Finally Matthew Kelly approached them, found the girls asleep, (in their
          lonesome bed I mean)
Matthew Kelly buried the hatchet in poor Clair's head deep.

Matthew Kelly walked to the electric chair with his hair combed out in a
          curl, (so lonesome and so blue)   (2)
Try on a brand new suit of clothes Matthew said "It will be the last I
          try on in this world."

Now if anybody should happen to ask you who in the world wrote such
          a sad song, (so lonesome, etc.)   (2)
Tell 'em it was Kid Coley and he never composed it wrong; – and it was
          no lie.[45]

Like Rabbit Brown's *Dunbar Child*, Kid Coley's *Clair and Pearley Blues* was not collected in the field. Another ballad of this type, *Betty and Dupree*, or simply *Dupree*, however, was noted by Odum and Johnson and published by them in 1926 as a "current story". They noted that it could be compared with *Frank Dupree*, a white ballad to be heard in Atlanta. Versions had been "taken" from Asheville, North Carolina and other places in Georgia and North Carolina, in all cases, in the twelve-bar blues form. It had been composed by a white street newspaper seller and evangelist, Andrew Jenkins. Born in Jenkinsburg, Atlanta in 1888, he was a prolific composer of ballads and religious songs; his *Frank Dupree* was based on the fate of a local murderer who was hanged for his crime in Atlanta on September 4, 1922.[46] The ballad was picked up by Willie Walker, who was the most celebrated guitarist in South Carolina. Also a blind man, he was born in 1896 and, shortly before World War I, was the lead musician in the Greenville String Band, which also included Blind Gary Davis. Greatly admired by Josh White, Gary Davis and Pink Anderson, Blind Willie Walker made only one record. But though he died in 1933, a tape of his *Dupree Blues* "literally opened doors and loosened tongues" when Bruce Bastin did research in Greenville thirty-six years later.[47] Walker sang:

> Betty told Dupree "I wants me a diamond ring" (2) (oh baby)
> "Now listen mama your daddy bring you most anything."
>
> He had to kill a policeman and he wound a detective too, (oh sugar)
> Killed a detective, wounded a policeman too, (oh babe)
> "See here mama, what you caused me to do."
>
> Hired him a taxi, said "Can't you drive me back to Main, (2) (say
> taxi)
> I've done a hangin' crime yet I don't never feel ashamed."
>
> Rested poor Dupree, placed him in the jail, (2) (oh Lord)
> He heard the mean old judge, went and refuse to sign him any bail.
>
> Wrote a letter to Betty, and this is the way the letter read, (2) (oh
> baby)
> "Come home to daddy, I'm almost dead."
>
> Betty went to the jailer, cryin' "Mister Jailer please, (2) (oh baby)
> Please Mister Jailer, let me see my used-to-be."[48]

Clearly this had some narrative order, and so did a variant by a more obscure singer, Kingfish Bill Tomlin, on which "Betty" sounded more like "Bertie" perhaps an abbreviation for Albertina. It shared the opening stanza but was different in its subsequent story:

> I went down Decatur Street, stepped inside a jewelry store (2)
> And a shot from my pistol, I went down there no more.
>
> "If you didn't want me Bertie, y' had no right to lie (2)
> Cause the day you leave me I swear that's the day you'll die."
>
> She said "Please Mister Dupree, change your name again, (2)
> At the end of this you might wind in the pen."
>
> He says "That's all right Bertie, all right the way you do, (2)

It was late las' night, y'know when I stole this ring for you."
"So I'm locked here in jail with my back turned to the wall,   (2)
An' you know Miss Bertie that you the cause of it all." [49]

Though the sequence is more compressed there still is continuity in this balladic-blues, as is the case with others of the genre.

   Old Timbrook Blues, Clair and Pearley Blues and *Dupree Blues* all have considerable sequential flow and the disconnected character of the nodal ballad certainly does not apply to them. Definitely in twelve-bar blues form, these balladic blues do not easily fit into the conventional view of the black ballad; though Dupree may be representative of the "bad man" ballad hero, he does not assume any heroic stature. Timbrook's rider, Billy Walker, could have been a black hero, but apart from identifying him as the jockey, the rest of the blues ballad is centered on the horse. There seems no special identification with Matthew Kelly either; his last gesture is not defiant enough to inspire admiration, not tragic enough to provoke sympathy. If they do not accord with Lawrence Levine's "epic figure, a culture hero whose exploits are performed in the name of the entire race",[50] they do correspond to the casual accounts of John Henry or Frankie on record.

   Old Timbrook Blues seems to have been based on a white original, but it does relate to an incident which was only a few years after the presumed date of John Henry's death in the C & O tunnel. Apart from these two ballads the events which the others record are much later: *Railroad Bill* in 1897, *Frankie and Albert*, 1899, *Stack O'Lee* perhaps at much the same time, the *Bo Weevil Ballad* after 1905, *The Titanic* after 1912. This makes them concurrent with the ragtime songs and the emergence of the blues, rather than being precursors of blues.

   Several of the ballads that were most popular with blacks were of a two-line and refrain form. Frequently, too, they were in a twelve-bar sequence with a chordal progression that was similar to blues. As I have suggested elsewhere, it seems likely that this musical frame influenced the hardening of the familiar twelve-bar blues form, combined with the more free-ranging improvisations of the field holler.

   Most early recordings of blues are of the nodal type, with several verses loosely drawn to a theme stated in one stanza; narrative, sequential blues may well have been influenced by composers of blues songs, by the requirements of record executives for blues with more of a story line, or simply the result of experimentation by the blues singers themselves. As many of the ballads that were popular among blacks at the time when blues was taking shape were also of a nodal type, this may have been a general tendency; it is one to be noted in many white ballads of the period also.

   There were many other ballads collected in the field which were not represented on Race records: *John Hardy, Batson, Bugger Burns, Po' Lazarus, Joe Mica, Bad Land Stone* among them. On record, they were more often to be found in the white "Favorite Songs" and "Hillbilly" lists. There is a strong possibility that ballads generally considered to be black were, in a number of instances, the work originally of white composers, remaining in the white tradition for years after they had been discarded by black songsters. Others were very likely of black origin, but continued to be popular with white songsters, the appeal of a good tune and a strong theme transcending race barriers. But the precise origin of many ballads must remain contentious. As many white and black songsters worked together in medicine shows and rural picnics and functions, they inevitably picked up or exchanged the songs of their respective cultural groups.

Indications of the factors that had bearing on the inclusion of ballads among their recordings, whether they were songsters who traveled or who stayed at home, are to be found in the experiences of typical performers. Two songsters who contributed a number of examples of ballads were Walter "Furry" Lewis and "Mississippi" John Hurt. In his early years, Lewis led a restless life working with traveling stock companies, doctor shows and with jug bands in Memphis. His range of songs reflects diversity of the contexts in which he played and the popularity of certain items; it also indicates those which he had learned to play effortlessly and was at ease with when making his records, among them it will be recalled, *Billy Lyons and Stack O'Lee*, *Kassie Jones* and *John Henry*. John Hurt on the other hand, lived all his life in a Mississippi hill town of only a few hundred people, never playing as a professional songster or leaving his rural background for any extended period. In his case the ballads of his youth remained the music that he knew and played in the 1920s and, like Furry Lewis, still played thirty-five years later when he was rediscovered.

Mississippi John Hurt was initially heard by the Okeh recording director Tommy Rockwell at the suggestion of two excellent white rural musicians, Willie Narmour and Shell Smith who also came from Avalon. Of Hurt's first eight titles, which included *Frankie* and an unissued *Casey Jones*, only two titles were issued, but he was invited by letter to record in New York: Rockwell wrote on November 8, 1928 explaining that "the first record that you made sold fairly well" but that the balance of the Memphis recordings was not satisfactory. He offered $20.00 a side and all expenses if Hurt would come to New York to record. "We would like to have you get together about eight selections at least four of them to be old time tunes, similar to selections 'Frankie' and 'Nobody's Business'. There are a great many tunes like these which are known throughout the South." [51] Hurt's later recordings included *Louis Collins*, *Stack O'Lee Blues* and *Spike Driver Blues*, one of the "John Henry" group. But the records did not sell well. In spite of attempts to get on record again John Hurt and his ballads were passed over by the recording companies.

Ballads on record add to our knowledge of the ways in which they had been sung and played and reveal important indications of the manner in which they were adapted and developed by the songsters. Whatever their provenance, or even the publication at a relatively early date of sheet music of a ballad, black singers seem to have had a genius for extending, elaborating and reconstructing them. It was a skill which found its fullest scope for development in the blues. Tastes were changing; the ballads, along with the minstrel songs, the medicine show repertoire and the old dance routines, were giving way rapidly to the new idiom, to which however, they played an important part in giving meaning and form.

9

Next Week, Sometime . . .?
Past recording and future research

This discussion of the recordings of the folk songsters and the "saints" of the working-class black churches commenced with some observations on the singing of Peg Leg Howell. Howell, it will be remembered, has been widely, and rightly, acknowledged as an important country blues singer in the Georgia tradition. But the rural compass of his songs on record indicated a greater range, while even in his blues there were to be found the traces of songs from other and older sources. In *The Story of the Blues* I wrote of Howell that "his blues are of special interest because they clearly represent the transition from old songs, work songs and ballads, to blues". On this Jeff Todd Titon sounded a note of caution. Quoting my observation, he acknowledged "certainly, Howell used widely collected traditional texts and tunes, borrowing from Anglo-American tradition as well as from Afro-American. But whether that proves that he represents a transition from work songs and ballads to blues – if there was such a transition – is arguable." [1]

Of course Titon is right to question such an assumption on what may be, ultimately, unknowable. However, there are only a limited number of alternative explanations for the evolution of the blues. Scarcely noted before 1902–3, the idiom appears to have had little impact, though a fairly wide distribution, until the end of the first decade of the century. If "transition" is accepted as the "passage, change, from one place or state or act or set of circumstances to another", then this is surely an appropriate description of the change in circumstances where the old songs declined in their appeal as the blues began to dominate black secular vocal traditions. While it is true that work songs of the "holler" type and ballads may not have been constituent elements in the forming of the blues, as I have argued in the same book, it is the explanation that most closely fits the evidence. In his exhaustive discussion of the "Folk and Popular Blues" David Evans finds my suggestion "the most plausible, that the field holler vocal was combined with one of the common harmonic accompaniment patterns of the blues ballad", to mold the blues form. [2]

As we have seen, Howell's songs included ballad and social song fragments, and blues based on street-cries and hollers; in this sense he may be said to *represent* the transition. It was one that took place during the active, musical part of his lifetime, and was not the total and immediate replacement of one

Former associate of Blind Blake, songster Bill Williams was first recorded in 1970. Three years after he died at his home in Greenup, Kentucky.   Photograph by Paul Oliver.

tradition by another. Kip Lornell and Bruce Bastin, among the few who have researched forms of black song apart from blues in recent years, have used the term "pre-blues" to describe these traditions; later Lornell settled for "non-blues". The former term is not wholly accurate, for while the song types existed before the advent of blues, and in this sense may be considered "pre-blues", they also existed in parallel with the blues, and with sufficient vigor for Lornell to record examples in the field in the mid-1970s. His later term of "non-blues" was unsatisfactory in describing the traditions collectively by what they were *not*, rather than by what they were.[3]

From the many examples quoted in the present work, there is substantial evidence of dance songs; minstrel and medicine show numbers; ragtime, coon and bully songs; social songs of fantasy and realism; parodies and comic songs; and ballads of various forms, all of which were known to the songsters and examples of which were still residual in their repertoires in the second half of the 1920s. A large proportion of these songs dated from the closing decades of the nineteenth century, some had words or stanzas that were of an earlier date and a number were composed or current before World War I. These were songs, then, which for the most part pre-dated blues, but which were still in currency or composed when blues was in its infancy.

Generally, black folk musicians of all generations learned their instruments at an early age, often playing music before the age of ten. In the company of a father, uncle, or other older musician, many started to play for functions when in their early teens. The songs that they learned at this time were often the popular themes of the day, and the ones that they remembered longest. To a considerable extent the repertoires of the singers were reflected by their generations, the oldest singers frequently recording a broad range of material, those ten or fifteen years younger combining them with blues, while the singers of a still younger generation were wholly committed to blues. There were some modifying factors: Peg Leg Howell, though born in 1888, did not start to play guitar until he was over twenty years old; Eddie 'Son' House, born in 1902, was of similar age when he began playing; Big Bill Broonzy, born in 1893, played fiddle when a child, but did not learn to play guitar until the 1920s.

Though Johnny Watson (Daddy Stovepipe) was born in 1867, few songsters who recorded were born before the 1880s; Henry Thomas, born in Texas in 1874 was an exception. Among those of the eighties generation were Papa Charlie Jackson, Simmie Dooley, Gus Cannon, Charley Patton, Frank Stokes, Peg Leg Howell, and probably Jim Jackson and Blind Blake. To these should be added Huddie Ledbetter (Leadbelly), who did not record in the 1920s. Singers of the early 1890s included Mississippi John Hurt, Walter Furry Lewis, Luke Jordan, Bo Carter and Pink Anderson (1900), all of whom were clearly songsters, and to whom should be added Jesse Fuller, Mance Lipscomb, and Bill Williams who did not record until after World War II. In the latter half of the nineties, the first generation of acknowledged blues singers was born, including Blind Lemon Jefferson, Memphis Minnie,

Tommy Johnson, Sleepy John Estes and Whistling Alex Moore. And born around the turn of the century, Texas Alexander, Barbecue Bob, Charlie Lincoln, Walter Vinson, Peetie Wheatstraw, Kokomo Arnold, Will Shade, Son House, Blind Willie McTell and Charlie Burse, most of whom had some elements of the songster's repertoire or approach in part of their recorded work.

Within a few years a generation of singers was born who reached their early teens in World War I. Few pianists apart from Charles Cow Cow Davenport (1894), Jimmy Yancey (1898) and Georgia Tom Dorsey were born before 1900, but the period 1904–7 witnessed the birth of a remarkable number of blues pianists including Pinetop Smith, Leroy Carr, Bumble Bee Slim, Big Maceo Merriweather, Roosevelt Sykes, Little Brother Montgomery, Henry Brown and Sunnyland Slim. Of this generation too, were the guitarists, Jazz Gillum, Ed Bell, Big Boy Crudup, Bukka White, Buddy Moss, Black Ace, and, by the end of the decade, Blind Boy Fuller, Aaron "T-Bone" Walker, Tommy McClennan, Washboard Sam, Jack Dupree and "Howling Wolf" Burnett. All but the last-named recorded before World War II when they were in their twenties or early thirties. Further particularization of, for example, the remarkable generation of blues singers born during the First World War who recorded after 1945, is unnecessary. That there was a songster generation of the 1880s and 90s, an intermediate phase of singers born around the turn of the century and a virtually total blues singing generation of around 1905 is all self-evident. [4]

When, or indeed how, the blues emerged is a question which has provoked much speculation but, not surprisingly, no incontestable evidence. Text references, and the reminiscences of such figures as W. C. Handy and Ma Rainey together point to the period around the turn of the century. Among the earliest recollections with a specific date was that of John Jacob Niles who, in 1898 heard Ophelia Simpson, known as "Black Alfalfa": "She did the current ragtime things, but was most effective in the native blues." Earlier, she had killed her man, one Henry "Dead Dog" Simpson, who worked at a fertilizer plant on the Ohio River near Louisville. After a brief period in the "Stony Lonesome" jail, Ophelia worked for Dr. Parker's Medicine Show where "she cooked, helped mix the tape-worm eradicator and shouted in the oleo". It was there that Niles heard her sing:

> I ain't got not a friend in dis town,   (2)
> Cause my New Orleans partner done turned me down.
>
> Po' gal wishin' for dat jail-house key,   (2)
> To open up de door and let herself go free.
>
> Stony Lonesome no place for a dog,   (2)
> Not even fitten for a razor-backed hog.
>
> High Sheriff said, "Gal don't be so blue,   (2)
> Cause dat jail-house keeper goin' to be good to you."

Jesse Fuller played guitar, harmonica, cymbals and "fotdella" – a foot
operated bass. He died aged 80, in 1976.   Photograph: *Good Time Jazz*.

and so on for eleven stanzas "in the style of the classic blues". Entitled "A
Night on Mobile Bay", the oleo constituted the second part of the evening
performance. It "presented a group of Negroes (not burnt cork) singing their
own native music. Some of it was unaccompanied and some of it was sung to
plucked strings, brasses and percussion instruments – all played by Negroes."

A previously unrecorded songster, Mance Lipscomb, playing outside his home in
Navasota, Texas at the time of his discovery in 1960. He died in 1976, aged 81.
Photograph by Paul Oliver.

Perhaps the earliest and most detailed of black performers on a medicine show, Niles's description placed Ophelia Simpson's blues in the context of "current ragtime things", a black band and a minstrel entertainment structure to the medicine show.[5]

Writing of the "Singer's Perspective", Jeff Todd Titon noted that many blues singers had toured with medicine shows and picked up "humorous songs that they were able to use later": he did not suggest that it was the *blues* that they may have picked up.[6] Yet this seems equally plausible. In the early days of the century, when medicine shows and minstrel shows were a commonplace and provided means of regular employment and travel to innumerable musicians, the blues in one form or another would have been readily assimilated by the songsters. The appeal of a new musical form would have been considerable to "professional" folk singers; the technical challenge would have been no problem to them.

Many indications have been given in this book of singers who worked with the medicine shows, both those who would be recognized as songsters and those whose preponderance of blues justifies their being termed "blues singers". Though there were both songsters and blues singers who were almost wholly local in their reputation and circle of friendships, influences and contacts, there were many others who were wanderers and hoboes traveling between juke joints and country functions and working with the shows when they were able. "You don't never see them little minister [sic] shows now, did you?" blues singer Mott Willis asked David Evans. "Oh we were around Clarksdale and Tutwiler and all around in there, Hollandale." "All around in there" implies that the small settlements and the townships were visited by the minstrel and medicine shows: "sometimes, kind of out in the country, you know, have a little old tent".[7]

When traveling musicians came to a town or settlement it was customary for them to seek out the "best" musicians in the locality and to demonstrate their skills, compete in performance and exchange songs. For the songsters working on the road shows the ability to produce "new" songs, and to acquire extensions to their repertoires was obviously to their advantage and the enhancement of their prestige. In addition to the "current ragtime things" the blues and blues-songs offered such additions, and the framework for inventing new ones.

Undoubtedly these and other types of show were effective in transmitting blues from district to district at a time when much of the populace was less mobile than it was to be later. Their performers frequently joined the shows where they were made up in the city, and the more literate among them may have responded to the advertisements seeking talent that appeared in *The Chicago Defender* and other black newspapers. Though a rural origin for the blues has often been stressed it is quite likely that it was equally popular in the cities. Most songsters gravitated to the cities – Memphis, Dallas or Atlanta for example – where they would have both heard and shared the blues with other singers.

Here could be heard, in the black tent shows and later in the Theater Owners Booking Agency venues, the professional singers on the vaudeville stage, of whom a great many were of the songsters' generation. Ma Rainey, Mamie Smith and Sara Martin were born in the 1880s; Bessie, Trixie and Clara Smith, Ada Brown, Esther Bigeou, Lottie Beamon, Rosa Henderson, Lucille Hegamin, Lizzie Miles, Ida Cox, Alberta Hunter and Leola B. Wilson were among those born in the nineties.[8] In many instances their careers on stage dated back to the decade before World War I and they were probably more instrumental in spreading blues than has been acknowledged outside of jazz writing. But how their blues related to the broad range of other song types on their records must be reserved for another work.

Folk musicians tend to refine their skills within an idiom and, having done so, to remain with their basic approach substantially unaltered for long periods. This has been the case with ethnic orchestras and singers of European or Mexican extraction, with rural white old-time musicians, and with blues singers of all generations. There are exceptions: in the blues, Muddy Waters changed his style from his Mississippi field songs to the forceful, Chicago music of his later years, but against such an example are scores of singers who changed little, if at all. The "rediscovery" of many blues singers after as much as thirty-five years away from the recording studio demonstrated this many times. Similarly, songsters like Mississippi John Hurt or Furry Lewis retained abilities that were, in effect, frozen in time. Folk singers tend to play and sing the music of their youth or the formative periods in their lives. Songsters were not exceptions in this respect but their keenness of ear and interest in extending their repertoires meant that as blues became dominant, they adopted them and incorporated them into their spectrum of performance. For the songsters, they constituted another idiom to be learned, composed, arranged and performed. Only sometimes, as in the case of Peg Leg Howell, did the songster use the blues as a vehicle for the expression of a more personal message; for the majority, blues were first, and probably always, performed as songs with a specific structure.

Songsters acquired blues as they picked up other songs, but they were doubtless subjected to some pressure by the record managers to perform blues as the popular music of the day. The part the record executives played in shaping their repertoires as they appeared on record is a significant issue. When Tommy Rockwell wrote to Mississippi John Hurt, he apparently had a concept of the kind of songs that he felt would sell, but much of the recording of black vocal traditions was based on less considered grounds. Lester Melrose, a former owner of a grocery store, opened a music shop on Cottage Grove, Chicago in 1922. "We carried a full stock of pop sheet music, piano rolls, small musical instruments and records." As business picked up they moved to a larger store and soon were handling the major labels. Inquiries came in "from various composers, including colored, about publishing their music, or getting it recorded on phonograph records. It was impossible for us to publish pop tunes at that time, so we decided to take a whirl at the blues. The blues selections started coming in and we soon had ten or twelve selections that we thought were good material."[9]

Paramount was one of the record companies to whom Melrose and the black promoter, J. Mayo "Ink" Williams sent the singers they wished to get on record. A young Englishman from Somerset, newly arrived in the USA, Art Satherley was soon responsible for making the records of black musicians for Paramount, while A. C. Laibley mainly supervised the hillbilly artists. "I didn't just say 'Sing this and go out and have a drink somewhere', I spent my time in that studio getting them ready for the people of the world . . . When I spoke to those Negroes, I would talk to them. I would tell them what we had to expect", Satherley explained. Taking full-page advertisements in *The Chicago Defender* at $1000 a time was his idea: "It was so new for the people of America to be able to buy what they understood and what they wanted that we quickly had several thousand people buying records daily", he claimed, adding that within a year they had a thousand dealers competing with those for Columbia and Victor.[10]

Victor's recording manager, formerly with Okeh, was Ralph Peer. Though he was forthcoming on his business acumen in securing the publishing rights for all his artist's songs, Peer was enigmatic on the subject of his taste, particularly the grounds for the selection of black singers. His immense success in recording the Carter Family and Jimmie Rodgers was evidence of his perception on hearing potentially best-selling performers. But they came to him in response to a news story which was run – at his suggestion – in the Bristol, Tennessee *News Bulletin* in July 1927: a few among the "deluge" of long-distance calls from hopeful singers which he received.[11] It was a technique that he may not have used to seek black singers, but it was employed

Where to Buy Okeh Race Records

Polangine Music Shop	Russian Music Store
917 Broadway .... Farrell. Pa	3507 Hastings St Detroit. Mich
Walker Thomas Furniture Co.	Scott's News Service
1913 Seventh St N W	451 Seventh St Milwaukee. Wic.
Washington. D C.	RECORDS SENT C. O. D.
Geo. W. Thomas Music Co.	Delux Music Shoppe
428 Bowen Ave ... Chicago. Ill	2234 Market St St Louis. Mo
Harmony Music Shop	Pastime Music Shop
4541 S State St Chicago. Ill	2339 Market St St. Louis. Mo.
Rialto Music Shop	A. Gressett Music House
330 S State St Chicago. Ill.	Meridian .. Mississippi
Richardson's Piano Store	J. A. Abrams
3603 S State St Chicago. Ill.	Gulfport ..... Mississippi
Vito Lunetto	Columbia Music Shop
103 W Oak St Chicago. Ill	451 Michigan Ave Buffalo. N. Y
Morris Music Shop	Brown Music Store
116 S Rampart St New Orleans La	4414 Central Ave Cleveland. Ohio
Melody Music Shop	Cedar Music Shoppe
4700 Hastings St Detroit. Mich	9907 Cedar Ave. Cleveland. Ohio
New York Russian Music Store	Sol Gershuny
2341 Hastings St .....Detroit. Mich.	554 W. Sixth St...Cincinnati. Ohio

A list of dealers handling Okeh Race records included Jesse Johnson's DeLux Music Shoppe in St. Louis. George W. Thomas in Chicago was also an active musician, composer and talent scout. *Paul Oliver collection.*

by others including Frank Walker, a recording executive for Columbia who was born in a farming and music-making community at Fly Summit, New York. "We had our list of 'old familiar tunes' and we had our 'race music'", he recalled. "We also had different serial numbers for them but you see the same area that produced the one produced the other." He arranged field trips through the South, generating interest in the local areas. "We built it up in advance – getting the word around that at a certain time of the year we were going to be there, and these people would show up sometimes from eight or nine hundred miles away. How they got there I'll never know, and how they got back I'll never know. They never asked you for money. They were just happy to sing and play, and we were happy to have them. Most of them we saw had something to go back with." [12] In Southern cities local talent scouts, usually associated with the music retail business, kept an eye open for singers, as did Polk Brockman in Atlanta who would "attend Atlanta's 81 Theater (TOBA circuit) weekly, visit black churches and occasionally accost musicians on the street". He too, would make it known that there would be a recording session for one of the major companies. "Merchants, furniture stores, record dealers were key sources of information for public and producer. News about coming auditions was communicated by word of mouth. On occasion Brockman would go to town and find '200 persons waiting to see me'. Yet most of the 'discoveries' . . . might be put to hard work and chance." But, reported Roger S. Brown, who interviewed him decades later, "his keen ear was accompanied by utter disinterest in the music. As his charming wife affectionately asserts: 'He liked the sound of the cash register'." [13]

To a large extent the record men relied upon the response to their advertising and their own hunches; they knew little about the music, but found ways to ascertain local interest. Explained Frank Walker: "I started going around the country and gathering people off the street by giving them a slip of paper telling them we wanted their opinion on a certain phonograph record, if they would be at such a place at a certain time in the afternoon. We would bring all the people up – from the bank president to the street cleaner. You watched the expression on their face. We were able to judge them because you were playing to America." [14]

A Jackson, Mississippi music salesman who was responsible for the recording of Charley Patton and other important figures, H. C. Speir "had no rules for picking blues singers beyond his personal taste. He felt that a singer should have 'harmony', by which he simply meant appeal to his ear. He never took into consideration the fact that a singer might have a reputation for popularity in the black community. He also never used blues singers as scouts." Relying on his own taste and the singers who came to his store, Speir complained that he "often had to buy 500 copies of a record from a company 'just to record some nigger'. This was proof to the company that he had confidence in the record sales potential" – if not respect for the artist. [15]

These were white recording managers and talent scouts, but blues singers were used for this purpose, and black record promoters were also seeking artists actively. Jesse Johnson, who managed the DeLux Music Shop in St. Louis was one. His widow, blues singer Edith Johnson recalled that he would come home at "two or three or five in the mornin'" seeking blues singers in the company of Jack Kapp. The pianist Roosevelt Sykes "seemed to be popular with the fellers that was runnin' the record business such as J. Mayo Williams and Jack Kapp – those fellers knowed pretty well about blues singers and that I knowed pretty good material when I heard it, so they asked would I go out and find some artists for them?" With a letter of introduction Sykes hunted talent in Mississippi, though "it was kinda difficult at times". In Memphis Jim Jackson was an active seeker for recording talent, as was Lonnie McIntorsh on occasion. So too was the singer Charley Jordan in St. Louis, while, in Dallas, Sam Price, a young black record salesman, dancer and pianist, also discovered talent and was responsible for the recording of both Blind Lemon Jefferson and Texas Alexander.[16]

It is evident that some recording executives and managers developed an ear for the kind of music that would sell. Ralph Peer, with an interest in securing the publication rights, laid emphasis on "original" songs, and this would possibly have favored blues rather than traditional songster material. With a change of title or arrangement, an old song could become a new and "original" one and it is by no means clear whether there was complicity in changing titles to avoid an old copyright or to secure a new one. In practice it seemed to have mattered little, though it could account for the different titles used for the same song, of which there are many examples in this book.

The preferences of record executives or the companies for which they were employed do not become apparent through any imbalance of songster material: Okeh, Victor, Columbia, Paramount and Vocalion all recorded substantial numbers of examples. Nor are preferences especially apparent when the recordings of a specific singer for different companies are compared: when, for example, Jim Jackson's Victor recordings are placed against those for Vocalion, or Frank Stokes's recordings for Paramount are compared with those that he made for Victor. There is a slight tendency towards a proportionately larger number of blues in later sessions by some songsters, probably reflecting some pressure to record the popular form, but it is not particularly marked.

To what extent the talent scouts screened aspiring artists prior to making a selection to advance to the record companies, and the degree to which they exercised control on the items that the singer chose to perform, is difficult to ascertain. Blues singer Nehemiah "Skip" James recalled that when H. C. Speir sent for him there was a "roomful" of singers there also auditioning; he claimed to be the only one to have been accepted. A further filter took place when the artist recorded. Eighteen of Skip James's titles were issued by Paramount, but he remembered making twenty-six items. The roomful of singers may have been the exaggeration of a very proud man, but James, who was intelligent and meticulous, was very likely correct in his recollection of the number of items that he cut; three matrices of recordings made at the time at any rate are untraced.[17] Unfortunately, with only a few exceptions, the recorded but unissued titles made by Paramount are unknown. Some of the major companies like Victor or Columbia kept more detailed files, and from the discographies compiled with this data it is possible to make tentative conclusions as to some of the songster material which did not appear on disc, even though it was recorded by the artists. The list is not a long one, and gives little confirmation that the songs were deliberately eliminated for their type or content. One that may have been was Bo Carter's first recording, *The Yellow Coon Has No Race*, but other unissued songs bear titles that appear innocuous.

Reliance on titles as an indication of content is in any case somewhat precarious. Sam Collins, for example, recorded as I have noted, a *Midnight Special Blues* which was the prison nodal ballad. On the other hand, Sodarisa Miller's recording entitled *The Midnight Special* was not a version of the ballad but a conventional railroad blues. An *11.29 Blues* by Romeo Nelson was, in fact, a version of *The Midnight Special*, even though the phrase " 11.29 " referred to a prison sentence of one day less than a year and not to the time of a train. Leroy Carr's later (1934) recording of *Eleven Twenty-Nine Blues* used this meaning of the phrase, but was not a version of *The Midnight Special*. Examples of the problem of titles abound but, nevertheless, conclusions may be drawn from other reliable evidence.

A desire to choose older songs is apparent in the small number made for Okeh by Blind Lemon Jefferson. His *Elder Green's In Town* was a version of *Alabama Bound*, while *Laboring Man Away From Home* is known to have been the Child ballad *Our Goodman*. A list of titles entered for copyright by Chicago Music on behalf of the Tappahannock barber, William Moore, appears to complete his total session of sixteen matrices. Among the titles were a version of *I Got Mine* and a tantalizing *Silas Green From New Orleans*, which may hint at the source of some of his songs.[18] Among the unissued titles by Winston Holmes and Charlie Turner are *Fleetin' John*, which is helpfully identified in the file as a version of *Lost John*; another, *Sanford Barnes*, is likely to have been *Way Down in Arkansas* in which this name sometimes occurs. It is reasonable to assume that Jim Jackson's unissued *Black But Sweet* was the same as the song recorded by Billy and Mary Mack as *Black But Sweet, Oh God*; there are no hints as to the nature of his *Goodbye Boys*. It is unlikely that Sam Collins's *Blue Heaven Blues* relates to the composition (though one songster, Spark Plug Smith did record it a couple of years later) but we might conjecture that his *Maybe Next Week Sometime* was the same song as Alec Johnson's *Next Week, Sometime*, and possibly that *Long Time Rubin* was the ballad *Reuben*. Unless the masters turn up we are unlikely to know, but in Sam Collins's case one has. Recently released as *My Road Is Rough and Rocky* it has been suggested that this was the master listed as *Toe-Nail Flang-Dang* (unlikely, for the files enter "no vocal" and the *Flang-Dang* is normally a Spanish tuning dance piece). Whichever master it is, Sam Collins's song turns out to be a distant relative of *Long Gone*.[19]

Among unissued recordings of ballads were Mississippi John Hurt's *Casey Jones* and Coley Jones's *Frankie and Albert*. Although no versions of the *Boll Weevil* in conventional ballad form appear to have been recorded by black singers, Joe Calicott's unissued *Mississippi Boll Weevil Blues* might have been one. Little recorded until his "rediscovery" in the 1960s, Calicott was a member of the group of songsters from Hernando, Mississippi, which included Garfield Akers, Jim Jackson and the somewhat younger Robert Wilkins. Sam Butler on Vocalion was the same man as Paramount's Bo Weevil Jackson. There is nothing in the records issued as by Bo Weevil Jackson to indicate why he had this nickname, but an unissued Vocalion master of Butler's *Devil and My Brown Blues*, recently released, turns out to be the blues-ballad *Boll Weevil*, thus explaining his nickname and suggesting that other significant items might be hidden by deceptive titles.[20]

Interesting but elusive connexions in the repertoires of songsters might be revealed if unissued items were traced: Furry Lewis's *The Panic's On* for instance, may have been the same as Hezekiah Jenkins's record. Both Henry Thomas and Archie Lewis made versions of *Honey Won't You Allow Me One More Chance?* (decades later to be re-composed by Bob Dylan). Archie Lewis also made *Chicken*, which is the title by which *Chicken You Can Roost Behind The Moon* (or *Chicken You Can't Roost Too High For Me*) is sometimes known. Was Henry Thomas's *Chicken Rag* also the same item? Another song by Henry Thomas, *Fishing Blues*, was noted by W. P. Webb as early as 1912. *Any Fish Will Bite* by the Carter Brothers may be another variant of the song for the phrase is a key one in its lyric. It's possible, for the other unissued title by the Carter Brothers (The Mississippi Sheiks) was *Some Folk Say a Preacher Won't Steal*, a song of considerable age related to Frank Stokes's *You Shall* and Kansas Joe and Memphis Minnie's *Preacher's Blues*.[21]

Purchasers of Race records had to rely on advertisements and record stores for details of the newest issues and they could have no knowledge either of forthcoming releases or of unissued recordings. The diversity of the songsters' repertoires can best be appreciated when issued and unissued recordings, often made for more than one company, are seen together. For example, Joe Evans and Arthur McClain were songsters from Fairmount, Eastern Tennessee who played guitars, violin, mandoline, piano and kazoos between them. Of their first sessions for Gennett only a popular number, *Little Son of a Gun (Look What You Done Done)* was issued; other unreleased titles included *They Wanted a Man To Lead the Lions Around* and *Mama Don't Turn Me Out In the Cold*, which suggest medicine show material. An ARC session spread over just two days in May 1931 produced dances like *Old Hen Cackle* and *Sourwood Mountain*, sentimental or novelty numbers like *Oh You Son of a Gun*, *So Sorry Dear* and *Georgia Rose*, nodal ballads like *John Henry* and *Two*

White Horses In a Line, blues standards like *Sittin' On Top of the World* and *Down In Black Bottom* and blues of various kinds and structures like *Cream and Sugar Blues, Shook It This Morning Blues* or *Mill Man Blues*. They even included a parody of the recent hit *Birmingham Jail* by the white hillbilly singers Darby and Tarlton, with their *New Huntsville Jail*, and what was probably a boogie woogie piano solo, *Boogity Woogity*. This last was unissued but the other titles appeared on the American Record Company (ARC) labels, Oriole, Romeo, Banner, Perfect, under their own names, together or singly, as The Two Poor Boys and, in the case of the instrumentals *Old Hen Cackle* and *Sourwood Mountain*, as by Colman and Harper when this coupling was also issued in the Perfect hillbilly series.[22]

Further examples comparing issued and unissued recordings, and sessions with different recording companies might be given for instance, of Sam Jones; Coley Jones, solo and with the Dallas String Band; Tommy Bradley and James Cole; Walter Taylor and John Byrd; Buford Threlkeld (Whistler) or Bo Carter. But the evidence cited is clear enough: some songsters drew upon a remarkable range of material and through motivation or opportunity, managed to get it before the recording machines, if not always actually on record. To what extent the unissued items represented poor performances on the part of the musicians, or selectivity on grounds of taste or marketing on the part of the recording managers, must remain an open question. I have already discussed at length in *Screening the Blues* the issue of censorship of Race records and the withholding of items regarded as too obscene for release, and must let the matter rest there.[23]

There were no substantial differences between the recording of secular and religious artists. The attitudes of the recording executives were very much the same. Agent Polk Brockman showed his customary business instincts when he signed up Reverend Gates to an exclusive contract: "I guess I stole him. He made his first record for Columbia but they let him wander around and didn't sign him up." In the recording studio "Uncle Art" Satherley put the religious singers into an appropriate mood. "I would ask 'Before we sing this spiritual which one of you lost a loved one in the last year or so?' And one would step forward. Then I would say to the fellow that had some preaching experience, 'Just say a little short prayer before we start preaching'." His aim was to give black people "what they wanted back. And the only way to get it back was to get what they felt in their souls. How many recording men know that?" Some were not very interested. Asked what the instrument was that the jack-leg evangelist Washington Phillips played, Frank Walker replied, "God knows, Nobody knows. He had no name for it; it was something he had made himself. Nobody on earth could use it except him. Nobody would want to, I don't think."[24]

Preachers and congregations were neither difficult to locate nor hard to bring to the recording units as were some songsters, for the nature of their worship identified them with specific churches and they were accustomed to singing collectively with the preacher in simple surroundings. They were generally literate and could respond to invitations to record on later sessions. Only the street evangelists presented problems akin to those posed by the irregular movements of the songsters, and at least one of these, Lonnie McIntorsh, worked as a talent scout.

Sessions with religious artists produced a low rate of unissued items. There were some that may have been rejected on grounds of obscurity, like Calvin P. Dixon's *Revivals Habakkuk 3.1*, of outspokenness, like Reverend Nix's *Throwing Stones*, of subject, like Reverend Weems's *The Hoodoo Lost His Hand*, or for being too pointed as Reverend Gates may have been on *Women Spend Too Much Money* or *Good-Bye Chain Stores*. Being sometimes more spontaneous, some Sanctified preachers may have marred their sermons; Reverend McGee on his *Beauty For Ashes* perhaps, or Elder Richard Bryant when preaching *Don't Forget the Family Prayer*. Some congregations may have been simply too rough or too disorganized; this could have been the case with the regrettably unissued session of Elder Tarleton Roberts, on whose titles, including *Death Went Creeping Through the Door*, Sisters Bessie Johnson and Malvina Taylor sang and Will Shade played. Other unissued sessions by Evangelist Anna Perry of the Church of the Living God, and Reverend Lionel Jackson who recorded a *Baptism At the River* in New Orleans, can only be guessed at. But the possibility that Brothers Wright and Williams, who were assisted by Sisters Jordan and Norman from Reverend Gates' congregation, may have been Macon Ed (Eddie Anthony) and Tampa Joe still tantalizes. The loss of Reverend Clayborn's *Sinking of the Titanic* is also unfortunate, while the recent release of formerly unissued titles such as Arizona Dranes's *God's Got a Crown* and Washington Phillips's *You Can't Stop a Tattler* are indications of the quality of some items that were viewed as unsuitable for issue at the time.[25]

When all factors are considered – the influence of the record men, the means whereby singers were sought or invited to record, the vagaries of the industry itself, the success in marketing by some firms and the failure of others, the vast distances between field locations, their timing in relation to the cycles of farm work, traveling shows and their own schedules, the frequent tours by some companies and the use only of northern urban recording locations by still others – one gains the impression that the reasons why folk musicians came to be recorded were largely fortuitous. Later, when the record men had established reliable contacts, some, at least, took pains to set up sessions before making field trips: a process which may have inhibited chance encounters with further unknown musicians.[26]

The question then arises as to how representative the music was that *did* appear on record. A certain initial innocence of the range of music and a degree of opportunism in recording those who presented themselves before the recording machines suggest that the random sampling achieved a relatively balanced cross-section of secular and sacred vocal traditions current among adult blacks in the South. There were omissions: street cries were represented only by the odd coupling by Ole Man Mose – Reverend Moses Mason from Texas – of *Shrimp Man* and *Molly Man* (the latter being a corruption of "Tamale Man"). The black scholar Willis Lawrence James attempted a *River Rousty Song* and a work song *Oh Cap'n* with less success, while a male vocal group calling itself the T. C. I. Section Crew produced some highly self-conscious and unconvincing imitations of *Track Linin'* and a *Section Gang Song*. In their authentic forms these were songs of work rather than of leisure and though there are several examples of work songs and hollers that have strongly influenced blues, as in the recordings of Texas Alexander or even Bessie Tucker, there were no documentary recordings of these work traditions on commercial record; nor would one expect there to be. Children's game and play songs were likewise missing; Race records were mainly aimed at the youth and adult markets who had the purchasing power. "Toasts" were barely hinted at, and then in hokum recordings – the genre was probably only emerging at the time. No doubt it was largely because of these omissions, and the folklorist's aversion to blues as a corrupting influence, that the Library of Congress recordings heavily featured work songs, hollers, play-party and game songs when collecting in the field commenced in 1933.[27]

How popular the records of songsters, preachers or evangelists were when compared with those by blues singers, quartets or vaudeville artists is difficult to ascertain. Though pressing figures have been published for some Columbia Race records they do not indicate sales but initial orders. While these are clearly related to expected sales, and the first repeat orders identify minimum sales, totals are lacking. That they may be a very inaccurate guide is evident by the fact that the first Bessie Smith record for which order figures are cited, *Yellow Dog Blues*, had an initial order of 12,075 and a follow-up order of 10,000, yet a sales figure of 780,000 copies in six months has been cited for her version of *Down Hearted Blues*. Hence it is difficult to know whether a first order of 4175 and a second order of 2500 for Blind Willie Johnson's 1928 release, *If I Had My Way*, is a reliable indication of its sales. By comparison Coley Jones's *Drunkard's Special* had orders that barely totalled 4000; but this was in 1930 and the industry was feeling the pinch of the Depression. The following year a mere 649 copies were ordered of Hezekiah Jenkins's *The Panic Is On*.[28]

Columbia records are not considered rare, their sales figures were probably better than those of some of their contemporaries. Much attention has been given to "rarity" by collectors; only "two known copies" were believed to exist of Richard "Rabbit" Brown's *The Sinking of the Titanic*, and only three of John Byrd's *Old Timbrook Blues*. Subsequent estimates were more generous, but fewer than five copies were thought to have survived of Sam Collins's *Midnight Special Blues* and Long Cleve Reed's *Original Stack O'Lee Blues* on Black Patti was termed "the rarest of all country blues records". A single copy of Charley Patton's *Joe Kirby* was "recovered" in 1977, and as late as 1982 the only known disc of Skip James's ballad *Drunken Spree* was found in Virginia, far from the singer's home state of Mississippi.[29] The rarity of these items may not be so much an indication of limited popularity as of limited availability; Black Patti records were pressed in very small numbers while the Patton and James on Paramount were among the last fifty items in a catalogue which had released more than 1150 records. While as many as 500 Race records were issued each year between 1927 and 1930, new releases plummeted to a mere 150 in 1933. These and other factors, including the price of records and eventually a collapsing economy, affected releases, distribution and sales.[30]

Assiduous "canvassing" of black homes in the South has brought satisfaction to several persistent collectors and the reissue of the many rare items they have recovered has made them generally available to enthusiasts. But the selective purchasing of rarities and the rapid off-loading of unwanted items has done a disservice to scholarship in at least one respect. Careful annotation of all the records that survived in homes in comparable black neighborhoods would have been highly instructive as to tastes in blues, gospel, folk vocal traditions, popular songs, jazz and instrumental music. From such documentation samplings could have been made that might have been a more accurate gauge of their respective popularity. Regretfully, it is probably too late for such research to be undertaken.

Similarly, although a number of record men, including talent scouts, have been interviewed who were often associated with the music and furniture (hence phonograph) sales business, the focus of interviewing has been on their recording activities and on obtaining more biographical data on blues singers. Opportunities have been missed for information that would throw light on the purchasing of records. We do not know whether more men bought records than women, nor whether under twenty-fives bought more than older people; we do not know if the same consumers bought sacred who bought secular records, or whether purchasing was divided along age, sex and caste lines. We have no information on what sales in different parts of the country were, or what the distribution of specific records or genres might have been.

Nevertheless, there is some relationship between records bought and phonographs owned, and on this at least there are some data. In 1927 a seven-year study of both white and black rural homes in Greene County, Georgia, approximately eighty miles east of Atlanta, and in Macon County, an equivalent distance south, was commenced under the auspices of the Georgia Committee on Inter-racial Cooperation. Of the 323 black homes intensively studied not one had a radio but 19 per cent had phonographs. Some 23 per cent had pianos or organs – though other instruments were not noted. Greene County had a higher proportion of pianos than Macon County, which had more phonographs, these being "most numerous among the cropper families". Owing to migration the population was somewhat older in Greene and had more furniture left behind by absent relatives. The ownership of phonographs.

phonographs might be compared with that of sewing machines (55 per cent of families) and cooking ranges (only 15 per cent).[31] A similar study was made in 1930 by Charles S. Johnson in Macon County, Alabama, east of Tuskegee: 612 black families were studied with a total membership of 2432 persons, or about a fifth of the population of the county. Rural and depressed, the conditions in the county were extremely poor, over half of the houses used open privies and nearly 300 had no sewage disposal; 258 used open wells for water and over eighty had no water supply at all. Nevertheless, even here, some seventy-six families, or one in eight, had a "victrola"; there were twenty-three organs, three pianos – but just one banjo.[32] Again, no guitars were listed.

A few years later, in 1935, a massive Consumer Purchases Study was conducted as a Works Progress Administration project. Some 300,000 Southern farm, village and city families were examined, of which some 25,000 were black. One large city, Atlanta, two smaller cities, Columbia, South Carolina and Mobile, Alabama and numerous towns, villages and farm counties were studied. Among the villages were eleven in Mississippi including such locations as Drew, Hollandale, Itta Bena, Leland, Moorhead, Mound Bayou and Rosedale; others, similar, were located in Georgia and North and South Carolina. Of the Georgia and Mississippi farm families, two per cent of black farm operators owned radios, five per cent had pianos but twenty-two per cent possessed phonographs; of the sharecroppers, five per cent owned a radio, seventeen per cent a phonograph but only one per cent a piano. In the Carolinas the percentages were fractionally higher: five per cent of black farm operators possessed a radio, and an equivalent number a piano, but thirty per cent had a phonograph; among the sharecroppers, two per cent a piano but twenty-four per cent owned a phonograph. In the city of Atlanta, forty-six per cent of black families had radios, half those of whites, but "race differences in the ownership of pianos were generally small with ownership in both groups increasing rapidly with income. In contrast, phonographs were reported more frequently by Negroes than by whites; moreover, ownership appeared to bear little relationship to income." Compiler Richard Sterner concluded that "provision for recreation in the home thus seemed to be more extensive among urban than rural families for both Negro and white families". Though extremely interesting in revealing the popularity of the phonograph in black homes, as might be expected, these studies did not extend to consideration of whether the records played were sacred or secular, nor how many a family might own.[33]

Statistical data and consumer sampling may be lacking, but the strongest evidence of the popularity of the songs that appeared on them was the issue of the records themselves. Between the spring of 1924 and the close of 1931 a steady succession of releases by songsters, preachers and evangelists came from the various Race labels. What then was the basis for the appeal of the records of songsters and saints; an appeal so considerable that Columbia and

Victor Race records were selling at 75 cents each at a time when the average annual income of black families in many Southern states was less than \$300.[34]

The period during which the constituents of the songster's repertoires emerged was a painful one for black people, who experienced the backlash of white post-Reconstruction frustration. Effectively, Reconstruction ended with the Compromise of 1877 when Northern Republicans and Southern Democrats reached the agreement that placed Rutherford Hayes in the White House. All the Confederate States were back in the Union and as the new President withdrew the troops, Southern landlords were again in power over black labor and blacks were soon losing the vote. Relations between the races gradually worsened in the eighties; riots, lynchings, the Ku Klux Klan and the convict lease system victimized blacks, with violence often being used as a means of terrorism rather than as summary punishment. Less extreme but ultimately more damaging was the fact that blacks had no economic power; millions were absorbed into the debt slavery of sharecropping. Those that migrated to the Northern cities, as hundreds of thousands did, found themselves swelling the black ghettoes that were beginning to take shape. Slowly social and political advances were made, but they were little felt or understood by the field hand in the cotton row.[35]

By far the majority of blacks remained in the South where their inferior position was being circumscribed with the force of law, most notably by systematic disenfranchisement, but for working-class blacks, more humiliatingly, by the statutes that curbed their freedom. Black Codes specified the "Jim Crow" laws that required separate accommodations for facilities that ranged from drinking fountains to railroad cars. In the 1880s Mississippi saloons served both whites and blacks at the same bar, and blacks could book public places for dances and other functions. Not so after 1890, when even the cemeteries were segregated. Discriminatory laws were progressively applied, many specifically affecting black entertainment. "Tent shows are to maintain separate entrances for different races. Any circus or other such traveling show" was required by the state of South Carolina in 1917 to have entrances for blacks plainly marked "For Colored Only". As late as 1926 a Virginia statute, with a fine parade of synonyms, stated that "it shall be the duty of any person, persons, firm, institution, or corporation, operating, maintaining, keeping, conducting, sponsoring, permitting, any public hall, theater, opera house, motion picture show or any place of public entertainment or public assemblage . . . to separate the white and colored race . . ." Blacks were thrown onto their own resources, reminded at every turn of their separate and inferior status.[36]

Yet, from the mid-nineties to the early twentieth century was also the period of the ragtime and coon songs. Many of these like the Bully songs, unsubtly reinforced the stereotypes of black features and behavior. "Ragtime" songs emphasized the presumed promiscuity of blacks, their alleged propensity for gambling, their love of dancing and "good times" and the duplicity of their preachers. The clichés were summarized perhaps, in Tom Logan's *The Coon's Trade Mark: A Watermelon, Razor, Chicken and a Coon* of 1897. It may well have been ironic, and presumably was when performed by Bert Williams, but the image of the razor-toting, watermelon-sucking, chicken-stealing black man was ingrained in the popular mind; so much so that in 1903 the State of Missouri actually made chicken stealing "a felony subject to imprisonment for five years or a fine of $200".[37]

On the other hand, there was a flow of sentimentalized coon songs coming off the presses which showed sympathetic lithographs of black mothers nursing beribboned "Topsy" piccaninnies, and idealized scenes of rustic cabins in a sunny, timeless Southland. Guilt may have played a part in the creation of these romanticized images but basically they represented the reverse of the same coin: blacks were either presented as sub-human, vicious, stupid, comic, dissolute, extravagant, amoral, or they were innocents, happiest in the carefree natural surroundings of a non-existent Alabammy or Swanee. Either way they were not to be trusted with the vote, not to be given equal opportunities or office but to be kept in place as wayward, immature, irresponsible or loveable children.

Against this the Broadway musicals featuring gifted black entertainers might seem to have been a potential antidote. After the success of Bob Cole's "Trip to Coontown" of 1898–9, Will Marion Cook and Paul Lawrence Dunbar's "Clorindy – The Origin of the Cakewalk", which introduced the dance to New York society the same year, and Williams and Walker's "In Dahomey" which played Times Square in 1902, the "Coon" image was softened. But it was no accident that the Broadway hit of 1903 was a virulent anti-black play about Reconstruction, "The Leopard's Spots" by a Southern white racist, Thomas Dixon Jr.[38] Black shows stayed in the North and mainly on the East coast, or they traveled to Europe; they had little power for good in the South, but the coon, bully and ragtime sheet music was distributed and printed everywhere.

There were many black composers of coon and ragtime songs as has been shown, and their compositions (those by the white minstrel John Queen apart) seem generally to have been assimilated more readily by the songsters than those by white composers. The reasons are doubtless complex, relating partly to marketing, and partly to a more ready use of black idiom, if not greater accuracy in the types portrayed. Ragtime songs composed by blacks differed only marginally – but perhaps significantly – from those by white authors.

If the black ragtime songs were still stereotyped, why did they appeal to such an extent that they were being played thirty years after being composed? Partly, it seems because many blacks believed in, and played up to, the stereotypes. Certainly life on the black main stem of many cities was not too far removed from the image depicted; life *was* rough, there was heavy gambling, drinking and prostitution, there *were* frequent killings and slashings – of this there is no doubt. In this milieu, in which the blues also flourished, the caricatures were larger-than-life projections of Aaron Harris in New Orleans or Bad Sam on Beale Street. This is not to say that all blacks accorded to the values, or lack of them, portrayed (any more than they are shared by the millions who watch crime films and television programmes today) but there was a vicarious pleasure to be gained from the mythic stature of their anarchic central figures.[39]

But stereotypical usage played another role, in that it offered a way for blacks to assume and master the image that whites had of them. They shared the stereotype, enjoyed the joke and to some extent defused the anger and humiliation it provoked. Songsters could trade on white fears and fantasies and mock them, while on the minstrel or medicine show stage, points could be made that arose out of both content and situation, as the sociologist Arthur F. Raper found at such a show in Oglethorpe, Georgia. "The whole troupe was doing a twisting, jiggling dance which was followed by a dialogue in which a black boy pleaded for the attention of a mulatto girl, only to be refused with: 'Who me? Why you don't know who I am; my daddy's the biggest planter in Georgia.'" A sketch with an entertainer singing "I'll leave my gun at home" followed, "and it seemed quite accidental that he was . . . pointing straight at a white man when he came to the line 'I'll leave my gun at home, if you'll leave my wife alone.'" Immediately the little company broke into another dance "with the biggest black man exhorting his associates in good Black Belt diction, 'Shake it, black boy; now you darkies is dancin'.'"[40] Innumerable opportunities for such shafts can be found in the songs on Race records.

At best such devices helped to restore self-esteem; at least they made life more bearable for those who lived through the excesses of segregation, even if, by so doing, they may at times have been over-accommodating. It may well have been a stage that had to be overcome before blacks could assert themselves. Ragtime songs offered figures and situations with which blacks could emphathize – when the hero of *I've Got Mine* outwitted his opponents, when the hustler exploited the good fortune of having a "gal in the white folk's yard", when the barber mockingly dreamed of being a millionaire, when Long John "got away lucky" or when the anti-hero John Henry "took sick and went to bed". Such items provided themes that were reworked in blues, while others survived because they also provided themes that blues did not handle well. Conversely, blues provided an opportunity for the development of themes that were not strong in the ragtime canon; for thirty years the blues and the songs complemented each other. There were many blues that canalized aggression but rather few that were humorous; what is often seen as humor in blues is the persistence of the minstrel song. On the other hand, ragtime songs seldom dealt with relationships between men and women that were other than humorous, exploitative or sentimental. Male blues singers were rarely sentimental and while they often adopted a chauvinistic stance towards women in their blues, they also sang of loneliness and broken affairs from a position of personal involvement.

Many examples in the foregoing chapters have shown how the songsters took popular, including published, themes and instead of merely repeating them, reworked them into virtually new songs, or marked variants of the original. In some cases the tunes were also considerably adapted, while verses were exchanged with other songs or new ones introduced. The black singer associated with his song and recomposed it to suit his needs, experience or audience. He had no qualms about introducing other songs or stanzas and, it seems, enjoyed doing so. It was a process which, as early as the 1860s had been noted often in connexion with the spirituals, and seems to have been carried on into secular song.[41] It is therefore hardly surprising that songs were amalgamated or edited into combination songs and medleys, that verses were transferred from one song to another, and that the lines, images and phrases of ragtime songs were adopted by the blues. Unfortunately pursuing a somewhat destructive argument, Stephen Calt has discussed the use of Biblical imagery and lines in the blues and, to a lesser extent, the borrowing of lines from popular song. In Calt's opinion "only a smattering of the figurative phrases found in country blues appear to have been coined by the musicians themselves. More often than not he [sic] makes use of the so-called 'dead metaphor' or the stock colloquialism of the nineteenth century in order to make a figurative statement."[42] Calt's observations, provocative though they were, fell short of tracing any phrases to the ragtime songs of the turn of the century, or of evaluating their importance in the process of blues composition. This was also missing from Jeff Todd Titon's valuable chapter on "Formulaic structure and meaning" which discusses the means whereby blues formulae are combined (usually, in his analysis, in half-lines) but does not consider their sources.[43]

Yet the occurrence of phrases and lines in the ragtime songs performed by the songsters which also appear in blues is everywhere apparent; what is less clear is whether the phrases were borrowed from the folk tradition in the first place, or whether they were inventive lines encapsulated in song. Did Chris Smith's *All In Down and Out* become the basis, even as a title, for Henry Thomas's *Lovin' Babe*: "Oh lovin' babe, I'm all out and down"? Did George Evans, the "Honey Boy", who composed *Standin' On the Corner Didn't Mean No Harm* – "with my Susan Melinda, up came a coon and he grabbed her by the arm" – written in 1895, provide another popular line for Reed and Hull's *Original Stack O'Lee Blues*? Did Irving Jones's *I'm Lending Money To the Government Now*, with its boast "I've got more money than the law allows" provide the source for Will Shade's comment on the early days in Memphis?[44] Perhaps such questions are unanswerable, but there is much evidence of a close relationship between the themes and idioms of the blues with those of the songs of the ragtime era and the medicine show stage.

Though the personalizing of lyrics in blues has been subject to much comment, there is no denying that blues singers were central to their songs, either by projection, or by personal narration. It is essential to the nature of the blues that the singer is also the subject, whether he fantasizes in that role, places himself in a conventionalized situation within the lyric or describes an incident in his own life. This aspect emerges in some of the ragtime songs but is rare; it is even rarer to find a blues which is not focused upon the blues singer himself. A blues singer finds and describes his identity, admittedly often through conventions, clichés or formulae, but also frequently through fragments of his own experience. It seems likely that record scouts and promoters played a part in this, encouraging "originals" and emphasizing the personality of the blues singer in publicity. There also appears to be a progression from loose aggregations of blues stanzas towards more structured and narrative blues through the period. If this is broadly true, it may have been through an increasing awareness of the potential of the blues by the singers themselves, or pressure on the part of the record men. In effect, it was probably both: blues singers responding to suggestions, and discovering for themselves the possibilities for thematic development.

Blues gained from its individualism, but it lost in a number of ways. The variety of tunes, the complexity of instrumental accompaniments and the dexterity of the musicians were reduced as blues guitarists and singers settled for an ever narrower range of stanza structures. They seldom varied the form within performances, and often exploited clichés of phrasing and instrumental mannerism which would have shamed some of the best of the songster-guitarists. Blues opened up the potential of music-making and expression to a far greater number of musicians, while its basic structure, if not its more subtle expression, could be learned very rapidly. In the face of this it was perhaps inevitable that the appeal of the old songs would wane.

Many of the factors which made the ragtime and minstrel songs significant for rural singers and their audiences for over three decades also had bearing on the religious music of the period. It too, was born out of segregation, providing a powerful and spiritual counter-force which inspired a new and passionate religious impulse. Perhaps the preachers accepted the stereotypes that were depicted in the popular songs too readily; certainly they inveighed against the behavior caricatured in the coon songs, sometimes with an extravagance which was a caricature in itself. The fundamentalist Baptists, and not a few of the store-front sects, were puritanical in their attitudes to dancing, drinking, gambling, smoking, fashion and much else, and the proscriptions of some of the churches were as restrictive as the life depicted in ragtime songs was undisciplined and libertine.

Pursuing the way of the Lord on earth, seeking sainthood through obedience, the congregations and evangelizing ministers had a faith on which to depend and a Word to follow. The themes of both sermons and spirituals were often traditional, though their interpretations of them were frequently original. Like the Biblical texts on which the sermons were based the spirituals and long-meter hymns provided a strong thread of continuity and tradition through the Baptist services on record.

Because of their emphases on baptism by fire, sanctification, spontaneous praise, speaking in tongues and, particularly, holy dancing and instrumental music, the Holiness churches were often viewed with outright hostility by the established churches. As the call to preach required neither literacy nor ordination the preachers were held in deep suspicion by those outside their churches and, almost in defiance, with passionate loyalty within them. In spite of this, the later recordings by Baptist preachers revealed in the use of contemporary themes, and even in occasional use of music, the influence of the Sanctified churches. The Church of God in Christ among the Sanctified, Holiness and Pentecostal churches was very influential in this respect, but, bearing in mind its proportionately small numbers, the extent of recording bore no proportional relationship to the membership of the church.

To what degree the secular elements in Sanctified song were sought or encouraged by the record companies is a matter of conjecture. It appears that these qualities were more apparent in the later records, on the threshold of the Depression, than on the earlier ones. This could have been a result of a desire to find singers of this type in order to increase potential sales in a difficult period, for it was a tendency that paralleled the increasing secular and worldly content of the sermons on record. But it may have been a direct reflection of a change taking place in the Sanctified church itself. There is evidence, as has been shown, of a shared repertoire, and an awareness of material by other singers on record which influenced newcomers to the recording studio. Street singers, camp meetings, the gospel song books of the white evangelical movement and even the radio broadcasts of Sister Aimee Semple McPherson and her Four-Square Gospel all helped to introduce popular elements into the services.[45] But whatever the sources of the process of secularization there is no doubt that recording helped to consolidate it.

Yet, of the preachers who recorded in the twenties, only Reverend J. M. Gates was recorded extensively in the following decade, with approximately forty titles, several being two-part sermons. A quarter of all sermons on record before World War II were by this most popular of Baptist preachers who could look back on a long and successful career. When he died in the 1940s, thousands lined the route of the cortège. Some of the most celebrated of the Sanctified preachers did not record again even though they made personal advances. Reverend Rice returned to Alabama having been made Bishop for his Pentecostal denomination; he was still preaching and broadcasting in the 1960s and died in Montgomery in 1973. Reverend McGee became Bishop of the Church of God in Christ in both Chicago and New York and died in 1971 having led a fulfilled life which had taken him to Mexico and even to the Holy Land. Their promotions indicated the tendency in the Sanctified churches to seek established status.[46]

Jack-leg preachers and street singers were in a sense outside the institutionalized structure; but though there were declared opponents to the denominations, like Washington Phillips, most jack-legs hoped for a chance to preach, endeavored to establish their own front parlor or store-front churches or joined the Church of God in Christ, where their fundamentalism and their music was welcome. There was also a marked decline in the number of evangelists recorded after the first phase; victims of the Depression perhaps, or aging and absorbed within the church. With the new songs of such gospel composers as Thomas A. Dorsey – the former blues singer and hokum artist Georgia Tom – the focus of the record industry was directed to the new, sharp, smart gospel quartets and swinging jazz-inflected rhythms of Elder Beck, or later, Sister Rosetta Tharpe.[47] Compared with them the street evangelist may have sounded archaic. The sermons and congregational singing, Sanctified churches with their music, and street evangelists with their self-accompanied songs in the first phase of Race records revealed the richness, variety, energy and conviction of the black churches: qualities that were to carry them through the years of stress which were to come. What distinguished the context of religious singers from that of the songsters was essentially the persistence of an institutional framework. The denomination provided a shelter for the singing congregations and a body with which to associate. Moreover, the preachers were differently motivated, their evangelizing and proselytizing being directed towards collectivity within the corporate churches.

Songsters had no such structure within which to work. A few minstrel shows like the dependable Silas Green and Rabbit Foot companies continued to operate but they offered a seasonal and precarious living. Like the record companies, they too were seeking new singers. Some of the old record companies, such as Paramount or Gennett closed down; others concluded their Race series, reshuffled or were bought up. New labels like Decca and Bluebird started Race series that featured young singers of the modern blues.

Of the former songsters on record for the Race labels in the twenties, only Charley Patton made a substantial number of titles. But, of around thirty items made under his own name or, in three instances, accompanying Bertha Lee, only a dozen were released. Important and extensively recorded songsters like Blind Blake, Gus Cannon, Jim Jackson, Sam Jones, Coley Jones, Henry Thomas, Furry Lewis, Mississippi John Hurt, Peg Leg Howell and Frank Stokes were not recorded commercially again. Only Papa Charlie Jackson made a few titles, which in 1934 already sounded out of date. The Memphis Jug Band was alone among the jug and string bands to make a significant number of recordings in the second phase – twenty, of which all but four were issued – mainly good-time music.

Those who survived and flourished in the thirties were the performers who combined the instrumental and inventive skills of the songster with an ability to respond to the increasing sophistication of the blues: Big Bill Broonzy, Bo Carter, Memphis Minnie, Lonnie Johnson, Tampa Red, Blind Willie McTell. Most slipped in the odd title of songster repertoire which can be traced in their extensive discographies. But, by 1938 Charley Patton, Blind Blake, Jim

Bo Carter (left) continued to record in the 1930s but Will Shade, leader of the Memphis Jug Band did not do so after 1934. Gus Cannon – Banjo Joe, made his last commercial records in 1930. All three continued to work in shows and for local events in Memphis and Mississippi through the 1940s. Photograph by Paul Oliver.

Jackson, Papa Charlie Jackson were all dead, though some of their contemporaries like Frank Stokes, Gus Cannon and Furry Lewis, adding more blues to their repertoires, continued to work the medicine shows or played for country suppers and local functions through the thirties and forties.

While the gospel quartets and solo singers satisfied the desire for an idiom appropriate to a modern religion which invited participation, gave free rein to emotional engagement, and which spoke for the fundamentalist beliefs in the black working class, the blues offered a framework for a secular individualized music which provided the outlets for self-expression while meeting the need for group entertainment. Blues and gospel as they matured in the thirties responded to the strains of the post-depression era, given further shape by the more knowing operations of the recording industry.[48]

The deep schisms in American society, in the relationships of blacks to whites and between the collective thrust of the church and the emergence of self-identification among the independent blacks were complemented by these growing musical forms.[49] Dance songs and routines, ragtime themes and medicine show entertainment, social songs and nodal ballads, in the secular traditions; fire-and-brimstone sermons, Sanctified gospel songs and the ballets of the street evangelists were eventually to be largely displaced by the blues and gospel song. But in varying degrees they mirrored the changes in society and the aspirations of the black masses, and these new forms owed their evolution and character to the music and song that had preceded them.

By comparing the recordings made by the songsters in the 1920s with the songs collected in the field in the previous decades; by examining these vocal traditions with the ragtime and dance songs of the nineties in mind; by considering the songs of the Baptist and Sanctified congregations and the street evangelists alongside the sermons, and comparing these with some of the published Pentecostal songs of the turn of the century, I hope to have pushed back the study of black song prior to recording by some thirty years, and in some cases by much more. The critical period from the end of Reconstruction to the First World War was a time when black music assumed its identity. Piano ragtime, instrumental ragtime, ragtime songs, ballads, black vaudeville and minstrelsy, New Orleans jazz, the blues and the songs of the Sanctified church all assumed their independent shape in this bitter period of segregation and Jim Crow laws. Some of them – piano ragtime, instrumental jazz, ballads and blues – have been given considerable critical attention; others, among them ragtime songs, social songs, vaudeville, minstrelsy, gospel song and sermons have received comparatively little. There is much that needs to be done.

In concluding this present work I wish to summarize what some of these areas of research might be. In the first place, this study has been mainly concerned with the songs and their lyrics, their possible sources and reasons for their survival and popularity. Quite the most pressing undertaking would be an examination of their musical structure and the transitional forms which accompaniments and vocal lines have taken. In particular, comparative studies of the differing approaches of various songsters would add to our knowledge of the creative process in the black community.

No less urgent is the need for a more searching examination of the relationship of the white song traditions with those of blacks. It may be noted that many white folk singers have acknowledged their debt to black musicians; the reverse influence of whites on blacks is far less frequently stated. Clearly the subject needs investigation in depth, with comparative repertoires, including their relationships and their differences, carefully noted.

Further research in text collections may reveal many more correspondences with published secular song. A wider knowledge of the songs that were in print may still make it possible to recover examples in the field. It is likely that phrases, even whole stanzas, that were passed into the blues could be traced to song texts, while a more concentrated search in the obscure publications of the early century, or in archives and private collections, may still turn up old field notes that could throw further light on the connexions between published song and the folk traditions. If some were uncovered from nineteenth-century collections, it might be possible to ascertain whether the published songs themselves incorporated stanzas that were in folk currency.[50]

Much work needs to be done on the sales and distribution of sheet music in music stores in Southern cities; similarly the question of sales of records, already mentioned here; their popularity and the kinds of audience that responded to the different categories of music could be the subject of useful research. But the whole question of the recorded artist and his record-purchasing public, the impact that records had on folk musicians, and the degree to which they stimulated others or, conversely, took their place in the jukes, is still largely unexplored.

More practicable might be the further documentation of dances, and hence the songs and music that accompanied them. As the present work has shown, the names of dances, and very probably many of their steps also, establish a thread of continuity which extends back into the slavery period; it is likely that some dances at least have survived to the present in country areas. As yet, plantation and rural dances have not been subject to much serious examination, the Stearnses' *Jazz Dance* concentrating on the black professional stage. On the other hand, the whole field of minstrel, vaudeville and stage entertainment for black audiences has had relatively little examination to date. In particular, the enormous quantity of recordings of vaudeville and "classic blues" singers has been as seriously disregarded as have the recordings of folk traditions. It is not merely a matter of hearing and comparing their songs and performances, though this remains to be done in depth; it is also a question of their links with the medicine show stage on one plane, and with the Broadway stage on another. Any inter-relationships of repertoire and performers that may have existed across the range of black

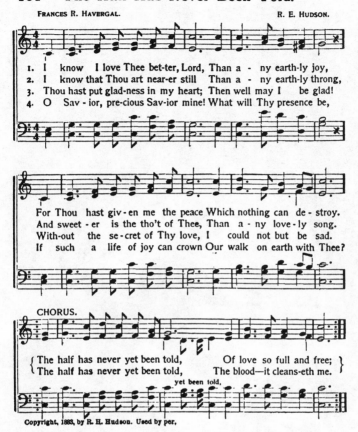

Havergal and Hudson's *The Half Has Never Been Told.* Philip P. Bliss wrote another version in the same year, 1883. *Paul Oliver collection.*

professional entertainment, including the interaction between black entertainers and white outside the minstrel show, also need reviewing.

Much of the latter can now only be deduced from recordings, for few veterans of the professional stage remain in the early 1980s. As for the vocal traditions within the less sophisticated or folk fields, there is evidence that a wide range of songs survived until recently, and probably still does. Field recordings since 1960 were, with a few notable exceptions, largely aimed at obtaining blues, yet they have produced many examples of gospel and evangelical songs, ballads, social songs, and occasional medicine show items. More broadly purposeful recording might have recovered many more – especially in the much neglected ragtime song genres.

In this book, which is concerned with the formative period, I have not attempted to examine these late recordings, but clearly this is work which

Walter "Furry" Lewis the last survivor of the songster generation who recorded in the 1920s, at his Memphis home, 1980. He died the following year, aged 88. Photograph by Paul Oliver.

should be undertaken, augmented wherever possible by further, systematic fieldwork. With the origins of some of the song forms now nearly a century away the chances for constructive research in the field diminish drastically with every year.

This leads me to acknowledge both my debt to the early collectors and my respect for their perception. As a writer on blues I shared with many others some exasperation for their lack of interest in the new genre, and did not regard sufficiently the breadth of their work. Only a small number of these collectors were extensively or professionally engaged in the field – Howard Odum, John A. Lomax, E. C. Perrow and Newman Ivey White among them. Many were students in Southern Universities and colleges, still others were interested friends of the compilers. The majority were amateurs in the best sense, who sent their manuscript notes to Newman White or Dorothy Scarborough who compared them with other versions in their compilations. Few had the benefit of a recording machine; most collectors seem to have depended on their ears and notebooks. Anyone who transcribes lyrics from records that can be played over many times knows how difficult this can be. That it is possible to compare the words of songs on record with many of those printed from their manuscript notes made in the field is an indication of their integrity, accuracy and catholicity, for which I have had growing admiration during the course of the present study. Would that the same could be said of those of us who have documented the blues in the past twenty-five years.

The half may never be told in full, but if we are to understand the sacred, secular and synthesized popular music of our time, we need to comprehend its origins, persistence and evolution, without prejudice or attitudes pre-conditioned by partiality for specific idioms.

Notes

Generally, where books and articles are cited once only, publication details are given in the Notes; those that are cited several times are listed in the Bibliography. Details of records and published sheet music are given in the Notes; see also the Index of Song Titles. For abbreviations see Index of Artists.

Introduction

1 Reverend F. W. McGee, pr, acc. unk., 4 vo, tmb, p, g, d, *The Half Ain't Never Been Told*, Victor 21492, Chicago, June 1, 1928.
2 Dixon and Godrich, *Recording the Blues*; Oliver, *The Story of the Blues*.
3 Handy, *A Treasury of the Blues*; Waters, *His Eye is on the Sparrow*; Broonzy, *Big Bill Blues*; Handy, *Father of the Blues*; Oliver, *Bessie Smith*.
4 Odum, "Folk-Song and Folk-Poetry"; Perrow, "Songs and Rhymes from the South", 1912,13,15; Thomas, *Some Current Folk-Song*; W. Prescott Webb, "Notes to the Folk-Lore of Texas"; J. Lomax, "Self-Pity in Negro Folk-Songs".
5 Talley, *Negro Folk Rhymes*; Odum and Johnson, *Negro Workaday Songs*; Scarborough, *On the Trail of Negro Folk-Songs*; Niles, critical text to Handy, *A Treasury of the Blues*; White, *American Negro Folk-Songs*, p. 388.
6 White, *American Negro Folk-Songs*, p. 390.
7 Johnson, *The Book of American Negro Spirituals*; *The Second Book of Negro Spirituals*; Kennedy, *Mellows*.
8 Sandburg, *The American Songbag*; V. Calverton, ed. *Anthology of American Negro Literature*, New York: The Modern Library, 1929; Sterling Brown, "The Blues as Folk Poetry", in B. A. Botkin, ed. *Folk-Say. A Regional Miscellany*, Norman, Okla: University of Oklahoma Press, 1930.
9 Lomax and Lomax, *American Ballads and Folk Songs; Negro Folk Songs; Folk Song, U.S.A.*; A. Lomax, *The Folk Songs of North America*.
10 B. A. Botkin, ed. *A Treasury of Mississippi River Folklore*, New York: Crown Publishers Inc., 1955; Courlander, *Negro Folk Music U.S.A.*.
11 Jan Harold Brunvand, *The Study of American Folklore*, New York: W. W. Norton and Co., 1968; Duncan Emrich, *Folklore on the American Land*, Boston: Little, Brown and Co., 1972.
12 Frederic Ramsey, Jr., and Charles Edward Smith, ed. *Jazzmen*, New York: Harcourt Brace, 1939; Iain Lang, *Background of the Blues*, Keynote Series Book 2, London: Worker's Music Association, 1942.
13 Ernest Borneman, *A Critic Looks at Jazz*, London: Jazz Music Books, 1946, p. 40; Rudi Blesh, *Shining Trumpets, A History of Jazz*, London: Cassell and Co., 1949, pp. 109–48.
14 Charters, *The Country Blues*; Oliver, *Blues Fell This Morning*.
15 Titon, *Early Downhome Blues*, p. 110.
16 Pete Welding, "The Art of Folk Blues Guitar", *Downbeat*, 32, No. 14, July 1, 1965, pp. 22–4, 56; Charles Keil, *Urban Blues*, Chicago: University of Chicago Press, 1966, Appendix C, "Blues Styles: An Annotated Outline", pp. 217–24.

288

17 Examples not elsewhere cited include: Derrick Stewart-Baxter, *Ma Rainey and the Classic Blues*, London: Studio Vista, 1970; William Ferris, *Blues From the Delta*, Garden City, N.Y.: Anchor Doubleday, 1978; Peter Guralnick, *Feel Like Going Home: Portraits in Blues and Rock 'n' Roll*, New York: Outerbridge and Dienstfrey, 1971; Harry Oster, *Living Country Blues*, Detroit: Folklore Associates, 1960; Paul Garon, *Blues and the Poetic Spirit*, London: Eddison, 1975; Eric Sackheim, *The Blues Line, A Collection of Blues Lyrics*, New York: Schirmer Books, 1975; Charles Sawyer, *The Arrival of B. B. King*, New York: Doubleday, 1980; Mike Rowe, *Chicago Breakdown*, London: Eddison Press, 1973; Giles Oakley, *The Devil's Music*, London: British Broadcasting Corporation, 1976; Richard Middleton, *Pop Music and the Blues*, London: Victor Gollancz Ltd., 1972; Michael Haralambos, *Right On: From Blues to Soul in Black America*, London: Eddison Press, 1974.
18 *Blues Unlimited*, Bexhill-on-Sea and London, 1963– . *Living Blues*, Chicago, 1970– . Examples of other Blues Magazines include: *Blues World*, U.K.: *Jefferson*, Sweden; *Blues Forum*, Germany; *Blues Life*, Austria; *B.N.*, Finland; *R and B Panorama*, Belgium; *Block*, Holland; *Il Blues*, Italy; *Juke*, Japan; *Alley Music*, Australia.
19 Harris, *Blues Who's Who*, p. 9.
20 Lydia Parrish, *Slave Songs of the Georgia Sea Islands*, New York: Farrar, Straus and Co., 1942; Miles Mark Fisher, *Negro Slave Songs in the United States*, Ithaca, N.Y.: Cornell University Press, 1953.
21 John Lovell Jr., *Black Song: The Forge and the Flame*, New York: Macmillan, 1972; Dena Epstein, *Sinful Tunes and Spirituals*, Urbana and Chicago: University of Illinois Press, 1977.
22 Robert William Fogel and Stanley L. Engerman, *Time on the Cross*, London: Little, Brown and Co., 1974; Paul A. David, Herbert G. Gutman *et al.*, *Reckoning with Slavery*, New York: Oxford University Press, 1976; John W. Blassingame, *The Slave Community*, New York: Oxford University Press, 1979. Albert J. Raboteau, *Slave Religion*, New York: Oxford University Press, 1978.
23 Raichelson, *Black Religious Folksong*; Ricks, *Some Aspects of the Religious Music of the United States Negro*; Heilbut, *The Gospel Sound*; Mahalia Jackson and Evan McLeod Wylie, *Movin' On Up*, New York: Hawthorn Books, 1966; Doug Seroff, Album notes to *Birmingham Quartet Anthology*, Clanka-Lanka CL144001/2, 1980; William Tallmadge, Album notes to *Jubilee to Gospel*, JEMF 108, 1980.
24 Bessie Jones and Bess Lomax Hawes, *Step It Down: Games, Plays, Songs, and Stories from the Afro-American Heritage*, Evanston, Ill.: Harper and Row, 1972; Bruce Jackson, *Wake Up Dead Man: Afro-American Worksongs from Texas Prisons*, Cambridge, Mass: Harvard University Press, 1972; Roger D. Abrahams, *Deep Down in the Jungle: Negro Narrative Folklore from the Streets of Philadelphia*, Hatboro, Penn: Folklore Associates, 1964.
25 For discussion see John Cowley, "The Library of Congress Archive of Folk Song Recordings" in Dixon and Godrich, *Blues and Gospel Records* (3rd edn) 1982; Harold Courlander, *Negro Folk Music U.S.A.*, 1963; Frederic Ramsey Jr., *Been Here and Gone*, New Brunswick, N.J.: Rutgers, the State University, 1960; Bob Groom, *The Blues Revival*, London: Studio Vista, 1970, pp. 25–38.
26 *The Rural Blues – Sacred Tradition 1927–1930*, Herwin 206; *Traditional Jazz in Rural Churches 1928–1930*, Truth Record TLP-101; microgroove reissues are listed in Godrich and Dixon, *Blues and Gospel Records 1902–1942* (2nd edn only).
27 For detailed accounts see Foreman, 'Jazz and Race Records'; Dixon and Godrich, *Recording the Blues*.
28 Charlie Gillett, *The Sound of the City: The Rise of Rock and Roll*, New York: Outerbridge and Dienstfrey, 1970.
29 LeRoi Jones, *Blues People: Negro Music in White America*, London: MacGibbon and Kee, 1965.
30 Dan Mahony, *The Columbia 13/14000-D Series: A Numerical Listing*, Stanhope, N. J.: Walter C. Allen, 1961; Brian A. L. Rust, *The Victor Master Book Volume 2 (1925–1936)*, Hatch End, Middlesex: 1969; Max E. Vreede, *Paramount 12000/13000 Series*, London: Storyville Publications, 1971; Brian Rust and Allen G. Debus, *The Complete Entertainment Discography from the Mid-1890's to 1942*, New Rochelle, N.Y.: Arlington House, 1973.
31 Chris Albertson, *Bessie*, London: Barrie and Jenkins, 1972; Sandra R. Lieb, *Mother of the*

Blues: A Study of Ma Rainey, Amherst, Mass: University of Massachusetts Press, 1981.

32   Bengt Olsson, *Memphis Blues and Jug Bands*, London: Studio Vista, 1970; a forthcoming book by Fred E. Cox, John Randolph and John Harris, *Jug Bands of Louisville* was announced in Storyville, No. 66, August–September 1976.

33   A discography of hillbilly and Old Time music is in preparation by Tony Russell. Name discographies have appeared in *Old Time Music*, London: 1971–2.

34   Frank C. Brown Collection, ed. White, 1952.

1   Dance songs and routines

1   George Mitchell, "An Interview with Peg Leg Howell", Note to *The Legendary Peg Leg Howell*, Testament T-204.

2   Peg Leg Howell, vo, g, *Coal Man Blues*, Columbia 14194-D, Atlanta, November 8, 1926: see also Charters, *Sweet as the Showers of Rain*, pp. 108–9.

3   Lomax, "Self Pity in Negro Folk Song", p. 14: see also, Oliver, *Story of the Blues*, p. 44.

4   Peg Leg Howell, vo, g, *Please Ma'am*, Columbia 14356-D, Atlanta, April 20, 1928; Mitchell, interview, *The Legendary Peg Leg Howell*.

5   Peg Leg Howell, vo, g, *Skin Game Blues*, Columbia 14473-D, Atlanta, November 9, 1927; see also, Oliver, *Blues Fell This Morning*, p. 155.

6   Peg Leg Howell, vo, g, poss. Ollie Griffin, vln, *Rolling Mill Blues*, Columbia 14438-D, Atlanta, April 10, 1929; Oliver, *Story of the Blues*, p. 44.

7   Judith McCulloh, "In the Pines: The Melodic-Textual Identity of an American Lyric Folk-Song Cluster", Indiana University, unpublished Ph. D. Thesis, 1970; The complex interweaving of the songs, *The Longest Train, In The Pines, Reuben's Train, Train 45* and *900 Miles* is discussed in Norm Cohen, *Long Steel Rail*, pp. 491–502, 503–17.

8   Odum, "Folk-Song and Folk-Poetry", pp. 258–9; W. H. Thomas, *Some Current Folk-Songs*, p. 5.

9· G. Malcolm Laws Jr., *American Balladry from British Broadsides*, Philadelphia: The American Folklore Society, 1957, pp. 47–9. For recent use of these terms see Mack McCormick, notes to Mance Lipscomb, *Texas Sharecropper and Songster*, Arhoolie F 1001, 1960; Little Brother Montgomery (1960) in Oliver, *Conversation with the Blues*, p. 62; Aaron Cleveland Sparks (1975, 1977) in Mike Rowe and Charlie O'Brien, "Well Them Two Sparks Brothers they been here and gone", *Blues Unlimited*, No. 144, Spring 1983.

10   Peg Leg Howell, vo, g, and Jim Hill, vo, mand, *Chittlin' Supper*, Columbia 14426-D, Atlanta, April 13, 1929.

11   Charles Dickens, *American Notes* (1850), London: Chapman and Hall, 1913, chap. 6.

12   Hans Nathan, *Dan Emmett*, pp. 73, 83; Charles Read Baskervill, *The Elizabethan Jig and Related Song Drama*, New York: Dover Publications, Inc., 1965, p. 361.

13   C. K. Ladzekpo and Olly Wilson, "Basic Anlo-Ewe Dance Form" in 'Introduction to the Music of the Anlo-Ewe People of Ghana', unpub. MS, chap. 5. The suggestion that minstrel dancing was copied from blacks has been contested by San Dennison, "The Roots of Blackface Minstrel Music", paper given to the Symposium on *American Popular Music and Its Impact on World Culture*, Dartmouth College, May 13–15, 1983.

14   Norman R. Yetman, *Life Under the "Peculiar Institution"*, p. 218; B. A. Botkin, *Lay My Burden Down*, p. 56.

15   Dena J. Epstein, *Sinful Tunes and Spirituals*, pp. 53–4; Federal Writers' Project, *The Negro in Virginia*, New York: Hartings House, pp. 92–3.

16   Yetman, *Life Under the "Peculiar Institution"*, pp. 190, 268.

17   George Rawick, *The American Slave*, see for example, *Mississippi Narratives*, Part 4. Jim Marlin, p. 1438, Harriett Miller, p. 1505, Glaccow Norwood, p. 1650.

18   Epstein, *Sinful Tunes and Spirituals*, pp. 139–60; Dena J. Epstein, "The Folk Banjo: A Documentary History", *Ethnomusicology*, Vol. 19, no. 5, September 1975, pp. 347–71; Courlander, *Negro Folk Music U.S.A.*, p. 000.

19   Rawick, *The American Slave*, Texas Narratives, Part 3, John Crawford, p. 975.

20 McCormick, *Henry Thomas*. Henry Thomas (Ragtime Texas), vo, g, quills, *Old Country Stomp*, Vocalion 1230, Chicago, June 13, 1928. Compare it with the account of plantation dances by "Maum Katie, a very old Negro woman" in Henry C. Davis, "Negro Folk Lore in South Carolina", *Journal of American Folk-Lore*, July–September 1914, pp. 241–54.

21 Thomas W. Talley, *Negro Folk Rhymes*, New York: Macmillan Co., 1922, pp. 303–6; George W. Cable, "The Dance in Place Congo", *Century Magazine*, February 1886, reprinted in *Creoles and Cajuns*, New York: Doubleday and Company, Inc., 1959, p. 371. See also Epstein, *Sinful Tunes and Spirituals*, p. 145, for additional information on quills.

22 Scarborough, *On The Trail of Negro Folk-Songs*, pp. 102–4.

23 Stovepipe No. 1, vo, g, hca, stovepipe, *Cripple Creek and Sourwood Mountain*, Columbia 201-D, New York, August 20, 1924; *Turkey in the Straw*, Columbia 201-D, New York, August 20, 1924.

24 Nathan, *Dan Emmett*, pp. 174–5. Peg Leg Howell, vo, g, and Eddie Anthony, vo, vln, *Turkey Buzzard Blues*, Columbia 14382–D, Atlanta, October 30, 1928.

25 Vernon Lane Wharton, *The Negro in Mississippi 1865–1890* (1947), New York: Harper and Row, 1965, p. 270.

26 Lafcadio Hearn, "Levee Life", pp. 227, 228–9.

27 Epstein, *Sinful Tunes and Spirituals*, pp. 141–4.

28 Ann Charters, *The Ragtime Songbook*, pp. 19–21; Blesh and Janis, *They All Played Ragtime*, pp. 151–2.

29 Blind Blake, vo, g, *West Coast Blues*, Paramount 12387, Chicago, c. September 1926.

30 Blind Blake, vo, g, unk. bones, *Dry Bone Shuffle*, Paramount 12479, Chicago, c. May 1927.

31 Nathan, *Dan Emmett*, p. 127.

32 William Moore, vo, g, *Barbershop Rag*, Paramount 12613, Chicago, c. January 1928; *Ragtime Crazy*, Paramount 12648, Chicago, c. January 1928.

33 Tom and Mary Anne Evans, *Guitars: From the Renaissance to Rock*, London: Paddington Press, 1977, pp. 220–59.

34 Ann Charters, "Negro Folk Elements in Classic Ragtime", *Ethnomusicology*, Vol. 5, no. 3, September 1961, pp. 174–82; Berlin, *Ragtime*, Part 1, pp. 1–56, Berlin gives extensive references on the "perceptions of ragtime", pp. 56–60.

35 Jim Jackson, vo, g, *Bye, Bye, Policeman*, Victor V38505, Memphis, September 7, 1928.

36 Ernest Hogan, *La Pas Ma La*, New York; M. Witmark and Sons, 1895.

37 Cannon's Jug Stompers, Gus Cannon, vo, bj, jug, acc. bj, vo, k, hca, *Walk Right In*, Victor V38611, Memphis, October 1, 1929; Max Hoffman, *Bom-Ba-Shay*, New York, M. Witmark and Sons, 1897; William Jerome and Jean Schwurz, *That Spooney Dance*, New York; Jerome H. Remick and Co., 1909; Ed Rogers and Saul Aaronson, *Alabama Bound*, New York: M. Witmark and Sons, 1916.

38 Jim Jackson, vo, g, *This Mornin' She Was Gone*, Victor V38003, Memphis, August 27, 1928.

39 Stearns, *Jazz Dance*, pp. 110, 111.

40 Evans, *Atlanta Blues*, p. 10. (Georgia Bill) Blind Willie McTell, vo, g, *Georgia Rag*, Okeh 8924, Atlanta, October 31, 1931.

41 Henry Williams, vo, g, and Eddie Anthony, vo, vln, *Georgia Crawl*, Columbia 14328-D, Atlanta, April 19, 1928.

42 Peg Leg Howell, vo, g, and His Gang, *Too Tight Blues*, Columbia 14298-D, Atlanta, November 1, 1927.

43 Barbecue Bob, vo, g, *Doin' the Scraunch*, Columbia 14591-D, Atlanta, December 5, 1930.

44 Stearns, *Jazz Dance*, p. 105; Sylvia Dannett and Frank Rachel, *Down Memory Lane*, New York: Greenberg, 1954, p. 94.

45 LeRoi Jones, *Blues People*, p. 17; Stearns, *Jazz Dance*, p. 112.

46 Jim O'Neal and Steve LaVere, "Too Tight Henry" in *Living Blues*, No. 34, 1977. Too Tight Henry, vo, g, *Charleston Contest*, Columbia 14374-D, Atlanta, October 27, 1928.

47 (Papa) Charlie Jackson, vo, bj, *Skoodle Um Skoo*, Paramount 12501, Chicago, c. July 1927; Seth Richard, vo, g, *Skoodeldum Doo*, Columbia 14325-D, New York, May 15, 1928.

48 Winston Holmes, vo, and Charlie Turner, g, *Kansas City Dog Walk*, Paramount 12815, Richmond, Ind., June 21, 1929. Stearns, *Jazz Dance*, p. 213.

49   Pink Anderson, vo, g, and Simmie Dooley, vo, g, k, *Gonna Tip Out Tonight*, Columbia 14336-D, Atlanta, April 14, 1928.

50   Oliver, Paul, *Juke Joint Blues*, Sleeve note for Blues Classics, BC 23, 1970, reprinted in *Blues Off the Record*; Zora Neale Hurston, *Mules and Men*, Philadelphia: Lippincott, 1935, p. 66; Zora Neale Hurston, in *Negro*, ed. Nancy Cunard, London: Nancy Cunard, 1934.

51   Hazekiah Jenkins (sic), vo, g, *Shout You Cats*, Columbia 14585-D, New York, January 16, 1931.

52   McKee and Chisenhall, *Beale Black and Blue*, p. 184.

53   Stearns, *Jazz Dance*, p. 13.

54   Scott Joplin, *Treemonisha – Opera in 3 Acts*, St. Louis and New York: Scott Joplin Music Company, 1911; Stearns, *Jazz Dance*, p. 21.

55   William Moore, vo, g, *Old Country Rock*, Paramount 12761, Chicago, c. January 1928.

56   Oliver, *Blues Fell This Morning*, pp. 163–5; Oliver, *The Story of the Blues*, pp. 83–4; Hughes and Bontemps, *The Book of Negro Folklore*, pp. 596–600.

57   Jim Clarke, vo, p, *Fat Fanny Stomp*, Vocalion 1536, Chicago, December 1929.

58   Nathan, *Dan Emmett*, pp. 130–1; 88–91; 72.

59   Georgia Tom, vo, p, and Hannah May, vo, acc. g, *Come On Mama*, Oriole 8033, New York, September 16, 1930.

2   Songs from the ragtime era

1   Newman I. White, "The White Man in the Wood pile", p. 210.

2   *Ibid.*, pp. 214–15, 213.

3   Spaeth, *Read 'Em and Weep*, pp. 108–10; Spaeth *History of Popular Music*, pp. 168–70.

4   Reginald Nettel, *Seven Centuries of Popular Song*, London: Phoenix House, 1956, pp. 209–10.

5   Blind Blake, vo, g, *Champagne Charlie Is My Name*, Paramount 3137, Grafton, Wis., c. June 1932.

6   James J. Geller, *Famous Songs and Their Stories*, New York: Macaulay, 1931, pp. 97–8.

7   The origins of the song are disputed. A discussion of the Bully songs appears in Norm Cohen, album notes to *Paramount Old Time Tunes*, JEMF 103, and notes to *Minstrels and Tunesmiths*, JEMF 109.

8   Memphis Jug Band, Ben Raney, vo, kazoo, acc.2g.j, *I'm Looking for the Bully of the Town*, Victor 20781, Chicago, June 9, 1927.

9   W. K. McNeil, "Syncopated Slander: The 'Coon Song' 1890–1900", *Keystone Folklore Quarterly*, Vol. 17, No. 2, Summer 1972, pp. 65–79.

10   W. F. Gates, "Ethiopian Syncopation; the Decline of Ragtime", quoted in Berlin, *Ragtime*, p. 341.

11   Berlin, *Ragtime*, p. 24; Tom Fletcher, *The Tom Fletcher Story: 100 Years of the Negro in Show Business*, New York: Burdge and Co., 1954, pp. 138–41.

12   Marks, *They All Sang*, p. 88.

13   Chris Smith, *Never Let the Same Bee Sting You Twice*, 1900, copy untraced, ref: Southern, *Biographical Dictionary*; Richard "Rabbit" Brown, vo, g, *Never Let the Same Bee Sting You Twice*, Victor 21475, New Orleans, March 11, 1927.

14   Elmer Bowman and Chris Smith, *Beans! Beans! Beans!*, New York: Lyceum Publishing Co., 1912; "Beans" Hambone, vo, g, and El Morrow, vo, g, *Beans*, Victor 23280, Charlotte, N.C., May 23, 1931. A full transcription appears in Richard K. Spottswood's album notes to *Songs of Humor and Hilarity*, Folk Music in America, Vol. 11, Library of Congress LBC 11.

15   Irving Jones, *Possumala Dance*, or, *My Honey*, New York: Willis Woodward and Co., 1894; G. Thomas, "South Texas Negro Work-Songs", p. 171.

16   Jim Jackson, vo, g, *I'm a Bad Bad Man*, Vocalion 1164, Chicago, January 23, 1928.

17   Blind Sammie (Willie McTell) vo, g, *Razor Ball*, Columbia 14551, Atlanta, April 17, 1930.

18   Odum and Johnson, *The Negro and His Songs*, p. 187; Irving Jones, *Let Me Bring My Clothes Back Home*, New York: F. A. Mills, 1898.

19 Webb, "Miscellany of Texas Folk-Lore", p. 48; Henry Thomas, vo, g, *Arkansas*, Vocalion 1286, Chicago, July 1, 1927.
20 Irving Jones, *My Money Never Gives Out*, New York: Feist and Frankenthaler, 1900.
21 Cannon's Jug Stompers, Gus Cannon, vo, bj, j, acc bj, hca, *My Money Never Runs Out*, Victor 23262, Memphis, November 28, 1930.
22 Irving Jones, *The Ragtime Millionaire*, New York: Feist and Frankenthaler, 1900.
23 William Moore, vo, g, *Ragtime Millionaire*, Paramount 12636, Chicago, c. January, 1928.
24 Irving Jones, *All Birds Look Like Chickens To Me*, New York: W. B. Gray and Co., 1899; Sweet Papa Stovepipe, vo, g, *All Birds Look Like Chicken To Me*, Paramount 12404, Chicago, November, 1926.
25 Irving Jones and Kerry Mills, *Under the Chicken Tree*, New York: F. W. Mills, 1908; Earl McDonald's Original Louisville Jug Band, McDonald, vo, *Under the Chicken Tree*, Columbia 14206-D, Atlanta, March 30, 1927.
26 Oliver, *Screening the Blues*, p. 39; Irving Jones and Maxwell Silver, *You Must Think I'm Santa Claus*, New York: F. A. Mills, 1904; Lil McClintock, vo, g, *Don't Think I'm Santa Claus*, Columbia 14575-D, Atlanta, December 4, 1930; Richard Raichelson, "Lil McClintock's Don't You Think I'm Santa Claus", *JEMF Quarterly*, Vol. 6, pt 3, Autumn 1970, No. 19, pp. 132–4.
27 The music sheets of Irving Jones's compositions are held in the Harding Collection, The Bodleian Library, Oxford.
28 Bureau of the Census, *Negro Population 1790–1915*, "Illiterates by Class of Population 1910", Table 27, p. 428; "Illiterates in the Negro Population in Rural and Urban Communities, 1910", Table 28, p. 429.
29 Marks, *They All Sang*, p. 93.
30 Hamm, *Yesterdays*, pp. 297–9; Oliver, *Screening the Blues*, p. 91; Hamm, *Yesterdays*, p. 300.
31 Blesh and Janis, *They All Played Ragtime*, p. 241.
32 Robert C. Toll, *Blacking Up: The Minstrel Show in Nineteenth Century America*, London: Oxford University Press, 1974, pp. 198–206.
33 *Ibid.*, pp. 275–80.
34 Ike Simond, *Old Slack's Reminiscence*, pp. 17, 9, 32; H. T. Sampson, *Blacks in Blackface*, pp. 6–7.
35 Southern, *Biographical Dictionary*; *New York Age*, February 19, 1912; *The Chicago Defender*, May, 1919 (courtesy Karl Gert zur Heide).
36 Marks, *They All Sang*, p. 96.
37 Oliver, *Screening The Blues*, pp. 174–5; Scott Middleton and Billy Smythe, *Hesitation Blues*, Chicago and Louisville, Kentucky: Billy Smythe Music Co., 1915; W. C. Handy, *The Hesitation Blues*, New York: Pace and Handy Music Co., 1915; Niles, "Historical and Critical Text" in Handy, *A Treasury of the Blues*, pp. 243–4; Handy, *Father of the Blues*, pp. 120–2.
38 Odum and Johnson, *The Negro and His Songs*, pp. 177–8.
39 Mississippi John Hurt vo, g, *Nobody's Dirty Business*, Okeh 8560 Memphis, February 14, 1928.
40 The sheet music is reproduced in Scarborough, *On the Trail of Negro Folk-Songs*, p. 268; Abbe Niles, "Notes to the Collection" in Handy, *A Treasury of the Blues*, p. 251; Scarborough, *On the Trail of Negro Folk-Songs*, pp. 266–7.
41 Jim Jackson, vo, g, *Long Gone*, Victor V38517, Memphis, September 7, 1928.
42 Papa Charlie Jackson, vo, g, *Long Gone Lost John*, Paramount 12602, Chicago, c. January 1928.
43 Dennis Jones (Little Hat Jones), vo, g, *Kentucky Blues*, Okeh 8815, San Antonio, Texas, June 14, 1930.
44 Henry Thomas, vo, g, *Bob McKinney*, Vocalion 1138, Chicago, October 5, 1927.
45 Frank Stokes, vo, g, Dan Sane, g, *Take Me Back*, Victor V38531, Memphis, August 30, 1928.
46 William Harris, vo, g, *Hot Time Blues*, Gennett 6707, Richmond, Ind., October 11, 1928.
47 George W. Lee, *Beale Street (Where the Blues Began)*, College Park, Maryland: McGrath Publishing Co., 1969, p. 153. Handy, *Father of the Blues*, pp. 93, 99–101.
48 Beale Street Sheiks, Frank Stokes, vo, g, Dan Sane, g, *Mister Crump Don't Like It*, Paramount 12552, Chicago, c. September, 1927.

49 Charlie Jackson, vo, bj, *Mama don't Allow It (And She Ain't Gonna Have It Here)*, Paramount 12296, Chicago, c. August, 1925.
50 Pat Rooney and Harry von Tilzer, *I've Got a Gal for Ev'ry Day in the Week*, Chicago and New York: Shapiro, Bernstein and Von Tilzer, 1900.
51 Papa Harvey Hull, vo, and Long Cleve Reed, vo, g, *Gang of Brown Skin Women*, Gennett 6122, Chicago, c. April 8, 1927.
52 Jim Jackson, vo, g, *My Monday Woman Blues*, Victor 21236, Memphis, January 30, 1928.
53 *Ibid.*

3   Songsters of the road shows

1 Sampson, *Blacks in Blackface*, p. 61: Southern, *Bibliographical Dictionary*.
2 Wittke, *Tambo and Bones*, p. 130; Oliver, *The Story of the Blues*, p. 60.
3 A. B. Spellman, *Four Lives in the Bebop Business*, London: McGibbon and Kee, 1967, pp. 98–9; Wittke, *Tambo and Bones*, p. 131.
4 "Stage–Music–Movies", *Chicago Defender*, various issues, 1929; Wittke, *Tambo and Bones*, pp. 130–1; Oliver, *The Story of the Blues*, pp. 58–64; Harris, *Blues Who's Who* (entries under named artists).
5 Leroy Carr, vo, p, acc. g, *Carried Water For the Elephant*, Vocalion 1593, Chicago, September 9, 1930.
6 Malcolm Webber, *Medicine Show*, Caldwell, Idaho: The Caxton Printers Ltd., 1941, pp. 100–2; Interview with Preston Love, *Sounds and Fury*, No. 7, 1965, p. 24.
7 White, *American Negro Folk-Songs*, pp. 389–90.
8 Stovepipe No. 1, vo, stovepipe, and David Crockett, g, *A Woman Gets Tired of the Same Man All the Time*, Okeh 8514, St. Louis, April 26, 1927.
9 Oliver, *Blues Fell This Morning*, pp. 222–3; Oliver, *Walter "Buddy Boy" Hawkins 1927–29*, Album notes to Matchbox Bluesmaster Series, MSE 202; Walter "Buddy Boy" Hawkins, vo, g, *How Come Mama Blues*, Paramount 12802, Richmond, Ind., June 14, 1929.
10 Ukelele Bob Williams, vo, uke, *West Indies Blues*, Paramount 12247, Chicago, c. November 1924.
11 Amy Jacques Garvey, *Philosophy and Opinions of Marcus Garvey* (Part I, 1923, Part II, 1925), London: Frank Cass, 1967, pp. XVII–XXI, Introduction to 2nd edn; Oliver, *Screening the Blues*, p. 172.
12 Ethel Waters with Charles Samuels, *His Eye Is on the Sparrow*, London: W. H. Allen, 1951, p. 149; Danny Barker, "A Memory of King Bolden", *Evergreen Review*, No. 37, September 1965, p. 68.
13 Stewart Holbrook, *Golden Age of Quackery*, pp. 198, 199, 204–7, 209–15.
14 Oliver, *Conversation With the Blues*, pp. 83–5; Interview with Sleepy John Estes and Hammie Nixon, *Living Blues*, No. 19, January/February 1975.
15 Odum and Johnson, *The Negro and His Songs*, p. 232; White, *American Negro Folk-Songs*, pp. 195–200.
16 "Big Boy" George Owens, *The Coon Crap Game*, Gennett 6006, Richmond, Ind., October 1926.
17 White, *American Negro Folk-Songs*, p. 195; John Queen and Charlie Cartwell, *I Got Mine*, New York: Howley, Haviland and Dresser, 1901.
18 Frank Stokes, vo, g, *I Got Mine*, Victor V38512, Memphis, August 27, 1928.
19 Bruce Bastin, *The Last Medicine Show*, Album notes to Flyright LP507/8; Brooks McNamara, *Step Right Up: An Illustrated History of the Medicine Show*, Garden City, N.Y.: Doubleday, 1976.
20 Rudi Blesh, *Keaton*, London: Secker and Warburg, 1966, pp. 15–21; Bill Malone, *Country Music U.S.A. – A Fifty Year History*, Austin: The University of Texas Press, 1968, pp. 19–20; Porterfield, *Jimmie Rodgers*, pp. 57–8; Mike Paris and Chris Comber, *Jimmy the Kid: The Life of Jimmie Rodgers*, London: Eddison Music Books, 1977, p. 31.
21 Paris and Comber, *Jimmy the Kid*, p. 29; Interview with Speckled Red, Oliver, *Conversation with the Blues*, p. 83.

22 Jim Jackson, vo, g, *He's In the Jailhouse Now*, Vocalion 1146, Chicago, January 22, 1928.

23 Porterfield, *Jimmie Rodgers*, p. 142 (Note 4); Llewellyn White, *The American Radio*, Chicago: University of Chicago Press, 1947, p. 13; Whistler and His Jug Band, Buford Threlkeld, vo, g, acc, vln, mand, *Jail House Blues*, Gennett 5614, Richmond, Ind., September 25, 1924.

24 Earl McDonald's Original Louisville Jug Band, Earl McDonald, vo, jug, acc. sax, bj, mand, *She's In the Graveyard Now*, Columbia 14255-D, Atlanta, March 30, 1927.

25 Blind Blake, vo, g, acc. bj, *He's In the Jailhouse Now*, Paramount 12565, c. November 1927.

26 Memphis Sheiks, Charlie Nickerson, vo, acc. hca, bj, mand, g, jug, *He's In the Jailhouse Now*, Victor 23256, Memphis, November 21, 1930.

27 Paris and Comber, *Jimmie The Kid*, p. 75.

28 Odum and Johnson, *Negro Workaday Songs*, p. 59; Don Kent, "On the Trail of Luke Jordan", *Blues Unlimited*, No. 66, p. 69.

29 Luke Jordan, vo, g, *Traveling Coon*, Victor 20957, Charlotte, North Carolina, August 16, 1927.

30 White, *American Negro Folk-Songs*, pp. 349–50.

31 Coley Jones, vo, g, *Traveling Man*, Columbia 14288-D, Dallas, December 4, 1927.

32 Jim Jackson, vo, g, *Traveling Man*, Victor V38517, Memphis, September 4, 1928.

33 Lawrence Levine, *Black Culture and Black Consciousness*, p. 405; White, *American Negro Folk-Songs*, p. 201.

34 Russell, *Blacks, Whites and Blues*, pp. 26, 47; Mack McCormick, *Henry Thomas*.

35 Alec Johnson, vo, acc. g, *Next Week Sometime*, Columbia 14416-D, Atlanta, November 2, 1928; Burris and Smith with Bert Williams, *Next Week! Sometime!! Not Now!!!*, New York: Gotham–Attucks Music, 1905.

36 Alec Johnson, vo, acc. p, vln, mand, *Mysterious Coon*, Columbia 14378-D, Atlanta, November 2, 1928.

37 McKee and Chisenhall, *Beale Black and Blue*, pp. 106, 195.

38 W. J. Simons, *There Is No Chicken That Can Roost Too High For Me*, Philadelphia: Wilsky Music Publishing Co., 1899; Beale Street Sheiks (Frank Stokes and Dan Sane) vo, g, *Chicken You Can Roost Behind the Moon*, Paramount 12576, Chicago, c. September, 1927.

39 Stovepipe No 1, vo, stovepipe; David Crockett, g, hca, *A Chicken Can Waltz the Gravy Around*, Okeh 8543, St. Louis, April 26, 1927.

40 E. C. Perrow, "Songs and Rhymes", No. 28, p. 135; White, *American Negro Folk Songs*, pp. 301–2; Frank C. Brown Collection, pp. 478, 547–8. Jim Jackson, vo, g, *What a Time*, Victor V38033, Memphis, August 28, 1928.

41 Jim Towel, vo, acc. p. *I've Been Hoodooed*, Brunswick 7060, Chicago, October 26, 1928; White, *American Negro Folk-Songs*, pp. 206–7; Gussie Davis, *I've Been Hoodoo'ed*, New York: Spaulding and Gray, 1894.

42 Bo Chatman, vo, vln, acc. mand, g, *Good Old Turnip Greens*, Brunswick 7048, New Orleans, c. December 1928; see also Russell, *Blacks, Whites and Blues*, p. 56.

43 Henry Thomas, vo, g, quills, *Charmin' Betsy*, Vocalion 1468, c. October 7, 1929; Jim Jackson, vo, g, *Going 'Round the Mountain*, Victor V38525, Memphis, September 4, 1928; White, *American Negro Folk-Songs*, pp. 316–21.

44 Odum and Johnson, *Negro Workaday Songs*, pp. 176–7; Ukelele Bob Williams, vo, uke, *Go Long Mule*, Paramount 12247, Chicago, c. November 1924; Odum and Johnson, *Negro Workaday Songs*, p. 178.

45 Genovese, *Roll, Jordan, Roll*, pp. 581–3; Levine, *Black Culture and Black Consciousness*, pp. 192–4; Epstein, *Sinful Tunes and Spirituals*, pp. 186–8.

46 Hearn, "Levee Life", p. 224; Odum and Johnson, *Negro Workaday Songs*, p. 115; Talley, *Negro Folk Rhymes*, p. 91; White, *American Negro Folk-Songs*, pp. 385–6.

47 Julius Daniels, vo, g, *Can't Put the Bridle on That Mule This Morning*, Victor 21359, Atlanta, October 24, 1927.

48 Scarborough, *On the Trail of Negro Folk-Songs*, p. 180; Barbecue Bob, vo, g, *Monkey and the Baboon*, Columbia 14523-D, Atlanta, April 23, 1930.

49 Constance Rourke, *American Humor*, Garden City, N.Y.: Doubleday and Company, Inc., 1931, pp. 88–90.

4 Fantasy, reality and parody

1   Interview with Carl Martin, *Living Blues*, No. 43, Summer 1979, p. 29 (interviewed by Pete Welding, Chicago, May 31, 1966); Interview with Eugene Powell (Sonny Boy Nelson), *Living Blues*, No. 43, Summer 1979, pp. 14–17 (interviewed by Simon J. Bronner, Greenville, Mississippi, June 21–3, 1976).
2   *Negro Population, 1790–1915*, Table 17, Occupation Negro Males, pp. 517–22; Table 18, Occupation Negro Females, p. 521; Table 19, Occupation, pp. 523–5.
3   Archie Lewis, vo, g, *Miss Handy Hanks*, Champion 16677, Richmond, Ind., March 30, 1933.
4   Oliver, *Screening the Blues*, pp. 119–22; Hambone Willie Newbern, vo, g, *Way Down in Arkansas*, Okeh 8693, Atlanta, March 13, 1929.
5   Henry Thomas, vo, g, *Arkansas*, Vocalion 1286, Chicago, July 1, 1927.
6   Botkin (ed), *Lay My Burden Down*, p. 10.
7   Zora Neale Hurston, MS of W.P.A. Federal Writers' Project, Florida, 1938, pp. 40–5, in Botkin, *A Treasury of Southern Folklore*, p. 479.
8   Blind Blake, vo, g, *Diddie Wa Diddie*, Paramount 12888, Richmond, Ind., August 17, 1929.
9   Blind Blake, vo, g, *Diddie Wa Diddie No. 2*, Paramount 12994, Grafton, Wis., c. May 29, 1930.
10 Gates Thomas, "South Texas Negro Work-Songs", p. 177; W. H. Thomas, *Some Current Folk Songs of the Negro*, p. 12; Gates Thomas, "South Texas Negro Work-Songs", p. 177; White, *American Negro Folk-Songs*, pp. 306–8, 353–4.
11 Ed Rogers and Saul Aaronson, *Alabama Bound*, New York: M. W. Witmark and Sons, 1910; Charlie Jackson, vo, bj, *I'm Alabama Bound*, Paramount 12289, Chicago, c. May 1925.
12 Papa Harvey Hull, vo, acc. vo, g, *Don't You Leave Me Here*, Gennett 6106, Chicago, c. April 8, 1927.
13 Shields McIlwaine, *Memphis Down In Dixie*, New York: E. P. Dutton and Co., 1948, Chap. 7; Oliver, *Conversation With the Blues*, pp. 85–6.
14 Charley Patton, vo, g, acc. vln, *Elder Greene Blues*, Paramount 12972, Grafton, Wis., c. October 1929.
15 W. H. Thomas, *Some Current Folk-Songs of the Negro*, pp. 3–5.
16 Troy Ferguson, vo, acc. g, *Good Night*, Columbia 14483-D, Atlanta, November 6, 1929.
17 Bill Moore, vo, g, *Tillie Lee*, Paramount 12613, Chicago, c. January, 1928.
18 Charlie Jackson, vo, bj, *Mama, Don't You Think I Know?*, Paramount 12305, Chicago, c. August 1925.
19 Charlie Jackson, vo, bj, *I'm Looking For a Woman Who Knows How To Treat Me Right*, Paramount 12602, Chicago, c. January 1928; Charlie Jackson, vo, bj, *I Got What It Takes But It Breaks My Heart To Give It Away*, Paramount 12259, Chicago, c. January 1925.
20 Oliver, *Blues Fell This Morning*, pp. 117–22.
21 Memphis Jug Band, Charlie Nickerson, vo, acc. hca, g, mand, *Move That Thing*, Memphis, November 28, 1930; for discussion of an early version collected by Gates Thomas, 1906, see Oliver, *Screening the Blues*, pp. 192–3; Webb, "Miscellany of Texas Folk-Lore", p. 49.
22 Charters, *The Country Blues*, pp. 184, 190–1; Oliver, *Screening the Blues*, pp. 190, 250; Tampa Red, vo, g, and Georgia Tom, vo, p, *It's Tight Like That*, Vocation 1216, Chicago, October 24, 1928.
23 Bruce Bastin, "Blue Harmony Boys, Rufus and Ben Quillian", *Blues Unlimited*, No. 113, May/June 1975, p. 21; Mike Rowe, "The Blue Harmony Boys – The Unusual", *Blues Unlimited*, No. 123, January/February 1977, pp. 23–5; Rufus and Ben Quillian, vo, acc, g, *Working It Slow*, Columbia 14584-D, Atlanta, December 7, 1930.
24 A considerable literature on the Dozens exists. For reprints of important articles by John Dollard, "The Dozens, Dialectic of Insult", and Roger D. Abrahams, "Playing the Dozens", and discussion of other texts, see Alan Dundes, *Mother Wit From the Laughing Barrel*, Englewood Cliffs, N.J.: Prentice-Hall, 1973, pp. 297–309; for discussion of the Dirty Dozens on record, see Oliver, *Screening the Blues*, pp. 239–46; Ben Curry, vo, bj, mand, acc. hca, *The New Dirty Dozen*, Paramount 13140, Grafton, Wis., c. January 1932.
25 Charley Jordan, vo, g, *Keep It Clean*, Vocalion 1511, Chicago, c. mid-June, 1930.

26 For a full discussion of these songs together with problems of censorship on record, see Oliver, *Screening the Blues*, "The Blue Blues", pp. 164–244; for *Stavin' Chain*, see Richard A. Noblett, "A Study of a Folk Hero", *Blues Unlimited*, No. 131/2, 1978, pp. 31–3; No. 134, pp. 14–17.

27 Gus Cannon, vo, bj, j, acc. hca, *Feather Bed*, Victor V38515, Memphis, September 9, 1928.

28 Booker T. Washington, *Up From Slavery* (1900), New York: Bantam Books, 1959, pp. 155–6.

29 Basil Mathews, *Booker T. Washington*, London: SCM Press Ltd., 1949, pp. 229–34.

30 Banjo Joe (Gus Cannon), vo, bj, acc. g, *Can You Blame the Colored Man?*, Paramount 12571, Chicago, c. November 1927.

31 Bengt Olsson, Album notes to *Cannon's Jug Stompers*, Herwin 208, New York, Herwin Records Inc.

32 W. E. Burghardt Du Bois, *The Souls of Black Folk* (1953), Greenwich, Conn., Fawcett Publications, 1961, pp. 48, 49, 50.

33 Mary Ellison, *The Black Experience (American Blacks since 1865)*, London: B. T. Batsford Ltd., 1974, pp. 48–56; J. W. Schulte Nordholt, *The People That Walk in Darkness*, London: Burke, 1960, pp. 182–7; Meier and Rudwick, *From Plantation to Ghetto*, pp. 177–200; Charles S. Johnson, *Patterns of Negro Segregation*, pp. 158–85.

34 Geeshie Wiley, vo, g, and Elvie Thomas, vo, *Pick Poor Robin Clean*, Paramount 13074, Grafton, Wis., c. March 1931.

35 Ralph Ellison, *Shadow and Act*, London: Secker and Warburg, 1967, p. 231 (excerpt from *Saturday Review*, July 28, 1962).

36 Oliver, *Blues Fell This Morning*, pp. 15–18; Johnson, *Shadow of the Plantation*, pp. 126–8.

37 Lil McClintock, vo, g, *Furniture Man*, Columbia 14575-D, Atlanta, December 4, 1930.

38 Luke Jordan, vo, g, *Cocaine Blues*, Victor 21076, Charlotte, N.C., August 16, 1927; *Furniture Man* was recorded in a number of versions, and under various titles by white singers, including Chitwood and Landress, the Georgia Crackers and others.

39 Meier, *Negro Thought in America*, p. 105; *Negro Population, 1790–1915*, Table 70, pp. 571–2; Part VI, Table 7, p. 461.

40 Will Bennett, vo, g, *Real Estate Blues*, Vocalion 1464, Knoxville, Tenn., August 28, 1929.

41 Johnson, *Shadow of the Plantation*, p. 120.

42 Spark Plug Smith, vo, g, *Vampire Woman*, Banner 32725, New York, January 6, 1933.

43 Winston Holmes, vo, and Charlie Turner, g, *Rounders Lament*, Paramount 12798, Richmond, Ind., June 21, 1929.

44 Frazier, *The Negro Family in the United States*, pp. 245–55; Johnson, *Shadow of the Plantation*, pp. 71–80; Gutman, *The Black Family in Slavery and Freedom, 1750–1925*, pp. 450–5.

45 Scarborough, *On The Trail of Negro Folk Songs*, pp. 274–5; Henry Thomas, vo, g, *Honey, Won't You Allow Me One More Chance?* Vocalion 1141, Chicago, October 7, 1927.

46 Webb, *Miscellany of Texas Folk-Lore*, p. 47; Henry Thomas, vo, quills, *Fishing Blues*, Vocalion 1249, Chicago, June 13, 1928.

47 Frazier, *The Negro Family in the United States*, p. 220.

48 Kid Coley, vo, g, acc. vln, *Tricks Ain't Walkin' No More*, Victor 23293, Louisville, Ky., June 13, 1931.

49 Richard N. Current, Harry T. Williams and Frank Freidel, *American History* (A Survey), New York: Alfred A. Knopf, 1961, pp. 529–616; White, *American Negro Folk-Songs*, pp. 350–1; Charles S. Johnson, "The New Frontage in American Life", *The New Negro: An Interpretation*, ed. Alain Locke, New York: A. and C. Boni, 1925, pp. 278–98.

50 Hazekiah Jenkins (sic), vo, g, *The Panic Is On*, Columbia 14585-D, New York, January 16, 1931.

51 Meier and Rudwick, *From Plantation to Ghetto*, pp. 219–20; John J. Niles, *Singing Soldiers*, New York: Charles Scribner's Sons, 1927, pp. viii, 94.

52 Coley Jones, vo, g, *Army Mule In No Man's Land*, Columbia 14288-D, Dallas, December 3, 1927.

53 Oliver, *Screening the Blues*, pp. 44–89.

54 Johnson-Nelson-Porkchop, vo, g, *G. Burns Is Gonna Rise Again*, Okeh 8577, Memphis, February 17, 1928.
55 Bogus Ben Covington, vo, hca, bj, *I Heard The Voice of a Pork Chop*, Paramount 12693, Chicago, c. September 1928.
56 Winston Holmes, vo, and Charlie Turner, g, *The Death of Holmes' Mule*, Paramount 12793, Richmond, Ind., June 21, 1929; Tony Russell, "Kansas City Dog Walkers", *Jazz Monthly*, No. 168, February, 1969, pp. 8–10.
57 T. O. Fuller, *History of the Negro Baptists of Tennessee*, Memphis: Roger Williams How College, 1936, pp. 50–1.
58 Sam Dennison, *Scandalize My Name*, pp. 383–93; The Three Deacons and Sister Lowdown, acc. harmonium, *John Jasper's Camp Meeting*, Okeh 8153, New York, c. July 1, 1924.
59 Jazz Baby Moore and Company, acc. p, *Morning Prayer*, Vocalion 1045, St. Louis, Mo., July 28, 1926.
60 Brother Fullbosom, acc. p, *A Sermon On a Silver Dollar*, Paramount 13078, Grafton, Wis., c. April 1931.

5 Baptist preachers and their congregations

1   Du Bois, *The Souls of Black Folk*, p. 141.
2   Foreman *Jazz and Race Records 1920–1932*, pp. 192–5; Mahony, *The Columbia 13/14000-D Series*, pp. 33–4; Rev. J. C. Burnett, pr, acc. 2 sisters, *The Downfall of Nebuchadnezzar*, Meritt 2203, Kansas City, 1926.
3   Woodson, *The History of the Negro Church*, Chap. 3, pp. 56–7; William E. Hatcher, *John J. Jasper: The Unmatched Negro Philosopher and Preacher*, New York: Fleming H. Revell Co., 1908. Both 1893 and 1901 have been given for the year of Jasper's death. Genovese, *Roll, Jordan, Roll*, pp. 269–270.
4   Richardson, "The Negro in American Religious Life", pp. 402, 403.
5   Lincoln, *The Black Experience in Religion*, pp. 65–7.
6   Myrdal, *An American Dilemma*, p. 861.
7   Frazier, *The Negro Church in America*, pp. 42, 45, 868.
8   Mays and Nicholson, *The Negro's Church*, pp. 59, 70.
9   James Weldon Johnson, *The Autobiography of An Ex-Colored Man* (1912), New York: Alfred A. Knopf, 1928, pp. 175, 177.
10 Zora Neale Hurston, *Dust Tracks on a Road*, New York: Hutchinson and Co., 1944, pp. 140–1.
11 James Weldon Johnson, *God's Trombones: Seven Negro Sermons in Verse*, New York: The Viking Press, 1927; Zora Neale Hurston, *Jonah's Gourd Vine*, London, Duckworth, 1934.
12 Dixon and Godrich, *Blues and Gospel Records*, 3rd edn, 1982.
13 Rosenberg, *The Art of the American Folk Preacher*, p. 31ff.
14 Rev. Sutton E. Griggs, vo, pr, acc. 5 vo, p, *A Hero Closes a War*, Victor 21706, Memphis, September 18, 1928; for details of the writings of Sutton Elbert Griggs, see Janheinz Jahn, *A Bibliography of Neo-African Literature*, London: Andre Deutsch, 1965, p. 256; for critical comments on Sutton Griggs' writings, see LeRoi Jones, *Blues People*, p. 132.
15 Rev. Jim Beal, pr, and cong., *The Hand of the Lord Was Upon Me (And I Went Out In the Spirit)*, Brunswick 7108, Chicago, August 24, 1929: See Dixon and Godrich, *Blues and Gospel Records*, 3rd edn, p. 64n.
16 Robert Anderson, *From Slavery to Affluence; Memoirs of Robert Anderson, ex-slave*, Hemingford, Neb., The Hemingford Ledger, 1927.
17 Rev. J. C. Burnett, pr, acc. 2 vo, p, *The Great Day of His Wrath Has Come*, Columbia 14225-D, New York: May 17, 1927.
18 Rev. J. C. Burnett, pr, acc. 2 vo, p, *The Gambler's Doom*, Columbia 14261-D, New York: September 21, 1927. The word 'sic' used in this sermon is the colloquial equivalent of 'seek'.
19 Evangelist Cal Ogburn, *One Hundred Illustrated Sermons*, Chicago: Rhodes and McClure, 1900; Rosenberg, *The Art of the American Folk Preacher*, pp. 29, 127–37, 254; personal communication: Jorge Carvalho, Queen's University, Belfast; Nick Toches, *Country: The Biggest Music in America*, New York: Dell Publishing Co., 1977, pp. 4–5.

20 *Music Memories*, Vol. 2, No. 5, Birmingham, Alabama; Hughes and Bontemps, *The Book of Negro Folklore*, pp. 315–16; for a partial transcription of *Black Diamond Express To Hell* see Oliver, "Down the Line", Sources of Afro-American Folk Song (2), *Music Mirror*, June 1954, p. 41 reprinted in Oliver, *Blues Off the Record*.

21 Rev. A. W. Nix, pr, and cong, *After the Ball Is Over*, Vocalion 1124, Chicago, June 29, 1927.

22 Rev. A. W. Nix, pr, and cong, *The White Flyer To Heaven*, Vocalion 1170, Chicago, June 29, 1927.

23 Mitchell, *Black Preaching*, pp. 188–9.

24 Lomax, *The Negro Revolt*, p. 86; Mitchell, *Black Preaching*, p. 163.

25 Lomax, *The Negro Revolt*, pp. 86–7.

26 Fischel and Quarles, *The Negro American: A Documentary History*, Glenview, Ill., Scott, Foresman and Co., 1967, pp. 135–6; Mitchell, *Black Preaching*, p. 208.

27 Calvin P. Dixon (Black Billy Sunday), *As an Eagle Stirreth Up Her Nest*, Columbia 14057-D, New York, January 14, 1925.

28 Rev. Isaiah Shelton, pr, *As the Eagle Stirreth Her Nest*, Victor 20583, New Orleans, March 8, 1927.

29 Rev. J. M. Gates, pr, and cong, *The Eagle Stirs Her Nest*, Okeh 8582, Memphis, February 22, 1928.

30 Rosenberg, *The Art of the American Folk Preacher*, p. 155.

31 Rev. B. L. Wrightman, pr, and cong, *The Soul's Physician*, Gennett 6517, Richmond, Ind., May 16, 1928.

32 Rev. J. M. Milton, pr, and cong, *Silk Worms and Boll Weevils*, Columbia 14562-D, Atlanta, November 5, 1929.

33 Rev. J. M. Milton, pr, and cong, *The Black Camel of Death*, Columbia 14501-D, Atlanta, November 5, 1929.

34 Rev. J. M. Gates, pr, and cong, *Speed On, Hell Is Waiting For You*, Okeh 8699, Atlanta, March 18, 1929.

35 Dixon and Godrich, *Recording the Blues*, pp. 38–40; Foreman, *Jazz and Race Records 1920–1932*, p. 160; on *Men and Women Talk Too Much*, Bluebird B8382, Atlanta, February 7, 1940, Rev. Gates gave details of his life.

36 Rev. J. M. Gates, pr, and cong, *Yonder Comes My Lord With a Bible In His Hand*, Victor 20650, Chicago, December 1, 1926.

37 Rev. J. M. Gates, pr, and cong, *God's Wrath in the St. Louis Cyclone*, Okeh 8515, Atlanta, October 6, 1927.

38 Rev. J. M. Gates, pr, and cong, *Hell Is In God's Jail House*, Okey 8547, Atlanta, October 3, 1927.

39 Rev. J. M. Gates, pr, acc. Deacon Davis and other voices, *Do It Yourself*, Victor 21523, Memphis, February 20, 1928.

40 Rev. J. M. Gates, pr, and cong, *The Woman and the Snake*, Okeh 8817, Atlanta, April 25, 1930.

41 Rev. J. M. Gates, pr, acc. Deacon Davis and sisters, *Praying For the Mourners*, Okeh 8452, New York, February 22, 1927.

42 Deacon Leon Davis, pr, acc. 2 sisters, *Experience Meeting*, Okeh 8527, Atlanta, October 6, 1927.

43 Rev. J. F. Forest, pr, and cong, *Sermon On Baptism*, Gennett 6262, Birmingham, Ala., c. August 21, 1927.

44 Julia Peterkin, *Roll, Jordan, Roll*, New York: Robert O. Ballou, 1933, p. 88.

45 Rev. R. M. Massey, pr, and cong, *Old Time Baptism*, Paramount 12618, Chicago, c. January 1928.

46 Rev. E. D. Campbell, pr, acc. 2 sisters and brother, *Take Me To the Water*, Victor 20546, Memphis, February 26, 1927.

6   Saints of the Sanctified churches

1   Elder J. E. Burch, pr, acc. cong, tam, g, dms, *Baptism By Water, And Baptism By the Holy Ghost*, Victor 21198, Atlanta, October 23, 1927.

2   Elder J. E. Burch, pr, acc.cong, tam, g, dms, *God's Dwelling Place*, Victor 21063, Atlanta, October 23, 1927; Elder J. E. Burch, pr, acc. cong, tam, g, dms, *The Church and the Kingdom*, Victor V38536, Atlanta, October 23, 1927; Elder J. E. Burch, pr, acc. cong, tam, g, dms, *Wash You, Make You Clean*, Victor 21063.

3   Elder J. E. Burch, pr, acc. cong, tam, g, dms, *Life and Death*, Victor 21476, Atlanta, October 23, 1927; Elder J. E. Burch, pr, acc. dms, *The Prayer Service*, Victor 21248, Atlanta, October 23, 1927; Elder J. E. Burch, pr, acc. dms, *Love Is My Wonderful Song*, Victor 21248, Atlanta, October 23, 1927.

4   George Eaton Simpson, "Black Pentecostalism in the United States", p. 203; early white gospel is discussed by James C. Downey, "Revivalism, The Gospel Songs and Social Reform", *Ethnomusicology*, IX, No. 2, May, 1965; Joseph R. Washington, *Black Sects and Cults*, p. 62.

5   Washington, Ibid., p. 208; Harry V. Richardson, "The Negro in American Religious Life", pp. 402–6; Charles V. Hamilton, *The Black Preacher in America*, pp. 75–7.

6   U.S. Bureau of the Census, *Religious Bodies*, 1936, Vol. 1, pp. 86, 851; Gunnar Myrdal, *An American Dilemma*, p. 864.

7   Ralph Alison Felton, *These My Brethren: A Study of 570 Negro Churches and 1542 Negro Homes in the Rural South.*

8   Bishop O. T. Jones and Elder J. E. Bryant, *Official Manual of the Church of God in Christ*, Chicago: Church of God in Christ, 1957; Hamilton, *The Black Preacher in America*, p. 76; Bernard Klatzko, *In the Spirit*, Album Notes, p. 11; Simpson, "Black Pentecostalism in the United States", p. 208; Frazier, *The Negro in the United States*, p. 353.

9   Rev. E. S. (Shy) Moore, pr, acc. vo group, p, g, j, *The Solemn Warning*, Victor 21737, Memphis, September 22, 1928.

10 Elder Richard Bryant, pr, acc. vo group, k, hca, bj, g, *The Master Came and Called To Me*, Victor 21357, Memphis, February 7, 1928.

11 Elder Bryant recordings cited were from sessions in February and September 1928; Klatzko, *In the Spirit*, p. 13.

12 Elder Curry, vo, g, acc. cong, Elder Charles Beck, p, *Memphis Flu*, Okeh 8857, Jackson, Miss., December 16, 1930.

13 Elder Curry, vo, g, acc. Elder Charles Beck, p, *Prove All Things*, Okeh 8910, Jackson, Miss., December 18, 1930; for the Sanctified church important passages from Psalm 149 included ". . . sing unto the Lord a new song, and his praise in the congregation of saints" (verse 1); "Let them praise His name in the dance; let them sing praises unto Him with the timbrel and harp" (verse 3) and "Let the saints be joyful in glory" (verse 5).

14 Frazier, *The Negro in the United States*, pp. 353–4; Myrdal, *An American Dilemma*, pp. 866–7.

15 Drake and Cayton, *Black Metropolis*, pp. 614, 615, 633, 866–7.

16 Spear, *Black Chicago: The Making of a Negro Ghetto*, pp. 91–4; Oliver, *Blues Fell This Morning*, pp. 179–181; Spear, *Black Chicago*, p. 169.

17 Oliver, Interview with Brother John Sellers, June 1958.

18 Rev. F. W. McGee, pr, acc. vo group, p, g, d, trb, *Three Ways, Part 1 and 2*, Victor 21581, Chicago, June 16, 1928.

19 Don Kent, "Interview with Reverend McGee", pp. 49–52; Reverend F. W. McGee recordings cited were from sessions between May 1927 and October 1929 except for the last recording on July 1930.

20 Rev. F. W. McGee, pr, p, acc. vo group, g, cornet, string bass, *Jonah in the Belly of the Whale*, Victor 20773, Chicago, June 7, 1927.

21 Rev. F. W. McGee, pr, p, acc. cong, g, g, d, *A Dog Shall Not Move His Tongue*, Victor 23296, New York, May 29, 1930.

22 Rev. F. W. McGee, pr, p, acc. cong, g, string bass, tam, *The Crooked Made Straight*, Victor 21090, Chicago, November 8, 1927.

23 Rev. F. W. McGee, pr, p, acc. vo group, trb, g, d, *Women's Clothes (You Can't Hide)*, Victor 23296, Chicago, October 23, 1929.

24 Rev. Emmett Dickinson and the Three Deacons, pr, vo, *Is There Harm In Singing the Blues?*,

Paramount 12925, Grafton, Wis., c. November 1929; see also Titon, *Early Downhome Blues*, Appendix B, p. 277–8.

25 Rev. Emmett Dickinson, pr, *Death of Blind Lemon*, Paramount 12945, Grafton, Wis., c. March 1930; see also Oliver, "Blind Lemon Jefferson", *The Jazz Review*, New York: 1956, reprinted Oliver, *Blues Off the Record*, which includes a full transcription.

26 Rev. F. W. McGee, pr, p, with Mother B. A. Hooks and Sister Coleman, vo, acc. cornet, 2 g, *Holes In Your Pockets*, Victor V38583, New York, January 28, 1930.

27 Wardlow, "Rev. D. C. Rice: Gospel Singer", pp. 164–5.

28 Wardlow, "Rev. D. C. Rice, 1928–1930, Sanctified Singing with Traditional Jazz accompaniment", Album Notes to Herwin 212.

29 Rev. D. C. Rice, pr, acc. cong, t, trb, p, str. bass, tam, d, *I'm In the Battlefield for My Lord*, Vocalion 1262, Chicago, February 22n 1929.

30 Rev. D. C. Rice, pr, acc. cong, trb, p, triangle, *Shall Not a Dog Move His Tongue*, Vocalion 1201, Chicago, August 11, 1928; other recordings cited were from sessions between August 11, 1928 and mid-January 1930.

31 Rev. D. C. Rice, pr, acc. cong, trb, p, mand, triangle, *Come and See*, Vocalion 1255, Chicago, June 13, 1928.

32 Rev. D. C. Rice and Sanctified Congregation, vo, acc, p, tam, bass, d, *Testify – For My Lord Is Coming Back Again*, Vocalion 1502, Chicago, c. mid-January 1930.

33 Rev. D. C. Rice, pr, acc. cong, p, percussion, Sister Black, Sister Rice testifying, *We Got the Same Kinda Power Over Here*, Vocalion 1647, Chicago, c. July 16, 1930.

34 Evangelist R. H. Harris and Pentecostal Sisters, pr, g, *Jesus Is Coming Soon*, Gennett 6148, Chicago, c. March 15, 1927.

35 Rev. Leora Ross, pr, with Church of the Living God Jubilee Singers, *God's Mercy to Colonel Lindbergh*, Okeh 8541, Chicago, December 14, 1927.

36 Missionary Josephine Miles pr, and Sister Elizabeth Cooper, vo duet, p, *You Have Lost Jesus*, Gennett 6676, Richmond, Ind., May 16, 1928; other recordings cited were from the same session.

37 Rev. Sister Mary M. Nelson, vo, acc. 2 vo, *Isaiah*, Vocalion 1110, New York, April 21, 1927.

38 Spear, *Black Chicago*, pp. 96, 176; Frazier, *The Negro Church in America*, p, 56; Drake and Cayton, *Black Metropolis*, pp. 643–5; Arthur Huff Fauset, *Black Gods of the Metropolis: Negro Religious Cults of the Urban North*, Philadelphia: University of Pennsylvania Press, 1944, pp. 13–21.

39 Nugrape Twins (Mark and Matthew), vo duet, acc. p, *Pray Children If You Want To Go To Heaven*, Columbia 14251-D, Atlanta, March 25, 1927.

40 Luther Magby, vo, acc. organ, tam, *Blessed Are the Poor In Spirit*, Columbia 14278-D, Atlanta, November 11, 1927.

41 Malcolm Shaw, "Arizona Dranes", Album Notes to Herwin 210; Malcolm Shaw, "Arizona Dranes and Okeh", *Storyville*, No. 27, February 1970, p. 85.

42 Nat Hentoff and Nat Shapiro, *Hear Me Talkin' To Ya*, London: Peter Davies, 1955, p. 227.

43 Arizona Dranes, vo, p, *It's All Right Now*, Okeh 8353, Chicago, June 17, 1926.

44 Arizona Dranes, vo, p, acc. Rev. F. W. McGee and Jubilee Singers, *The Lamb's Blood Has Washed Me Clean*, Okeh 8419, Chicago, November 11, 1926.

45 Arizona Dranes, vo, p, and Choir, acc. mand, *Just Look*, Okeh 8646, Chicago, July 3, 1928.

46 Jessie May Hill, vo, acc. cong, p, g, *The Crucifixion of Christ*, Okeh 8490, Chicago, May 5, 1927.

47 Jessie May Hill, vo, acc. cong, p, g, *Earth Is No Resting Place*, Okeh 8501, Chicago, May 5, 1927.

48 Southern, *Biographical Dictionary*.

49 Laura Henton, vo, acc. p, g, brass bass, *Heavenly Sunshine*, Columbia 14388-D, Dallas, December 5, 1928.

50 Laura Henton, vo, acc. p, g, string bass, *Plenty Good Room In My Father's Kingdom*, Brunswick 7144, Kansas City, early November 1929.

51 Mother McCollum, vo, acc.2g, *When I Take My Vacation In Heaven*, Vocalion 1532, Chicago, c. mid-June 1930.

52   Mother McCollum, vo, acc. 2g, *Jesus Is My Air-O-Plane*, Vocalion 1616, Chicago, c. mid-June 1930.
53   Oliver, *Blues Fell This Morning*, pp. 242–5.
54   Sister Cally Fancy, vo, acc. p, tam, *Everybody Get Your Business Right*, Brunswick 7110, Chicago, August 15, 1929.
55   Oliver, *Blues Fell This Morning*, pp. 233–41; Sister Cally Fancy, vo, acc, hca, g, *I'm Gonna Tell My Jesus Howdy*, Brunswick 7157, Chicago, August 15, 1929.
56   Elders McIntorsh and Edwards, vo duet, with Sisters Johnson and Taylor, vo, tam, acc. 2g, *The 1927 Flood*, Okeh 8647, Chicago, December 4, 1928.
57   Elders McIntorsh and Edwards, vo duet, with Sisters Johnson and Taylor, vo, tam, acc. 2g, *The Latter Rain Is Fall* (sic), Okeh 8698, Chicago, December 4, 1928.
58   Memphis Sanctified Singers; Bessie Johnson, Melinda Taylor, Sally Sumler, vo, acc. Will Shade g, *He Got Better Things For You*, Victor V38559, Memphis, October 1, 1929.
59   Elders McIntorsh and Edwards, vo duet, with Sisters Johnson and Taylor, vo, tam, acc. 2g, *What Kind of Man Jesus Is*, Okeh 8647, Chicago, December 4, 1928.
60   Eddie Head and His Family, vo, acc. g. tam, *Down On Me*, Columbia 14548-D, Atlanta, April 22, 1930.
61   Holy Ghost Sanctified Singers, vo group, acc. poss, Will Shade, hca, g, j, *Thou Carest Lord, For Me*, Brunswick 7162, Memphis, c. February 21, 1930.

7   Jack-leg preachers and evangelists

1   Washington Phillips, vo, dulceola, *Denomination Blues – Parts 1 & 2*, Columbia 14333-D, Dallas, December 5, 1927.
2   Washington Phillips, vo, dulceola, *I Am Born To Preach the Gospel*, Columbia 14448-D, Dallas, December 4, 1928.
3   Washington Phillips, vo, dulceola, *Train Your Child*, Columbia 14448-D, Dallas, December 4, 1928.
4   Washington Phillips, vo, dulceola, *I Had a Good Father and Mother*, Columbia 14566-D, Dallas, December 2, 1929.
5   Myrdal, *An American Dilemma*, p. 876: Drake and Cayton, *Black Metropolis*, pp. 630–1.
6   Rev. W. M. Mosley, pr, and cong, *You Preachers Stay Out of Widows' Houses*, Columbia 14635-D, Atlanta, November 2, 1931.
7   Stovepipe No. 1, vo, g, hca, *Lord Don't You Know I Have No Friend Like You*, Columbia 210-D, New York, August 19, 1924.
8   Julius Daniels, vo, g, acc. Bubba Lee Torrence, g, *Slippin' and Sliding' Up the Golden Street*, Victor 20499, Atlanta, February 19, 1927.
9   Charley Patton, vo, g, *Lord I'm Discouraged*, Paramount 12883, Richmond, Ind., June 14, 1929.
10   Charley Patton, vo, g, *You're Gonna Need Somebody When You Die*, Paramount 13031, Grafton, Wis., c. October 1929.
11   W. D. Pearson, "Going Down to the Crossroads: The Bluesmen and Religion", *Jazz and Blues*, April 1972, pp. 13–15; David Evans, "Interview with the Reverend Rubin Lacy. Part 3" *Blues Unlimited*, No. 42, 1967, p. 5; John Fahey, *Charley Patton*, London: Studio Vista, 1970, p. 20.
12   Gayle Dean Wardlow, "The Huff Brothers", *Blues Unlimited*, No. 56, September 1968, p. 4.
13   Leola Manning, vo, acc. p, g, *He Fans Me*, Vocalion 1446, Knoxville, Tenn., August 28, 1929.
14   Leola Manning, vo, acc. p, g, *The Blues Is All Wrong*, Vocalion 1529, Knoxville, Tenn., April 4, 1930; Leola Manning, vo, acc. p, g, *Laying In the Graveyard*, Vocalion 1529, Knoxville, Tenn., April 4, 1930.
15   Blind Roosevelt Graves, vo, g, and Uaroy Graves, vo, tam, *Telephone To Glory*, Paramount 12874, Richmond, Ind., September 20, 1929.
16   Oliver, *Screening the Blues*, pp. 44–89.
17   The Guitar Evangelist (Edward W. Clayborn), vo, g, *Death Is Only a Dream*, Vocalion 1096, Chicago, April 19, 1927.

18   The Guitar Evangelist (Edward W. Clayborn), vo, g, *In Time of Trouble Jesus Will Never Say Goodbye*, Vocalion 1162, Chicago, January 21, 1928.

19   The Guitar Evangelist (Edward W. Clayborn), vo, g, *Let That Lie Alone*, Vocalion 1093, Chicago, April 19, 1927.

20   Max Jones, "Interview with Josh White", *Blues Unlimited*, No. 55, July 1968, p. 17; Don McLean, "Josh White; A Farewell", *Sing Out!*, Vol. 19, No. 4, Winter 1969, p. 9.

21   Blind Joe Taggart, vo, g, acc. Joshua White, vo, g, *There's a Hand Writing On the Wall*, Paramount 12717, Chicago, c. October 1928.

22   Blind Joe Taggart, vo, g, and Emma Taggart, vo, *I Wish My Mother Was On That Train*, Vocalion 1063, New York, November 8, 1926.

23   Blind Joe Taggart, vo, g, *God's Gonna Separate the Wheat From the Tares*, Vocalion 1123, Chicago, June 30, 1927.

24   Blind Joe Taggart, vo, g, *Religion Is Something Within You*, Paramount 12744, Chicago, c. December 1928.

25   Blind Joe Taggart, vo, g, acc. unk., vo, g, vln, *Been Listening All the Day*, Paramount 12611, Chicago, c. January 1928; Blind Joe Taggart, vo, g, acc. unk. vo, g, vln, *Goin' To Rest Where Jesus Is*, Paramount 12611, Chicago, c. January 1928.

26   David Evans, "Blind Willie McTell", *Atlanta Blues*, album notes to JEMF 106.

27   Blind Benny Paris, vo, g, and Wife, vo, *Hide Me In the Blood of Jesus*, Victor V38503, Atlanta, October 22, 1928.

28   A. C. Forehand, vo, hca, g, acc. Blind Mamie Forehand, hand cymbals, *I'm So Glad Today, Today*, Victor 20547, Memphis, Tenn., February 25, 1927.

29   Blind Mamie Forehand, vo, hand cymbals, acc. A. C. Foreman, g, *Honey In the Rock*, Victor 20574, Memphis, Tenn., February 28, 1927.

30   Gayle Dean Wardlow, "Biographical Notes" to *In The Spirit*, album notes for Origin 12/13; Blind Willie Davis, vo, g, *Your Enemy Cannot Harm You*, Paramount 12726, Chicago, c. December 1928.

31   Blind Willie Davis, vo, g, *I Believe I'll Go Back Home*, Paramount 12979, Grafton, Wis., c. October 1929.

32   Blind Willie Davis, vo, g, *Trust In God and Do the Right*, Paramount 12979, Grafton, Wis., c. October 1929.

33   Blind Willie Harris, vo, g, *Where He Leads Me I Will Follow*, Vocalion 1273, New Orleans, c. February 1929.

34   Blind Roger Hays, vo, g, hca, *I Must Be Blind, I Cannot See*, Brunswick 7047, New Orleans, November 1928.

35   Bruce Bastin, *Crying For the Carolines*, London: Studio Vista, 1971, p. 188; Blind Gussie Nesbit, vo, g, *Pure Religion*, Columbia 14576-D, Atlanta, December 4, 1930.

36   Charters, *The Country Blues*, pp. 156–65; Charters, *Blind Willie Johnson*, album notes to Folkways FG 3585; Charters, *Blind Willie Johnson*, album notes to RBF 10.

37   Blind Willie Johnson, vo, g, *I Know His Blood Can Make Me Whole*, Columbia 14276-D, Dallas, December 3, 1927.

38   Blind Willje Johnson, vo, g, acc. Angeline Johnson, vo, *You'll Need Somebody On Your Bond*, Columbia 14504-D, New Orleans, December 11, 1929; Blind Willie Johnson, vo, g, acc. Angeline Johnson, vo, *You're Gonna Need Somebody On Your Bond*, Columbia 14530-D, Atlanta, April 20, 1930.

39   Blind Willie Johnson, vo, g, acc. Angeline Johnson, vo, *If It Had Not Been For Jesus*, Columbia 14556-D, Atlanta, April 20, 1930.

40   Blind Willie Johnson, vo, g, acc. Angeline Johnson, vo, *Go With Me To That Land*, Columbia 14597-D, Atlanta, April 20, 1930; Blind Willie Johnson, vo, g, acc. Angeline Johnson, vo, *John the Revelator*, Columbia 14530-D, Atlanta, April 20, 1930.

41   Blind Willie Johnson, vo, g, acc. Angeline Johnson, vo, *The Rain Don't Fall On Me*, Columbia 14537-D, Atlanta, April 20, 1930.

42   Other cited records made between December 1927 and April 1930; Charters, *The Country Blues*, pp. 164–5.

43   Mrs. C. H. Morris, *Sweeter As the Years Go By*, Chicago: Charles H. Gabriel, 1912; Thoro Harris and Howard B. Smith, *Jesus Is Coming Soon*, Chicago: Thoro Harris, 1914; J. B.

Herbert (arr), *You Better Run*, Chicago: Homer A. Rodeheaver, 1923; J. B. Herbert (arr), *Shine On Me*, Chicago: Homer A. Rodeheaver, 1923; Charles Albert Tindley, *Leave It There*, Chicago: Hope Publishing Co., 1916.

44 P. B. Bliss et al. *Gospel Hymns Consolidated*, New York: Biglow and Main, 1883; selected by Henry Date, *Pentecostal Hymns, No. 2. A Winnowed Collection*, Chicago: The Hope Publishing Co., 1895; *Gospel Pearls*, Chicago: The National Baptist Convention, 1921; *Full Gospel Songs*, Chicago: Thoro Harris, c. 1923.

45 Homer Rodeheaver, *Negro Spirituals*, Chicago & Philadelphia: The Rodeheaver Co., 1923, p.2.

46 J. H. Fillmore et al. e.g. *Quartets and Choruses for Men, A Collection of New and Old Gospel Songs*, Cincinnati: Fillmore Music House, 1913; *Favorite Gospel Songs*, Dallas: Stamps-Baxter Music and Print Co., n. d.; Alfred B. Smith, *Singspiration Gospel Songs and Choruses*, Wheaton, Ill., Alfred B. Smith, 1940–6.

47 White, *American Negro Folk Songs*, Appendix 11, pp. 413–26; Frank C. Brown Collection, pp. 663–7.

48 Kennedy, *Mellows*, pp. 11–18.

49 Blind Willie Johnson, vo, g, *If I Had My Way I'd Tear the Building Down*, Columbia 14343-D, Dallas, December 3, 1927.

50 Henry Thomas, vo, g, *Jonah In the Wilderness*, Vocalion 1140, Chicago, October 7, 1927.

51 William Baltzell, *The Wreck of the Titanic*, Chicago, Aubrey Stauffer & Co., 1912; Richard "Rabbit" Brown, vo, g, *Sinking of the Titanic*, Victor 35840, New Orleans, March 11, 1927; Edith M. Lessing, *Just As The Ship Went Down*, New York, Harold Rossiter Music Co., 1912.

52 Blind Willie Johnson, vo, g, *God Moves on the Water*, Columbia 14520-D, New Orleans, December 11, 1929; Dorothy Scarborough, *From A Southern Porch*, New York, 1919, pp. 305–7.

53 William Smith, Versey Smith, vo duet, g, tam, *When That Great Ship Went Down*, Paramount 12505, Chicago, c. August 1927.

54 Frank C. Brown Collection, Vol III, pp. 663–7.

55 William Smith, Versey Smith, vo duet, g, tam, *Everybody Help the Boys Come Home*, Paramount 12505, Chicago, c. August 1927.

56 Blind Willie Johnson, vo, g, acc. Angeline Johnson, vo, *When the War Was On*, Columbia 14545-D, New Orleans, December 11, 1929.

57 Blind Willie Johnson, vo, g, acc. Angeline Johnson, vo, *Jesus Is Coming Soon*, Columbia 14391-D, Dallas, December 5, 1928; Blind Willie Johnson, vo, g, *God Don't Never Change*, Columbia 14490-D, New Orleans, December 10, 1929.

58 White, *American Negro Folk-Songs*, pp. 424–5.

59 Sister Cally Fancy's Sanctified Singers, vo, acc. group, p, *Death Is Riding Through the Land*, Parts 1 & 2, Vocalion 1663, Chicago, October 28, 1931; The song relates to *Little Black Train Is A-Comin'*, Frank C. Brown Collection, Vol III, p. 551.

8 Survivors of the ballad tradition

1 Scarborough, *On The Trail of Negro Folk-Songs*, pp. 33–64.

2 Lomax, *Adventures of a Ballad Hunter*, pp. 165–79.

3 Francis James Child, *The English and Scottish Popular Ballads*, New York: Houghton, Mifflin and Co., 1884–1898; Vol. 5, No. 274, "*Our Goodman*," pp. 88–95.

4 Coley Jones, vo, g, *Drunkard's Special*, Columbia 14489-D, Dallas, December 6, 1929; this version is discussed by John Minton, "'Our Goodman' and 'The Maid' at the Sookey Jump; two Afro-American variants of Child Ballads on commercial disc," *J.E.M.F.Q.* Vol. XVII, Spring/Summer 1981, No. 65/66, pp. 31–5. (The second ballad is Leadbelly's *Gallis Pole*, 1935–42.)

5 For collected versions see Sandburg, *The American Songbag*, pp. 228–31; Scarborough, *On the Trail of Negro Folk-Songs*, p. 94; for published versions see Oliver, *Early Blues Songbook*, London: Wise Publications, 1982, pp. 11, 58; for "Derby Ram" see Oliver, *Screening the Blues*, pp. 193–5.

6 Guy B. Johnson, *John Henry: Tracking Down a Negro Legend*, Chapel Hill, N.C.: University

of North Carolina Press, 1929: Louis W. Chappell, *John Henry: A Folk-Lore Study*, Jena: Frommarsche Verlag, Walter Biedermain, 1933; for further bibliography see *A Brief List of Materials Relating to "John Henry"*, Washington: The Library of Congress Archive of Folk Song, 1970.

7 For examples of early collected versions see Odum and Johnson, *Negro Workaday Songs*, pp. 221–40; Scarborough, *On the Trail of Negro Folk-Songs*, pp. 218–22; White, *American Negro Folk-Songs*, pp. 189–90; Frank C. Brown Collection, Vol. 2, pp. 623–7; Vol. 4, pp. 298–302; Laws, *Native American Balladry*, p. 246; Norm Cohen, *Long Steel Rail*, pp. 61–89; John Harrington Cox, *Folk Songs of the South*, Cambridge, Mass: Harvard University Press, 1925, pp. 175–88.

8 The Two Poor Boys, (Evans and McClain) vo, g, mand, *John Henry Blues*, Perfect 181, New York, May 20, 1931.

9 Furry Lewis, vo, g, *John Henry (The Steel Driving Man)* Parts 1 & 2, Vocalion 1474, Memphis, September 22, 1929.

10 Henry Thomas, vo, g, quills, *John Henry*, Vocalion 1094, Chicago, July 1, 1927.

11 Birmingham Jug Band, vo, hca, g, mand, j, *Bill Wilson*, Okeh 8895, Atlanta, December 11, 1930.

12 Cohen, *Long Steel Rail*, pp. 79–89.

13 Richard M. Dorson, *American Folklore*, Chicago: University of Chicago Press, 1959, p. 182; Levine, *Black Culture and Black Consciousness*, pp. 420–7.

14 Mississippi John Hurt, vo, g, *Spike Driver Blues*, Okeh 8692, New York, December 28, 1928; for transcript see Oliver, *Blues Fell This Morning*, pp. 28–9; Sackheim, *The Blues Line*, p. 226.

15 Lomax and Lomax, *American Ballads and Folk Songs*, pp. xxvii, 203; Spaeth, *A History of Popular Music*, pp. 206–9; *St. Louis Post-Dispatch*, October 20, 1899; Sandburg, *The American Songbag*, pp. 75–86; Spaeth, *Read 'Em and Weep*, pp. 34–40; Scarborough, *On the Trail of Negro Folk-Songs*, pp. 80–5; White, *American Negro Folk-Songs*, p. 213; for other references see Laws, *Native American Balladry*, pp. 247–8.

16 Mississippi John Hurt, vo, g, *Frankie*, Okeh 8560, Memphis, February 14, 1928; for transcript see Sackheim, *The Blues Line*, p. 231.

17 Charley Patton, vo, g, *Frankie and Albert*, Paramount 13110, Grafton, Wis., c. October 1929; see also John Fahey, *Charley Patton*, London: Studio Vista, 1970, pp. 86–7.

18 Nick Nichols, vo, acc. p, g, *Frankie and Johnny (The Shooting Scene)* Part 1, *(The Courtroom Scene)* Part 2, Columbia 2071-D, Dallas, December 5, 1929; Ren Fields and Leighton Brothers, *Frankie and Johnny*, New York: Shapiro, Bernstein, 1912.

19 Richard E. Buehler, "Stacker Lee: A Partial Investigation into the Historicity of a Negro Murder Ballad", *Keystone Folklore Quarterly*, No. 12, 1967, pp. 187–91; Shields McIlwaine, *Memphis Down In Dixie,* New York: E. P. Dutton & Co., 1948, pp. 184–219; Odum, "Folk-Songs and Folk-Poetry", pp. 288–9; Odum and Johnson, *The Negro and His Songs*, pp. 196–8; Scarborough, *On the Trail of Negro Folk-Songs*, pp. 91–3; see also Laws, *Native American Balladry*, pp. 253–4; Levine, *Black Culture and Black Consciousness*, pp. 413–15, 502.

20 Long "Cleve" Reed, Little Harvey Hull – Down Home Boys, vo duet, acc. 2 g, *Original Stack O' Lee Blues*, Black Patti 8030, Chicago, c. May 1927.

21 Furry Lewis, vo, g, *Billy Lyons and Stack O' Lee*, Vocalion 1132, Chicago, October 9, 1927; for transcript see Sackheim, *The Blues Line*, p. 255.

22 Mississippi John Hurt, vo, g, *Stack O' Lee Blues*, Okeh 8654, New York, December 28, 1928.

23 "Ma" Rainey, vo, acc. her Georgia Band, c,trb, cl, p, bj, bass saxophone, *Stack O' Lee Blues*, Paramount 12357, New York, c. December 1925.

24 Levine, *Black Culture and Black Consciousness*, pp. 410–12; Carl Carmer, *Stars Fell On Alabama*, London: Lovat Dickson and Thompson, 1935, pp. 124–41; Cohen, *Long Steel Rail*, pp. 122–31; Odum, "Folk-Songs and Folk Poetry", pp. 289–92.

25 Will Bennett, vo, g, *Railroad Bill*, Vocalion 1464, Knoxville, Tenn., August 28, 1929.

26 Spaeth, *Read 'Em and Weep*, pp. 119–22.

27 Cohen, *Long Steel Rail*, pp. 132–57; Perrow, "Songs and Rhymes from the South", 1913, pp. 165–7; Odum, "Folk-Songs and Folk Poetry", pp. 351–2; Odum and Johnson, *Negro Workaday Songs*, p. 126.

28 Alan Lomax, *The Folk Songs of North America*, pp. 553–5.

29 Furry Lewis, vo, g, *Kassie Jones*, Parts 1 and 2, Victor 21664, Memphis, August 28, 1928.
30 Earl McDonald's Original Louisville Jug Band, Earl McDonald, vo, jug, acc, sax, bj, mand, *Casey Bill*, Columbia 14371-D, Atlanta, March 30, 1927.
31 Henry Thomas, vo, g, *Bob McKinney*, for transcript see McCormick, *Henry Thomas*. Mississippi John Hurt, vo, g, *Louis Collins*, Okeh 8724, N.Y.C. December 12, 1928.
32 Richard "Rabbit" Brown, vo, g, *The Mystery of the Dunbar's Child*, Victor 35840, New Orleans, March 11, 1927.
33 Marina Bokelman, 'The Coon-Can Game: A Blues Ballad Tradition', unpublished Master's Thesis, U.C.L.A. 1968; Cohen, *Long Steel Rail*, p. 126; Evans, *Big Road Blues*, pp. 44–7.
34 Sandburg, *The American Songbag*, pp. 26–7, 217; Mack McCormick, "A Who's Who of 'The Midnight Special'", *Caravan*, No. 19, January 1960, pp. 11–21; Cohen, *Long Steel Rail*, p. 481(n2).
35 Sam Collins, vo, g, *Midnight Special Blues*, Gennett 6307, Richmond, Ind., September 16, 1927.
36 Perrow, "Songs and Rhymes from the South", Vol. 26, p. 128; White, *American Negro Folk-Songs*, p. 207; Frank C. Brown Collection, Vol. III.
37 Jim Jackson, vo, g, *Old Dog Blue*, Vocalion 1146, Chicago, January 22, 1928; see Odum and Johnson, *Negro Workaday Songs* for "silver spade" motif, pp. 129, 198.
38 Oliver, *Blues Fell This Morning*, pp. 18–19; for a contemporary description see C. P. Brooks *Cotton*, New York: Span and Chamberlain, 1898, pp. 186–8.
39 Gates Thomas, "South Texas Negro Work Songs", pp. 173–5; Lomax and Lomax, *American Ballads and Folk Songs*, pp. 2–7; White, *American Negro Folk-Songs*, pp. 352–3; Scarborough, *On the Trail of Negro Folk-Songs*, pp. 76–9, quotes these references.
40 Charley Patton, vo, g, *Mississippi Boweavil Blues*, Paramount 12805, Richmond, Ind., June 14, 1929.
41 Charlie "Dad" Nelson, vo, g, kazoo, *Cotton Field Blues*, Paramount 12401, Chicago, c. September 1926.
42 Jean Thomas, *Ballad Makin' In The Mountains of Kentucky*, New York: Henry Holt Co., 1939, p. 134 & n; Richard Spottswood, *Local History and Events*, album notes to LBC 12, p. 7.
43 John Byrd, vo, g, *Old Timbrook Blues*, Paramount 12997, Grafton, Wis., c. March 1930.
44 Olive Woolley Burt, *American Murder Ballads*, New York: Oxford University Press, 1958, pp. 29–32; Jean Thomas, *Ballad Makin' In the Mountains of Kentucky*, pp. 138–42.
45 Kid Coley, vo, p, acc. vln, *Clair and Pearley Blues*, Victor 23293, Louisville, Ky., June 13, 1931.
46 Odum and Johnson, *The Negro and his Songs*, pp. 55–9; Laws, *Native American Balladry*, pp. 21–2; Frank C. Brown Collection, Vol. III, pp. 570–1; Archie Green, *Only A Miner*, Urbana: University of Illinois Press, 1972, pp. 123–7.
47 Bastin, *Crying for the Carolines*, p. 71.
48 Willie Walker, vo, g, acc. Sam Brooks, vo, *Dupree Blues*, Columbia 14578-D, Atlanta, December 6, 1930; for a full transcription see Titon, *Early Downhome Blues*, pp. 251–2.
49 "Kingfish" Bill Tomlin, vo, acc. p. *Dupree Blues*, Paramount 13057, Grafton, Wis., c. November 1930.
50 Levine, *Black Culture and Black Consciousness*, p. 429.
51 Richard Spottswood, *Mississippi John Hurt*, album notes to Piedmont 13157.

9 Past recording and future research

1 Oliver, *The Story of the Blues*, p. 43; Titon, *Early Downhome Blues*, p. 126.
2 H. W. Fowler and F. G. Fowler, *The Concise Oxford Dictionary*, Oxford: Clarendon Press, p. 1357; Evans, *Big Road Blues*, p. 44.
3 Kip Lornell, "Pre-Blues Black Music in Piedmont, North Carolina" *North Carolina Folklore Quarterly*, Vol. 22, No. 1, February 1975, pp. 26–32; Bruce Bastin, "Black Music in North Carolina", *North Carolina Folklore Journal*, Vol. 27, No. 1, May 1979, pp. 3–19; Kip Lornell, *Virginia Traditions: Non-Blues Secular Black Music*, album notes to Blue Ridge Institute BR1001.

4   See Harris, *Blues Who's Who* for birth dates of these and other blues singers.
5   John Jacob Niles, "Shout, Coon, Shout!", *The Musical Quarterly*, Vol. 16, No. 4, October 1930, pp. 516–30.
6   Titon, *Early Downhome Blues*, p. 56.
7   Evans, *Big Road Blues*, pp. 188–9.
8   Harris, *Blues Who's Who*, contains many other comparable birth dates for professional stage singers.
9   Lester Melrose, "My Life in Recording", *American Folk Music Occasional*, No. 2, eds. Chris Strachwitz and Pete Welding, New York: Oak Publications, 1970, pp. 59–61.
10 Norm Cohen, "'I'm a Record Man', Uncle Art Reminisces", *John Edwards Memorial Foundation Quarterly*, No. 8, 1972, pp. 18–22.
11 Charles K. Wolfe, "Ralph Peer at Work: The Victor 1927 Bristol Sessions", *Old Time Music*, No. 5, ed. Tony Russell, London: Summer 1972, pp. 10–15.
12 Mike Seeger, Interview with Frank Walker, "Who Chose These Records?", *Anthology of American Folk Music*, eds. Josh Dunson et al. New York: Oak Publications, 1973, pp. 8–17.
13 Roger S. Brown, "Polk Brockman, Recording Pioneer", *Living Blues*, No. 23, Chicago: Living Blues Publications, September/October 1975, p. 31; Foreman, *Jazz and Race Records*, p. 159.
14 Seeger, "Who Chose These Records?", p. 15.
15 David Evans, "Interview with H. C. Speir", *John Edwards Memorial Foundation Quarterly*, No. 8, 1972, p. 72.
16 Oliver, *Conversation With the Blues*, pp. 115–16.
17 Peter Guralnick, *Feel Like Going Home*, New York: Outerbridge and Dienstfrey, 1971, p. 94.
18 John Cowley, personal communication.
19 Sam Collins, vo, g, *My Road is Rough and Rocky*, Yazoo L1038; for speculations see Dixon and Godrich, *Blues and Gospel Records*, 3rd edn, p. 168: other unissued titles mentioned in the text are listed under the artist's names in Dixon and Godrich, *ibid.*
20 Sam Butler, vo, g, *Devil and My Brown Blues*, Matchbox Bluesmasters MSE 202; for discussion see Oliver, album notes to this release.
21 cf. transcript of *Fishing Blues* in this work, p. 131, for *You Shall*, see Oliver, *Screening the Blues*, p. 58.
22 For the background on Evans and McClain I am indebted to Terry Zwigoff; Dixon and Godrich, *Blues and Gospel Records 1902–1943*, 3rd edn, pp. 228–9.
23 Oliver, *Screening the Blues*, pp. 164–261.
24 Foreman, *Jazz and Race Records*, p. 160; Cohen, *Long Steel Rail*, p. 20; Foreman, *Jazz and Race Records*, p. 125.
25 Arizona Dranes, vo, p, and choir *God's Got a Crown*, Herwin 210, formerly Okeh unissued; Chicago, July 3, 1928; Washington Phillips, vo, dulceola, *You Can't Stop a Tattler*, Parts 1 & 2, Agram Blues AB2006, formerly Columbia unissued; Dallas, December 2, 1929.
26 See also Oliver, "Special Agents", *The Jazz Review*, New York: July 1956, reprinted in Oliver, *Blues Off the Record*.
27 Dixon and Godrich, *Blues and Gospel Records*, has details of Library of Congress field sessions.
28 Mahony, *The Columbia 13/14000-D Series, A Numerical Listing*.
29 "78 Presents The Rarest 78's", *78 Quarterly*, No. 1, 1967, and *78 Quarterly*, No. 2, 1968, New York; Bernard Klatzko, album notes to Herwin 201; Charley Patton's *Joe Kirby* was reissued on Herwin 203; and Skip James's *Drunken Spree* on Matchbox Bluesmasters MSE 207.
30 Dixon and Godrich, *Recording the Blues*, pp. 70–4; Foreman, *Jazz and Race Records*, pp. 172–7.
31 Arthur F. Raper, *Preface to Peasantry*, p. 66.
32 Charles S. Johnson, *Shadow of the Plantation*, pp. 15, 100, 184.
33 Richard Sterner, *The Negro's Share*, pp. 157, 159.
34 Dixon and Godrich, *Blues and Gospel Records*, p. 67; Foreman, *Jazz and Race Records*, pp. 179–180; Frazier, *The Negro in the United States*, p. 209.
35 For detailed discussions see W. E. B. Du Bois, *Black Reconstruction in America 1860–1880*,

New York: Harcourt, Brace and Co., 1935; and C. Vann Woodward, *Origins of the New South, 1877–1913*, Baton Rouge: Louisiana State University Press, 1951.

36 Wharton, *The Negro in Mississippi*, p. 232; Charles S. Johnson, *Patterns of Negro Segregation*, pp. 171–2.

37 Dennison, *Scandalize My Name*, pp. 383–415; Charles S. Johnson, *Patterns of Negro Segregation*, p. 170.

38 James Weldon Johnson, *Black Manhattan*, New York: Alfred A. Knopf, 1930, pp. 102–8; W. J. Cash, *The Mind of the South*, New York: Alfred A. Knopf, 1941, p. 197.

39 Oliver, *Blues Fell This Morning*, pp. 179–90, 193–203; Oliver, *Conversation With the Blues*, pp. 54–8, 85–9; Alan Lomax, *Mister Jelly Roll*, London: Cassell and Co. Ltd., 1952, pp. 131–2, 139–40.

40 Raper, *Prelude to Peasantry*, pp. 392–4; note that "Black Belt diction" means *white* Southern speech.

41 e.g. William Francis Allen, Charles Pickard Ware and Lucy McKim Garrison, *Slave Songs of the United States*, New York: A. Simpson and Co., 1867, p. iv; Natalie Curtis-Burlin, *Negro Folk Songs*, Book II, New York: G. Schirmer, 1918, p. 8.

42 Stephen Calt, Stefan Grossman and Hal Grossman, *Country Blues Songbook*, New York: Oak Publications, 1973, p. 15.

43 Titon, *Early Downhome Blues*.

44 Oliver, *Conversation With the Blues*, p. 86.

45 Allene M. Sumner, "The Holy Rollers of Shin Bone Ridge", *The Nation*, July 29, 1925, pp. 137–8; Shelton Bissell, "Vaudeville at Angelus Temple", *The Outlook*, May 23, 1928, p. 126.

46 Wardlow, "Rev. D. C. Rice: Gospel Singer", pp. 167, 183; Kent, "Interview with Reverend McGee", p. 52.

47 Heilbut, *The Gospel Sound: Good News and Bad Times*, passim.

48 Oliver, "Up Today and Down Tomorrow", in *From Fear, Free*, eds. Stephen W. Baskerville and Ralph Willett, Manchester: University of Manchester Press, 1984.

49 Oliver, "Blues and the Binary Principle", *Popular Music Perspectives*, eds. David Horn and Philip Tagg, Göteborg and Exeter: International Association for the Study of Popular Music, 1982, pp. 163–173; Oliver, "Twixt Midnight and Day: Binarism, Blues and Black Culture", *Popular Music 2*, eds. Richard Middleton and David Horn, Cambridge: Cambridge University Press, 1982, pp. 179–200.

50 Important work in this respect has been commenced in the field of white folk song; see Norman Cohen, "Tin Pan Alley's Contribution to Folk Music", *Western Folklore*, Vol. 29, 1970; and Anne and Norm Cohen, "Tune Evolution as an Indicator of Traditional Musical Norms", *Journal of American Folklore*, Vol. 86, No. 339, January–March, 1972.

Bibliography

Principal works consulted are listed below. Other references are given in the Notes.

Bastin, Bruce, *Crying for the Carolines*, London: Studio Vista, 1971

Berlin, Edward A., *Ragtime: A Musical and Cultural History*, Berkeley, Los Angeles, London: University of California Press, 1980

Blesh, Rudi and Janis, Harriet, *They All Played Ragtime*, London: Sidgwick and Jackson, 1958

Botkin, B. A. (ed), *Lay My Burden Down (A Folk History of Slavery)*, Chicago: University of Chicago Press, 1945

A Treasury of Southern Folklore, New York: Crown Publishers, 1949

Broonzy, William (as told to Yannick Bruynoghe), *Big Bill Blues*, London: Cassell, 1955

Bureau of the Census, see *Negro Population 1790–1915*

Calt, Stephen, "The Country Blues as Meaning", *Country Blues Songbook*, ed. S. Grossman, H. Grossman, S. Calt, New York: Oak Publications, 1973

Charters, Ann, *The Ragtime Songbook*, New York: Oak Publications, 1965

Charters, Samuel B., *The Country Blues*, New York: Rinehart and Co. Inc., 1959

The Bluesmen, New York: Oak Publications, 1967

Sweet as The Showers of Rain, New York: Oak Publications, 1973

Cohen, Norm, *Long Steel Rail: The Railroad in American Folk Song*, Urbana: University of Illinois, 1981

Courlander, Harold, *Negro Folk Music U.S.A.*, New York: Columbia University Press, 1963

Cunard, Nancy, *Negro, An Anthology*, London: Nancy Cunard, 1934

Denisoff, Serge and Peterson, Richard A. *The Sounds of Social Change*, New York: Rand McNally and Co., 1982

Dennison, Sam, *Scandalize My Name, Black Imagery in American Popular Music*, New York: Garland Publishing Co., 1982

Department of Commerce, see *Negro Population 1790–1915*

Dixon, Robert M. W. and Godrich, John, *Recording the Blues*, London: Studio Vista, 1970

Blues and Gospel Records 1902–1943 (3rd edn) London: Storyville Publications, 1982 (see also Godrich, for 2nd edn)

Drake, St. Clair and Cayton, Horace R., *Black Metropolis: A Study of Negro Life in a Northern City*, New York: Harcourt, Brace and Co., 1945

Du Bois, W. E. Burghardt, *The Souls of Black Folk, Essays and Sketches*, Chicago: McClurg, 1903

Epstein, Dena J., *Sinful Tunes and Spirituals: Black Folk Music to the Civil War*, Urbana: University of Illinois Press, 1977

Evans, David, "An Interview with H. C. Speir", *Blues Unlimited* 56, 1968 Bexhill-on-Sea, Sussex: England.

Tommy Johnson, London: Studio Vista, 1971

Big Road Blues: Tradition and Creativity in the Folk Blues, Berkeley: University of California Press, 1982

"Blind Willie McTell", *Atlanta Blues*, album notes to JEMF 106

Felton, Ralph Alison, *These My Brethren. A Study of 570 Negro Churches and 1542 Negro Homes in the Rural South*, Madison, N.J.: Department of Rural Church, Drew Theological Seminary, 1950

Foreman, Ronald C. Jr., 'Jazz and Race Records 1920–1932', Ph. D. Dissertation, University of Illinois, 1968

Frank C. Brown Collection of North Carolina Folklore, ed. Newman I. White, Durham, NC: Duke University Press, 1952–62. Vol. 2 *Folk Ballads* (1952), Vol. 3 *Folk Songs* (1952) ed. H. M. Belden and Arthur Palmer Hudson

Frazier, E. Franklin, *The Negro in the United States*, New York: Macmillan, 1949
The Negro Family in the United States, New York: The Dryden Press, 1951
The Negro Church in America, New York: Schocken Books, 1964

Fuller, T. O., *History of the Negro Baptists of Tennessee*, Memphis, Tenn: Roger Williams How College, 1936

Genovese, Eugene D., *Roll, Jordan, Roll: The World the Slaves Made*, New York: Pantheon Books, 1974

Godrich, John and Dixon, Robert M. W., *Blues and Gospel Records 1902–1942* (2nd edn), London: Storyville Publications, 1969

Gutman, Herbert G., *The Black Family in Slavery and Freedom 1750–1925*, Oxford: Basil Blackwell, 19

Hamilton, Charles V., *The Black Preacher in America*, New York: William Morrow and Co. Inc., 1972

Hamm, Charles, *Yesterdays: Popular Song in America*, New York: W. W. Norton and Co., 1970

Handy, W. C., *A Treasury of the Blues*, ed. Abbe Niles, New York: Charles Boni, 1926
Father of the Blues, London: Sidgwick and Jackson, 1957

Harris, Sheldon, *Blues Who's Who*, New Rochelle, New York: Arlington House Publishers, 1979

Hearn, Lafcadio, "Levee Life", *Cincinnati Commercial*, March 17, 1876, reprinted in *The Selected Writings of Lafcadio Hearn*, ed. Henry Goodman, New York: The Citadel Press, 1949

Heilbut, Tony, *The Gospel Sound: Good News and Bad Times*, New York: Simon and Schuster, 1971

Holbrook, Stewart H., *The Golden Age of Quackery*, New York: The MacMillan Co., 1959

Hughes, Langston and Bontemps, Anna (eds), *The Book of Negro Folklore*, New York: Dodd, Mead and Co., 1958

Johnson, Charles S., "The New Frontage in American Life", *The New Negro: An Interpretation*, ed. Alain Locke, New York: A. and C. Boni, 1925
Shadow of the Plantation, Chicago: Chicago University Press, 1934
Patterns of Negro Segregation, London: Victor Gollancz, 1944

Johnson, James Weldon, *The Book of American Negro Spirituals*, New York: The Viking Press, 1925
The Second Book of Negro Spirituals, New York: The Viking Press, 1926

Jones, LeRoi, *Blues People*, New York: William Morrow and Co. Inc., 1963

Kennedy, R. Emmett, *Mellows: A Chronicle of Unknown Singers*, New York: Albert and Charles Boni, 1925

Kent, Don, "Interview with Reverend McGee", *American Folk Music Occasional*, eds. Chris Strachwitz and Pete Welding, New York: Oak Publications, 1970, pp. 49–52

Klatzko, Bernard, *In The Spirit*, album notes to Origin OJL 12 and OJL 13

Laws, G. Malcolm Jr., *Native American Balladry* (rev. edn), Philadelphia: The American Folklore Society, 1957

Levine, Lawrence W., *Black Culture and Black Consciousness*, Oxford: Oxford University Press, 1977

Lincoln, Eric C., *The Black Experience in Religion*, New York: Doubleday Anchor, 1974

Lomax, Alan, *The Folk Songs of North America*, London: Cassell, 1960

Lomax, John A., "Self-Pity in Negro Folk-Songs", *The Nation*, 105, July–December 1917, pp. 141–5.
Adventures of a Ballad Hunter, New York: The Macmillan Co., 1947

Lomax, John A. and Lomax, Alan, *American Ballads and Folk Songs*, New York: Macmillan, 1934

Negro Folk Songs as Sung by Lead Belly, New York: Macmillan, 1936

Folk Song U.S.A. New York: Duell, Sloan and Pearce, Inc., 1947

Lomax, Louis, *The Negro Revolt*, London: Hamish Hamilton, 1963

Mahony, Dan, *The Columbia 13/14000-D Series, A Numerical Listing* (rev. edn), Stanhope, N.J.: Walter C. Allen, 1966

Marks, Edward B., *They All Sang*, New York: The Viking Press, 1934

Mays, Benjamin E. and Nicholson, Joseph W., *The Negro's Church*, New York: Institute of Social and Religious Research, 1933

McCormick, Mack, *Henry Thomas*, album notes and transcriptions, Herwin 209, Glen Cove, New York: 1974

McKee, Margaret and Chisenhall, Fred, *Beale Black and Blue*, Baton Rouge and London: Louisiana State University Press, 1981

McNeil, W. K., "Syncopated Slander: The 'Coon Song' 1890–1900", *Keystone Folklore Quarterly*, 17, 1972

Meier, August, *Negro Thought in America, 1880–1915*, Ann Arbor, Michigan: The University of Michigan Press, 19

Meier, August and Rudwick, Elliott M., *From Plantation to Ghetto* (1966) London: Constable, 1970

Mitchell, Henry H., *Black Preaching*, Philadelphia and New York: J. B. Lippincott Co., 1970

Myrdal, Gunnar, *An American Dilemma*, New York and Evanston: Harper and Row, 1944

Nathan, Hans, *Dan Emmett and the Rise of Early Negro Minstrelsy*, Norman, Oklahoma: University of Oklahoma Press, 1962

Negro Population, 1790–1915, Department of Commerce, Bureau of the Census, Sam L. Rogers, Director, Washington, DC: Government Printing Office, 1918

Niles, John J., "Shout, Coon, Shout!" *The Musical Quarterly*, 16, 1930

Singing Soldiers, New York: Charles Scribner's Sons, 1927

Odum, Howard W., "Folk-Song and Folk-Poetry as Found in the Secular Songs of the Southern Negroes", *Journal of American Folklore*, 24, 1911, pp. 255–94, 351–96

Odum, Howard W. and Johnson, Guy B., *The Negro and His Songs*, Chapel Hill: University of North Carolina Press, 1925

Negro Workaday Songs, Chapel Hill: University of North Carolina Press, 1925

Oliver, Paul, *Bessie Smith*, London: Cassell, 1959

Blues Fell This Morning: The Meaning of the Blues, London: Cassell, 1960

Conversation With the Blues, London: Cassell, 1965

Screening the Blues: Aspects of the Blues Tradition, London: Cassell, 1968

The Story of the Blues, London: Barrie and Jenkins, 1969

Savannah Syncopators: African Retentions in the Blues, London: Studio Vista, 1970

Blues Off the Record: Thirty Years of Blues Commentary, Tunbridge Wells: Midas Books, 1984

Olsson, Bengt, *Memphis Blues and Jug Bands*, London: Studio Vista, 1970

Cannon's Jug Stompers, album notes and transcriptions, Herwin 208, Glen Cove, New York: 1973

Paskman, Dailey and Spaeth, Sigmund, *Gentlemen, Be Seated: A Parade of Old-Time Minstrels*, Garden City, N.Y.: Doubleday, Doran and Co. Inc., 1928

Perrow, E. C., "Songs and Rhymes from the South", *Journal of American Folklore*, 25 (1912), pp. 137–55; 26 (1913), pp. 123–73; 28 (1915), pp. 129–90

Peterkin, Julia, *Roll, Jordan, Roll*, New York: Robert O. Ballou, 1933

Porterfield, Nolan, *Jimmie Rodgers: The Life and Times of America's Blue Yodeler*, Urbana: University of Illinois Press, 1979

Raichelson, Richard, "Black Religious Folksong: A Study in Generic and Social Change", Philadelphia: University of Pennsylvania, unpub. diss. 1974

Raper, Arthur F., *Preface to Peasantry*, University of North Carolina Press (1936), reprinted New York: Atheneum, 1968

Rawick, George (ed), *The American Slave: A Composite Autobiography*, (31 Volumes) Westport, Conn: Greenwood Press, 1972–8

Richardson, Harry V., "The Negro in American Religious Life", *The American Negro Reference Book*, J. P. Davis (ed), N.J.: Prentice Hall Inc., 1966

Ricks, George Robinson, *Some Aspects of the Religious Music of the United States Negro: An Ethnomusicological Study with a Special Emphasis on the Gospel Tradition* (1960) Arno Press, 1977

Rosenberg, Bruce A., *The Art of the American Folk Preacher*, New York: Oxford University Press, 1970

Russell, Tony, *Blacks, Whites and Blues*, London: Studio Vista, 1970

Sackheim, Eric, *The Blues Line: A Collection of Blues Lyrics*, New York: Grossman Pub. 1969

Sampson, Henry T., *Blacks in Blackface: A Source Book on Early Black Musical Shows*, Metuchen, N.J.: The Scarecrow Press Inc., 1980

Sandburg, Carl, *The American Songbag*, New York: Harcourt, Brace and Co., 1927

Scarborough, Dorothy, *On the Trail of Negro Folk-Songs*, Cambridge, Mass: Harvard University Press, 1925

Seeger, Mike, "Who Chose These Records? A Look into the Life, Tastes and Procedures of Frank Walker", *Anthology of American Folk Music*, Josh Dunson and Ethel Raim (eds), New York: Oak Publications, 1973

Shaw, Malcolm, "Arizona Dranes and Okeh", *Storyville*, No. 27, February 1970

Simond, Ike, *Old Slack's Reminiscence and Pocket History of the Colored Profession from 1865 to 1891*, Robert Toll (ed), Bowling Green, Ohio: Bowling Green University Press, 1971

Simpson, George Eaton, "Black Pentecostalism in the United States", *Phylon*, Atlanta University Review of Race and Culture, Vol. 35, No. 2

Southern, Eileen, *The Music of Black Americans*, New York: W. W. Norton and Co., 1971
Biographical Dictionary of Afro-American and African Musicians, Westport, Conn: Greenwood Press, 1982

Spaeth, Sigmund, *Read 'Em and Weep*, Garden City, N.Y.: Doubleday, Page and Co., 1927
A History of Popular Music in America, New York: Random House, 1948

Spear, Allan H., *Black Chicago: The Making of a Negro Ghetto 1890–1920*, Chicago: The University of Chicago Press, 1967

Stearns, Marshall, *The Story of Jazz*, New York: Oxford University Press, 1956

Stearns, Marshall and Stearns, Jean, *Jazz Dance: The Story of American Vernacular Dance*, London: The Macmillan Co., 1968

Sterner, Richard, *The Negro's Share: A Study of Income, Consumption, Housing and Public Assistance*, New York: Harper and Brothers, 1943

Talley, Thomas W., *Negro Folk Rhymes*, New York: Macmillan, 1922

Thomas, Gates, "South Texas Negro Work-Songs: Collected and Uncollected", *Rainbow in the Morning*, Publications of the Texas Folklore Society, No. 5, J. Frank Dobie (ed), 1926

Thomas, Will H., *Some Current Folk-Songs of the Negro and Their Economic Interpretation*, Austin: Folk-Lore Society of Texas, pamphlet 1, 1912

Titon, Jeff Todd, *Early Downhome Blues: A Musical and Cultural Analysis*, Urbana: University of Illinois Press, 1977

Toll, Robert, *Blacking Up: The Minstrel Show in Nineteenth Century America*, London: Oxford University Press, 1974

Vreede, Max E., *Paramount 12000/13000 Series*, London: Storyville Publications, 1971

Wardlow, Gayle Dean, *In The Spirit*, Vols 1 and 2, Biographical Notes to Origin Jazz Library, OJL–12, OJL–13, Berkeley, California: 1966
"Rev. D. C. Rice: Gospel Singer", *Storyville* No. 23, June–July 1969, pp. 164–7, 183

Washington, Joseph R., *Black Sects and Cults*, New York: Anchor Press, Doubleday, 1972

Waters, Ethel, *His Eye is on the Sparrow*, London: W. H. Allen, 1951

Webb, W. Prescott, "Notes to Folk-Lore of Texas", *Journal of American Folklore*, No. 28 (1915) pp. 290–9
"Miscellany of Texas Folk-Lore", Frank Dobie (ed), *Coffee in the Gourd*, Publication of the Texas Folk-Lore Society, Vol. 11, Austin, Texas: 1923

Webber, Malcolm, *Medicine Show*, Caldwell, Idaho: The Caxton Printers, 1941

Wharton, Vernon Lane, *The Negro in Mississippi 1865–1890* (1947), New York: Harper and Row, 1965

White, Newman I., *American Negro Folk-Songs*, Cambridge, Mass: Harvard University Press, 1928

"The White Man in the Woodpile: Some Influences on Negro Secular Folk-Songs", *American Speech*, No. 4, October 1928–August 1929, pp. 207–15

Wittke, Carl, *Tambo and Bones*, Durham, N. Carolina: Duke University Press, 1930

Woodson, Carter G., *The History of the Negro Church*, Washington: The Associated Publishers Inc., 1921

Yetman, Norman R. (ed), *Life Under the "Peculiar Institution" Selections from the Slave Narrative Collection*, New York: Holt, Rinehart and Winston Inc., 1970

A guide to reissued recordings

Two volumes of long-playing records, *Songsters and Saints*, comprising four discs in all have been produced to coincide with the publication of this book. Included on the records are examples of social songs, dance songs, ballads, Baptist and Sanctified preaching with congregations and gospel songs, illustrating every chapter. Most major songsters and sacred singers and preachers are represented. The volumes are available on Matchbox MSEX 2001/2002 and Matchbox MSEX 2003/2004. They may be obtained from specialist record shops and dealers, or through the distributors:

Matchbox Records, The Barton, Inglestone Common, Badminton, Glos. GL9 1BX, England
Down Home Music, 10341 San Pablo Avenue, El Cerrito, Cal. 94530, U.S.A.
Qualiton Imports Ltd, 39–28 Crescent St., Long Island City, NY 11101, USA.

Matchbox Records MSEX 2001/2002
Songsters and Saints Volume One

A. Dances and Traveling shows

1. Peg Leg Howell and Eddie Anthony	*Turkey Buzzard Blues*
2. Pink Anderson and Simmie Dooley	*Gonna Tip Out Tonight*
3. Beans Hambone and El Marrow	*Beans*
4. Earl McDonald's Original Louisville Jug Band	*Under the Chicken Tree*
5. Alec Johnson	*Mysterious Coon*
6. "Big Boy" George Owens	*The Coon Crap Game*
7. Memphis Jug Band	*He's in the Jailhouse Now*
8. Charley Patton	*Elder Greene Blues*
9. Hambone Willie Newbern	*Way Down in Arkansas*

B. Comment, parodies and ballad heroes

1. Lil McClintock	*Furniture Man*
2. Julius Daniels	*Can't Put the Bridle on That Mule This Morning*
3. Hezekiah Jenkins	*The Panic Is On*
4. Bogus Ben Covington	*I Heard the Voice of a Pork Chop*
5. Johnson – Nelson – Porkchop	*G. Burns Is Gonna Rise Again*
6. Bo Chatman	*Good Old Turnip Greens*
7. Two Poor Boys	*John Henry Blues*
8. Will Bennett	*Railroad Bill*
9. Kid Coley	*Clair and Pearley Blues*

C. Baptist and sanctified sermons

1. Rev. Jim Beal	*The Hand of the Lord Was Upon Me*
2. Rev. A. W. Nix	*After the Ball Is Over*
3. Rev. Isaiah Shelton	*As the Eagle Stirreth Her Nest*
4. Rev. J. M. Milton	*Silk Worms and Boll Weevils*
5. Rev. R. M. Massey	*Old Time Baptism – Part 2*

314

6. Rev. J. E. Burch	*Baptism by Water, And Baptism by the Holy Ghost*
7. Rev. E. S. (Shy) Moore	*The Solemn Warning*
8. Elder Curry	*Prove All Things*
9. Rev. Leora Ross	*God's Mercy To Colonel Lindberg*

D. Gospel soloists and evangelists

1. Missionary Josephine Miles	*You Have Lost Jesus*
2. Mother McCollum	*When I Take My Vacation in Heaven*
3. Eddie Head and His Family	*Down On Me*
4. Washington Phillips	*I Am Born to Preach the Gospel*
5. Blind Roosevelt Graves and Brother	*Telephone to Glory*
6. The Guitar Evangelist (E. W. Clayborn)	*Death Is Only a Dream*
7. Blind Willie Davis	*Your Enemy Cannot Harm You*
8. Blind Nesbit	*Pure Religion*
9. William and Versey Smith	*When That Great Ship Went Down*

Matchbox Records MSEX 2003/2004
Songsters and Saints Volume Two

A. Medicine show songsters

1. Papa Charlie Jackson	*I'm Alabama Bound*
2.	*Long Gone Lost John*
3. Cannon's Jug Stompers	*My Money Never Runs Out*
4. Banjo Joe (Gus Cannon)	*Can You Blame the Colored Man*
5. Jim Jackson	*Bye Bye Policeman*
6.	*My Monday Woman Blues*
7.	*Old Dog Blue*
8. Beale Street Sheiks (Stokes and Sane)	*Mr. Crump Don't Like It*
9.	*Chicken You Can Roost Behind the Moon*

B. Songsters East and West

1. Stovepipe No. 1 and David Crockett	*A Chicken Can Waltz the Gravy Around*
2.	*A Woman Gets Tired of the Same Man All the Time*
3. Henry Thomas	*Old Country Stomp*
4.	*Bob McKinney*
5.	*Arkansas*
6. Luke Jordan	*Traveling Coon*
7.	*Cocaine Blues*
8. Blind Blake	*He's in the Jail House Now*
9.	*Dry Bone Shuffle*

C. The straining preachers

1. Rev. J. C. Burnett	*The Downfall of Nebuchadnezzar*
2.	*The Gambler's Doom*
3. Rev. J. M. Gates	*Yonder Comes My Lord With a Bible in His Hand*
4.	*God's Wrath In the St. Louis Cyclone*
5.	*The Eagle Stirs Her Nest*
6. Rev. F. W. McGee	*The Half Ain't Never Been Told*

7.   *Jonah in the Belly of the Whale*
8. Rev. D. C. Rice   *Come and See*
9.   *We Got the Same Kinda Power Over Here*

D. Saints of church and street

1. Arizona Dranes   *It's All Right Now*
2.   *Just Look*
3. Blind Joe Taggart   *God's Gonna Separate the Wheat From Tares*
4.   *There's a Hand Writing on the Wall*
5. Blind Willie Johnson   *If I Had My Way I'd Tear the Building Down*
6.   *God Moves on the Water*
7.   *The Rain Don't Fall On Me*
8. Elders McIntosh and Edwards   *The Latter Rain Is Fall*
9. Memphis sanctified singers   *He Got Better Things For You*

Other reissues

Many recordings by songsters have been reissued and a number by preachers and evangelists. Among the following long-play albums there is some duplication of titles, while many isolated items appear in other collections not listed here. Details of microgroove reissues up to 1969 were included in Godrich and Dixon, *Blues and Gospel Records*, 2nd edition only. Many Reissue albums have been withdrawn from circulation, but may often be obtained through specialist dealers in folk, blues and jazz records.

Songsters

Blind Blake	*Blues in Chicago*	Riverside RLP 8804
	1926–1930 Vol 1	Biograph BLP 12003
	1926–1932 Vol 2	Biograph BLP 12023
	Vol 3	Biograph BLP 12031
	1926–1931 Vol 4	Biograph BLP 12037
Tommy Bradley/J. Cole	*1931–1932*	Matchbox MSE 211
Cannon's Jug Stompers	*1928–1930*	Roots 336
Coley Jones and the Dallas String Band	*1927–1929*	Matchbox MSE 208
Mississippi John Hurt	*1928 Sessions*	Yazoo 1065
Peg Leg Howell	*1928–1929*	Matchbox MSE 205
Peg Leg Howell and his Gang	*1927–1930*	Origin OJL 22
Papa Charlie Jackson	*Fat Mouth*	Yazoo 1027
	Papa Charlie Jackson	Biograph BLP 12042
	Papa Charlie Jackson	Matchbox MSE 225
Jim Jackson	*Jim Jackson*	Agram Blues AB 2004
Furry Lewis	*In His Prime 1927–1928*	Yazoo 1050
Mississippi Sheiks/ Beale St. Sheiks	*1927–1932*	Biograph BLP 12041
Blind Willie McTell	*The Early Years*	Yazoo 1005
	1927–1935 Recordings	Yazoo 1037
	1929–1935 Recordings	Roots 324
Charley Patton	*Founder of the Delta Blues*	Yazoo L–1020
	Patton, Sims and Bertha Lee	Herwin 213
	The Remaining Titles	Wolf WSE 103
Frank Stokes	*Frank Stokes and Will Batts and Dan Sane*	Roots 308

	Creator of the Memphis Blues	Yazoo 1056
	Remaining Titles	· Matchbox MSE 218
Henry Thomas	"Ragtime Texas" 1927–1929	Herwin 209

Collections

The following collections largely feature songsters. (Featured artists given in parentheses.)

Country Blues – The First Generation (Papa Harvey Hull/Richard Rabbit Brown)	Matchbox MSE 201
Early Folk Blues, Vol 1 "Skoodle Um Skoo"	Matchbox SDR 199
The East Coast States [Georgia – Carolinas – Virginia], Vol 1	Roots RL 318
The East Coast States, Vol 2	Roots RL 326
The Great Jug Bands	Origin OJL 5
Next Week, Sometime (Alec Johnson)	Nugrape CBR 001
Ragtime Blues Guitar (William Moore)	Matchbox MSE 204
Sunshine Special (Earl McDonald)	VJM VLP 39

Saints

Arizona Dranes	Barrelhouse Piano with Sanctified Singing 1926–1928	Herwin 210
Bessie Johnson	1928–1929	Herwin 202
Blind Willie Johnson	His Story	Folkways 3585
	Praise God I'm Satisfied	Yazoo 1058
	Let Your Light Shine On Me 1927–1930	Earl BD 607
Rev. F. W. McGee	Rev. F. W. McGee	Roots 338
Washington Phillips	Denomination Blues	Agram Blues AB 2006
Rev. D. C. Rice	Sanctified Singing with Traditional Jazz Accompaniment	Herwin 212
Blind Joe Taggart	A Guitar Evangelist 1926–1931	Herwin 204

Collections

Black Diamond Express to Hell, Vol 1	Matchbox SDX 207
Christ Was Born on Christmas Morn	Historical HLP 34
Guitar Evangelists, Vol 1 1927–1936	Truth TLP 1002
Guitar Evangelists, Vol 2 1927–1941	Truth TLP 1003
In The Spirit, Vol 1	Origin OJL 12
In The Spirit, Vol 2	Origin OJL 13
Nearer My God To Thee	Roots RL 304
Living Humble – A Gospel Compilation	Nugrape CBR 002
Negro Religious Music, Vol 1 The Sanctified Singers	Blues Classic's BC LP 17
Negro Religious Music, Vol 2 The Sanctified Singers	Blues Classic's BC LP 18
Negro Religious Music, Vol 3 Singing Preachers and Their Congregations	Blues Classic's BC LP 19
The Rural Blues – Sacred Tradition (McCollum, Head, Clayborn)	Herwin 206
The Sanctified Jug Bands	Matchbox MSE 226
Southern Sanctified Singers	Roots RL 328
Ten Years of Black Country Religion	Yazoo L 1022
Traditional Jazz in Rural Churches	Truth TLP 1001
Whole World in His Hands (Graves, Bryant)	Herwin 207

Index of song titles

Italic numerals indicate pages on which transcriptions also appear.

Index of artists

including singers, musicians, preachers and composers

In the Notes and Indices the following abbreviations are used:
bj banjo; comp composer; coll collector; d drums; ent entertainer; g guitar; hca harmonica;
j jug; mand mandolin; p piano; pr preacher; prom promoter; tam tambourine; trb trombone;
tpt trumpet; vln violin; vo vocal, uke ukelele; wbd washboard; other instruments written in
full.

General index

331